SOCIAL INTERACTION AND THE DEVELOPMENT OF KNOWLEDGE

SOCIAL INTERACTION AND THE DEVELOPMENT OF KNOWLEDGE

Edited by

Jeremy I. M. Carpendale
Simon Fraser University

Ulrich Müller
Pennsylvania State University

 LAWRENCE ERLBAUM ASSOCIATES, PUBLISHERS
2004   Mahwah, New Jersey   London

Lawrence Erlbaum Associates, Inc., Publishers
10 Industrial Avenue
Mahwah, New Jersey 07430

Library of Congress Cataloging-in-Publication Data

Social interaction and the development of knowledge / edited by Jeremy I. M. Carpendale
    and Ulrich Müller.
      p.   cm.
    Includes bibliographical references and index.
    ISBN 0-8058-4124-5 (alk. paper)
      1. Piaget, Jean, 1896–   2. Social learning.   3. Social interaction.   4. Social interaction in
children.   5. Knowledge, Sociology of.   6. Social epistemology.   I. Carpendale, Jeremy I.
M., 1957–   II. Müller, Ulrich, 1964–

HQ783.S564   2003
303.3'2—dc21   2003052860
                                                                                              CIP

Books published by Lawrence Erlbaum Associates are printed on acid-free paper,
and their bindings are chosen for strength and durability.

Printed in the United States of America
10 9 8 7 6 5 4 3 2 1

This book is dedicated to the memory of Michael Chapman. Michael was an esteemed colleague and valued friend of many of the contributors to this volume. Michael's outstanding scholarship influenced the work of many developmentalists, including the editors—one of us (JC) was a former student. Michael's brilliant career was cut short by his untimely death in 1991, but his continuing influence is evident in the way that his work is cited in many of the chapters in this book. We wish to acknowledge Michael's important contributions to Piagetian scholarship, his work in extending and reformulating Piagetian theory, and in particular his ideas concerning the topic of this volume—the role of social interaction in the development of knowledge.

Contents

1 Social Interaction and the Development
of Rationality and Morality: An Introduction 1
Jeremy I. M. Carpendale and Ulrich Müller

2 A Relational and Embodied Perspective
on Resolving Psychology's Antinomies 19
Willis F. Overton

3 Piaget's Social Epistemology 45
Richard F. Kitchener

4 Individualism and Collectivism: A Dynamic
Systems Interpretation of Piaget's Interactionism 67
Jan Boom

5 Coordinating Operative and Figurative Knowledge:
Piaget, Vygotsky, and Beyond 87
Tamer G. Amin and Jaan Valsiner

6 The Social Ontology of Persons 111
Mark H. Bickhard

7   The Development and Overcoming of
    "Universal Pragmatics" in Piaget's Thinking   133
    Rainer Döbert

8   A Bridge too Far: On the Relations Between Moral
    and Secular Reasoning   155
    Bryan W. Sokol and Michael J. Chandler

9   Developmental Epistemology and Education   175
    Leslie Smith

10 Social Interaction and the Construction of Moral
    and Social Knowledge   195
    Larry Nucci

11 From Joint Activity to Joint Attention: A Relational
    Approach to Social Development in Infancy   215
    Ulrich Müller and Jeremy I. M. Carpendale

12 Piaget's Theory and Children's Development
    of Prosocial Behavior: The Force of Negation   239
    Orlando Lourenço

13 Wittgenstein's Internalistic Logic and Children's
    Theories of Mind   257
    Timothy P. Racine

Author Index   277

Subject Index   285

SOCIAL INTERACTION AND THE DEVELOPMENT OF KNOWLEDGE

Social Interaction and the Development of Rationality and Morality: An Introduction

Jeremy I. M. Carpendale
Ulrich Müller
Simon Fraser University & Pennsylvania State University

One of the most important questions that can be asked about development is how the psychological development of the individual is influenced by society. Any complete developmental theory must address this issue, and the task of conceptually clarifying the role of society in development raises many important epistemological questions. Chief among these are the multifaceted problems of how to conceptualize (a) the relation between the individual and society or collective, and (b) the contribution of society to the emergence of rational and moral norms. A major goal of this book is to elaborate on the process of socialization and the epistemological issues involved in this process. These issues are the topics of a number of chapters of this book and are dealt with from a variety of theoretical perspectives.

Another goal of this book is to present and evaluate Piaget's (1977/1995) unique but still widely bypassed treatment of these issues (Kitchener, 2000). Piaget is considered one of the giants of developmental psychology, but his theoretical and empirical contributions are mostly placed in the domain of individual cognitive development. Serious consideration of the social dimension of development is not credited to Piaget. In fact Piaget's theory has been and still is considered by many psychologists (e.g., Bruner, 1997; Tappan, 1997) to be the avatar of an individualist approach to development. A number of chapters in this book (e.g., Amin & Valsiner, chap. 5; Boom, chap. 4; Döbert, chap. 7; Kitchener, chap. 3; Smith, chap. 9; Lourenço, chap. 12) show that Piaget's theory is fundamentally social. Piaget's ideas about social interaction and development are, however, complex and need to be examined and evaluated.

In this introductory chapter, we begin with a few words on the social dimension in Piaget's theory. Next we describe and critically assess different ways in which the relation between the individual and collective has been conceptualized. Then we sketch different approaches to explaining the role of social interaction in development. Finally, we examine the issue of how society contributes to the development of rational and moral norms, which raises the problem of relativism. We also outline how Piaget and the contributing authors address these topics.

THE SOCIAL DIMENSION IN PIAGET'S THEORY

As mentioned earlier, it is still common to think that Piaget ignored the social dimension of development. Although this view has become entrenched in textbooks, it is incorrect (Chapman, 1988, 1992; Lourenço & Machado, 1996; Smith, 1982, 1993, 1996). In fact in Piaget's (1923/1955, 1924/1928, 1932/1965) early work, social factors were clearly important. The early Piaget assumed that reasoning originates in interpersonal argumentation, and autonomous morality is the product of cooperation. Even in his later work, Piaget was not silent on the social dimension of development. This is clear from Piaget's statements that, "the need to belong to a particular society is one of the essential parts of 'human nature' " (Piaget, 1970a, p. 3) and the individual is a socialized entity "from the time of his birth until he dies" (Piaget, 1970b, p. 27; see also Piaget, 1977/1995, pp. 33, 35, 217, 278, 287). However, at a surface level, the social dimension of psychological functioning did not receive the same attention in Piaget's later writings. One reason for Piaget's apparent neglect of the role of social factors in development may have been his rejection of social transmission as sufficient in accounting for the development of new knowledge (Chapman, 1988). In addition, Piaget's thinking about how social factors contribute to development changed considerably in his later work. Döbert (chap. 7) argues that this change in Piaget's thinking represents an advance rather than a retreat because at a deeper level the social dimension became a more integral part of Piaget's theory.

Because the social dimension of Piaget's writings is largely unfamiliar, Piaget's theory is frequently pitted against Vygotsky's, with the assumption that Piaget neglected and Vygotsky emphasized social factors in development. Amin and Valsiner (chap. 5, this volume), however, refer to the debate between Piaget (1962/2000) and Vygotsky (1934/1986) over the phenomenon of egocentric speech to show that Piaget and Vygotsky's theories are complementary, merely differing in what they emphasized. Piaget emphasized the operative aspect of knowledge, whereas Vygotsky emphasized the figurative aspect. Amin and Valsiner suggest that Piaget's interest in the social dimension in development was largely formal, and that he was not concerned with the specific content of social conventions. In contrast, Vygotsky emphasized the influence of the specific content of external structuring resources; although he acknowledged that internalization is a constructive process, he did not elaborate on this process. Amin and Valsiner propose that an integrative framework, giving equal emphasis to both components, raises new questions and generates new ideas about the process of development. They illustrate this framework with examples from recent theory and research on semantics. However, their integrative framework has yet to be applied within developmental psychology.

NEITHER INDIVIDUAL NOR COLLECTIVE: A THIRD ALTERNATIVE

With respect to the conceptualization of the relations between the individual and society, three different positions can be distinguished: (a) methodological individualism, (b) sociological or dualistic holism, and (c) relational structuralism or systemism (Bunge, 2000; Moessinger, 2000; Piaget, 1977/1995). For Piaget, the question of how to conceptualize the relation between the individual and society is part and parcel of the larger problem of how to conceptualize the relation between elements or parts and wholes (Piaget, 1968/1971b; see Chapman, 1988, pp. 11–30). Accordingly, Piaget (1968/1971b) found the same types of solutions being suggested to the problem of the relation between the individual and society as to the problem of the relation between part and whole.

According to methodological individualism, all phenomena in the social sciences must eventually be reducible to individuals and their properties, and individuals should be used as the units of analysis for explanation (Bunge, 2000; Lenk, 1987). Methodological individualism has been endorsed by Weber (1978) and Homans (1961) among others.

Dualistic or sociological holism argues that social facts are irreducible to the behavior and cognition of the individual and thus constitute supraindividual entities. Accordingly, societal phenomena should be explained in terms of the properties of the whole societies analyzed. Piaget believed that Durkheim (1982; see Giddens, 1977, for a discussion) endorsed dualistic holism. According to Durkheim, sociological phenomena cannot be reduced to individual behavior because they possess the power to exert outside pressure on individual consciousness. In addition, Durkheim (1982) claimed that, in some unknown way, the fusion of members constitutes a whole with a psychic life of its own: "By aggregating together, by interpenetrating, by fusing together, individuals give birth to a being, psychical if you will, but one which constitutes a psychical individuality of a new kind" (p. 129). For Durkheim (1953, p. 26) psychical individuality of a new kind is manifest in supraindividual cognitive phenomena such as collective representations.

Closely tied to the individualist and collectivist positions are specific views on whether the individual or the collective should receive major force in explaining social facts (Dahlbäck, 1998). Whereas for many individualistic approaches individual behavior is the primary force, proponents of collectivist approaches often declare all aspects of persons inherently and completely social (i.e., they reduce the psychology of the person to the "fusion" with the social world [Lave, 1988] or to rhetorics [Shotter, 1990]; see Lawrence & Valsiner [1993]). Furthermore, in collectivist approaches, the collective is viewed as imposing itself on and structuring individuals (Piaget, 1970/1973, p. 21), and individuals' behavior patterns and mental activities are reduced to functions of the collective (Piaget, 1977/1995, p. 39).

Both methodological individualism and sociological holism have been criticized for a variety of reasons (see e.g., Bunge, 2000; Elias, 1978; Lenk, 1987; Piaget, 1977/1995). Methodological individualism has been criticized for failing to take into account the internal relation that exists between the individual and society: Our actions are often formed and guided by anticipations of the reactions of others, which cannot be captured by the reduction of society to properties of individuals (Lenk, 1987). In addition, by reducing society to properties of individuals, methodological individualism does not provide any possibility to study and compare different cultures and institutions—the macroscopic analysis of culture and society is essentially ruled out by methodological individualism. Furthermore, moral rules and duties are social phenomena and cannot be reduced to factors of a purely individual psychology (Piaget, 1932/1965, p. 196). Finally, as Piaget (1977/1995) remarked, methodological individualism leads to the "attribution to individual consciousness of a set of ready-made faculties" (p. 40), thereby ignoring that socialization is constitutive of and transforms individual consciousness.

Sociological holism has also drawn numerous criticisms (Bunge, 2000). First, it has been remarked that sociological holism reifies and mystifies structures (e.g., institutions). Reification has been defined as "the apprehension of human phenomena as if they were things, that is, in nonhuman or possibly supra-human terms. . . . The reified world is, by definition, a dehumanized world" (Berger & Luckmann, 1966, p. 89). Durkheim's notion of collective representations as supraindividual entities provides an example of reification because representations are by necessity always individual because they can only be localized within individual persons and their brains (Boesch, 1989; Bunge, 2000). Reification leads to overlooking the point that social facts and phenomena are produced and continuously reproduced by human beings; they depend on human action and cannot be considered independent of human actions (Berger & Luckmann, 1966; Elias, 1978).

A second criticism leveled against sociological holism is that it does not provide an analysis of social structures (Bunge, 2000), and thus ignores the heterogeneity of social relations (Piaget, 1932/1965, p. 395; 1977/1995, p. 217). In contemporary developmental psychology, the same type of criticism has been leveled against the apprenticeship model of cultural learning or participation theory (Duveen, 1997; Valsiner, 1998). According to participation theory (see Matusov, 1998; Matusov & Hayes, 2000; Rogoff, 1998), "development is a process of transformation of participation" that occurs through participation in social practices under the guidance of an expert (Rogoff, 1998, p. 695). In participation theory, the dualism between individual and collective is collapsed because the individual is said to never leave the flow of sociocultural activity, and the focus is on the transformation of participation (Matusov, 1998). The lack of analysis of social relations ensues from the failure to recognize the dualism between individual and collective (Valsiner, 1998). As a consequence, different abilities and knowing levels among participants are not captured—a point nicely illustrated in the following example from Smith (1996): "In a family trip to a supermarket, there is one social unit. But it does not follow that each member has access to the same set of operations" (p. 260).

Third, sociological holism has the tendency to be conservative and "makes no room for original and particularly nonconformist thinking" (Bunge, 2000, p. 400; Smith, 1996). With respect to the explanation of morality, Piaget (1932/1965) noted that the danger of sociological holism is that "it may compromise morality by identifying it with reasons of state, with accepted opinions, or with collective conservatism" (p. 344). The same social conservatism also applies to participation theory because it focuses "exclusively on the reproduction of existing social relations. One can legitimately ask how social change can be brought about through a process of apprenticeship" (Duveen, 1997, p. 82).

Finally, sociological holism leans toward cultural relativism because it fosters the view that each community has its own set of beliefs and values, which are neither better nor worse than those of other communities. Relativism eschews the search for objective truth, which transcends cultures and is universal, and it ultimately leads to epistemological anarchism: "Because it denies the universal canons of valid argument, relativism does not even make rational debate possible among people from different cultures or even subcultures" (Bunge, 2000, p. 400; see also Chandler, 1997; Overton, chap. 2, this volume).

The dead ends into which both methodological individualism and sociological holism lead are due to fictions: on the one hand, the fiction of isolated individuals in methodological individualism; on the other hand, the fiction of a supraindividual whole in sociological holism. In the "Sociological Studies," Piaget (1977/1995) elaborated a unique solution to the problem of the relation between the individual and society that neither reduces the individual to the collective nor the collective to the individuals. Rather, Piaget (1970/1973) referred to his position as "relational structuralism" (p. 22) because the relations between elements that form structures are primary. Relational structuralism posits "systems of interactions or transformations as the primary reality and hence subordinating elements from the outset to the relations surrounding them and, reciprocally, conceiving of the whole as the product of the composition of these formative interactions" (Piaget, 1970/1973, p. 22; see also Piaget, 1977/1995, p. 136). As a result, Piaget (1977/1995) conceived of the collective as a "system of interactions which modify the very structure of individuals" (p. 42; see also Piaget, 1970b, p. 26; Kitchener, 1996).

Relational structuralism opens the door for a critical analysis of the totalities constituted by individuals. Piaget (1932/1965, p. 362) rejected the notion of society with a capital "S." Instead he argued that, "it is always necessary to make clear what kind of society is at issue and the problem is to replace the mysterious 'whole' to which Durkheim repeatedly appeals . . . by basic and clearly defined social relations" (Piaget, 1977/1995, p. 188): "It is therefore not 'social life' as a whole that psychology must invoke, but a series of relationships established in all possible combinations between individuals of distinct levels of mental development, and as a consequence of various types of interaction (coercion, co-operation, imitation, discussion, etc.)" (Piaget, 1945/1962, p. 4). Piaget's relational position has important implications for the development of morality and rationality because different types of interindividual relationships are related to and enable or constrain specific structures of rationality and morality (Piaget, 1932/1965, 1977/1995).

By analyzing social facts from a developmental perspective, Piaget's relational position avoids the reification of social phenomena and pays attention to the heterogeneous and often conflictual nature of social phenomena. The developmental psychological perspective examines the very construction and continuous reconstruction of social phenomena, thereby reconciling structures and genesis. At the same time, Piaget acknowledged the importance of macroscopic sociological analysis. Institutions as objectivated human activity must be studied simultaneously from the outside as objective structures and from the inside as being constituted by human actions, and there is no conflict between developmental psychological analysis and structural sociological analysis (Piaget, 1932/1965, pp. 360, 372).

Piaget's relational position is similar to Elias's (1978) "figurations" and contemporary systemism (Bunge, 2000; Moessinger, 2000). Elias (1978) proposed that society is formed by interdependent human beings who, through their basic dispositions and inclinations, are directed toward and linked with each other, making up webs of interdependence or *figurations* of many kinds. From the perspective of systemism, individuals are viewed as part of a social system, and the relations between the individuals give rise to systemic or emergent properties that amount to a new ontological level. Overton (chap. 2, this volume) explicates the relational approach on which Piaget's work is based and contrasts the metatheoretical assumptions underlying the relational approach with the assumptions underlying *split* approaches. According to *split* approaches, behavior is understood as a combination of apparently competing alternatives such as the individual versus society, and the question becomes which one is primary. In contrast to this *split* metatheory, Overton argues that the relational approach avoids this and other similar dichotomies that have plagued developmental psychology and psychology in general by viewing such polarities as differentiating from an inclusive activity matrix.

DEVELOPMENT AND SOCIAL INTERACTION

Any attempt to determine the role of social interaction in development encounters three major questions: (a) To what extent are social interaction skills and competencies internally transmitted (i.e., hereditary) and to what extent are they acquired? (b) What are the specifics of the process of social transmission? (c) Are social competence and social knowledge domain-specific or are there developmental relations between cognitive and social aspects of intelligence? In this section, we briefly outline and discuss various answers to these questions.

There are a variety of views regarding the extent to which the human way of life in general and human social competencies in particular are genetically determined. According to the influential nativist position proposed by Cosmides and Tooby (2002), the mind largely consists of a series of modules or cognitive mechanisms that were selected over evolutionary time and evolved to solve particular problems present in the ancestral environment. Each module is a specific mental mechanism adapted to deal with particular problems in the domain in question. Social competencies are seen to be no exception, and Cosmides and Tooby (2002) suggested that a number of social competencies are based on innate modules.

However, it is doubtful whether any nativist position captures what distinguishes human beings from other animals. In particular, human beings lack any specialization for a species-specific environment and are far more flexible than other animals. In contrast to other animals, human beings have a sociocultural history in the course of which they transform the environment to adapt it to their genetic makeup. Furthermore, nativism does not account for normative or justified knowledge (see Kitchener, chap. 3, this volume; Smith, chap. 9, this volume). All these characteristics of human beings cannot easily be reconciled with the rigidity of innate skills.

To account for these essentially human characteristics, Piaget (1967/ 1971a) proposed that phylogenesis has led to an increasing disappearance of innate fixations and in human beings to a "bursting" of the instinct (pp. 366–367). What remains in terms of human social competencies is only a biological drive or tendency, but no social instinct in the form of a complete hereditary action scheme (Piaget, 1977/1995, p. 288). As a consequence, human societies depend almost exclusively on educational transmission and development and have an essentially educational character (Piaget, 1977/1995, p. 290; see Smith, chap. 9, this volume, on Piaget's views on education). Piaget (1968/1971b) also noted the constructive aspect of the human condition that sharply differs from the condition of other animals: "Whereas other animals cannot alter themselves except by changing their species, man can transform himself by transforming the world and can structure himself by constructing structures; and these structures are his own, for they are not eternally predestined either from within or from without" (pp. 118–119).

A similar view was expressed by Elias (1978). If it is specific to human beings that human societies can change without change in the biological constitution of human beings, then, according to Elias, the crucial question in demand of an answer is: " 'Which biological characteristics of man make history possible?'. Or, to phrase it in sociologically more precise terms: 'Which biological characteristics are prerequisites for the changeability, and particularly for the capacity for development, shown by human societies?' " (p. 107).

This question was partly answered by Portmann's (1944/1990) zoological research. Portmann argued that, compared with nonhuman primates and other similar mammals, human infants are born 1 year too early because to attain the degree of development characteristic of other primates at birth, human pregnancy would have to last for about 21 months (which is realized in other species such as elephants and whales). This gives humans an *extrauterine year*—a period of dependency that does not take place in the constrained environment of the womb where species-specific behavior appropriate for a genetically assigned environment matures.

Rather, already during this formative period of rapid growth infants interact with the physical and social environment. In contrast to other species, human development "corresponds to the situation of a creature open to the world. . . . Our mental structures do not mature through self-differentiation to become finished behavior patterns, capable only of the slightest subtleties, as we know maturation to occur in animals" (Portmann, 1944/1990, p. 94). The upshot of Portmann's position is that our sociocultural history and biology are not two separate strata, one added on the other. Rather, the particular human biological constitution already embodies the dialectic between openness to the world and mediation through culture (see Grene, 1974, ch. 16; Plessner, 1926, 1976).

The claim that humans are socially constituted is addressed by Bickhard in chapter 6 (this volume). Human beings are not only biologically and psychologically constituted, they are also, as persons, fundamentally socially constituted. Bickhard outlines a model of how the social dimension of persons emerge from the biological and psychological dimensions. Humans are highly adapted to complex social interaction, and therefore they enter into highly complex interactions that generate a typically human social reality. Bickhard characterizes the emergence of social reality from individual psychology as consisting of situation conventions or common understandings of the social situation. Language is then a means to elaborate on and modify such situation conventions. The emergence of social reality in interactions between people is the first step in Bickhard's argument. The second step is to explain how persons become able to participate in these social realities. Bickhard argues that understanding human sociality is not possible from the perspective of most contemporary approaches and requires starting from an action framework such as Piaget's.

If the social competencies characteristic of human beings are not innate, then their development and construction must be explained. In chapter 11, we (Müller & Carpendale) describe and explain the development of an important social skill that emerges during infancy: the ability to coordinate attention with others. This ability is essential to language development, further social development, and further cognitive development. Accounts of such early social development tend to fall into either individualist or relational epistemological frameworks. The individualist framework begins with the individual and suggests that the infant first comes to know her own mind through introspection and then infers the existence of other minds through analogical reasoning. Because the individualist approach to social development faces insurmountable problems, we propose, as an alternative, a relational approach to social development. According to the relational approach, neither self nor other is primary. Rather, development begins from a point of relative nondifferentiation between self and other. Gradually, through differentiating and coordinating

action schemes, and constructing more complex relations among themselves, other persons, and objects, infants develop distinctions between
subject and object, and self and other.

The capacity for joint attention is essential for further social cognitive
development, which in early childhood leads to the emergence of what
has been called a "theory of mind." Racine (chap. 13, this volume) critiques many of the approaches within the "theory of mind" literature, as
well as related theories, by explicating Wittgenstein's internalistic logic.
This logic underlies Wittgenstein's (1968) argument against the possibility of a private language, his notion of language games, and, more generally, his philosophy of psychology. Racine shows that these aspects
jointly motivate Wittgenstein's rejection of a causal view of meaning and
mind. (Sokol and Chandler [chap. 8, this volume] also deal with a causal
view of the mind with regard to Piaget's concept of structure.) An implication relevant for social development that follows from Wittgenstein's
arguments is that children must learn the meaning of words referring to
the psychological world through the interaction with others in the context of shared practices.

We now turn to the issue of how to conceptualize the process through
which society influences the individual—a process frequently described
in terms of the notion of internalization: "Internalization refers to the
process by which material that is held out for the individual by social others is imported into the individual's intra-psychological domain of thinking and affective processes, where social others may be persons, social
institutions, or culturally constructed external mediating devices" (Lawrence & Valsiner, 1993, p. 151). However, the general concept of internalization still needs to be elaborated in terms of what materials get imported
by the individual and in what ways this process operates (Lawrence &
Valsiner, 1993, p. 151). The process of internalization has traditionally
been viewed in one of two possible ways (see also Arievitch & van der
Veer, 1995; Matusov, 1998). First, it can be viewed as

> simple cultural transmission, as exemplified in most viewpoints on social-
> ization and enculturation, in which the course of transmission is seen as *uni-
> directional*. The "knower" (parent, teacher, expert) provides the "not-yet-
> knower" (child, student, novice) samples of completed knowledge, and the
> recipients of such prepackaged messages are expected to accept these as
> given, in passive (or at least not reconstructive) ways. This transmission
> process does not entail reorganization of what is transmitted. . . . Alterna-
> tively, internalization can be viewed as the *transformation* of culturally pro-
> vided input into the person's active process of co-construction of the self.
> This conceptual approach is based on a *bidirectional* culture transmission
> model. (Lawrence & Valsiner, 1993, p. 152)

In the case of internalization as transformation, internalization is not seen as an automatic copying or transmission operation, but as one involving coordination of the new with the old and restructuring of both (see Bickhard, chap. 6). Others contribute to this coordination and provide a frame within which the individual pieces are built into the individual's mental structure. The active and constructive role of the developing person is necessary for psychological development to take place.

Piaget endorsed a transformation model of how society influenced the individual. The child does not submit passively to the pressure of social life, "he actively selects among available possibilities, and reconstructs them and assimilates them in his own manner" (Piaget, 1977/1995, pp. 33, 36; see also Piaget, 1970b, p. 44). Although this reconstruction can be speeded up through sociocultural transmission (Piaget, 1977/1995, p. 37), it still follows a developmental logic that leads through the differentiation and integration of knowledge structures from less complex to more complex forms of knowledge. Knowledge cannot be taken over as ready made. Rather, "each individual is called upon to think and rethink the system of collective notions on his own account and by means of his own logic" (Piaget, 1977/1995, p. 138; see also Piaget, 1968/1971b, p. 117).

The transformation view of internalization has ramifications for the interpretations of how cultural tools influence development. The fact that higher psychological functions are mediated by cultural tools (e.g., Gauvain, 1995; Wertsch, 1985) does not, in itself, explain how the individual comes to understand the function and meaning of cultural tools. Cultural tools only contain information, and this information does not constitute knowledge or meaning. Knowledge and meaning result from the individual's constructive activity. As argued by Boesch (1992), the "multiple information contained in, and offered by culture will become knowledge through individual assimilation, which entails selective perception, transformation and integration in order to fit the cultural messages into the action structures of the individual" (p. 89). Thus, sociocultural conditions provide constraints and offer possibilities for development, but they produce this or that effect only if individuals act in a certain way (Bunge, 2000), and through their interactions individuals reconstruct culture (i.e., give meaning to institutions, practices, and tools; Giddens, 1984).

For Piaget, social interaction is one important motor and cause of development. Interaction can take different forms—between subject and object, between subject and other subjects—and both types of interactions are inseparable from each other (Piaget, 1977/1995, p. 41). Boom (chap. 4, this volume) discusses these forms of interaction as well as interaction between levels within the subject. Because of the central role given to interactions, Piaget's theory can be viewed as an early dynamic systems theory. Boom points out that a criticism of Piaget's theory, known as the learning paradox or the novelty problem (i.e., that more powerful structures cannot arise from less powerful structures), can be dealt with because dynamic systems theories can account for emergent properties.

The role of social interaction in the development of moral knowledge takes center stage in Nucci's chapter (10, this volume). Nucci builds on Piaget's insight that moral knowledge is constructed by children in the context of social interaction, rather than being transmitted from previous generations. Piaget (1932/1965, p. 349) argued that heteronomous morality, "which consecrates the existing order of ideas," and autonomous morality, which "allows the emancipation of what ought to be from what is," are based on different social processes: Whereas heteronomous morality is based on constraint, autonomous morality is based on cooperation. Nucci makes the case that Piaget too strongly linked constraining, heteronomous, parent–child interactions to heteronomous morality, and cooperative, autonomous, child–child interactions to autonomous morality. In contrast, Nucci argues for a more differentiated view of social relations and suggests that these different patterns of social interaction result in the development of differing domains of social cognition. In particular, the conceptual systems of morality, social convention, and personal autonomy develop from different aspects of children's social experience. In situations in which individuals' actions do not directly affect the welfare of others (areas in which choices do not conflict with others' rights), decisions are influenced by social convention or personal autonomy. The line between these domains of custom and personal choice varies cross-culturally and is negotiated within families during the transition from childhood to adolescence.

The issue of distinct domains of children's cognition is also tackled by Sokol and Chandler (chap. 8, this volume). They describe the clash between domain-general versus domain-specific accounts of development as it played out in the areas of moral and epistemic development. In an effort to bridge the divide between moral and epistemic development, Sokol and Chandler point to an ambiguity in Piaget's notion of structure, which can be interpreted either in a causal or functional sense, as the hidden cause of manifest behavior, or, alternatively, as a formal description of a pattern of activity (Chapman, 1988). Kohlberg subscribed to the former interpretation, which then led him to postulate domain general structures of reasoning. However, Sokol and Chandler suggest that the latter interpretation of structures is more consistent with the general thrust of Piaget's writings. Structures as formal descriptions are not causal, disembodied mental principles, but rather are located in activity—in the various systems of relations in which children are engaged. This relational reading of Piaget is consistent with domain-specific accounts of development (i.e., development is specific to the different relations children experience).

Lourenço (chap. 12, this volume) focuses on the implications of Piaget's cognitive concepts for social development. In particular, Lourenço shows the relevance of Piaget's concepts of affirmation and negation for the development of children's prosocial behavior. Consistent with this application of Piagetian cognitive theory to the development of prosocial behavior, Lourenço reports empirical evidence that children's increasing capacity to understand negation is positively related to their tendency to think of prosocial acts in terms of material, psychological, and moral gain rather than in terms of material cost as well as to their prosocial behavior.

FACTS, NORMS, AND RELATIVISM

As described earlier, structural holism implies relativism (i.e., rational and moral norms can be evaluated only relative to their specific cultures; for a discussion, see Chandler, 1997). From a relativist perspective, truth is just what everyone agrees with (i.e., it is culturally specific). Piaget (1977/1995) opposed such a relativistic stance, which in his eyes confuses ideology and rational logic and makes it impossible to distinguish between rational beliefs and inconsistent ideologies (pp. 24, 81, 135).

Part and parcel of Piaget's opposition to relativism was his rejection of structural holism. If the individual is subordinated to society, it becomes impossible to distinguish between opinion and justified knowledge (e.g., to account for the differences between the way children come to understand the Pythagorean theorem and the way they might be convinced of the dogmas of the Hitler Youth; Piaget, 1977/1995; Smith, 1995). If social transmission is explained as the unilateral transmission of moral and rational norms, as is the tendency in sociocultural approaches (e.g., Tappan, 1997), there is no way to distinguish irrational collective beliefs from knowledge that is grounded in good reasons. Truth does not simply result from verbal agreements—"as though history . . . did not abound in examples of collective errors" (Piaget, 1977/1995, p. 81). Furthermore, simple social transmission cannot explain why, at a certain level of development, morality and rationality are no longer experienced as something external to the individual—something into which the individual was blindly socialized.

In adopting a relational position and approaching rationality and morality from a developmental perspective, Piaget's theory offers an alternative to the relativist position by exploring the relations between intraindividual structures of operations and interindividual cooperation. For Piaget this raises the following question: Is it that individual intellectual development makes interpersonal cooperation possible or that interpersonal cooperation leads to the development of intraindividual structures? The answer given in his later work is that intra- and interindividual structures share a common nucleus (Piaget, 1968/1971b, p. 98). That is, the same logic is at work in the coordination of actions of one individual and the coordination of actions between individuals.

Cooperation and free discussion play an essential role in the development of knowledge because they constitute the most favorable condition for counteracting individual centrations on certain aspects of the issue at hand. Drawing on the importance of cooperation for cognitive development, pragmatic theories go even further and explain cognitive development mainly in terms of the formal procedures that are, for example, involved when in free discussion a consensus is reached. Döbert (chap. 7, this volume), however, argues that a reliance only on pragmatics leaves out the substantive connection to the world: "An appropriate procedural theory of rationality would thus have to operate in the triangle delineated by the individual, the substantive dimension, and the social dimension."

Döbert's conclusion is similar to Chapman's (1991, 1999) argument that the development of knowledge involves an "epistemic triangle" consisting of the relations among an active child, another person, and their object of knowledge. According to Chapman (1991), both the child and other person "have direct acquaintance with the object by virtue of their respective operative interactions with it, and they acquire knowledge of each other (and each other's experience) through communicative interaction (cf. Habermas, 1982). Further, the ability of agents to communicate with each other allows them to exchange knowledge of the object as well as to coordinate their actions in cooperative action" (pp. 211–212).

Development of knowledge implies better or more adequate forms of knowledge. This raises the distinction between how social conditions may cause the formation of belief versus the role of social conditions in the development of valid, warranted, and justified knowledge. Knowledge develops in relation to the natural world; as such the natural world is a causal condition for the development of knowledge, but epistemic norms somehow arise from psychological processes. Both Kitchener (chap. 3, this volume) and Smith (chap. 9, this volume) address this problem. Smith argues that developmental psychology tends to neglect the normative aspect of knowledge. Normative facts have both empirical and normative properties. They are empirical in origin, but they are not simply causal facts because norms have content based on reasons the use of which serves in their legitimation or justification. Based on Piaget's theory, Smith proposes an inclusive unit of analysis that combines the empirical investigation of causal facts in developmental psychology with the empirical study of normative facts in developmental epistemology. Key to Smith's proposal is that causal psychology (concerned with the causal origins of knowledge) and normative epistemology do not exhaust all the options of studying development; a third approach, which is also empirical—developmental epistemology— is possible and required to study the actual development of the normative aspect of knowledge. Smith applies this approach to the particular case of education and corrects many misconceptions regarding Piaget's view of education, notably the long-standing—but almost universally disregarded— commitment in Piagetian pedagogy to the design of instructional contexts for group learning in the classroom.

Kitchener (chap. 3, this volume) explores the question of whether Piaget has a social epistemology. The upshot of this question is not whether social conditions causally influence knowledge—they certainly do. Rather, this question aims to determine whether, given that social conditions influence belief formation, social factors are necessary in transforming belief into justified, warranted knowledge. Knowledge is grounded in interaction with the world and other people; the natural world and other persons are thus causal conditions for the development of knowledge, yet there is also a normative aspect to knowledge. Assuming that epistemic and moral norms do not exist before individuals and societies, we must explain how norms develop from the non-normative: "One must show how to secure a place for the normative within the natural" (Kitchener, chap. 3, this volume). Piaget's answer to how the individual constructs norms was through cooperative interaction in which individuals come to understand others' points of view. That is, logical and moral norms do not arise from social conformity to group norms nor from the activity of isolated individuals, but rather norms emerge from the cooperative social interaction of individuals.

Kitchener shows that social interaction has an essential part in Piaget's theory and that it would be a misconception to think otherwise. For Piaget, objectivity presupposes an awareness of other people with different perspectives. Thus, rationality is essentially social in nature: "social life is a necessary condition for the development of logic" (Piaget, 1977/ 1995, p. 210).

CONCLUSION

We have argued that social interaction is of central importance in the development of rationality and morality. Therefore, this is a fundamental issue to be dealt with in theories in the social sciences. We briefly introduced some of the epistemological issues that arise when we consider how to conceptualize the role of social interaction in development (e.g., the individual vs. the collective, issues arising concerning social interaction and development, as well as the normative dimension to development). These and other issues concerning social interaction and the development of knowledge as well as Piaget's contributions to these debates are taken up in greater depth in the remaining chapters in this volume.

ACKNOWLEDGMENTS

We thank Orlando Lourenço, Tim Racine, and Les Smith for comments on an earlier draft of this chapter. We also thank Michael Chandler, Orlando Lourenço, Bill Overton, and Les Smith for advice and encouragement in the planning of this book. The preparation of this chapter was supported by a Social Sciences and Humanities Research Council of Canada operating grant to the first author.

REFERENCES

Arievitch, I., & van der Veer, R. (1995). Furthering the internalization debate: G'alperin's contribution. *Human Development, 38,* 113–126.

Berger, P. L., & Luckmann, T. (1966). *The social construction of reality.* Garden City, NY: Doubleday.

Boesch, E. E. (1989). Cultural psychology in action-theoretical perspective. In C. Kagitcibasi (Ed.), *Growth and progress in cross-cultural psychology* (pp. 41–51). Berwyn: Swets North America.

Boesch, E. E. (1992). Culture—individual—culture—The cycle of knowledge. In M. v. Cranach, W. Doise, & G. Mugny (Eds.), *Social representation and the social bases of knowledge* (pp. 89–97). Lewiston, NY: Hogrefe & Huber.

Bruner, J. (1997). Celebrating divergence: Piaget and Vygotsky. *Human Development, 40,* 63–73.

Bunge, M. (2000). Ten modes of individualism—none of which works—and their alternatives. *Philosophy of the Social Sciences, 30,* 384–406.

Chandler, M. J. (1997). Stumping for progress in a post-modern world. In E. Amsel & K. A. Renninger (Eds.), *Change and development* (pp. 1–26). Mahwah, NJ: Lawrence Erlbaum Associates.

Chapman, M. (1988). *Constructive evolution: Origins and development of Piaget's thought.* New York: Cambridge University Press.

Chapman, M. (1991). The epistemic triangle: Operative and communicative components of cognitive development. In M. Chandler & M. Chapman (Eds.), *Criteria for competence: Controversies in the conceptualization and assessment of children's abilities* (pp. 209–228). Hillsdale, NJ: Lawrence Erlbaum Associates.

Chapman, M. (1992). Equilibration and the dialectics of organization. In H. Beilin & P. B. Pufall (Eds.), *Piaget's theory: Prospects and possibilities* (pp. 39–59). Hillsdale, NJ: Lawrence Erlbaum Associates.

Chapman, M. (1999). Constructivism and the problem of reality. *Journal of Applied Development Psychology, 20,* 31–43.

Cosmides, L., & Tooby, J. (2002). Unraveling the enigma of human intelligence: Evolutionary psychology and the multimodular mind. In R. J. Sternberg & J. C. Kaufman (Eds.), *The evolution of intelligence* (pp. 145–198). Mahwah, NJ: Lawrence Erlbaum Associates.

Dahlbäck, O. (1998). The individualism-holism problem in sociological research. *Journal for the Theory of Social Behavior, 28*, 237–272.

Durkheim, E. (1982). *The rules of the sociological method and selected texts on sociology and method* (W. D. Halls, Trans.). New York: The Free Press.

Durkheim, E. (1953). *Sociology and philosophy* (D. F. Pocock, Trans.). London: Cohen & West.

Duveen, G. (1997). Psychological development as a social process. In L. Smith, J. Dockrell, & P. Tomlinson (Eds.), *Piaget, Vygotsky and beyond* (pp. 67–90). London: Routledge.

Elias, N. (1978). *What is sociology?* New York: Columbia Press. (Original work published 1970)

Gauvain, M. (1995). Thinking in niches: Sociocultural influences on cognitive development. *Human Development, 38*, 25–45.

Giddens, A. (1977). *Studies in social and political theory.* New York: Basic Books.

Giddens, A. (1984). *The constitution of society: Outline of a theory of structuration.* Berkeley, CA: University of California Press.

Grene, M. (1974). *The understanding of nature.* Dordrecht: D. Reidel.

Habermas, J. (1982). *Theorie des kommunikative handelns* [Theory of communicative action] (2 Vols.). Frankfurt: Suhrkamp.

Homans, G. C. (1961). *Social behavior: Its elementary forms.* London: Routledge & Kegan Paul.

Kitchener, R. (1996). The nature of the social for Piaget and Vygotsky. *Human Development, 39*, 243–249.

Kitchener, R. (Ed.). (2000). Special issue: Piaget's sociological studies. *New Ideas in Psychology, 18*, 119–275.

Lave, J. (1988). *Cognition in practice.* New York: Cambridge University Press.

Lawrence, J. A., & Valsiner, J. (1993). Conceptual roots of internalization: From transmission to transformation. *Human Development, 36*, 150–167.

Lenk, H. (1987). Der methodologische Individualismus ist (nur?) ein heuristisches Postulat [Methodological individualism in (only?) a heuristic postulate]. In H. Lenk (Ed.), *Zwischen Sozialpsychologie und Sozialphilosophie* (pp. 67–82). Frankfurt am Main: Suhrkamp.

Lourenço, O., & Machado, A. (1996). In defense of Piaget's theory: A reply to 10 common criticisms. *Psychological Review, 103*, 143–164.

Matusov, E. (1998). When solo activity is not privileged: Participation and internalization models of development. *Human Development, 41*, 326–349.

Matusov, E., & Hayes, R. (2000). Sociocultural critique of Piaget and Vygotsky. *New Ideas in Psychology, 18*, 215–239.

Moessinger, P. (2000). *The paradox of social order.* New York: Aldine de Gruyter.

Piaget, J. (1928). *Judgment and reasoning in the child.* London: Routledge & Kegan Paul. (Original work published 1924)

Piaget, J. (1955). *The language and thought of the child.* Clevelman: Meridian. (Original work published 1923)

Piaget, J. (1962). *Play, dreams and imitation in childhood.* New York: Norton. (Original work published 1945)

Piaget, J. (1965). *The moral judgment of the child.* New York: The Free Press (Original work published 1932)

Piaget, J. (1970a). *The place of the sciences of man in the system of sciences.* New York: Harper Torchbooks.

Piaget, J. (1970b). *Main trends in psychology.* London: George Allen & Unwin.

Piaget, J. (1971a). *Biology and knowledge.* Chicago: University of Chicago Press. (Original work published 1967)

Piaget, J. (1971b). *Structuralism*. London: Routledge & Kegan Paul. (Original work published 1968)

Piaget, J. (1973). *Main trends in interdisciplinary research*. London: George Allen & Unwin. (Original work published 1970)

Piaget, J. (1995). *Sociological studies*. London: Routledge. (Original work published 1977)

Piaget, J. (2000). Commentary on Vygotsky criticism of language and thought of the child and judgement and reasoning in the child. *New Ideas in Psychology, 18,* 241–260. (Original work published 1962)

Plessner, H. (1926). *Die Stufen des Organischen und der Mensch* [The levels of the organic and the human being]. Berlin: Göschen.

Plessner, H. (1976). *Die Frage nach der Conditio Humana* [The quest for the human condition]. Frankfurt: Suhrkamp.

Portmann, A. (1990). *A zoologist looks at humankind*. New York: Columbia University Press. (Original work published 1944)

Rogoff, B. (1998). Cognition as collaborative process. In W. Damon (Series Ed.), D. Kuhn & R. S. Siegler (Vol. Eds.), *Handbook of child psychology: Vol. 2. Cognition, perception, and language* (5th ed., pp. 679–744). New York: Wiley.

Shotter, J. (1990). *Knowing of the third kind*. Utrecht: ISOR.

Smith, L. (1982). Piaget and the solitary knower. *Philosophy of the Social Sciences, 12,* 173–182.

Smith, L. (1993). *Necessary knowledge*. Hove, UK: Lawrence Erlbaum Associates.

Smith, L. (1995). Introduction to Piaget's sociological studies. In J. Piaget (Ed.), *Sociological studies* (pp. 1–22). London: Routledge.

Smith, L. (1996). With knowledge in mind: Novel transformation of the learner or transformation of novel knowledge. *Human Development, 39,* 257–263.

Tappan, M. B. (1997). Language, culture, and moral development: A Vygotskian perspective. *Developmental Review, 17,* 78–100.

Valsiner, J. (1998). Dualisms displaced: From crusades to analytic distinctions. *Human Development, 41,* 350–354.

Vygotsky, L. S. (1986). *Thought and language*. Cambridge, MA: MIT Press.

Weber, M. (1978). *Economy and society* (G. Roth & C. Wittich, Eds.). Berkeley, CA: University of California Press. (Original work published 1922)

Wertsch, J. V. (1985). *Vygotsky and the social formation of mind*. Cambridge, MA: Harvard University Press.

Wittgenstein, L. (1968). *Philosophical investigations* (3rd ed.). Oxford: Blackwell.

A Relational and Embodied Perspective on Resolving Psychology's Antinomies

Willis F. Overton
Temple University

Throughout their histories, general psychology and developmental psychology have been captives of numerous fundamental antinomies. These have included mind–body, nature–nurture, biology–culture, intrapsychic–interpersonal, structure–function, stability–change, continuity–discontinuity, observation–reason, universal–particular, matter–ideas, unity–diversity, and individual–society. Operating from the base of a 19th-century empiricism and an early 20th-century neopositivism, the standard approach to resolving these and others has been to privilege the significance of one member of the antinomy pair and deny or marginalize the other. Jean Piaget's work stands virtually alone in the field of psychology in offering a systematic contemporary resolution to antinomies based on the recognition that seemingly contradictory pairs may be more profitably understood as co-equal and indissociable complementarities rather than exclusive alternatives. However, in the vast majority of Piaget's writings, the details of this resolution are embedded in his empirical, methodological, and theoretical concerns about the specific nature of knowing and development. The ultimate effect of this embeddedness has been that Piaget is often read in the context of the standard resolution rather than the co-equal complementarity resolution. This reading, in turn, has generated serious misunderstandings (see Lourenço & Machado, 1996) about Piaget's theory and empirical findings concerning the nature and development of mind, and human functioning generally.

In this chapter, I describe two interrelated metatheories that articulate the co-equal indissociable complementarity resolution to antinomies and provide the grounding for a psychological theory of mind, human functioning, and development. These metatheories consist of a *relational* metatheory that resolves the antinomies and a *developmentally oriented embodied action* metatheory that grounds human experience and development within this resolution. In the discussion of these metatheories, I argue that they provide a coherent and reasonable context for the understanding of Piagetian theory, and that this coherence enhances the scientific meaningfulness of Piagetian empirical research and empirical findings. Although several of the antinomies are illustrative, the individual–social or person–sociocultural serves as the focus of attention.

All concepts and methods are contextualized by some metatheoretical framework. A metatheory provides basic constructs that articulate the meaning of concepts and methods in a domain of inquiry. A metatheoretical frame offers advice, guidelines, and criteria for decisions concerning the nature and the adequacy or inadequacy of a theoretical and methodological approach to the domain under investigation. A metatheory is prescriptive in the sense that it defines what is meaningful and meaningless, what is acceptable and unacceptable, and what is central and peripheral to inquiry. To grasp the guidelines and criteria that relational metatheory offers for the co-equal indissociable complementarity resolution of the antinomies, it is necessary to understand the metatheory that frames the standard resolution. This has been referred to as a *split metatheory*. Relational and split metatheories compose the world in different ways: Relational metatheory paints the world as systems of dynamic changing part–whole relations, whereas split metatheory paints the world as aggregates of dichotomous elements.

SPLIT METATHEORY

Split metatheory entails several basic defining principles, including *splitting*, *foundationalism*, and *atomism*. *Splitting* is the separation of components of a whole into mutually exclusive pure forms that are taken to describe basic elements. To split one must accept the twin principles of *foundationalism* and *atomism*. These are the metatheoretical axioms that there is ultimately a rock bottom unchanging nature to reality (the foundation of foundationalism), and this rock bottom is composed of elements—pure forms (the atoms of atomism)—that preserve their identity regardless of context. A corollary principle here is the belief that all complexity is *simple complexity* in the sense that any whole is taken to be an additive combination of its elements.

Splitting, foundationalism, and atomism are all principles of decomposition—breaking an aggregate down to its smallest pieces, to its bedrock. This process also goes by other names including *reductionism* and *the analytic attitude* (Overton, 2002a). Split metatheory requires another principle to reassemble or recompose the whole. This is the principle of *unidirectional and linear (additive) associative or causal sequences*. The elements must be related either according to their contiguous co-occurrence in space and time or according to simple efficient cause–effect sequences that proceed in a single direction (Bunge, 1962; Overton & Reese, 1973). In fact, split metatheory admits no determination other than individual efficient causes or these individual causes operating in a conjunctive (i.e., additive) plurality. That is, no truly reciprocal causality is admitted (Bunge, 1962; Overton & Reese, 1973).

All antinomies emerge from a split metatheoretical context. For example, the individual–social, individual–collective, or person–social antinomy represents all behavior and action as the additive product of elementary bedrock pure forms identified as person and sociocultural. Arising from this splitting, behavior is understood as an aggregate composed of these two pure forms, and the question becomes one of the primacy or privileged quality of one or the other. Nativism–empiricism is a closely related antinomy in which the pure forms consist of, on the one hand, some basic biological form or element (e.g., DNA, genes, neurons), and, on the other hand, some basic environmental element (e.g., parents, society, culture). Piaget's own work is characterized by a pervasive antipathy to the splitting of nativism–empiricism (see e.g., Piaget, 1987; see also his description of himself as "neither empiricist nor apriorist but rather constructivist or partisan of dialectic," 1992, p. 215).

Recently, the pursuit of the person–sociocultural antinomy has been a defining characteristic of contemporary sociocultural (e.g., Cole & Wertsch, 1996; Wertsch, 1991) and social constructivist approaches (e.g., Gergen, 1994). These follow the work of Marx, who pursued the broader ideas–matter antinomy and claimed a bedrock foundational primacy for material sociocultural objects—hence his presentation of dialectical *materialism*. Wertsch acknowledged Marx's contribution and framed his own work within the person–social antinomy by endorsing both a split interpretation of Vygotsky (i.e., "In pursuing a line of reasoning that reflected their concern with Marxist claims about the *primacy of social forces* Vygotsky and his colleagues . . . contended that many of the design features of mediational means *originated in social life*," 1991, p. 33; italics added) and a split interpretation of Luria:

As stated by Luria (1981), "in order to explain the highly complex forms of human consciousness one must go beyond the human organism. One must seek the origins of conscious activity and 'categorical' behavior *not in the re-*

cesses of the human brain or in the depths of the spirit, *but in* the external conditions of life. Above all, this means that one must *seek these origins in the external processes of social life,* [emphasis added] in the social and historical forms of human existence" (p. 25). (Wertsch, 1991, p. 34)

At times social constructivist and sociocultural splitting becomes more subtle. For example, Cole and Wertsch (1996) began one article by acknowledging, on the basis of several direct Piagetian quotes, that Piaget— a traditional villain of both socioculturalist and social constructivists, who is often inaccurately accused of privileging the person—"did not deny the co-equal role of the social world in the construction of knowledge" (p. 251). However, these authors then switched the ground of the issue from the social world specifically to culture mediation entailed by the social world and argued, both in headings (i.e., "The Primacy of Cultural Mediation," p. 251) and text, that culture is to be privileged:

Social origins take on a special importance in Vygotsky's theories that is less symmetrical than Piaget's notion of social equilibration. . . . *For Vygotsky and cultural-historical theorists more generally, the social world does have primacy over the individual* in a very special sense. Society is the bearer of the cultural heritage. . . . (p. 353; italics added)

RELATIONAL METATHEORY

Within a relational metatheoretical context, the antinomies dissolve because such dichotomous exclusive pairs come to be treated as truly co-equals; and if they are truly co-equals, there can be no issue of primacy or privilege. Yet to say that they are co-equals is one thing and to demonstrate their co-equal status is another. It is the task of relational metatheory to (a) establish that seemingly contradictory categories can be co-equal and indissociable while maintaining their individual identity (i.e., their complementarity); (b) demonstrate that the co-equality of categories need not involve an absolute relativism; and (c) demonstrate that this metatheory facilitates scientific inquiry. A related task for this chapter is to clarify that Piagetian theory represents an instantiation of relational metatheory and, hence, establish that Piagetian theory avoids all antinomies, including person–culture.

Holism

The basic principle that guides a relational metatheory is *holism*—the assertion that the identities of objects and events derive from the relational context or system in which they are embedded. Here the whole is not an aggregate of discrete elements, but an organized and self-organizing system of parts, each part being defined by its relations to other parts and to the whole. Complexity in this context is *organized complexity* (Luhmann, 1995; von Bertalanffy, 1968a, 1968b), in that the whole or system is not decomposable into elements arranged in additive linear sequences of cause–effect relations (Overton & Reese, 1973). Nonlinear dynamics are a defining characteristic of this type of complexity. In the context of holism, principles of splitting, foundationalism, and atomism are rejected as meaningless approaches to analysis, and fundamental antinomies such as person–culture are similarly rejected as false dichotomies.

The Piagetian theoretical commitment to this broad principle of relational metatheory is demonstrated in numerous assertions made by Piaget in a variety of sources:

> Wholes do not result from putting together a bunch of parts; parts result from differentiation of the whole. This means that autoconservative properties of the whole provide a cohesive force that distinguishes the whole from inorganic psychochemical totalities. (1985, p. 20)

> Wholeness is a defining mark of structures . . . all structuralists . . . are at one in recognizing as fundamental the contrast between *structures* and *aggregates*, the former being wholes, the latter composites formed of elements that are independent of the complexes into which they enter. To insist on this distinction is not to deny that structures have elements, but the elements of a structure are subordinated to laws, and it is in terms of their laws that the structure *qua* whole or system is defined. Moreover, the laws governing a structure's composition are not reducible to cumulative one-by-one associations of its elements: they confer on the whole, as such, over-all properties distinct from the properties of its elements. (1970a, pp. 6–7)

> Structure is a totality; that is, it is a system governed by laws that apply to the system as such, and not only to one or another element in the system. (1970b, p. 22)

> The concept of totality expresses the interdependence inherent in every organization. . . . The correlative of the idea of totality is . . . the idea of *relationship*. Every totality is a system of relationships just as every relationship is a segment of totality. (1952, p. 10)

> In the living organism, the reflexes form organized totalities and not juxtaposed mechanisms. (1952, p. 127)

With holism as the superordinate principle, relational methatheory moves to specific principles that define the relations among parts and the relations of parts to wholes. In other words, relational metatheory articulates principles of analysis and synthesis necessary for any scientific inquiry. These are the principles of (a) The Identity of Opposites, (b) The

Opposites of Identity, and (c) The Synthesis of Wholes (see Overton [2003] for an extended discussion).

The Identity of Opposites

The principle of the *identity of opposites* establishes the identity among fundamental parts by casting them not as exclusive contradictions as in the split methodology, but as differentiated polarities (i.e., co-equals) of a unified (i.e., indissociable) inclusive matrix—as a relation. As differentiations, each pole is defined recursively; each pole defines and is defined by its opposite. There are a number of ways to articulate this principle, but perhaps the clearest articulation is found in considering the famous ink sketch by Escher entitled "Drawing Hands." In this sketch, a left and a right hand assume a relational posture according to which each is simultaneously drawing and being drawn by the other. In this relational matrix, each hand is identical—thus co-equal and indissociable—with the other in the sense of each drawing and each being drawn. This is a moment of analysis in which the law of contradiction (i.e., Not the case that A = notA) is relaxed and identity (i.e., A = notA) reigns. In this *identity moment of analysis*, pure forms collapse and categories flow into each other. Here each category contains and, in fact, *is* its opposite. As a consequence, there is a broad inclusivity established among categories. If we think of inclusion and exclusion as different moments that occur when we observe a reversible figure (e.g., a necker cube or the vase-women illusion), then in this identity moment we observe only inclusion. In the next (opposite) moment of analysis, the figures reverse, and there again we will see exclusivity as the hands appear as opposites and complementarities.

Within the identity moment of analysis, it is a useful exercise to write on each hand one of the bipolar terms of a traditionally split antinomies (e.g., person and culture) and explore the resulting effect. This exercise is more than merely an illustration of a familiar bidirectionality of effects suggested by many scientific investigators. The exercise makes tangible the central feature of the relational metatheory; seemingly dichotomous ideas that are often been thought of as competing alternatives can, in fact, enter into inquiry as co-equal indissociable supportive partners. It also concretizes the meaning of any truly nonadditive reciprocal determination (Overton & Reese, 1973).

If inquiry concerning person, culture, and behavior is approached according to the principle of the identity of opposites, various constraints result because constraints are imposed by any metatheory. An important example of such a constraint is that behavior, traits, styles, and so on cannot be thought of as being decomposable into the independent and additive pure forms of person and culture. Thus, from the perspective of relational metatheory, the goals of sociocultural or social constructivist approaches in attempting to elevate society and culture to a privileged primary position simply represent a meaningless approach to inquiry.

If the principle of the identity of opposites introduces constraints, it also opens possibilities. The most important possibility is the recognition that, to paraphrase the philosopher Searle (1992), the fact that a behavior is biologically or person determined does not imply that it is not socially or culturally determined, and the fact that it is socially or culturally determined does not imply that it is not biologically or person determined. In other words, the identity of opposites establishes the metatheoretical position that genes and culture, like culture and person, and brain and person, and so on operate in a truly interpenetrating manner, and further that any concept of interaction (e.g., interaction, co-action, transaction) must be interpreted not as the cooperation or competition among elements, but as the interpenetration among parts. With this recognition, any debate based on antinomies—whether it be nativism–empiricism, person–culture, or any other—ceases to have merit. That is, given the denial of pure forms implied by the identity of opposites, it is impossible to cast questions of development as having a nativistic, empiricist, person, or social origins. It is impossible to claim that the social world has primacy over the individual in any sense, just as it is impossible to claim that the individual has primacy over the social world in any sense.

The identity of opposites establishes that traditional splits or dichotomies are better understood as bipolarities of a system whose parts are co-equals and indissociable. This message pervades Piagetian theory at every level. The most general and abstract explanatory concepts that frame Piagetian theory are *structure* and *function*. As an antinomy, structure–function has divided psychology from the structuralism of Titchener and Wundt and the functionalism of James and Dewey to visions of functionalism described by contemporary cognitivist approaches (Overton, 1994a, 1994b). Cast in antimonic form, Piaget has been described both as a static structuralist and as a contemporary functionalist (Beilin, 1983). However, Piaget himself argued that mental structures, understood as dynamic self-organizing systems, and functions, understood as the activity of those systems, can never be dissociated. "Structures are inseparable from performance, from functions" (Piaget, 1970a, p. 69). Further, as concepts specifically applicable to organisms, structure and function become translated as organization and adaptation, and, again at this level, Piaget was insistent that there can be no antinomy:

> Organization is inseparable from adaptation: . . . The first being the internal aspect of the cycle of which adaptation constitutes the external aspect. (Piaget, 1952, p. 7)

The "accord of thought with things" and the "accord of thought with itself" expresses this dual functional invariant of adaptation and organization. These two aspects of thought are indissociable: It is by adapting to things that thought organizes itself and it is by organizing itself that it structures things. (Piaget, 1952, p. 8)

The organism and the environment form an indissoluble entity, . . . there are adaptional variations simultaneously involving a structuring of the organism and an action of the environment, the two being inseparable from each other. (Piaget, 1952, p. 16)

Virtually all of the remaining basic concepts of Piagetian theory are nested within the identity of opposites of structure–function (i.e., organization–adaptation) and are presented as such identities. Piaget insisted that all the basic concepts of the theory are co-equals and indissociable, and thus defined a unity that resides in the "fact that they actually are two terms in a dialectical relation, and therefore two poles in a cycle that prevails from the outset and grows as a spiral throughout development" (Piaget & Garcia, 1991, p. 8). The action of adaptation arises out of mental organization, but as action it is composed of the bipolarity of assimilation–accommodation and "assimilation and accommodation represent two inseparable poles and not two distinct types of behavior" (1985, p. 35).

Assimilation–accommodation constitutes the basic mechanism of development. Assimilation is the act of projecting mental organization onto the world, thus giving the world meaning; accommodation is the act of modifying organization (meaning) in the context of resistances assimilation meets in the world. This basic explanation is incorporated into the more general explanatory bipolarity equilibration–reflective abstraction. Equilibration represents the structural side of the coin, and optimizing equilibration (Piaget, 1985) describes the process by which, as a result of action, the dynamic self-organizing system (i.e., mental organization) differentiates and becomes reintegrated (differentiation and integration being yet another bipolarity) at increasingly adapted levels of organization. Reflective abstraction is the functional side of the same coin describing assimilation–accommodation action specifically as it participates in the movement to these novel levels of mental organization. Finally, reflective abstraction is composed of a polarity. "Reflective abstraction includes two indissociable activities. One is 'reflecting or projecting onto a higher level. . . . The other is . . . 'reflexion' in the sense of cognitive reconstruction or reorganization of what is transferred" (Piaget, 1985, p. 29).

Beyond the context of structure–function, there are several other identities within the Piagetian system, including, for example, physical and logical-mathematical experience (Piaget, 1977), figurative and operative thinking (Piaget, 1967), and positive and negative feedback (Piaget, 1985).

However, the most general identity—the one that is most significant for the person–culture relationship—is the identity of subject (person) and object (social world). Here as in all other places, Piaget (1977) insisted on a unity that precludes the possibility of antinomy:

> The subject S and the objects O are therefore indissociable, and it is from this indissociable interaction S←–→O that action, the source of knowledge, originates. The point of departure of this knowledge, therefore, is neither S nor O but the interaction. (p. 31)

The Opposites of Identity

Although the identity of opposites sets constraints and opens possibilities—although it establishes the co-equal and indissociable character of basic polarities—it does not, in itself, establish the complementary nature of these polarities. Establishing the identities as complementarities within relational metatheory requires moving to a second moment of inquiry. In this second moment, the identity of categories that flow into each other fades into the background, figure and ground are reversed, and the moment becomes dominated by exclusivity and the opposite features of the polarity. Thus, in this opposite moment of analysis, it becomes clear that despite identity Escher's sketch shows a right hand and a left hand and these are opposites. In this moment the law of contradiction (i.e., Not the case that A = notA) is reasserted, and categories again exclude each other and become opposites. As a consequence of this exclusion, parts exhibit unique identities that differentiate each from the other as complementarities.

Piagetian theory does not explicitly articulate the nature of the two moments of inquiry, but Piaget's writings clearly indicate an appreciation of the necessary interrelationship of co-equal, indissociable, and complementary:

> Organization is inseparable from adaptation: They are two complementary processes. (Piaget, 1952, p. 7)

> I shall begin by making a distinction between two aspects of thinking that are different, although complementary. One is the figurative aspect, and the other I call the operative aspect. (Piaget, 1967, 14)

> Each individual has at his disposal two main cognitive systems that are complementary to one another. The presentative system . . . [and] the procedural system. . . . The first system constitutes the *epistemic* subject and the second refers to the *psychological* subject. (Piaget, 1987, p. 5)

And, focusing directly on the person–social relation that under a split interpretation would understand psychological explanation and sociological explanation as competing alternatives, not complements, Piaget (1995) stated: "The two complement each other in revealing the dual aspect, individual and inter-individual, of all behaviour patterns in human society" (p. 41).

A second important feature of the opposites of identity is that this moment rescues relational metatheory, and theories constructed within a relational metatheoretical context, from accusations of introducing an absolute relativism into the world of science (see Overton, [2003] for an extended discussion). Split metatheories generate absolutist positions. Empiricism generated the idea of attaining an absolute bedrock certainty through the reduction of all ideas and events to the foundational material world. Postmodern social constructivist (e.g., Gergen, 2001) and some sociocultural positions—while explicitly denying both the foundationalism of empiricism and foundations generally—take an implicit foundationalist position through the claim of privilege and primacy for the sociocultural world. Because the social is contingent, this foundationalism leads to an absolute relativism as found, for example, in discussions of cultural relativism (see Latour, 1993). In the moment of identity, relational metatheory also establishes a relativism as categories flow into each other. However, this relativism is not absolute because, in the moment of opposition, category boundaries are reestablished and categories again exclude each other (e.g., left hand is a left hand not a right, and right hand is right not left; the person is not culture, and culture is not the person). At this moment, each term of a bipolarity is no longer relative to its complement; it has its own individual identity and fixed features. This position becomes what Latour (1993) termed a *relative relativism*. It is a relativism that allows inquiry to proceed within a stable framework; stability is discovered in instability.

The stable frameworks act as platforms for launching scientific inquiry. These platforms are generally termed *standpoints, points of view, or lines of sight* in recognition that they do not reflect absolute foundations (Harding, 1986). Again consider Escher's sketch as illustrative: When left hand as left hand or right as right hand are the focus of attention, it becomes quite clear that—were they large enough—one could stand on either hand and examine the structures and functions of that hand. Thus, to return to the person–culture example, although explicitly recognizing that as Piaget (1995) says, "everything in the individual is always at once biological, psychological, and social" (p. 216), alternative points of view permit the scientist to analyze the behavior from an individual or, sociocultural standpoint. Person and culture no longer constitute competing alternative explanations. Rather they are two points of view on an object of inquiry created by and only fully understood through multiple viewpoints. To state this more generally, the unity that constitutes human identity and human development becomes discovered only in the diversity of multiple interrelated lines of sight.

Piaget consistently acknowledged the significance of points of view in two ways. On the one hand, his writings are replete with *point of view* as a phrase used to designate a view from one or another complementary pole. One such reference, directly relevant to the person–sociocultural complementarity, illustrates his acknowledgment that stable platforms are necessary for analytic scientific work:

> Since the demands of analysis initially require the separate study of each different aspect of society ... we are bound to distinguish systematically between the synchronic *viewpoint*, associated with equilibrium, and the diachronic or developmental *viewpoint*. This is the reason for the existence of two different types of explanation in sociology. (1995, p. 49; italics added)

Other references more broadly illustrate his use of point of view to describe inquiry from one or another complement:

> Psychological explanation and sociological explanation complement each other in revealing the dual aspect, individual and inter-individual, of all behaviour patterns in human society. (1995, p. 41)

> But a physiological explanation of this kind does not exclude the psychological point of view which we have taken. (1952, p. 39)

> From the biological point of view, intelligence is a particular instance of organic activity. (1952, p. 4)

> To describe this assimilation clearly one can do so either from the point of view of consciousness or from that of behavior. (1952, p. 140)

> From the subject's point of view, this amounts to saying that an assimilatory scheme confers meaning on the object it assimilates and assigns goals to the actions it organizes. (1985, p. 16)

The second way that Piaget acknowledged that the complements of basic polarities constitute analytic standpoints is found in the structure of his publications. Each of Piaget's major writings constitutes an inquiry into the development of knowing from an alternative complement. Thus, for example, *Biology and Knowledge* represents inquiry primarily from the biological point of view; *The Construction of Reality in the Child*, *The Moral Development of the Child*, and so on represent inquiry taken primarily from the person's viewpoint; and *Sociological Studies* represents inquiry primarily from a sociocultural viewpoint.

The Synthesis of Wholes

Engaging fundamental bipolar concepts as relatively stable standpoints opens the way and takes an important first step toward establishing a broad stable base for empirical inquiry within a relational metatheory. However, this solution is incomplete because it omits a key relational component—the relation of parts to the whole. The oppositional quality of the bipolar pairs reminds us that their contradictory nature still remains and continues to require a resolution. Further, the resolution of this tension cannot be found in the split approach of reduction to a bedrock reality. Rather, the relational approach to a resolution is to move away from the extremes to the center and above the conflict, and to here discover a novel system that will coordinate the two oppositional systems. This is the principle of the synthesis of wholes, and this synthesis will constitute yet another standpoint.

At this point, the Escher sketch fails as a graphic representation. Although Drawing Hands illustrates the identities and opposites, and although it shows a middle space between the two, it does not present a coordination. In fact the synthesis for this sketch would be an unseen hand that is drawing and being drawn by the drawing hands. The synthesis of interest for the general metatheory would be a system that is a coordination of the most universal bipolarity that can be imagined. Although there may be several candidates for this level of generality, the polarity between matter or nature and society seems sufficient for present purposes (Latour, 1993). Matter and society represent systems that stand in an identity of opposites. To say that an object is a social object in no way denies that it is matter, and to say that an object is matter in no way denies that it is social. Further, the object can be analyzed from either a social or physical standpoint. The question for synthesis becomes the question of what system will coordinate these two systems. Arguably the answer is that it is *life* or living systems that coordinate matter and society. Because our specific focus of inquiry is the psychological, we can reframe this matter–society polarity as the polarity of *biology* and *culture*. In the context of psychology then, as an illustration write *biology* on one and *culture* on the other Escher hand and consider what system coordinates these systems? It is the human organism, the *person* (see Fig. 2.1a). Persons—as an integrated self-organizing dynamic system of cognitive, emotional, and motivational processes and behaviors this systems expresses—represent a novel level or stage of structure and functioning that emerges from and constitutes a coordination of biology and culture (see Magnusson & Stattin, 1998).

At the synthesis, there is a standpoint that coordinates and resolves the tension between the other two members of the relation. This provides a particularly broad and stable base for launching empirical inquiry. A per-

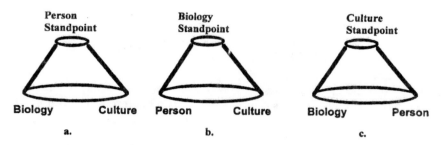

FIG. 2.1.   Relational standpoints in psychological inquiry: Person, biology, and culture.

son standpoint opens the way for the empirical investigation of universal dimensions of psychological structure–function relations (e.g., processes of perception, thought, emotions, values), their individual differences, and their development across the lifespan. Because universal and particular are themselves relational concepts, no question can arise here about whether the focus on universal processes excludes the particular, it clearly does not as we already know from the earlier discussion of polarities. The fact that a process is viewed from a universal standpoint in no way suggests that it is not contextualized.

Piaget's (1995) affirmation of the broad issue of synthesis is illustrated in the already quoted statement, "Obviously, everything in the individual is always at once biological, psychological, and social" (p. 216) and in statements such as, "The mental . . . exists between the biological and the social" (p. 33) and "there is no series of three successive terms: biology → psychology → sociology, but rather a simultaneous link from biology to psychology and sociology" (p. 33). Further, Piaget (1995) was explicit in his recognition of the temptation found among some contemporary researchers to ignore the person or psychological synthesis:

> Certain collective [i.e., sociocultural] interactions and a certain level of organic [i.e., biological] maturation are necessary. . . . In such cases, the link, on the one hand, and the differences, on the other hand, between biological explanation and sociological explanation are so evident that many authors renounce psychological explanation altogether and assimilate psychology to neurology and the social. (p. 32)

In response to such exclusive uses of biological and social explanations, Piaget (1995) argued that, "this does not mean that the psychological factor is negligible, however, because the existence of a *synthesizing factor* cannot be denied" (p. 294; italics added).

As a remedy to this tendency to ignore the person-centered synthesis as one of several possible standpoints, Piaget offered his own theory of cognitive development, which, like the theories of Werner (1957, 1958), Baldwin (1985), Stern (1938), and Sullivan (1953), among others, is a person-centered and developmentally oriented theory—where person includes both the epistemic and psychological subject. In his various writings, Piaget often called attention to the person-centered orientation of a particular discussion by opening a sentence or paragraph with one of several standpoint phrases, including "from the psychological point of view" (1952, p. 38), "from the point of view of behavior" (1952, p. 141), "from the subject's point of view" (1985, p. 16), "from the point of view of consciousness" (1952, p. 170), and "from the point of view of awareness" (1952, p. 35).

It is important to emphasize here that one standpoint of synthesis is relative to other synthesis standpoints. Life and Society are coordinated by Matter; thus, within psychological inquiry, *biology* represents a *standpoint* as the synthesis of *person and culture* (Fig. 2.1b). The implication of this is that a relational biological approach to psychological processes investigates the biological conditions and settings of psychological structure–function relations and the behaviors they express. This exploration is quite different from split—foundationalist approaches to biological inquiry that assume an atomistic and reductionistic stance toward the object of study. Neurobiologist Damasio's (1994, 1999) work on the brain–body basis of a psychological self and emotions is an excellent illustration of the biological relational standpoint. Damasio (1994) argued:

> A task that faces neuroscientists today is to consider the neurobiology supporting adaptive supraregulations [e.g., the psychological subjective experience of self] . . . I am not attempting to reduce social phenomena to biological phenomena, but rather to discuss the powerful connection between them. . . . Realizing that there are biological mechanisms behind the most sublime human behavior does not imply a simplistic reduction to the nuts and bolts of neurobiology. (pp. 124–125)

A third synthesis standpoint recognizes that Life and Matter are coordinated by Society; again granting that the inquiry is about psychological processes, culture represents a standpoint as the synthesis of person and biology (Fig. 2.1c). Thus, a relational cultural approach to psychological processes explores the cultural conditions and settings of psychological structure–function relations. From this cultural standpoint, the focus is on cultural differences in the context of psychological functions as complementary to the person standpoint's focus on psychological functions in the context of cultural differences.

This standpoint is illustrated by cultural psychology or developmentally oriented cultural psychology. It is also illustrated in Piaget's (1995) writings when, for example, in his *Sociological Studies*, he presented the "sociological point of view" (p. 185). However, not all cultural psychologies emerge from relational metatheory. For example, when a cultural psychology makes the social constructivist assertion that social discourse is "prior to and constitutive of the world" (Miller, 1996, p. 99), it becomes clear that this form of cultural psychology has been framed by split foundationalist background ideas.

A recent example of a relational developmentally oriented cultural standpoint is found in the work of Valsiner (1998), which examines the "social nature of human psychology." Focusing on the social nature of the person, Valsiner stressed the importance of avoiding the temptation of trying to reduce person processes to social processes. To this end, he explicitly distinguished between the dualisms of split foundationalist metatheory and dualities of the relational stance he advocated. Boesch (1991) and Eckensberger (1990) also presented an elaboration of the cultural standpoint. Boesch's cultural psychology and Eckensberger's theoretical and empirical extensions of this theory draw from Piaget's cognitive theory, Janet's dynamic theory, and Kurt Lewin's social field-theory, and Boesch specifically argued that cultural psychology aims to integrate individual and cultural change—an integration of individual and collective meanings, a bridging of the gap between subject and object (see e.g., Boesch, 1991).

As a final point concerning syntheses and the view from the center, it needs to be emphasized that a relational metatheory is not limited to three syntheses. For example, discourse or semiotics may also be taken as a synthesis of person and culture (Latour, 1993). In this case, biology and person are conflated, and the biological/person and culture represent the opposites of identity that are coordinated by discourse.

As a general summary to this point, the argument has been made that metatheoretical principles form the ground out of which grow the concepts and methods of any domain of empirical inquiry. Split metatheory produces dichotomous understandings of the world and methods that rely exclusively on the analytic ideal of the reduction of psychological process and behaviors to elements, followed by the additive linear causal recomposition of elements. Split metatheory in fact creates the antinomies, including the person–culture antinomy. Relational metatheory, in contrast, resolves the antinomies; it produces inclusive holistic understandings of the world and methods that operate within an analytic (identity and opposites)–synthetic relational frame. This frame promotes inquiry into psychological processes and behaviors from several co-equal, indissociable, and complementary standpoints, including the person standpoint, biological standpoint, and sociocultural standpoint. Piagetian theory emerges from and consequently needs to be read in the context of relational metatheory. To read Piagetian theory within the frame of split metatheory leads to confusion, misunderstanding, and incoherence.

Theories and methods refer directly to the empirical world, whereas metatheories refer to theories and methods themselves. A *metatheory* is a set of rules, principles, or story (narrative) that describes and prescribes what is acceptable and unacceptable as theory—the means of conceptual exploration of any scientific domain—and as methods—the means of observational exploration—in a scientific discipline. When metatheoretical ideas are tightly interrelated and form a coherent set of concepts, the set is often termed a *model* or *paradigm*. These coherent sets can form a hierarchy in terms of increasing generality of application. Relational metatheory constitutes such a model operating at a high level of generality. A developmentally oriented embodied action metatheory is a model that operates within the framework of the relational model. However, the embodied action model functions at a lower level of generality—a level that specifically frames inquiry into psychological and developmental psychological processes. Understanding a developmentally oriented embodied action model further clarifies the relational resolution of the various antinomies as they apply to psychological processes and further clarifies Piagetian theory as a broadly systematic effort designed to understand human knowing and development without resorting to the dichotomous understandings prevalent in the models of empiricism, nativism, and positivism.

DEVELOPMENTALLY ORIENTED EMBODIED ACTION METATHEORY

Embodiment

Several basic terms define a developmental oriented embodied action model (see Overton [2003] for an extended discussion). Each term is associated with relational principles, but for the present discussion *embodiment* is the most central of these basic concepts because embodiment is a concept of synthesis that bridges and integrates biological, sociocultural, and person-centered approaches to psychological inquiry (see Fig. 2.2).

Most simply stated, embodiment is the affirmation that the lived body counts in our psychology. It is not a split-off, disengaged agent that simply moves around peeking at a preformed world and drawing meaning directly from that world. It is not a set of genes that causes behavior, nor a brain, nor a culture. Behavior emerges from the embodied person actively engaged in the world. The concept of embodiment was first fully articu-

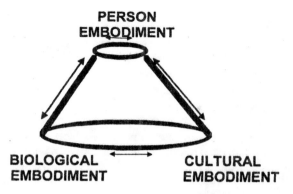

FIG. 2.2.   Embodiment as syntheses of person, biology, culture.

lated in psychology by Merleau-Ponty (1962, 1963). It represents a relational movement away from any split understanding of behavior as an additive product of biological and sociocultural determinants.

Embodiment is the claim that perception, thinking, feelings, and desires (i.e., the way we behave, experience, and live the world) is contextualized by our being active agents with this particular kind of body
(Taylor, 1995). In other words, the kind of body we have is a precondition
for our having the kind of behaviors, experiences, and meanings that we
have. As Johnson (1999) stated, "Human beings are creatures of the flesh.
What we can experience and how we make sense of what we experience
depend on the kinds of bodies we have and on the ways we interact with
the various environments we inhabit" (p. 81).

As a relational concept, embodiment includes not merely the physical
structures of the body, but the body as a form of lived experience actively
engaged with the world of sociocultural and physical objects. The body as
form references the biological, the body as lived experience references the
psychological person, and the body actively engaged with the world represents the sociocultural. Within a relational system, embodiment is a concept that bridges and joins in a unified whole these several research standpoints without any appeal to splits, foundationalism, elements, atomism,
or reductionism.

Biological Embodiment.   Contemporary neuroscience has increasingly endorsed the significance of embodiment as an essential component
of the biological standpoint as it addresses psychological issues. For example, Damasio (1994, 1999), exploring the neurological dimension of
emotions, Edelman (1992; Edelman & Tononi, 2000), exploring the neurological dimensions of consciousness, along with LeDoux (1996), exploring
the neurological dimension of emotions, all supported an embodied ap-

proach to biological–psychological inquiry, and all argued that the cognitive, affective, and motivational meanings that constitute mind can no longer be thought of as the direct expression of genetic modularities (as nativists such as Pinker [1997] would claim). Nor can they be thought of as a functionalist piece of software, nor even as merely a function of brain processes. Rather, they argued, these meanings must be considered in a fully embodied context. As Damasio (1994) said:

> Mind is probably not conceivable without some sort of embodiment.... This is Descartes' error: the abyssal separation between body and mind.... The Cartesian idea of a disembodied mind may well have been the source, by the middle of the twentieth century, for the metaphor of mind as software program ... [and] there may be some Cartesian disembodiment also behind the thinking of neuroscientists who insist that the mind can be fully explained in terms of brain events [i.e., connectionism], leaving by the wayside the rest of the organism and the surrounding physical and social environment—and also leaving out the fact that part of the environment is itself a product of the organism's preceding actions. (pp. 234–250)

Sociocultural Embodiment. From the cultural standpoint, recently some social constructivists not committed to a split metatheoretical approach (e.g., Harré, 1995; Sampson, 1996) have embraced embodied action as a relational anchoring to the relativism of split-off discourse analysis. For example, Sampson (1996) argued for "embodied discourses" as these "refer to the inherently embodied nature of all human endeavor, including talk, conversation and discourse itself" (p. 609; see also Csordas, 1999; Ingold, 2000; Overton 1997). Perhaps the most fully articulated contemporary employment of embodiment in a developmentally oriented cultural psychology is found in Boesch (1991). Boesch's presentation of "The I and the body" is a discussion of the centrality of embodiment for a cultural psychology. Thus, he stated, "The body, obviously, is more than just an object with anatomical and physiological properties: *it is the medium of our actions*, it is with our body that we both conceive and perform actions" (p. 312; italics added).

Embodiment, Action, and Person

The person-centered standpoint frames the major focus of Piagetian theory. To describe the nature and role of embodiment at this third point of synthesis, several interrelated concepts need to be distinguished. First, a person-centered standpoint refers to a theoretical and empirical focus of inquiry on the psychological processes and patterns of psychological processes as these explain the individual's actions and behaviors in the world. This orientation to psychological inquiry generally, and to developmental inquiry specifically, is perhaps best defined by contrast with its complement, which has been termed a *variable approach*. From a variable standpoint, the focus of inquiry is not on the action systems that characterize the person's acts and behaviors, but on biological, cultural, and individual variables as these are understood to operate as predictors, correlates, or antecedent causes of behavior. Magnusson (1998) noted that from a variable approach various individual and contextual variables are understood as the explanatory actors in the processes being studied, whereas from a person-centered approach action systems operate as the main vehicles of explanation.

The person-centered standpoint entails four basic interwoven concepts: person, agent, action, embodiment.

Person–Agent. Person and agent are complementary Escherian levels of analysis of the same whole. The person level is constituted by genuine psychological concepts (e.g., thoughts, feelings, desires, wishes) that have intentional qualities, are open to interpretation, and are available to consciousness (Shanon, 1993). In other words, at the person level these concepts have psychological meaning for the person. The agent level—called the *subpersonal level* by some (Dennett, 1987; Russell, 1996)—refers to action or dynamic self-organizing systems. *Schemes, operations, ego, attachment behavioral system*, and *executive function* are some of the concepts that describe these action systems. Broadly, the agent level corresponds to the epistemic subject of Piagetian theory (from the viewpoint of structure and function), and the person level corresponds to the psychological subject (from the viewpoint of consciousness, from the viewpoint of awareness, from the viewpoint of the individual). Throughout his writings, Piaget attempted to maintain a clear distinction between the agent and person levels (e.g., "Structures . . . do not belong to the subject's consciousness but to his operational behavior, which is something quite different" [Piaget, 1970a, p. 68]).

Taken as a whole, the person–agent forms the nucleus of a psychological theory of mind. In this context, *mind* is defined as a self-organizing dynamic system of cognitive (knowings, beliefs), emotional (feelings), and conative or motivational (wishes, desires) meanings or understandings, along with procedures for maintaining, implementing, and changing these meanings. Most important, a person-centered theory of mind is not an encapsulated cognitive model, but rather an approach that includes emotions, wishes, and desires as well as cognition. Further, there is no question about where mind is located. Mind emerges from a relational biocultural activity matrix. In the present context, mind is a person-centered concept because the approach being described takes the person standpoint. As a person-centered concept, mind bridges naturally to both the biological and sociocultural, and again no antinomies emerge among these domains.

Action, Intention, Behavior, and Experience.   Person–agency is the source of action, and a person-centered approach establishes the framework for what has traditionally been termed an *action theory* (Brandstadter, 1998; Brandstadter & Lerner, 1999; Müller & Overton, 1998). At the agent level, *action* is defined as the characteristic functioning of any dynamic self-organizing system. For example, a plant orients toward the sun. Weather systems form high and low pressure areas and move from west to east. Human systems organize and adapt to their biological and sociocultural worlds. At the person level, *action* is defined as intentional activity (i.e., meaning giving activity). Action is often distinguishable from *behavior* because the action of the person–agent implies a transformation in the intended object of action, whereas behavior often simply implies movement and states (von Wright, 1971). Thus, when the infant chews (action)—something that from a sociocultural environmental standpoint is called a *basket*—the infant from a person-centered standpoint is transforming this part of her actual known world into a practical action—chewable.

Of course, action is central to Piagetian theory: Function, assimilation, accommodation, operation, and reflective abstraction all reference action. Further, Piaget repeatedly made the point:

> I think that human knowledge is essentially active. To know is to assimilate reality into systems of transformations. To know is to transform reality. . . . To my way of thinking, knowing an object does not mean copying it—it means acting upon it. (1967, p. 15)

> To know an object . . . is to act on it so as to transform it. (1977, p. 30)

> The subject will . . . have to be defined in the terms we earlier proposed, as the center of activity. (1967, p. 70)

Further, Piaget (1995) did not limit the significance of action to the person; when discussing the sociological standpoint, he noted: "Social cooperation is also a system of actions, interpersonal rather than simply individual, but actions all the same and consequently subject to the laws of action" (p. 145).

Action serves at least three major functions in the development of mind. First, action expresses cognitive/affective/conative meaning. Here it is important to recognize that meaning has a bipolar relational status (Overton, 1994b). "I mean" (what the subject intends) and "it means" (the object referent) operate in a relational matrix. The former is concerned with person-centered meanings, whereas the latter is concerned with sociocultural meanings and reference. From a person-centered stand-point, the focus of analysis is on "I mean" and secondarily on how "I mean" comes to hook up with "it means." Considered in its expressive moment, action entails the projection of person-centered meanings (i.e., Piagetian assimilation), thus transforming the objective environmental world (i.e., an object point of view) into an actual world as known, felt, and desired. *World* here is another bipolar concept. The actual world is the world of meanings constructed by the person—the known world; the environmental or objective world is the world examined from a socio-cultural standpoint.

The second function that action serves is the instrumental function of communicating and adjusting person-centered meanings. Communication, dialogue, discourse, and problem solving all call attention to the relational to and fro movement between the expression of the self-organizing system and instrumental adaptive changes. Completely adapted action (i.e., successful) entails only projection. Partially adapted action (i.e., partially successful) results in exploratory action or variations. Adaptive exploratory action leads to reorganization of the system (transformational change) and, hence, new meanings.

This general cycle of expressive transformational action projected as meanings and exploratory variational action as the transformation (i.e., Piagetian accommodation) of these meanings to resistances encountered in the objective world constitutes the third and most general function of action: Action defines the general mechanism of all psychological development. From a person-centered developmental action standpoint, all development is explained by action. However, action is also identified with experience, thus it is possible to say that all development is explained by experience. Yet caution is necessary here because *experience*, like *meaning* and *world*, is a bipolar relational concept. From a person-centered perspective, experience is the person–agent action of observing, manipulating, and exploring. From a sociocultural and objective environmental point of view, experience is often identified as an event or stimulus that is independent of the person and imposes on or is imposed on the person. For purposes of clarity, it would be better to retain the former action definition as experience and redefine the latter as opportunity for experience. Similarly, it should be pointed out that when experience is described as a feeling, the reference here is the person-centered felt meaning of the observational, manipulative, and explorative actions.

In defining *experience* as the developmental action cycle of projection–transformation (of the known world)–exploration–transformation (of the system), experience also becomes the psychological bridge between biological and cultural systems. There is no sense here of an isolated, cut-off, solitary human psyche. Person-centered experience emerges from a biosociocultural relational activity matrix (see e.g., Gallese, 2000a, 2000b; Suomi, 2000), and this experience both transforms and is transformed by the matrix. Person development is neither a split-off nativism, nor a split-off environmentalism, nor a split-off additive combination of the two. The neonate is a dynamic system of practical action meanings. These meanings represent the outcome of 9 months of the interpenetrating action of biology–environment, and this interpenetration stretches all the way down to DNA (Gottlieb, 1997, 2002; Lewontin, 1991, 2000). Finally, it should be explicitly understood that to say that development is explained by experience is not to deny that development is explained by biology and development is explained by culture. What is denied is the absolute exclusivity of any of these standpoint explanations.

Person–Agent Embodied Actions. Person–agency is the source of action, and action is the source of meaning, but this action is embodied. As discussed earlier, embodiment is the claim that our perception, thinking, feelings, and desires—that is, the way we experience or live the world—is contextualized by our being active agents with this particular kind of body. At the agent level, embodiment specifies the characteristic nature of the activity of any living system (e.g., the actual world of the fly is necessarily shaped by the nature of the fly's embodied acts). At the person level, embodiment affirms that from the beginning bodily acts constrain and inform the nature of intentionality (Margolis, 1987). Intentionality is not limited to a symbolic, reflective, or transreflective system of psychological meanings. Intentionality also extends to a system of psychological meanings that characterize practical embodied actions operating at the most minimum level of consciousness (Zelazo, 1996). These most basic meanings and all others "come from having a body with particular perceptual and motor capabilities that are inseparably linked" (Thelen, Schoner, Scheier, & Smith, 2001, p. 1). That is, they arise—as Piaget repeatedly insisted—from the sensory-motor functioning that represents a concrete instantiation of embodied actions: "Starting from primitive perceptual and motoric structures and before any language, the infant succeeds in constituting a 'sensory-motor intelligence' " (Piaget, 1995, p. 140).

CONCLUSIONS

In this chapter, I argued and presented evidence that within the context of a relational metatheory a developmentally oriented embodied action model—and the research paradigm it entails—bridges and joins together in a unified whole several complementary research standpoints without any need to appeal to split Cartesian concepts involving foundationalism, elements, atomism, and reductionism. I also argued and presented evidence that Piagetian theory is most coherently interpreted within this frame. When the domain of inquiry is any topic that directly or indirectly touches on issues of the place of biology, culture, and the person in explanations of human functioning and development, a relational embodied action model offers an alternative to classical split approaches that is conceptually coherent and empirically productive. This embodied understanding of human behavior and development impacts on the way science is thought about and the way science is done (see Overton [2003] for an extended discussion). From an embodied perspective, it no longer makes sense to ask questions about genetic influences on, cultural influences on, or the influence of individual characteristics on human behavior and development. *Influence on* is the language of a causal reductionism and a bedrock foundationalism. Similarly it makes no sense to argue about the primacy of any of these standpoints. Within a relational embodied action model, questions and research strategies focus on functional intra- and interrelations among dynamic self-organizing systems including biological, cultural, and person systems as these arise and develop from the body as a form of lived experience actively engaged with the world of sociocultural and physical objects.

REFERENCES

Baldwin, J. M. (1985). *Mental development in the child and the race: Methods and process.* New York: Macmillan.

Beilin, H. (1983). The new functionalism and Piaget's program. In E. K. Scholnick (Ed.), *New trends in conceptual representation: Challenges to Piaget's theory?* (pp. 3–40). Hillsdale, NJ: Lawrence Erlbaum Associates.

Boesch, E. E. (1991). *Symbolic action theory and cultural psychology.* Berlin, Germany: Springer-Verlag.

Brandtstädter, J. (1998). Action perspectives on human development. In W. Damon (Series Ed.) & R. M. Lerner (Vol. Ed.), *Handbook of child psychology: Vol. 1. Theoretical models of human development* (5th ed., pp. 807–863). New York: Wiley.

Brandtstadter, J., & Lerner, R. M. (Eds.). (1999). *Action and self-development: Theory and research through the life span.* London: Sage.

Bunge, M. (1962). *Causality: The place of the causal principle in modern science.* New York: World Publishing Company.

Cole, M., & Wertsch, J. V. (1996). Beyond the individual–social antinomy in discussions of Piaget and Vygotsky. *Human Development, 39,* 250–256.

Csordas, T. J. (1999). Embodiment and cultural phenomenology. In G. Weiss & H. F. Haber (Eds.), *Embodiment: The intersection of nature and culture* (pp. 144–162). New York: Routledge.

Damasio, A. (1994). *Descartes' error: Emotion, reason, and the human brain.* New York: Avon.

Damasio, A. (1999). *The feeling of what happens: Body and emotion in the making of consciousness.* New York: Harcourt Brace.

Dennett, D. (1987). *The intentional stance.* Cambridge, MA: MIT Press.

Eckensberger, L. H. (1990). On the necessity of the culture concept in psychology: A view from cross-cultural psychology. In F. J. R. van de Vijver & G. J. M. Hutschemaekers (Eds.), *The investigation of culture. Current issues in cultural psychology* (pp. 153–183). Tilburg, Germany: Tilburg University Press.

Edelman, G. M. (1992). *Bright air, brilliant fire: On the matter of the mind.* New York: Basic Books.

Edelman, G. M., & Tononi, G. (2000). *A universe of consciousness: How matter becomes imagination.* New York: Basic Books.

Gallese, V. (2000a). The acting subject: Towards the neural basis of social cognition. In T. Metzinger (Ed.), *Neural correlates of consciousness* (pp. 325–334). Cambridge: MIT Press.

Gallese, V. (2000b). The "shared manifold hypothesis": From mirror neurons to empathy. *Journal of Consciousness Studies, 8,* 33–50.

Gergen, K. (2001). Psychological science in a postmodern context. *American Psychologist, 56,* 803–813.

Gergen, K. J. (1994). The communal creation of meaning. In W. F. Overton & D. S. Palermo (Eds.), *The nature and ontogenesis of meaning* (pp. 19–40). Hillsdale, NJ: Lawrence Erlbaum Associates.

Gottlieb, G. (1997). *Synthesizing nature-nurture.* Mahwah, NJ: Lawrence Erlbaum Associates.

Gottlieb, G. (2002). Developmental-behavioral initiation of evolutionary change. *Psychological Review, 109,* 211–218.

Harding, S. (1986). *The science question in feminism.* Ithaca, NY: Cornell University Press.

Harré, R. (1995). The necessity of personhood as embodied being. *Theory & Psychology, 5,* 369–373.

Ingold, T. (2000). Evolving skills. In H. Rose & S. Rose (Eds.), *Alas, poor Darwin: Arguments against evolutionary psychology* (pp. 273–297). New York: Harmony.

Johnson, M. (1999). Embodied reason. In G. Weiss & H. F. Haber (Eds.), *Embodiment: The intersection of nature and culture* (pp. 81–102). New York: Routledge.

Latour, B. (1993). *We have never been modern.* Cambridge, MA: Harvard University Press.

LeDoux, J. (1996). *The emotional brain: The mysterious underpinnings of emotional life.* New York: Touchstone.

Lewontin, R. C. (1991). *Biology as ideology: The doctrine of DNA.* New York: Harper Perennial.

Lewontin, R. C. (2000). *The triple helix: Gene, organism and environment.* Cambridge, MA: Harvard University Press.

Lourenço, O., & Machado, A. (1996). In defense of Piaget's theory: A reply to 10 common criticisms. *Psychological Review, 103,* 143–164.

Luhmann, N. (1995). *Social systems.* Stanford, CA: Stanford University Press.

Magnusson, D. (1998). The logic and implications of a person-oriented approach. In R. B. Cairns, L. R. Bergman, & J. Kagan (Eds.), *Methods and models for studying the individual* (pp. 33–63). London: Sage.

Magnusson, D., & Stattin, H. (1998). Person-context interaction theories. In R. M. Lerner (Ed.), *Theoretical models of human development. Volume 1 of the Handbook of child psychology* (5th ed., pp. 685–760). New York: Wiley.

Margolis, J. (1987). *Science without unity: Reconciling the human and natural sciences.* New York: Basil Blackwell.

Merleau-Ponty, M. (1962). *Phenomenology of perception* (C. Smith, Trans.). London: Routledge & Kegan Paul.

Merleau-Ponty, M. (1963). *The structure of behavior* (A. Fisher, Trans.). Boston: Beacon.

Miller, J. G. (1996). Theoretical issues in cultural psychology. In J. W. Berry, Y. H. Poortinga, & J. Pandey (Eds.), *Handbook of cross-cultural psychology: Theory and method* (pp. 85–128). Boston: Allyn & Bacon.

Müller, U., & Overton, W. F. (1998). Action theory of mind and representational theory of mind: Is dialogue possible? *Human Development, 41,* 127–133.

Overton, W. F. (1994a). The arrow of time and cycles of time: Concepts of change, cognition, and embodiment. *Psychological Inquiry, 5,* 215–237.

Overton, W. F. (1994b). Contexts of meaning: The computational and the embodied mind. In W. F. Overton & D. S. Palermo (Eds.), *The nature and ontogenesis of meaning* (pp. 1–18). Hillsdale, NJ: Lawrence Erlbaum Associates.

Overton, W. F. (1997). Beyond dichotomy: An embodied active agent for cultural psychology. *Culture and Psychology, 3,* 315–334.

Overton, W. F. (2002). Understanding, explanation, and reductionism: Finding a cure for cartesian anxiety. In L. Smith & T. Brown (Eds.), *Reductionism* (pp. 29–51). Mahwah, NJ: Lawrence Erlbaum Associates.

Overton, W. F. (2003). Development across the life span: Philosophy, concepts, theory. In R. M. Lerner, M. A. Easterbrooks, & J. Mistry (Eds.), *Comprehensive handbook of psychology: Developmental psychology* (Vol. 6). New York: Wiley.

Overton, W. F., & Reese, H. W. (1973). Models of development: Methodological implications. In J. R. Nesselroade & H. W. Reese (Eds.), *Life-span developmental psychology: Methodological issues* (pp. 65–86). New York: Academic Press.

Piaget, J. (1952). *The origins of intelligence in children.* New York: International Universities Press.

Piaget, J. (1967). *Six psychological studies.* New York: Random House.

Piaget, J. (1970a). *Structuralism.* New York: Basic Books.

Piaget, J. (1970b). *Genetic epistemology.* New York: Norton.

Piaget, J. (1977). The role of action in the development of thinking. In W. F. Overton & J. M. Gallagher (Eds.), *Knowledge and development* (pp. 17–42). New York: Plenum.

Piaget, J. (1985). *The equilibration of cognitive structures.* Chicago: The University of Chicago Press.

Piaget, J. (1987). *Possibility and necessity: The role of possibility in cognitive development* (Vol. 1). Minneapolis, MN: University of Minnesota Press.

Piaget, J. (1992). *Morphisms and categories: Comparing and transforming.* Hillsdale, NJ: Lawrence Erlbaum Associates.

Piaget, J. (1995). *Sociological studies.* New York: Routledge.

Piaget, J., & Garcia, R. (1991). *Toward a logic of meanings.* Hillsdale, NJ: Lawrence Erlbaum Associates.

Pinker, S. (1997). *How the mind works.* New York: Norton.

Russell, J. (1996). *Agency: Its role in mental development.* London: Taylor & Francis.

Sampson, E. E. (1996). Establishing embodiment in psychology. *Theory and Psychology, 6,* 601–624.

Searle, J. (1992). *The rediscovery of the mind.* Cambridge, MA: MIT Press.

Shanon, B. (1993). *The representational and the presentational: An essay on cognition and the study of mind.* New York: Harvester Wheatsheaf.

Stern, W. (1938). *General psychology: From the personalistic standpoint.* New York: Macmillan.

Sullivan, H. S. (1953). *The interpersonal theory of psychiatry.* New York: W.W. Norton.

Suomi, S. J. (2000). A behavioral perspective on developmental psychopathology: Excessive aggression and serotonergic dysfunction in monkeys. In A. J. Sameroff, M. Lewis, & S. Miller (Eds.), *Handbook of developmental psychopathology* (2nd ed., pp. 237–256). New York: Plenum.

Taylor, C. (1995). *Philosophical arguments.* Cambridge, MA: Harvard University Press.

Thelen, E., Schoner, G., Scheier, C., & Smith, L. (2001). The dynamics of embodiment: A field theory of infant perseverative reaching. *Behavioral and Brain Sciences, 24,* 1–86.

Valsiner, J. (1998). *The guided mind: A sociogenetic approach to personality.* Cambridge, MA: Harvard University Press.

von Bertalanffy, L. (1968a). *General system theory.* New York: George Braziller.

von Bertalanffy, L. (1968b). *Organismic psychology and systems theory.* Barre, MA: Barre.

von Wright, G. H. (1971). *Explanation and understanding*. Ithaca, NY: Cornell University Press.

Werner, H. (1957). The concept of development from a comparative and organismic point of view. In D. B. Harris (Ed.), *The concept of development: An issue in the study of human behavior* (pp. 125–148). Minneapolis: University of Minnesota Press.

Werner, H. (1958). *Comparative psychology of mental development*. New York: International Universities Press.

Wertsch, J. V. (1991). *Voices of the mind: A sociocultural approach to mediated action*. Cambridge, MA: Harvard University Press.

Zelazo, P. D. (1996). Towards a characterization of minimal consciousness. *New Ideas in Psychology, 14*(1), 63–80.

Piaget's Social Epistemology

Richard F. Kitchener
Colorado State University

In this chapter, I explore this question: In what sense does Jean Piaget have a social epistemology? When I use the term *social epistemology*, I am using it in the sense in which traditional epistemologists use the term *epistemology* and not in the much looser sense in which many scientists use the term. What is that sense?

Epistemology can be taken in a purely descriptive (empirical) sense or a normative sense. In the purely *descriptive* sense, epistemology would be concerned with the study of belief formation and change: How are beliefs and other cognitive representations formed, retained, and revised? An account of such belief formation would presumably be purely factual in nature, concerned with the question of what causal conditions explain this trajectory. These causal conditions might be individualistic in nature—internal states of the individual—or environmental events external to the individual.

A likely candidate for such external events would be social factors because many (if not most) of our beliefs are formed as a result of processes of social interaction with others—parents, teachers, and peers. It would be surprising if at least some of our beliefs were not reflections of the beliefs or interests of larger social groups to which we belong. Hence, this limited social epistemology would be of considerable significance because a complete causal account of the acquisition, maintenance, and revision of our beliefs would involve social factors.[1]

---

[1]Not every epistemologist would accept this view in an unqualified way. They would argue that causal factors of a social type are appropriate only for irrational beliefs, whereas

Many social scientists view the program of explaining scientific knowledge in this way. For example, Barnes (1977; one of co-founders of the *Strong Programme in the Sociology of Knowledge*) said:

> An immediate difficulty, which faces any discussion of the present kind, is that there are so many different conceptions of knowledge. Some of these can be set aside, for sociological purposes, by taking knowledge to consist of accepted belief, and publicly available, shared representations. The sociologist is concerned with the naturalistic understanding of what people take to be knowledge, and not with the evaluative assessment of what deserves to be so taken. (p. 1)

"Instead of defining [knowledge] as true belief—or perhaps justified true belief—knowledge for the sociologist," said Bloor (1991), "is whatever people take to be knowledge" (p. 5). For the sociologist, knowledge is merely belief—what the social group believes. What these sociologists seem to be ruling out is a naturalistic account of knowledge—real, genuine knowledge—and not just a naturalistic account of belief.

However, there is another type of social epistemology—what can be called a *normative social epistemology*. According to the more traditional account of epistemology, knowledge is not the same as belief. Knowledge might be a cognitive state of a certain kind, but a special kind of cognitive state: not just a belief of any type, but rather one that was warranted, reasonable, justified, backed by adequate evidence, and so on. These latter notions—*warrant, evidence, reason, justification*—are not ordinary run-of-the-mill type of empirical properties; they are normative (evaluative) ones. They concern issues not just of what a person *does* believe, but also of what he *should* believe; they concern the question of whether a belief was a *good* or *proper* one to adopt, whether the belief had *adequate evidence* in support of it, and so on. On this stronger, normative conception of social epistemology, one would be concerned not just with how a belief depends on social conditions, but how knowledge, justification, rationality, and warrant depend on these factors.

With respect to this normative social epistemology, the question is not merely what are the social factors that go into the causal explanation of a subject's cognitive state, but what are the social factors that transform belief into knowledge, that make a belief justified or warranted? In short, the question is: What (if anything) is epistemic about the social?

There was a time, at least in analytic epistemology and philosophy of science, when social epistemology was not an *au courant* topic. Indeed, most of 20th-century analytic epistemology and philosophy of science

rational beliefs require no such causal account. This is sometimes called the *asymmetry principle of explanation.*

was devoted to a particular conception of the nature of epistemology and the philosophy of science, one in which the isolated individual knower was deemed to be the epistemic subject in question. This was an inheritance of Descartes and Locke, who set the agenda for epistemology and philosophy of science for over 300 years (Kitchener, 2002). Fortunately, all of this has changed in recent years, and there are now several schools of (or rather approaches to) social epistemology, both continental in orientation and analytic.

Focusing on analytic epistemology, we can define *normative social epistemology* as "the study of the social dimensions of knowledge of information" (Goldman, 2001, p. 1), "the conceptual and normative study of the relevance of social relations, roles, interests, and institutions to knowledge" (Schmitt, 1994, p. 1). In particular, following Schmitt's (1994, 1999) suggestion, we can distinguish three branches of normative social epistemology: (a) the role of social conditions for individual knowledge, (b) the division of epistemic labor, and (c) the nature of collective knowledge. The first question, which has guided my previous remarks, concerns the issue of whether there are any social factors involved in individual knowledge (e.g., what is the role of the testimony of others in the individual's acquisition of knowledge?). The division of cognitive labor concerns the question of how the cognitive effort of individuals, their responsibilities, privileges, and rewards, should be distributed to maximize the accumulation of knowledge. This question has largely concerned the issue of the social organization of large-scale epistemic enterprises such as science. Finally, the issue of collective knowledge involves the question of whether there is something called *collective knowledge* over and above individual knowledge, and, if so, what is its nature?

In the case of Piaget's genetic epistemology, these same questions arise. They arise if one believes that his genetic epistemology is not merely a genetic psychology, but a genetic epistemology—a theory about the origin, maintenance, and development of epistemic states, with such states constituting a certain kind of relation between the subject and natural/social world. A genetic explanation of these states does not consist merely of a genetic explanation of a belief state, but an explanation of them as knowledge states. This involves special kinds of developmental explanations (Kitchener, 1986, 2002).

If Piaget has a genetic epistemology and not merely a genetic psychology, then raising questions about his social epistemology will undoubtedly raise questions about the role of social factors in the epistemic enterprise. Although the division of cognitive labor is not a topic Piaget's account has much to offer (but see Piaget & Garcia, 1983/1999), he wrote much that is relevant to the two other questions. First, Piaget has an important contribution to make to the issue, what is the nature of collective knowledge? His answer is that collective knowledge can be reduced to the certain kinds of social relations between individual knowers. Therefore, there is nothing irreducibly holistic about knowledge. Second, with respect to the role of the social in individual knowledge, Piaget has an account of how certain kinds of epistemic norms emerge from certain kinds of social interactions between individuals. Hence, certain kinds of social relations are necessary for the development of epistemic norms. In fact, according to Piaget, one can say that rationality is essentially social in nature. In short, I suggest that Piaget has a normative social epistemology and that it has a considerable contribution to make toward answering some of the problems addressed by contemporary analytic social epistemology.

THE SOCIAL VERSUS THE RATIONAL

To set the proper epistemological background for Piaget's social epistemology and its importance, I first introduce what I take to be an epistemological dilemma: the dilemma of the social versus the rational. On the one hand, knowledge and rationality seem to require an epistemic individualism; on the other hand, knowledge and rationality seem to require an irreducibly social dimension. Yet these two are incompatible. Hence, we have a paradox or dilemma not easily solved because there are strong arguments on both sides.

The Cartesian Knower and Its Paradox

Our modern concept of epistemology derives from the epistemological program of Descartes (and Locke, who was a kind of Cartesian), who gave us the epistemological model of the isolated, solitary knower. Suppose you begin, as Descartes did, with the assumption that many of our current beliefs—not only about what is known, but how they are known—are incorrect. These current beliefs were those basically inherited from late Medieval Aristotelian scholasticism, together with its epistemological stance of naive empiricism. To motivate his readers to reject these prejudices, Descartes employed skepticism. Yet to answer skepticism, Descartes had to make the revolutionary suggestion that only what is certain to your immediate consciousness counts as knowledge. After all, if you begin with skepticism, how will you know what is a case of knowledge? Only what is clear and distinct to one's immediate consciousness, only what one cognizes by immediate intellectual intuition. This revolutionary turn toward inward subjectivity and immediacy marks the distinctive feature of Cartesian epistemology. Obviously, if this is one's initial starting point, it follows that the knower must be solitary—alone in the world—and isolated from other knowers because one's criterion for what counts as knowledge must be something internal to the knower.

Given this initial starting point, it follows that knowledge must be lodged in the mind of the knower, and that it is the individual knower who is and must be the ultimate epistemological authority. For example, Rule 3 of the *Discourse* reads: "Concerning objects proposed for study, we ought to investigate what we can clearly and evidently intuit or deduce with certainty, and not what other people have thought or what we ourselves conjecture" (Descartes, 1637/1985, p. 13). Now it is true that Descartes does call on the cooperation of other knowers to assist him in the march of science: "Thus, by building upon the lives and labours of many, we might make much greater progress working together than anyone could make on his own" (Descartes, 1637/1985, p. 143). Yet it seems clear that such a notion has an unclear status in Descartes' system for how can we trust the epistemic endeavors of others? We can call this *the problem of epistemic trust*. If we are to trust others at all, it would seem that we can only do so as a result of our having ascertained that they are reliable knowers; this must mean that we have checked their results according to our own epistemic lights and have certified them. Yet we can never exhaustively do this. The status of testimony is thus problematic in a Cartesian epistemology.

This point emerges in even clearer relief when we pursue this question: Should we accept the experimental results of other researchers? Descartes distrusted the experimental results of other researchers and accepted them only after he subjected them to check (Descartes, 1637/1985, p. 148). Yet no scientist can subject every experimental result reported by other scientists to his or her own personal corroboration.

Descartes distrusted the naive employment of the senses, which must always be illuminated and corrected by reason: Because there are errors reported by other investigators, this "shows how little faith we must have in observations which are not accompanied by true reason" (Descartes, 1637/2001, p. 342). However, empiricists such as Locke and Hume, who placed their confidence more in the senses than in reason, had a similar problem. If one believes that everything one knows must have its source in the individual's sense experience, the problem of epistemic trust rears its head. Both rationalists such as Descartes and empiricists such as Locke and Hume advocated an epistemology of the solitary knower, but this is incompatible with trusting the epistemic reports of others. However, scientific knowledge would not be possible without such epistemic trust. Thus, we seem to have a paradox: To have genuine knowledge, one must have a social epistemology, but such an epistemology is incompatible with an individualistic epistemology. It would seem that to escape from this dilemma, we must somehow come up with a social epistemology committed to individualism and yet, at the same time, allow for the social to play an important epistemic role. Piaget's account, I believe, is one plausible way to do this.

The Social Psychology of Trust

Much of modern thought, including modern epistemology and philosophy of science, seems committed to the model of the solitary Cartesian knower. This is true even of those working in social psychology. For example, in his article "Social Influence and Conformity," Moscovici (1985) began with these thoughts:

> To the best of my knowledge, it was the West, and the West alone, that produced and refined the concept of humanity as autonomous, rational, self-directed individuals. By this exacting definition individuals were held fully accountable for their actions, they were assumed to evaluate reality solely on the basis of their own observations, and they were expected to be convinced only by arguments grounded on solid evidence. (p. 347)

If it is the isolated knower that is the paragon of rationality, then, as Moscovici proceeded to point out, we seem to have another example of the epistemic problem mentioned earlier—that of reconciling this conception of rationality with the role of the social in generating knowledge. According to Moscovi, it also generates a paradox: "Taken singly, all individuals are rational in their behavior, but then collectively, they cease to be rational—as witnessed by the outbursts of violence, panic, enthusiasm, and cruelty in which crowds indulge" (p. 347). If it is the autonomous individual who is rational, it must be the social that is irrational. How else can one explain the irrational behavior of individuals in groups? Now of course one could deny that, "taken singly, all individuals are rational in their behavior," but let us assume for the moment that this is true. Then it must be that when individuals enter into relations with others, "reason is set aside" by these social influence, and the individual abandons his autonomous rationality by conforming to the group's views. Reason is thus hypnotized by the group. If this view is correct, the prospects of a social rationality or social epistemology seem dim.

   Is it true that "reason is hypnotized by the group"? Is it true that the individual, left to himself, keeps to the rational path, but that the social group forces him to stray off course and follow the path of irrationality, prejudice, and error? Such questions appear to be natural ones for social psychologists to investigate experimentally. If one is serious about establishing the possibility of a social epistemology along naturalistic lines, then at some point the relevant evidence should be consulted. Although I do not have the space to look at all the relevant studies, there are two classic experiments in what can be called the *social psychology of trust* that are relevant here: the Asch studies and the Sherif studies. However, a brief examination of these two research programs show that they point to two quite different accounts of the role of the social in the process of individual rationality.

The Muzafer Sherif Studies. Sherif's (1935) classic study was a test of a certain hypothesis about what Sherif called a *frame of reference*. Sherif believed that individuals confronted by an ambiguous, unstructured stimulus situation experienced uncertainty and were consequently motivated to structure this situation. This required a frame of reference in relation to which the ambiguous stimulus situation was changed into one that made sense; it was structured or patterned with equilibrium. A frame of reference, Sherif suggested, could be developed by the individual subject alone or could be the outcome of social interaction with others. In the latter case, this social frame of reference could be called a *social norm*, which he defined to be: "an evaluative scale . . . designating an acceptable latitude and an objectionable latitude for behavior, activity, events, beliefs, or any other object of concern to members of a social unit" (Sherif & Sherif, 1969, p. 141). His famous experiment (1935) was designed to examine the process by means of which such social norms are formed, which (according to him) meant that social norms are the outcome of social interaction. Following Durkheim, Sherif believed that there were collective social properties (e.g., social norms) that were emergent vis-à-vis the individuals involved.

In Sherif's (1935) experiment involving the autokinetic effect, a subject viewing a stationary pinpoint of light in a completely dark room experienced the light moving. His task was to judge the distance the light moved. Sherif performed several experiments, first demonstrating that an individual over the course of time will establish a frame of reference (or anchor) in relation to which he will judge the distance the light moves. In a subsequent experiment, he examined the relation between these individual judgments and the judgments of others. He found that, as a result of social interaction, individual judgment shifted toward a common range and around a common mode (i.e., these judgments converged toward a certain point, which was a common social norm). For example, consider one example given by Sherif—that of three individuals S_1, S_2, and S_3, with their corresponding judgments of distance. He found the judgments of individual S_1, which had a median judgment of 8 inches, the judgment of S_2, which had a median of 2, and the judgment of S_3, with a median of 1, all converged toward a value of 2—a graph with a funnel shape. It is important to note that this was a common shifting of judgments among all the individuals—a case of collaboration or cooperation—and not that of an individual shifting toward a stable group median judgment—a case of conformity. Later these social norms were internalized by the individuals and subsequently functioned as their own individual frames of reference.

Now there are several important epistemological questions to raise of the Sherif experiment, but we can bypass most of these and focus on one: Was this process of norm formation, in which an individual's judgment changed and converged on that of the others as a result of social interaction, a rational and objective process? If it is rational, what makes it rational? Is the process merely one of social conformity or cooperation? For an individualist like Descartes, the answer seems to be clear: To be rational, the individual should have stayed with her own judgments instead of converging toward those of the others. She should have followed the epistemic principle, "Stand on your own two epistemic feet." For the social epistemologist, however, the individual should have taken into consideration the others' judgments. Why? One possible answer is this: In the autokinetic phenomenon, one feels uncertain about the correctness of one's answer. If so, one cannot trust one's subjective impression of distance. The only rational thing to do would be to consult the judgments of others according to the epistemic principle, "Two epistemic heads are better than one." Now in the case of the autokinetic phenomenon, there is no correct answer to the question of how far the light moved because it did not move at all.[2] But suppose there was a correct answer; suppose an individual knew this answer, but suppose the judgment of others were wrong. Here trusting others would be misleading. One can imagine Descartes saying, "From time to time I have found that the testimony of others deceives, and it is prudent never to trust completely those who have deceived us even once."

The Solomon Asch Study.   Asch (1952) believed that Sherif's results indicated the depressing conclusion that subjects would blindly copy the opinions of others and behave irrationally. Asch believed the opposite—that individuals were rational as individuals, but that in a group setting individuals would change their opinions in a rational way; every individual would judge for herself what was the case and would not submit to group pressure. Therefore, norms would not be social in nature, but rational in nature, and this meant rational in an individualistic way.

Asch's (1952) design is well known. An individual is shown a sample length of a line and then shown three lines of varying length. The subject must then judge which of these is identical to the sample. There were 12 trials with varying lengths. Solomon varied the experimental conditions

---

[2]This is true despite the instructions, "The light will start to move."

in a variety of epistemologically important ways. For example, in the most famous experimental arrangement, there were several other individuals (7–9) who also made judgments of the length prior to the judgment of the experimental subject. However, they were instructed to make incorrect judgments beginning with Trial 3 (i.e., there were 9 incorrect responses made by the stooge group). The lone experimental subject, as it were, had to choose between judging the length according to his own subjective impression or agreeing with the group, thereby making an incorrect judgment. Here individual autonomy is pitted against group pressure (conformity).

The results are interesting from a number of different points of view, but I limit my remarks to one: In 217 trials with 31 subjects, a change of opinion toward the false judgments occurred about one third of the time. This is hardly what could be called massive irrationality, nor does it seem to be correct to say (as Moscovici, [1985] did) that, "these individuals were more inclined to believe what others said the evidence was than to trust the report of their visual perception" (p. 349). On the contrary, as Asch (1952) put it, "the preponderance of estimates was, under the given conditions, correct and independent" (p. 457). Therefore, it seems somewhat exaggerated to conclude that social conformity and group pressure can lead individuals to abandon their individual rationality and epistemic autonomy and succumb to group pressure, although this is the conclusion many draw. Clearly, however, individuals sometimes abandon their own judgments and accept the false ones of the group. This is the group average it should be noted. As one might expect, there were interesting individual differences: one fifth of the 31 experimental subjects were not influenced at all, one fourth made only 1 error; in all 42% of the subjects (13 out of 31) "were not appreciably affected by the experimental conditions" (p. 458) because they made 0 to 1 errors, and 61% were affected only somewhat, making 0 to 2 errors. Still an individualist might have expected the subjects to do much better than they did (although how much better is unclear).

Asch argued that these results were consistent with a model of individual rationality on the grounds that the subject initially experienced disequilibrium because of the difference between her judgments and those of the group. On the one hand, the subject obviously trusted her own perceptions as a source of knowledge; on the other hand, the reports of others were often trusted as a source of knowledge. Therefore, we have a state of dissonance produced by accepting both of these as sources of knowledge. How can one explain this incompatibility? If one trusts one's own judgment in the face of overwhelming group disagreement, there is dissonance because both are reliable sources of knowledge. How, in the face of this, can the subject explain the group's judgment? However, if one trusts the group's judgment, then what about reliability of one's own perception? That would also have to be explained. So it would appear that agreeing with the group's opinions is one way to restore equilibrium. Clearly this works only on the assumption that the testimony of others is a reliable source of knowledge along with that of oneself. Yet to assume this is to assume that rationality is not lodged exclusively in the internal, subjective realm of the individual.

We seem to have two different models of rationality here—an individualist model of Descartes, which would counsel you to ignore the group judgment because it is not a reliable source of information, and a collective or social model of rationality, which would counsel you to consider the evidential testimony of others. In the Asch experiment, we have the rather rare situation of the entire group being wrong and the individual being correct. How often does this occur? This surely seems to be an anomaly because we usually assume (with good reason) that other individuals are a reliable source of knowledge (i.e., that such a social process is reliable). We often resort to the judgments of others when we are uncertain as to whether our subjective impression of warmth is a reliable indicator of how hot it really is and with good reason.

The prior discussion of the Sherif and Asch experiments point to two things. First, these social psychological studies show that we are pulled in two different directions about the epistemic problem of trust. Often knowledge requires the existence of other knowers who are a source of knowledge (e.g., we simply must use the testimony of others when engaged in scientific pursuit). Yet others can be wrong—massively wrong. Therefore, we are faced with the problem of epistemic trust: Should I trust only myself or should I also trust others?

Second, these studies point to two quite different social processes at work when adjudicating individual judgment versus the judgment of the group: The Sherif experimental paradigm shows that there is a group process of cooperation, whereas the Asch experimental paradigm illustrates the social process of conformity. These are different group processes with correspondingly important epistemological differences: Conformity is (usually) epistemically a vice, whereas cooperation is epistemically a virtue. When discussing the influence of social processes on individual rationality, therefore, it is important to keep these differences in mind; the individual knower should avoid conformity and seek cooperation. Correlatively, cooperation (unlike conformity) is an epistemically virtuous form of social interaction explaining the development of rationality, whereas conformity does not; at least such is the hypothesis advanced in Piaget's program of genetic epistemology. According to Piaget, it is not social relations and forms of interactions in general that are epistemic or rational, but only social relations of a certain kind—cooperation between equals.

GENETIC EPISTEMOLOGY AND COLLECTIVE KNOWLEDGE: SOCIOLOGICAL HOLISM VERSUS INDIVIDUALISM

One of the issues analytic social epistemology takes as important concerns the question of collective knowledge: Who can be a knower? Can there be collective knowers in addition to individual knowers? For example, does it make sense to say of a group that it has a belief—a *collective belief* (Gilbert, 1992)? How is such a collective belief different from and related to the beliefs of individual members making up that group? Can a group collectively hold a belief that none of its members holds? Similarly, are there such things as collective knowledge, collective justification, and collective rationality? For example, is collective knowledge just the summative addition of the knowledge of individuals (and hence reducible to it)?

This issue of individualism versus collectivism in the realm of knowledge is an instance of the long-standing debate between individualism and holism in the social and cultural sciences, with the individualist side being championed most prominently by Weber and the holism side defended by Durkheim. Throughout his many discussions of the nature of the social, Piaget systematically defended a position intermediate between individualism and holism—that of relationalism or interactionism. I suggest that this view can be fruitfully applied to the issue of collective knowledge.

According to sociological holism, *social facts are irreducible wholes because the (social) whole has properties none of the individual members possesses.* These holistic properties modify, influence, or constrain the individual members and emerge as a result of the individual members forming a group. As we see, the studies of Sherif and Asch are directly related to this issue.

Durkheim's (1895/1938) sociological holism has a complex basis, but part of the reason he believed in such holistic entities as the collective conscience was his belief that the moral order provides the basis for society and hence that no individualistic theory, such as the social contract theory, rational self-interest, or capitalism, could account for the origin and justification of society. Only an irreducible social theory could do this, and morality had precisely this function: Individuals engage in social interaction because of superindividual norms (feelings of obligation) that guide this behavior and provide necessary sanctions. Durkheim believed the moral order, in turn, resulted from social constraint, conformity, or socialization in which adults and other authorities instill such moral standards into the youth. The work of Sherif was largely inspired by the views of Durkheim because the former wanted to investigate the processes by means of which external social norms emerge and then constrain the individual.

Opposed to Durkheim's holism, the individualism of individuals such as Weber (1922/1947) and Tarde (1890/1933) denied sociological emergence and holism and claimed that society is merely an aggregate of individuals in interaction. According to individualism, *all collective and social properties can be reduced to the properties of individuals.*

Piaget's alternative to these views is termed a sociological relativism, relationalism, or interactionism (Kitchener, 1985): "the social totality is neither a combination of pre-existing elements, nor a novel entity, but a system of relationships each of which in it own right brings about a transformation of the elements thus related" (Piaget, 1977/1995, p. 41). According to relationalism, the whole is not the simple addition of the individual properties of the members forming the whole, but neither is it an emergent (nonpredictable) entity somehow existing over and above (and hence independently of) the individual parts. Rather the social whole is the resulting addition of all the relations among the individual members.[3]

Relationalism is a central feature of Piaget's social psychology, genetic epistemology, and social epistemology. For Piaget, society is explained in terms of the relations among individuals (e.g., relations of constraint, cooperation, social role taking, etc.), not in terms of the nonrelational properties of individuals (e.g., schemes or habits).

These three sociological views can be applied to epistemology resulting in the following: Epistemological holism is the view that there is collective knowledge not reducible to the summation of individual knowledge; epistemological individualism is the view that all collective knowledge can be analyzed in terms of (and is reducible to) the knowledge of the individual members; and epistemological relationalism is the view that all collective knowledge can be analyzed in terms of the relational knowledge of the individuals. Suppose, for example, we consider the epistemic concept of collective justification. Then group G, consisting of individuals A, B, C, . . . , would be (collectively) justified in (collectively) believing that p just in case there were the appropriate kind of justification obtaining among the individuals in G. This could occur by virtue of the testimony of certain of the individuals in G, by virtue of evidence accumulated by a team of researchers working in collaboration, by virtue of a consensus judgment obtained as a result of a long discussion among the members, or by virtue of an experimental measurement obtained by group effort. These are just some possible epistemic relations among individuals that would constitute collective epistemic justification, which would be the outcome of cooperative types of interaction among group members.

The prior account of collective knowledge is sketchy and certainly needs to be worked out. However, I believe this epistemic relationalism

---

[3]The situation is more complex than this, however, because Piaget (1977/1995) recognized another type of social whole—a probabilistic mélange.

provides an interesting and important alternative to the other two accounts of collective knowledge, and hence has the potential to provide a solution to one of the main problems in contemporary analytic social epistemology.

THE SOCIAL EXCHANGE OF VALUES:
THE EMERGENCE OF EPISTEMIC NORMS

Piaget claimed that all social facts can be reduced to interactions among individuals. There are three types of such interindividual interaction: rules (systems of obligation), values of exchange, and conventional signs. These correspond, respectively, to the cognitive, affective, and symbolic aspects of individual behavior. *Rules* (or norms of obligations) include linguistic, moral, legal, and logical principles. *Signs* are social conventions relating a signifier to the signified (e.g., mathematics, language, social rites, etc.). Finally, social *values* involve systems of exchange among individuals. An individual (by virtue of his or her interests, desires, and affects) has certain things she values. In interacting with others who have their own values, she exchanges values with them. Such values of exchange are obviously similar to the economic exchange of goods, but they are also different in that the social exchange of values is felt as obligatory, whereas the economic exchange of value is not. It is this aspect of Piaget's account that provides the backbone for much of the rest of his thinking about social epistemology (although his theory of rules is also essential). It is to this theory that I now turn because it explains how epistemic norms can emerge from empirical facts and how the individual is motivated to adopt certain rational normative principles.

In the standard case of a social exchange of values, there are two individuals (a and a') and four components or relations between them: an action (r), a satisfaction (s), a debt (t), and a valorization (v). Suppose, for example, there is an exchange of ideas. Here,

> (1) individual a asserts a certain proposition r_a (true or false in varying degrees); (2) Partner a' finds himself in agreement (or not, in varying degrees), his agreement being designated by $s_{a'}$; (3) The agreement (or disagreement) of a' is binding for the series of exchanges between a' and a, whence $t_{a'}$; (4) This engagement of a' confers value or validity v_a (positive or negative) on the proposition r_a or, in other words, renders it valid or not insofar as future exchanges between the same individuals are concerned. (Piaget, 1977/1995, p. 147)

As a result of acknowledging the proposition asserted by a, the satisfaction received by a' is exchanged for a value received by a. Here, however, it is not an *actual* exchange of values (as when a' would actually give *a* some economic good), but a *virtual* exchange. As a result of receiving this satisfaction (or what we might call an *epistemic gain*), a' concurs with the proposition expressed. As a result, a kind of intellectual obligation is incurred to continue to agree with this proposition (on pain of inconsistency). Hence, *a* may now count on a' agreeing to the proposition in the future, and thus the proposition is valued or has validity.

Piaget set out several equations constituting various types of logical relations; some of these relations are more equilibrated than others. In particular, there is an ascending order of equilibrated structures—rhythms, regulations, and groupings—that play a crucial part in Piaget's account.

Rhythms, regulations, and groupings form three different degrees (or kinds) of equilibria depending on the respective amounts of causality and logical implication present in each: The more logical implication present and causality absent, the more equilibrated the structure. *Rhythms* are purely factual (basically causal) patterns in nature. *Regulations* contain elements of both implication and causality, but with less causality and more logical implication than rhythms have (e.g., preoperational intelligence or a purely economic exchange of values). Hence, although these are more equilibrated, they are not fully equilibrated. *Groupings*, in contrast, are fully equilibrated, possessing full implicatory relations such as addition, inversion, identity, association, tautology, and so on, and hence no causality. Therefore, a grouping involves a fully normative (rational) exchange of values—something not present in an economic exchange of values.

Given that one can define an equibrated exchange of values, what is an individual's motivation to preserve this equilibrium? Why do *a* and a' respect the equivalence $(r_a = s_{a'}) = (t_{a'} = v_a)$? In such an equilibrium, values are conserved over time, and this requires norms of obligation.

One can see why norms of obligation are required if we contrast a virtual exchange of values with an actual exchange of values. In the case of an actual exchange of values (e.g., an exchange of goods in the open market place), there is no need for norms of obligation because everyone can immediately see during the actual exchange of goods what obligations have been incurred. This perceived or *intuitive reciprocity* (as Piaget called it) is an example of intuitive or preoperational thought—a kind of thought or intelligence relying exclusively on currently perceived matters of fact. Such a preoperational intelligence has a certain degree of equilibrium (i.e., is a regulation), but it is inadequate precisely in just those cases where intuitive matters of fact are insufficient (viz., where one is reasoning about nonpresent, nonperceptual states of affairs; e.g., about the constancy of invisible objects, a virtual exchange of values, etc.). In these cases, norms of reasoning about, say, transitivity of relations are required. These rules of reasoning are normative obligations that are binding on the individual.

Here Piaget drew on a presumed similarity between object and value constancy: To guarantee that objects are conserved over time (even when they disappear from view), operatory reversibility is required (i.e., a logical rule of inference or operation is required that allows one to reason backward and forward in time, and to conclude that an object should be in a certain place even when it is not currently perceived). Similarly, in the case of a virtual exchange of values, there is an analogous situation in which object constancy is replaced by value constancy and in which the maintenance of value constancy over time requires a normative operation that underwrites our inferences about future obligations as well as others' obligations to us. In short, reasoning requires normative principles of inference, the most adequate of which is *normative reciprocity* (i.e., those norms governing all relevant points of view in which the reciprocal duties and rights of each party are specified in an impartial and disinterested way. (This provides the rationale for much of Piaget's theory of the social nature of objectivity discussed next and for this moral theory.)

One way to illustrate what Piaget has in mind here is to consider an intellectual discussion or dialogue—an intellectual exchange of ideas—that is an example of interindividual action and a social exchange of values. If Piaget is correct, then norms or rules are required to guarantee an equilibrated intellectual discussion. However, in this case, we have the cognitive counterpart to moral norm—logical norms.[4]

Therefore, suppose a asserts a proposition p and thereby communicates a judgment to a' (r_a). Suppose a' agrees with a and hence also attributes validity to a's proposition ($s_{a'}$). As a result of a''s recognition of the validity of this proposition, a' becomes committed to conserving this accord of a and a'. This is $t_{a'}$. Finally, this results in a's valorization (i.e., this confers a value or validity on a's proposition).

Yet what guarantees equilibrium here? According to Piaget, several things are necessary and sufficient for an equilibrium of exchange: a common scale of values, rules of communication (consisting of the principle of identity and (non) contradiction), and the possible actualization of the virtual values, which requires reversibility (if $r_a = s_{a'} = r_{a'} = v_a$, then $v_a = t_{a'} = r_{a'} = s_a$) and a reciprocity of points of view ($r_a = r_{a'}$, $s_a = s_{a'}$, etc.). Therefore, the exchange of intellectual values can be said to be in equilibrium on the condition that there is a norm obliging us to conserve these respective values. This shows that moral and logical norms are really much closer than most

---

[4]As I have argued elsewhere (Kitchener, 1991), there are important and interesting parallels here between the views of Piaget and those of Jürgen Habermas (and Paul Grice). Unfortunately, I cannot pursue these issues here.

people suspect and in fact are isomorphic to each other—they are two aspects of the same thing (a system of equilibrated operations characterized as a grouping). Thus, there is a parallelism between the intellectual exchange of values (cognition) and the affective exchange of values (ethics).[5]

The distinction among rhythms, regulations, and groupings is central to much of Piaget's thinking about the social foundations of rationality and epistemology. As we have seen, a regulation is an exchange of values with a certain degree of equilibrium but lacking conservation. A grouping is an operatory structure that is fully equilibrated because it is purely implicational. Corresponding to these two types of equilibrated structures is the difference between the social relation of constraint and cooperation. According to Piaget, constraint is a social relation leading to regulations (and is isomorphic to it), but only cooperation can lead to a grouping. This takes us back to our earlier discussion of individualism versus holism and to the Sherif and Asch experiments on the social psychology of trust.

To illustrate Piaget's claim that cooperation involves a system of interactions having a fully equilibrated structure, consider the following example. Two individuals on opposite banks of a river are each building a pillar of stones across which a plank will go as a bridge (Piaget, 1977/1995). If these two individuals are cooperating with each other, what is the logical structure of this cooperation? Piaget's answer is that *cooperation is co-operation* (i.e., each is operating in mutual accord with the other so that the actions of both are adjusted by means of new operations). Each party is adjusting his actions in relation to the actions of the other. Some of the actions are similar to each other and thus correspond to each other with regard to their common characters (e.g., each is making a pillar of the same form and in the same vertical direction). This correspondence is an operation performed on other actions. Some actions are reciprocal or symmetrical (e.g., both parties are orienting the vertical slopes of the pillars so as to face each other and be inclined in opposite directions). Reciprocity like correspondence is also an operation. Finally, some operations may be complementary (e.g., one of the banks of the river is higher than the other), thus requiring a supplementary action on the part of one of the parties. Thus, not only are the two parties each individually acting in cer-

---

[5]Piaget's theory of social exchange is thus similar in certain ways to modern social exchange theory, but also different. I have discussed these differences in Kitchener (1981, 1991). The basic way in which it differs from that of Pareto (1935) and Homans (1958, 1961) is that it is based on a Durkheimian conception of social exchange—one based on morality—rather than on an economic model of rational self-interest or individual rewards. On this distinction, see Blau (1964, 1968). In short, most modern social exchange theory is based on a model of the egoistic individual trying to maximize his gain, and this conception is rejected by Piaget (and Durkheim): Self-interest cannot underlie the principle of reciprocity or justice and neither can utilitarianism or classical capitalism.

tain ways, but their actions have a certain logical structure to them—one we can characterize as a series of operations: correspondence, reciprocity, addition or subtraction of complementary actions, and so on.

Therefore, cooperation is equilibrated and has a logical structure isomorphic to logical thought. It is a necessary condition for equilibrated thought (and moral development), and thus (contrary to Durkheim) constraint as a form of social relations will not adequately account for the development of equilibrated thinking.

Constraint is a form of social relations involving an authority (e.g., parents), which enforces social agreement via some sanction, resulting in conformity. According to Piaget, constraint is not an adequate explanation of the moral or logical order. If individuals are not equals (the situation of constraint), there is no reciprocity and reversibility, which are present in cooperation, and hence there is no normative obligation. As Piaget (1977/ 1995) surprisingly put it, autism and constraint are not really different from each other because both are cases of affirming a proposition without proof.

Social pressure and the enforced conformity of family, school, and peer group pressure cannot account for the nature of logic. The views of sociological holism, epistemic holism, and with it the kind of conformity to be found in the Asch studies are inadequate as a social account of rational belief formation and revision. Yet so are the theses of sociological individualism and epistemic individualism. Logic does not arise because of the social conformity to group norms or merely from the activity of isolated individuals. Instead it arises from the interactions among individuals—an interaction and relation of cooperation among equals seen, for example, in the Sherif studies. Cooperation is thus essential for the development of logic and rational operations because it is only in cooperation with others (seen as equals) that reciprocity of viewpoints arises and with this general, disinterested normative rules governing how all parties should reason and act. It is the experimental paradigm of Sherif, not Asch, that shows us the social nature of rationality.

Given the rise of naturalistic epistemology in the 1960s, the place of epistemic norms in such a naturalistic account became the subject of many discussions. I refrain from discussing any of the vast literature on this topic except to point out the following: If one adopts the naturalistic perspective in epistemology and if one also believes it is crucial for epistemology to retain the normative (evaluative) nature of epistemology, one must show how to secure a place for the normative within the natural. If we suppose that no individual, species, or society begins its existence with such epistemic norms and values, one must show how such norms emerge or develop—how they come about from the non-normative. This is one of the central tasks of Piaget's genetic epistemology as Smith (1993) documented. We can take the question, therefore, to be: How does the individual construct epistemic norms? Piaget's theory of social exchange provided the basis for an answer.

Epistemic norms emerge from certain kinds of social relation among individuals—those involving cooperation. If this is correct, Piaget has shown that the paradigm case of the emergence of epistemic norms is not the Asch-type social situation of group conformity, but the Sherif-type social situation of cooperation and negotiation.

THE SOCIAL IS THE RATIONAL: OBJECTIVITY IS SOCIAL

It is widely believed that Piaget's cognitive developmental theory ignores or underestimates the importance of social factors. This seems to be a misconception based partly on a lack of acquaintance with Piaget's (1977/1995) social theory. As we have seen, Piaget maintained that the social is an essential factor in the development of knowledge, and one cannot understand the development of rationality merely by looking at the isolated individual. In fact he claimed that there is a distinctive kind of rationality and objectivity that is social in nature—rationality consists in certain forms of social interchange (Goldman, 1992). If so certain social conditions are necessary for the individual to possess certain kinds of knowledge.

Piaget often insisted that the social is a necessary condition for the development of knowledge and rationality: ". . . social life is a necessary condition for the development of logic. Thus, we believe that social life transforms the very nature of the individual, making him pass from an autistic state to one involving personality" (1977/1995, p. 210). Elsewhere he said: ". . . human knowledge is essentially collective and social life constitutes one of the essential factors in the formation and increase of pre-scientific and scientific knowledge" (1950, p. 187).

This claim was defended in several of Piaget's early works (1923/1955, 1924/1959, 1932/1965, 1927/1969, 1937/1971), in which he argued that rationality and objectivity presuppose other social agents. If one were really autistic or egoistic, and thus unaware of others, he argued, one would be unaware of oneself; objectivity would thus be impossible because objectivity entails the distinction between the self (the "subjective") and reality (the "objective"), and this distinction develops as a result of social interactions with others. Being objective means, among other things, not confusing the subjective with the objective. This requires an awareness that what one thinks—the subjective—may not coincide with what is true—the objective (Longino, 1990). Lacking such a distinction, the individual fails to recognize his own beliefs for what they are—representations—and instead takes them to be veridical. Thus:

> In order to be objective, one must have become conscious of one's "I." Objective knowledge can only be conceived in relation to the subjective, and a mind that was ignorant of itself would inevitably tend to put into things its own pre-notions and prejudices, whether in the domain of reasoning, of immediate judgment, or even of perception. An objective intelligence in no way escapes from this law, but, being conscious of its own "I," it will be on its guard, it will be able to hold back and criticize, in short it will be able to say what, roughly, is fact and what is interpretation. (1927/1969, pp. 241–242)

Objectivity presupposes self-consciousness, which presupposes the awareness of others. Likewise, rationality and objectivity—the giving of proof, evidence, justification, reason, and so on for what one believes—depends on the existence of others. Otherwise in the absence of other persons and their divergent points of view, there would be no need to defend one's own point of view. "Only under the pressure of argument and opposition will he seek to justify himself in the eyes of others . . ." (1924/1959, p. 137).

> Anyone who thinks for himself exclusively and is consequently in a perpetual state of belief, i.e. of confidence in his own ideas will naturally not trouble himself about the reasons and motives which have guided his reasoning process. Only under the pressure of argument and opposition will he seek to justify himself in the eyes of others and thus acquire the habit of watching himself think, i.e. of constantly detecting the motives, which are guiding him in the direction he is pursuing. (Piaget, 1924/1959, p. 137)

When forced to give reasons to someone else for what one believes, the epistemic subject comes to be able to evaluate his own reasons by taking up the other person's point of view and evaluating his own ideas accordingly. External dialogue thus gives rise to internal dialogue.

Piaget made two points here. First, objectivity is social because being objective involves discounting the purely subjective and attaining a state of objectivity in which the world is seen as containing different perspectives integrated into a single account. An objective account of the world, therefore, is one in which an account can be given of why someone perceives something from her particular point of view. Second, the resistance offered by others to our beliefs is the occasion for us to engage in reflection on our beliefs.

Both of these features are missed in the Cartesian account. Descartes insisted that one takes up the purely subjective point of view and trusts nothing else. Yet clearly we are sometimes mistaken, as Descartes admitted, in our subjective beliefs. If so, how do we determine when this subjective perspective is veridical? (It is certainly no solution to invoke God to guarantee that our subjective impressions of "clear and distinct" ideas are true.) In fact if there were no other epistemological perspectives for Descartes to consider—namely, skepticism—he never would have been forced to construct his theory of knowledge. One of Descartes' primary objectives was to get his contemporaries to subject their accepted beliefs to critical scrutiny, and for this reason he invoked methodological skepticism. Yet this involves a different perspective—one that serves as a critical basis for subjecting a set of beliefs to scrutiny. This is why Descartes really cannot be a epistemological solipsist, for if he were, he would (as Piaget pointed out) not feel the need to justify his beliefs. In effect, Descartes' epistemological program contains a tacit assumption that epistemic criticism is valuable. Yet epistemic criticism presupposes an epistemological pluralism or perspectivism. It thus appears that knowledge and rationality, in one important sense, are essentially social in nature.

CONCLUSION

In this chapter, I set out three aspects of Piaget's social epistemology: (a) his solution to the issue of epistemological holism versus epistemological individualism, which is epistemological relationalism; (b) his theory of the social exchange of epistemic values; and (c) his account of the social nature of rationality. These three aspects form three pillars of what can be called his *social epistemology*. As I tried to show, this brief sketch of his views has much to offer certain concerns of analytic social epistemology—namely, the issue of collective knowledge and the social nature of individual knowledge. I have lacked the space to discuss the important connection between his social epistemology and contemporary continental social epistemology. My discussion has been sketchy and incomplete, but I hope I have convinced the reader that there is something called Piaget's social epistemology and that a careful reading of his *Sociological Studies* (Piaget, 1977/1995) is worth the effort.

If we view Piaget merely as an ordinary psychologist, we surely misunderstand his program of genetic epistemology. Any such program, which is interested in how knowledge develops, is clearly concerned with knowledge. Therefore, this must involve (as Piaget always insisted) a consideration of the normative dimension of knowledge as well as the factual dimension. The normative cannot be eliminated. Yet as I understand Piaget, he was also a naturalistic epistemologist, and this means being committed to certain views about the nature of reality and the methodology to employ in constructing an epistemology. Any epistemic norm, therefore, must be grounded in the natural world, with the normative realm supervening on the natural. Epistemic norms are thus developmental outcomes of earlier naturalistic psychological processes.

When it comes to understanding the role of the social in this epistemological enterprise, what must be shown is that epistemic norms emerge from the social interaction of individuals. Just as the normative cannot be eliminated or reduced to the purely factual, so the social cannot be eliminated or reduced to properties of the isolated Cartesian knower. The social does play an essential role in Piagetian genetic epistemology. Hence, there is every reason to think that Piaget does have a social epistemology.

ACKNOWLEDGMENT

The author would like to thank Jeremy Carpendale and Ulrich Müller for the invitation to contribute to this collection of essays and for making many helpful comments and suggestions for the improvement of this manuscript.

REFERENCES

Asch, S. E. (1952). *Social psychology*. New York: Prentice-Hall.

Barnes, B. (1977). *Interests and the growth of knowledge*. London: Routledge.

Blau, P. M. (1964). *Exchange and power in social life*. New York: Wiley.

Blau, P. M. (1968). Interaction: Social exchange. In D. L. Sills (Ed.), *International encyclopedia of the social sciences* (Vol. 7, pp. 452–457). New York: Macmillan.

Bloor, D. (1991). *Knowledge and social imagery* (2nd ed.). Chicago: University of Chicago Press.

Descartes, R. (1985). Discourse on the method of rightly conducting one's reason and seeking the truth in the sciences. In J. Cottingham, R. Stoothoff, & D. Murdoch (Eds. & Trans.), *The philosophical writings of Descartes* (Vol. 1, pp. 111–151). Cambridge: Cambridge University Press. (Original work published 1637)

Descartes, R. (2001). Meteorology. In *Discourse on method, optics, geometry, and meteorology* (P. J. Olscamp, Trans.). Indianapolis: Hackett. (Original work published 1637)

Durkheim, E. (1938). *The rules of the sociological method* (W. Hollis, Trans.). New York: The Free Press. (Original work published 1895)

Gilbert, M (1992). *On social facts*. Princeton: Princeton University Press.

Goldman, A. (2001). Social epistemology. Stanford Encyclopedia of Philosophy. http://plato.stanford.edu/entries/epistemology-social.

Goldman, A. I. (1992). *Liaisons: Philosophy meets the cognitive and social sciences*. Cambridge, MA: MIT Press.

Homans, G. C. (1958). Social behavior as exchange. *American Journal of Sociology, 63*, 597–606.

Homans, G. C. (1961). *Social behavior: Its elementary forms*. New York: Harcourt, Brace.

Kitchener, R. F. (1981). Piaget's social psychology. *Journal for the Theory of Social Behavior, 11*, 255–277.

Kitchener, R. F. (1985). Holistic structuralism, elementarism and Piaget's theory of "relationalism." *Human Development, 28,* 281–294.

Kitchener, R. F. (1986). *Piaget's theory of knowledge: Genetic epistemology and scientific reason.* New Haven, CT: Yale University Press.

Kitchener, R. F. (1991). Jean Piaget—the unknown sociologist. *British Journal of Sociology, 42,* 421–442.

Kitchener, R. F. (2002). *Developmental epistemology: Cognitive development and naturalistic epistemology.* Manuscript in preparation.

Longino, H. (1990). *Science as social knowledge: Values and objectivity in scientific inquiry.* Princeton: Princeton University Press.

Moscovici, S. (1985). Social influence and conformity. In G. Lindzey & E. Aronson (Eds.), *Handbook of social psychology* (3rd ed., Vol. 2, pp. 347–412). New York: Random.

Pareto, V. (1935). *The mind and society.* New York: Harcourt, Brace. (Original work published 1916)

Piaget, J. (1950). *Introduction á l' épistémologie génétique: Vol. III. La Pensée biologique, la pensée psychologique et la pensée sociologique.* Paris: Presses Universitaires de France.

Piaget, J. (1955). *The language and thought of the child* (M. Gabain, Trans.). New York: Meridian Books. (Original work published 1923)

Piaget, J. (1959). *Judgment and reasoning in the child* (M. Warden, Trans.). Totowa, NJ: Littlefield, Adams. (Original work published 1924)

Piaget, J. (1965). *The moral judgment of the child* (M. Gabain, Trans.). New York: The Free Press (Original work published 1932)

Piaget, J. (1969). *The child's conception of physical causality* (M. Gabain, Trans.). Totowa, NJ: Littlefield, Adams. (Original work published 1927)

Piaget, J. (1971). *The construction of reality in the child* (M. Cook, Trans.). New York: Ballantine. (Original work published 1937)

Piaget, J. (1995). *Sociological studies* (2nd ed.; L. Smith, Ed., L. Smith et al., Trans.). London/ New York: Routledge. (Original work published 1977)

Piaget, J., & Garcia, R. (1999). *Psychogenesis and the history of science* (H. Feider, Trans.). New York: Columbia University Press. (Original work published 1983)

Schmitt, F. (1994). Socializing epistemology: An introduction through two sample issues. In F. Schmitt (Ed.), *Socializing epistemology: The social dimensions of knowledge* (pp. 1–27). Lanham, MD: Rowman & Littlefield.

Schmitt, F. (1999). Social epistemology. In J. Greco & E. Sosa (Eds.), *The Blackwell guide to epistemology* (pp. 354–382). Oxford: Blackwell.

Sherif, M. (1935). A study of some social factors in perception. *Archives Psychology,* No. 187, 5–60.

Sherif, M., & Sherif, C. W. (1969). *Social psychology* (rev. ed.). New York: Harper & Row.

Smith, L. (1993). *Necessary knowledge.* Mahwah, NJ: Lawrence Erlbaum Associates.

Tarde, G. (1933). *The laws of imitation* (E. C. Parsons, Trans.). New York: Holt. (Original work published 1890)

Weber, M. (1947). *The theory of social and economic organization* (A. M. Henderson & T. Parsons, Trans.). New York: The Free Press. (Original work published 1922)

Individualism and Collectivism: A Dynamic Systems Interpretation of Piaget's Interactionism

Jan Boom
University of Utrecht

Because of the role it gives to interactions, Piaget's constructivist theory of developmental process can be seen as an embryonic dynamic systems theory. The significance of nonlinear dynamic systems theories in this context is that they are capable of explaining emergent properties; objections to the idea that more powerful structures can arise from less powerful structures in development (known as the *novelty problem* or *learning paradox*) are no longer valid. This is important because such arguments have been used to deny the possibility of any novel or epigenetic process of development at all.

Construction, emergence, novelty, and *epigenesis*: All these terms relate to an aspect of Piagetian developmental theory that is recognized as central but at the same time can appear vague and elusive. This elusiveness has been seized on by both nativists and sociointeractionists who have tried to abolish the problem of emergence by shifting it to evolutionary biology and social interaction, respectively. However, against nativists it can be argued that dynamic systems theory has shown that emergence through interactions is possible, and against socio-interactionists it should be pointed out that social interaction is addressed and acknowledged to be essential by Piaget.

Although no less than three different kinds of interaction were discussed by Piaget at length, these deliberations have not proved convincing in explaining the dynamics of the developmental process. First, the interaction between subject and object in relation to development is thoroughly analyzed by Piaget (1975/1985) in his well-known book, *The Equilibration of Cognitive Structures*. Second, interactions within the subject are the focus of the recently translated *Studies in Reflecting Abstraction* (Piaget, 1977/2001). For example, in this account of reflecting abstraction, mutual interactions between operations or interactions among different hierarchical levels of cognitive organization are shown to be involved in an explanation of development. Third, the interaction between subject and subject is addressed by Piaget (1977/1995) in *Sociological Studies*. The role attributed by Piaget to this kind of interaction as an exchange of values and ideas appears to be even less recognized by developmentalists.

The criticism voiced by social interactionists against Piaget—that he neglected subject–subject interaction—is therefore wholly unjustified. His theorizing is interactionist in a profound way, and, moreover, he offered an overall framework for analyzing these interactions. In addition, by putting interactions at the heart of his explanation of process, Piaget was close to a dynamic systems theory. Even an extremely simple nonlinear dynamic system can be shown to display emergent behavior. By demonstrating the possibility of emergent properties, one of the main objections against the Piagetian type of constructive interactionism is thus neutralized.

Although we are still far from a complete and satisfying explanation of development, I (a) analyze the novelty problem in more detail, (b) evaluate attempts to base a solution to the novelty problem on interactionism, and (c) clarify what dynamic systems theory can add to the analysis of interactions. Finally, I conclude that interactionism is a viable option for explaining development.

THE PROBLEM OF EXPLAINING DEVELOPMENT

According to Piaget, a fundamental feature of development is the joint emergence of constructive novelty and adaptive improvement in cognitive development. This is the main theme in his equilibration theory (Piaget, 1975/1985; see Boom, 1997; Chapman, 1992). Although *novelty* and *improvement* are logically independent concepts, in that a novel stage does not necessarily imply a better one and a better stage is not necessarily qualitatively or structurally new (although it must be different in some respect), Piaget insisted on their intrinsic relatedness. Piaget's interactionism and constructivism purported to explain true novelty in cognitive functioning. Therefore, one of the most serious theoretical attacks to Piaget's theory—and on developmental psychology in general—was Fodor's denial of the possibility of the emergence of novel cognitive structures in development.

Novelty

The novelty problem was articulated by Fodor some 25 years ago. Fodor (1980) provided a modern formulation of the ancient (Plato) learning paradox (see also Pascual-Leone, 1980), making it directly relevant to the conception of stage development as entertained by Piaget. He concluded that it is impossible to learn something fundamentally new. Novel knowledge cannot be derived completely from old knowledge or it would not be new. Yet the new transcendent element of it cannot be wholly new either because then it could never be understood.

Fodor was primarily concerned with the issue of concept learning, which he believed to be a confused notion. He claimed that all actual learning theories were based on inductive extrapolation, and therefore must acknowledge hypothesis formation and confirmation among the processes involved in learning. He then showed that given such premises there can be no such thing as concept learning or achieving a new stage in development as Piaget would have it.

The line of argument entertained in learning theories (specifically within the empiricist tradition), and Fodor's objections to it, can be reconstructed in three steps: (a) First, a subject has to have an idea of what he or she wants to learn. A representation of it (e.g., a hypothesis specifying a general rule) must be present: the input. (b) Second, the subject should test these ideas to see whether they conform with experience: The hypothesis must be put to the test, which is why it has to be representable in the first place. In concept learning, testing would amount to verifying whether the concept is used correctly after the inference of a rule that specifies the correct use. In this case, correction is carried out by other competent speakers (who are treated in this model as environmental feedback). The predicate *learned* is only justified (or the claim of novel knowledge) after confirmation of the hypothesis. Thus, something is learned if and only if this step has been completed: the output of the learning process. (c) Third, a problem of circularity arises in the special case where the input and output are of the same kind. In this case, the learning process presupposes as input that which is only available as output.

This problem also arises in the acquisition of a new stage structure (in the Piagetian sense). Any representation that contains a hypothesis concerning a new structure presupposes an initial stage structure that is sufficiently complex to permit the representation. Yet the new—still to be attained—structure must typically transcend the old structure and thus can never be adequately represented by the old structure (Fodor, 1980). In both cases, the input paradoxically requires essential parts of the output (see Boom, 1991, 1997).

Actually there was an extensive debate between Piaget and Fodor during a conference in 1975 (see Piattelli-Palmarini, 1980) during which Fodor launched his attack. Piaget did not answer Fodor's arguments in much detail during their famous debate. He merely pointed out that Fodor's extreme nativistic position would lead to absurd consequences, apparently not realizing the impact that Fodor's argument would have. Subsequently, Fodor and the nativists were perceived to have won the debate. Nevertheless, the novelty debate continued (Boom, 1991; Campbell & Bickhard, 1987; de Graaf, 1999; Fodor, 1981; Jukes, 1991; Molenaar, 1986; Molenaar & Raijmakers, 2000; Prawat, 1999; Smith, 1993). Meanwhile, Piaget published several books relevant to the topic. In this more recent work (recent particularly in terms of translation dates), his constructive and interactionist ideas have become much clearer and perhaps contain an answer to nativism after all.

CONSTRUCTIVISM AND INTERACTIONS

The term *interactionism* is commonly used in psychology to denote a focus on social interactions. Indeed the focus is frequently on the social rather than the interaction (Wertsch, 1985). Interactionism thus appears as a legitimation of the insistence on stressing the nonuniversal, the individual differences, and the cultural influences, whereas the formal properties of interaction tend to be neglected. In contrast, Piaget's constructivism is based on a formal analysis of the dynamics of interactions. However, as far as Piaget's work is acknowledged to be interactionist, this is mostly taken to be an interactive adaptation to the external world (to attain equilibrium). What is less well known is Piaget's view that development can be seen not only as the result of interaction between subject and object, but also as resulting from interaction between levels within the subject or as a result of interaction between subject and subject.

Subject–Object Interactions

Our first question is whether the denial of novelty is inherently a problem for the subject–object interaction model or whether this model can provide a satisfactory answer. Piaget's (1975/1985) later theory of equilibration and his theory regarding the construction of negations (Piaget, 1974/1980) includes models for transcending contradictions that perhaps offer a viable alternative to nativism.

Let us begin by reviewing the process of achieving equilibrium. The effort to achieve equilibrium is fundamentally related to the interaction between subject and object. To compensate for disturbances in the empirical domain, some form of contact between subject and object is needed. On the one hand, Piaget claimed that external disturbances to the cognitive domain are possible (e.g., a failure to achieve one's goal). On the other hand, he admitted that external reality can only be known through cognitive structures. This would seem to reduce external disturbances to internal ones. Piaget's solution to this dilemma requires that we first understand the detailed account he gives of the struggle for equilibrium.

Because the object cannot be known in a direct unmediated fashion, Piaget introduced into his theory the distinction between observables and coordinations. The term *observables* refers to what a given subject perceives as the facts. *Coordination* refers to the inferences that go beyond the readily perceptible. For example, two events can be observed, and those two observables might be coordinated by thinking of a causal connection between them. The causal connection is not something that can be seen; it is inferred. Yet what can be perceived and what needs to be inferred depends on the stage of development of the subject concerned; what is difficult for a 4-year-old to construct might be so evident to a 10-year-old that this older child takes it as an observable fact.

Of course coordinations may be implicit and perceptions may be illusory. The point to emphasize here, however, is that what is to count as observable is not absolutely given; it is stage dependent (based on previous constructions). Nevertheless, seen from the perspective of a certain stage, an observable is a given and, more important, functions as a given in the sense that it can conflict with accompanying coordinations. Cognitive disturbances do not result from discrepancy with some absolutely given external reality, but from discrepancy between what is observable (e.g., as indicated by changes to the object) on the one hand and knowledge and expectations derived from the actions of the subject on the other hand. Restoring the balance (e.g., between expectations and observables) may require further differentiation of the schemes employed. Thus, the earlier scheme x is not wrong and need not be immediately discarded. On the contrary, the disturbance arises precisely because the scheme x is employed in a situation where it is not entirely adequate. An appropriate response to this inadequacy—this experience of imbalance between expectations and observables—would therefore be a differentiation of scheme x to scheme x', which is possible only when the difference between what is needed and what had previously been available is not too great.

Therefore, compensations cannot be understood as motivated by adaptation to a fixed, subject-independent reality. Although Piaget accepted that there is a subject-independent reality at the ontological level, and he assumed that the overall stage pattern is such that this ultimate reality is approached as a limit, this limit plays no immediate role in his account of knowledge construction. At the epistemological level, he remains a constructivist. Compensations are the instruments of adaptation to a subject-dependent reality. With development the possibilities for interaction increase for the subject. Thus, there is a kind of developmental progress, but this progress is not the advance of knowledge toward some form of absolute knowledge of reality. What develops are the fundamental possibilities of interaction.

With these qualifications in mind, one might ask about the mechanisms involved in such changes. To stay with the subject–object model, perhaps the best example of a developmental mechanism in Piaget's theory is the way contradictions in natural thought are overcome (Piaget, 1974/1980). Piaget claimed that all sorts of contradictions in the thinking of the children he had studied could be reduced to one basic formula: "incomplete compensations between affirmations (attributing the quality a to the class A) and negations (attribution of non-a to the complementary class A' under $B = A + A'$)" (Piaget, 1974/1980, p. 288; see Chapman, 1988). An incomplete compensation might take the form of an incomplete opposition between classes of objects that should be disjunct because one entails the negation of certain properties of the other.

For example, the images of capital letters seen in the mirror are reversed as children readily notice. However, when shown an M in the mirror, some children insist that it is not reversed. Others are aware of the problem and deny that the M can be a real letter. Here we have two classes (normal letters and reversed letters), which should be disjunct. Contradictions arise when a symmetrical letter like M is thought to belong to both classes or when the class of reversed letters is judged to lack an M. If this is accepted, transcending contradictions comes down to completing the compensation between affirmations and negations. A child may readily perceive affirmations, but the difficulty lies in arriving at the proper negations (in Piaget's technical sense). These negations have to be constructed by the child. Only when affirmations and negations are available within a system is compensation possible and a new level of equilibrium capable of being attained. In the preceding example, the confusions are overcome when a subject is able to construct the concepts *reversed* and *nonreversed* as necessary complements. Thus understood, the negation always refers to something not directly observable. The negation has to be constructed (is not relatively easy to observe) because it is precisely its general or necessary (unobservable) nature that counts.

The reactions of the children encountered in this example with mirrored letters can be generalized to three phases in handling disturbances. At first a subject can try to ignore the contradiction—for example, by simply forgetting what has happened. In the second phase, a subject is aware of contradictions, but is only capable of inventing ad hoc solutions and exceptions to neutralize the disturbance (e.g., such a child concludes that some letters just do not turn around in the mirror, whereas others do). Not until the third phase do subjects reconstruct these disturbances as negations of at least some part of their already attained knowledge. For example, the idea that each letter necessarily has its reverse has to be constructed for only then can it be seen that the reversed capital letter is essentially (although it is not actually) the same as the normal letter. Handling disturbances in this third way is thus crucial for development. According to Piaget (1974/1980), a new transcending point of view is constructed in this way, and a new stage in development can be attained.

Unfortunately, it is still not clear from the prior discussion exactly how this happens, and one may wonder whether this whole explanation is not circular. When subjects are in a transitional phase, they have to construct negations to overcome the limitations of their lower level knowledge, but this construction of negations requires an anticipation of the higher level knowledge (see Piaget, 1974/1980). Therefore, it may seem that in the Piagetian framework the construction of the negation would require an anticipation of an insight belonging to the subsequent stage (see Boom, 1991). This brings us to Piaget's ideas on reflecting abstraction, which concerns an internal mechanism in which interactions among operations, and in particular among different levels of organization, are explicitly addressed.

Subject–Internal Interactions

To understand what Piaget meant by reflecting abstraction, let us consider the following. If we reflect on something, we take something we have done or observed in a prereflexive manner out of its original context by thinking about it. In abstracting in this way, thinking it out of its spatial and temporal context, we become conscious of new aspects, distinctions, and relations. These are the elements of Piaget's definition of *reflecting abstraction*. Whereas the usual term *reflection* typically pertains to adult thinking and is used in the context of becoming consciously aware of something, Piaget defined a more general mechanism—a mechanism that also underlies the cognitive processes of very young children, but still a mechanism that preserves the idea of structuring previous cognitive structuring (as in the term *reflection*). In fact for Piaget conscious reflection is only one extreme variety of this mechanism. The other extreme he posited is pseudoempirical abstraction, a process by which material properties of an object or action are abstracted. Empirical abstraction (concerning, e.g., weight, color, movement, and force) does not go beyond the observable features, is not by itself creative, and is always dependent on earlier reflecting abstractions.

The general definition given by Piaget (1977/2001) reads: "Reflecting abstraction proceeds from the actions or operations of a subject and transfers to a higher plane what has been taken from a lower level of activity; it leads to differentiations that necessarily imply new, generalizing compositions at the higher level" (p. 29).

Reflecting abstraction involves two steps: first, projecting the structure implied in the coordination to the next higher level where the coordination ceases to be a coordination and becomes an action observable; and second, reorganizing this structure, which meanwhile has become a substructure.

The first step consists of bringing structures of the lower level to the next level, thereby constituting this higher level (Piaget, 1977/2001). In the more technical description, a coordination pertaining to actions of a subject at level x becomes an action observable for level $x + 1$. In this way, a new level is linked to the foregoing level. The step is constructive because a new level of abstraction is constituted. To give an example of an elementary form of this kind of projection, consider the case when a concept is formed—*concept* here taken in the elementary and restricted sense of a class. For example, take the concept *toy*, defined as any small thing with which one can play. The sensorimotor equivalent for this concept *toy* is the collection of objects that can be assimilated to the action scheme of playing. In this first step, projection, the observable properties of these actions are interiorized, and a reintegration of these objects into a whole is possible on the basis of their common property of being an object of playing. The projection in this example comes down to the formation of a concept.

The second step, reorganization or *réflexion*, is needed because the transposition of the structures of the lower level to the next higher level gives rise to multiple disequilibria (Piaget 1977/2001) that result from the various kinds of new relations introduced by the first step. This second step is constructive in a double sense, according to Piaget. In the first place with the projection, generalization over several instances has become possible. "Even if the coordination that projection thereby transfers from the plane of action to the conceptual plane remains the same, this very projection creates a new morphism or correspondence between the coordination on the conceptual plane and the practical situations in which the coordinated action is repeatedly carried out" (Piaget, 1977/2001, p. 308). In the second place, these first organizations also lead to the discovery of related content, which was not assimilable into the earlier structure, but which has now become assimilable by further (perhaps minor) transformation of the structure, and so becomes integrated within a larger and therefore partly novel structure (cf. Piaget & Garcia, 1989). In other words, this step consists of interactions in the form of reciprocal assimilations and accommodations between substructures.

Although it is easy to see how reflecting abstraction should lead to novelty—this follows directly from its constructive character—Piaget's argument supporting his claim of improvement is less clear despite that he wrote numerous volumes dealing with this issue. The question is: In what sense are these constructions, described as reflecting abstractions, supposed to lead to improved forms of knowledge? Part of the answer to this question relates to the fact that only the purely internal formal relations between the previous form of knowledge and the next have been dealt with. This formal account only takes us so far if we want to understand why this differentiation should not merely affect subjective criteria, but why it is also adaptive (see Boom, 1997).

More worrisome, however, is that it is still not clear how the very process itself is possible. If the mechanism works, the paradox is solved (at least for novelty), but does and can it work? In the absence of any causal explanation, the model remains merely a prescription for what would be required if we are to understand the process of cognitive development.

Subject–Subject Interactions

We turn to another type of interaction, the subject–subject model, based on internalization as advanced by social interactionists. Unilateral transmission will not do, but Chapman (1992) proposed that joint activity, in which subjects come to share the knowledge that each possesses, can lead to the construction of new knowledge neither individual possessed before. Such an idea was worked out originally and in some detail by Miller (1986; see also Döbert, chap. 7, this volume).

Miller claimed that it is possible to experience disturbances in a relevant and meaningful way without reference to the subsequent stage. However, he claimed this is only possible by means of discussion among a group of peers who seriously try to resolve a dispute. Miller maintained that cognitive development can be adequately explained only if the structures and processes of social cooperation are taken into account as a "reality sui generis" and as a necessary factor in development (Miller, 1987). In collective argumentation, which is the model for all argumentation, the primary goal is to develop a joint argument that answers a disputed question by relating it to collectively accepted knowledge.

In Miller's view, discussion between peers sharing the same developmental level is of the greatest significance (Miller, 1986). On the basis of theoretical considerations as well as empirical research, he claimed that under such circumstances a disturbance can be understood and something novel can be learned. Such collective arguments, he said, are regulated by a specific set of rules and, more specifically, three principles of cooperation. These three basic cooperative principles of argumentation can operate (in some form) among young subjects. They function as a coordinating mechanism that determines the processes of argumentation in such a way that, in principle, a set of collectively valid statements can be found and agreed on.

The principle of generalizability specifies that a statement is justified if it (a) is either immediately acceptable (belongs to the collectively valid) or (b) can be converted to the collectively acceptable. The principle of objectivity states that if a statement cannot be denied (i.e., its denial cannot be converted into a collectively valid statement), it belongs to the realm of the collectively valid, whether it confirms or falsifies some participants' points of view. The principle of consistency forbids that contradictions should enter into—or (once they have been discovered) remain in—the realm of the collectively valid (Miller, 1986, 1987). These conditions governing collective argument are much more restrictive than those governing individual thinking. An isolated individual could easily ignore conflicting information. However, in a collective argument, this is not acceptable as long as the goal—the development of a joint argument that gives an answer to a disputed question—is retained.

Assuming that these principles indeed operate, it is conceivable that one participant in the argument might assert proposition A while another participant asserts proposition B, with both statements mutually exclusive and traceable to the same shared base of collectively accepted knowledge. Consider the well-known balance scale task. If two or more children address this problem, one child may claim that the one arm is heavier because of a greater number of weights, whereas another child maintains that the other arm is heavier because of the greater distance of the weights from the fulcrum. Because both children are at a stage in which they acknowledge only one of the variables, they must in principle be able to understand each other's reasoning (albeit with difficulty). What they were unable to do is coordinate both points of view and see their interconnectedness.

The first conclusion that Miller drew from this example is that a child can no longer simply ignore what is going on and is bound to experience some form of contradiction. At least he or she will be made aware that his or her current knowledge is not sufficient to reach a consensus (Miller, 1986). Collectively accepted knowledge is knowledge that cannot be denied and yet is not necessarily completely comprehended. Thus, it creates the possibility of experiencing contradictions without reference to the subsequent stage.

In contrast, in the Piagetian model, a contradiction gains relevance only if the observations that constitute the contradiction are perceived to violate a necessary rule (i.e., allow no exceptions). The subject must be aware of the contradiction, although not necessarily be able to explain it in words. Hence, it is not sufficient for an expectation that was only highly probable to be violated. For example, in the well-known balance scale task, the necessary rule consists of knowing that an argument for why the right side should go down also implies (negatively) an argument for why the left side must go up. This relationship and its necessary character are presupposed in experiencing the contradiction, according to Piaget. However, this relationship requires knowledge that constitutes the subsequent stage, which, Miller rightly observes, is precisely what remains to be learned.

In Miller's case, subjects have a much easier task to accomplish. They can experience a relevant contradiction without a necessary negation because as participants in a discussion they are bound by the principles of argumentation, specifically the principles of objectivity and consistency. These principles function as an alternative source for experiencing contradictions without reference to necessary relations known only at the subsequent stage. If we accept Miller's point of view thus far, we have an alternative for Piaget's model of stage transition that eliminates the circularity inherent in Piaget's account.

I would contend, however, that the learning paradox is not yet resolved because it is unclear how the boundaries of the cognitive stage are transcended by the peers. Miller explained only how the shortcomings of the current knowledge can be recognized, but this does not bring the subject to the subsequent stage. Miller claimed that it is conceivable that the participants in the discussion, when they find themselves in a deadlock, experience the shortcomings of the present foundation of the collectively known. This might encourage reflecting abstraction, with the possible outcome of transcending the boundaries of the present stage. Thus far it is unclear how this would be possible. For Piaget, experiencing the contradiction in a meaningful way could lead to the subsequent stage because it is already involved in a way, but this is precisely the circularity Miller wanted to avoid.

Another way of putting it is this: Granted that a conclusion is reached through cooperation and has become part of the collectively valid, and thus emergent properties have arisen in the interaction, then what happens when the interaction is discontinued? How are such emergent properties consolidated and used in future situations? Invoking the notion of interiorization here would meet the same objection as has already been raised against reflecting abstraction. How?

In view of these problems, we turn again to Piaget, for not only has he considered subject–subject interactions himself, but he also placed these interactions in a broader context (Piaget, 1977/1995).

Interaction in Sociological Studies

One of the core features of Piaget's (1977/1995) sociological studies is a formal analysis of social exchanges. These exchanges may concern values, ideas, or propositions. His goal was a description in terms of possible forms of equilibrium. Two interesting points emerge from this that are not addressed explicitly in Piaget's more recent work, but are relevant for the learning paradox. He (a) argued that subject–subject and subject–object interactions are both instantiations of a deeper logic of interaction, and (b) pointed out the complicated relation among types of explanation, kinds of systems involved, and development.

In the main chapter of this book, Piaget gave a lengthy argument to show that the individual structures of logical thought and the structures of ideal cooperation are two sides of the same coin. For Piaget the conditions for equilibrium in an intellectual exchange are the same as for equilibrium in the logic used by individuals to group their formal operations (Piaget, 1977/1995, see pp. 80–94). Thus, he suggested a close correlation between the logical operations of the individual and certain forms of interindividual cooperation. Piaget presented logic as the product of cooperation, which has an active exchange of values at its core. He even claimed that the ultimate criterion of truth is the agreement among minds (see p. 80). However, it is not just any agreement that guarantees truth as history has shown us. According to Piaget, the problem is to distinguish between ideology and rational logic (scientific logic), which can both follow from agreement between minds. In terms of development, an individual would never be able to achieve equilibrium in operations without coordinating different points of view to some extent. At the same time, however, cooperation presupposes a certain level of cognitive organization among participants. Piaget ended his essays by remarking that, "it is the common equilibrium that is axiomatized in formal logic" (p. 94). The parallels drawn at this fundamental level, with subject–object and subject–subject interactions interwoven in this way, argue against the idea that subject–subject interactions are alone or even primarily responsible for overcoming the learning paradox (or vice versa).

Piaget observed a basic distinction between kinds of explanation, between causal (or real) explanations and formal axiomatization, and between diachronic and synchronic perspectives (which may be compared with horizontal and vertical reconstructions; van Haaften, Korthals, & Wren, 1997). In analyzing forms of social equilibrium, the same structures are found as were found for individual mental development: ". . . the transition from causality to implication involves three basic steps having distinct properties of these two sorts of relationship: rhythms, regulations, and groupings" (Piaget, 1977/1995, p. 56). Groupings (of operations) are the sole exchanges that can achieve complete equilibrium in the form of logic. Logic is the axiomatization of operations or the common expression of intra- and interindividual operatory mechanisms. Piaget argued that to understand logic as an operatory structure with perfect equilibrations, an axiomatic reconstruction of the implications involved in operatory mechanisms is needed. In contrast, rhythms only concern simple relationships that require causal explanations. Regulations are somewhere in between, requiring perhaps partly causal and partly implicational analysis.

The learning problem can be reformulated now in a true Piagetian spirit as the problem of giving a causal explanation for the transformation of regulations (but only for certain types of problems) to groupings (of operations or groupings of exchanges of propositions). The most directly relevant description for this process is undoubtedly reflecting abstraction. However, the problem with the idea of reflecting abstraction as a process is that, although it is a plausible description of what might be going on, it fails to convince as an explanation (let alone a causal explanation). An obvious retort is that it is not clear what kind of explanation would be possible (cf. Piaget, 1975/1985). I do not go into that discussion, but instead turn to the language of nonlinear dynamic systems. From this perspective, I interpret reflecting abstraction as a form of self-organization.

DYNAMIC SYSTEMS

Piaget recognized the importance of dynamic systems:

> It is important to recall at the outset that by a cognitive equilibrium (which is analogous to the stability of a living organism) we mean something quite different from mechanical equilibrium (a state of rest resulting from a balance between antagonistic forces) or thermodynamic equilibrium (rest with destruction of structures). Cognitive equilibrium is more like what Glansdorff and Prigogine call "dynamic states"; these are stationary but are involved in exchanges that tend to "build and maintain functional and structural order in open systems" far from the zone of thermodynamic equilibrium. (Piaget, 1977/2001, p. 312; see also Piaget, 1975/1985)

Elsewhere in his writings, Piaget (1977/1995) also suggested the importance of dynamic system theories: "If we could have rewritten today the pages which follow, we would have placed much more emphasis on the self-regulating processes of equilibration" (p. 26). For additional hints as to why Piaget's theory is an incipient systems theory, see Chapman (1992).

However, self-organization as spontaneous organization toward a higher level of order is still an elusive concept. Fortunately, recent progress in dynamic systems theory makes it increasingly clear that dynamic systems theory can supplement Piagetian theory. The foundations are laid by Prigogine's nonequilibrium thermodynamics (Nicolis & Prigogine, 1977), Thom's (1975) catastrophe theory, and Haken's (1983) synergism (see Molenaar & Raijmakers, 2000). I attempt to show that interactions (as described earlier by Piaget) satisfy the conditions necessary for nonlinear dynamic systems to generate new behavior (with emergent properties and reorganizations).

Nonlinear Dynamic Systems

First, nonlinear dynamic systems (NLD) need to be defined or at least described in more detail. In NLD theory, only the form of behavior over time (or time evolution) is at issue. Take as an example the simplest relevant system possible: Suppose we have a system with only two possible states (0 and 1) and two observations at different time points (t_1 and t_2). In that case there are only four possible patterns. The behavior over time of the entire system is adequately described by one variable with two values over two realizations. However, we could have decided that we needed 1,000 variables with 1,000 values each over 1,000 time points to adequately describe some system. That would of course result in an astronomical number of possible patterns. Luckily, however, the next state of the system often depends on the previous state, which reduces the possible states of the system enormously (not so for a dice, but we are talking mainly about living systems). With these examples in mind, we should now define some key terms:

System—a set of variables changing over time with some natural connectedness among the variables.

Dynamic system—present state of all variables and their derivatives is dependent to a certain degree on the previous state.

Deterministic dynamic system—completely dependent on the previous states.

Linear dynamic system—all dependence can be expressed as a combination of linear equations.

Nonlinear dynamic system—dependence cannot be expressed entirely as a combination of linear equations. This is the more general case; linearity is in fact a limiting case.

Stochastic linear dynamic system/nonlinear dynamic system—when a random term is added to a linear dynamic system/nonlinear dynamic system equations.

Chaotic—exhibits sensitive dependence on initial conditions (practically with starting value differences much smaller then measurement error) as is explained later. Chaotic is not the same as random.

Whatever scale we choose to describe the behavior of the system, we only consider the variables; everything we are interested in should be the result solely of the equations governing these variables. Although this may seem a stark reduction, surprisingly good results can be obtained in this way, and one can always turn to a finer scale. Moreover, this approach is well suited to the study of epigenesis and therefore is developmental to the bones. I now turn to the bottom–up definition of *self-organization*, avoiding describing systems or structures as living entities (which would presuppose what we want to show).

Self-Organization

Surprising behavior can emerge in nonlinear systems. A difference or differential equation describes the changes in values over time (e.g., if we define that at $t + 1$ the value is 10 greater than the value at t, we have a linear growth over time). Nonlinearity generally obtains when a quadratic or higher order term is involved in the equation (e.g., $x_{t+1} = x_t r (1 - x_t) = r x_t - r x_t^2$. In this equation, an important role is played by the parameter r. With respect to time, r is a constant, but when we vary r, different patterns in time can emerge. Another important element is the starting value: x_0 can have any numerical value except zero. Even in this simple example of an equation (actually this is a famous equation that describes growth under limited resources), it can easily be shown that depending on r the time behavior of this mathematically defined system can be strange: With values of r between 0 and 2, differences in the value of the initial value are reflected proportionally in the x value, and over longer time all converge to the same final value for x. However, with an r around 2.7, the pattern becomes totally unpredictable for very small changes in the initial value, and x varies wildly and irregularly and continues to do so. In this situation, the slightest perturbation in the starting values leads to radical changes in behavior (expressed in the variable x). For these particular values of r (> 2.7), the system is chaotic. By a gradual variation of one of the parameters of the system, a radical change in type of behaving can be simulated.

However, it is also possible (even in simple systems like the one earlier) that for some values of the parameters the system is governed by an attractor, which means that almost irrespective of initial value the system's temporal evolution will end at a certain fixed value or in an oscillation between few values. The famous example here is the pendulum. Perturbations can be considerable and still the system rather quickly settles back to its desired position.

The point to take from these two examples is that when one of the parameters in a nonlinear dynamic system is changed slowly in (as under the influence of changing external or internal environmental conditions), it is conceivable that a radically new behavioral pattern suddenly emerges. The slow gradual change in one of the parameters might stand for effects of e.g. slow increase in some relevant capacity or resource. The variation in the dependent variable over short time is the behavior of the system. Because *suddenly* is not a precise term here, it would be better to define the character of the emergence as follows: Without external planning and without planned prespecification, a real discontinuity in behavior (in the time-dependent main variable) is possible. Such analyses have been used with success in movement science, and more recently were introduced into developmental psychology (e.g., van Geert, 1994).

The examples given before are extremely simple, but with slightly more complex systems we can illustrate equilibrium states. Equilibrium obtains when the equations alluded to earlier are such that around a certain time point there is no change in the variables. However, because the equations typically contain one or more parameters, this equilibrium also depends on the parameters and may even disappear when one of the parameters changes. The relation between smooth changes in the parameters and equilibrium states in these systems is central to the mathematical theory of self-organization. For most properties described previously, rigorous mathematical proof exists or is possible (see Raijmakers, 1996). The whole idea of destabilizing and stabilizing through reorganization is an integral part of nonlinear dynamical thought. It also bears a strikingly close resemblance to the terms Piaget used to describe the cognitive developmental process. In addition, we can now be more clear and precise about what interaction does.

Interaction Revisited

It is essential to the prior account that the dependence of the system from the previous state is a nonlinear dependence. Only then can abrupt qualitative changes in the equilibria show up and self-organization be possible. The prior example involved a term with x to the power 2, but why should such nonlinearity ever occur?

Let us consider interaction. The basic feature of interaction is that action A at t influences B at t_{+1} and, consequently, B influences A again at t_{+2}. All forms of interaction boil down to such a schematization. However, from this we can conclude that A at t_{+2} is indirectly influenced by A at t_0. In addition, A at t_{+2} is influenced by A at t_{+1}. Here we see that at any moment A is influenced by a function that contains A at least more than once—like a term that involves A to the power 2 (or more). The same goes for B. Of course these influences are often toned down in realistic interactions, but when the influence of A from earlier moments is completely eliminated no interaction can be said to have existed.

Therefore, the first conclusion is that true interaction always involves nonlinear dependencies. Interaction means that influence returns, so we are dealing with a kind of circular causality. This is true irrespective of whether we are dealing with organism–environment or organism–organism interactions.

The second conclusion is that the particular features of interaction do not follow from the recombination as such. The interaction itself (when in a balanced way) may have self-organizing properties. When self-organization is possible, this may lead to reorganizations. In a geometrical metaphor (see Molenaar & Raijmakers, 2000), the abrupt qualitative changes in the set of equilibria are like sudden earthquakes that completely reorganize the existing topological pattern of domains of attraction in state space.

Two qualifications are in order: The first is that the developmental pathways of systems regulated by interactions are not easy to follow. Most of our methodology is focused on linear dependencies and is therefore not adequate because predictions are extremely difficult. However, more adequate methodological tools such as latent class analysis (e.g., Boom, Hoijtink, & Kunnen, 2001; Jansen & Van der Maas, 1997) are nowadays available.

The second qualification is that the picture sketched here is highly simplified. It would be more interesting to model reorganizations that lead to one part of the system monitoring other parts or even itself. For such transitions, quite complicated coupled nonlinear dynamic systems would be needed (but certain types of neural networks might be promising). The way the nonlinear dynamic systems approach can be really helpful at present, however, can best be illustrated by catastrophe theory. Because indicators exist signaling discontinuities and in turn discontinuities signal reorganizations, we can show, for instance, whether empirically observed changes in behavior are due to internal reorganizations or not. Only the first case is to be associated with qualitatively different thinking, whereas in the second case any suggestion of radical difference is probably more apparent than real. For example, Raijmakers (1996) showed that the connectionist simulation of learning to predict the workings of a balance scale by McClelland and Jenkins (1991) does not involve discontinuities at all contrary to their claim to have modeled abrupt changes. Data of children for this task reveal distinct rules consistent with real discontinuities, although admittedly it is difficult to ascertain all criteria specified by Raijmakers (1996; see also Boom, Hoijtink, & Kunnen, 2001).

CONCLUSION

Three forms of interaction were analyzed: Development can be seen as the result of interactions between subject–object, subject–subject, or within the subject. However, these independently described forms of interaction all prove inadequate to resolve the ultimate construction problem that underlies the learning (or novelty) paradox.

Next, the suggestion by Piaget was taken up that individual structures of logical thought (embodied in subject–object interactions) and the structures of ideal cooperation (embodied in subject–subject interactions) are both instantiations of a deeper logic of interaction, or at least that is what development should lead to for Piaget. The problem with Piaget's account of this process, in terms of reflecting abstraction, is that it fails to convince as a causal explanation and therefore leaves room for doubt as to whether such developmental mechanisms are possible at all.

Finally, I have shown that interactions in a dynamic system may lead to the emergence of new structures and sudden reorganizations. That reorganization can take place quite suddenly and have rather severe consequences is not only possible, but even plausible for systems as complex as the human mind. This can even be demonstrated with simple simulations in a spreadsheet program as van Geert (1994) showed. In addition, we can be clearer and more precise as to what role interaction plays in this respect. Seen from the perspective of nonlinear dynamics theory, the Piagetian idea of interactions and reorganizations leading to a sequence of destabilization and stabilization in cognitive functioning is at least possible, and therefore arguments against novelty do not carry conviction any longer.

REFERENCES

Boom, J. (1991). Collective development and the learning paradox. *Human Development, 34,* 273–287.

Boom, J. (1997). Cognitive development. In A. W. van Haaften, M. Korthals, & T. Wren (Eds.), *Philosophy of development: Reconstructing the foundations of human development and education* (pp. 101–117). Dordrecht: Kluwer.

Boom, J., Hoijtink, H., & Kunnen, E. S. (2001). Rules in the balance: Classes, strategies, or rules for the balance scale task? *Cognitive Development, 16*(2), 717–735.

Campbell, R. L., & Bickhard, M. H. (1987). A deconstruction of Fodor's anticonstructivism. *Human Development, 30,* 48–59.

Chapman, M. (1988). *Constructive evolution: Origins and development of Piaget's thought.* Cambridge: Cambridge University Press.

Chapman, M. (1992). Equilibration and the dialectics of organization. In H. Beilin & P. B. Pufall (Eds.), *Piaget's theory: Prospects and possibilities* (pp. 39–59). Hillsdale, NJ: Lawrence Erlbaum Associates.

de Graaf, J. W. (1999). *Relating new to old*. Unpublished doctoral dissertation, Universiteit Groningen, Groningen.

Fodor, J. (1980). Fixation of belief and concept acquisition. In M. Piattelli-Palmarini (Ed.), *Language and learning: The debate between Jean Piaget and Noam Chomsky*. Cambridge, MA: Harvard University Press.

Fodor, J. (1981). The present status of the innateness controversy. In J. Fodor (Ed.), *Representations* (pp. 257–316). Brighton: Harvester Press.

Haken, H. (1983). *Advanced synergetics*. Berlin: Springer.

Jansen, B. R. J., & Van der Maas, H. L. J. (1997). Statistical test of the rule assessment methodology by latent class analysis. *Developmental Review, 17*, 321–357.

McClelland, J. L., & Jenkins, E. (1991). Nature, nurture, and connections. In K. van Lehn (Ed.), *Architectures for intelligence: The twenty-second Carnegie Mellon Symposium on cognition* (pp. 41–73). Hillsdale, NJ: Lawrence Erlbaum Associates.

Miller, M. (1986). *Kollektive Lernprozesse [Collective learning processes]*. Frankfurt a/M: Suhrkamp.

Miller, M. (1987). Argumentation and cognition. In M. Hickmann (Ed.), *Social and functional approaches to language and thought* (pp. 225–250). New York: Academic Press.

Molenaar, P. C. M. (1986). On the impossibility of acquiring more powerful structures: A neglected alternative. *Human Development, 29*, 245–251.

Molenaar, P. C. M., & Raijmakers, M. E. J. (2000). A causal interpretation of Piaget's theory of cognitive development: Reflections on the relationship between epigenesis and nonlinear dynamics. *New Ideas in Psychology, 18*, 41–55.

Nicolis, G., & Prigogine, I. (1977). *Self-organization in non-equilibrium systems: From dissipative structures to order through fluctuations*. New York: Wiley.

Pascual-Leone, J. (1980). Constructive problems for constructive theories. In R. Kluwe & H. Spada (Eds.), *Developmental models of thinking* (pp. 263–296). New York: Academic Press.

Piaget, J. (1980). *Experiments in contradiction*. Chicago: University of Chicago Press. (Original work published 1974)

Piaget, J. (1985). *The equilibration of cognitive structures*. Chicago: University of Chicago Press. (Original work published 1975)

Piaget, J. (1995). *Sociological studies*. London: Routledge. (Original work published 1977)

Piaget, J. (2001). *Studies in reflecting abstraction*. Hove: Psychology Press. (Original work published 1977)

Piattelli-Palmarini, M. (Ed.). (1980). *Language and learning: The debate between Jean Piaget and Noam Chomsky*. Cambridge, MA: Harvard University Press.

Prawat, R. S. (1999). Dewey, Peirce, and the learning paradox. *American Educational Research Journal, 36*, 47–76.

Raijmakers, M. (1996). *Epigenesis in neural networks models of cognitive development*. Unpublished doctoral dissertation, Universiteit van Amsterdam, Amsterdam.

Smith, L. (1993). *Necessary knowledge: Piagetian perspectives on constructivism*. Hillsdale, NJ: Lawrence Erlbaum Associates.

Thom, R. (1975). *Structural stability and morphogenesis*. Reading, MA: Benjamin.

van Geert, P. (1994). *Dynamic systems of development: Change between complexity and chaos*. New York: Harvester Wheatsheaf.

van Haaften, A. W., Korthals, M., & Wren, T. (1997). *Philosophy of development: Reconstructing the foundations of human development and education*. Dordrecht: Kluwer.

Wertsch, J. V. (1985). *Vygotsky and the social formation of mind*. Cambridge, MA: Harvard University Press.

5

Coordinating Operative and Figurative Knowledge: Piaget, Vygotsky, and Beyond

Tamer G. Amin
American University of Beirut

Jaan Valsiner
Clark University

Piaget and Vygotsky certainly belong to a class of thinkers with a broad, integrative perspective on developmental issues. There were many other such thinkers in the first half of the 20th century—William Stern, Ernst Cassirer, Karl Bühler, and Jakob von Uexkyll, to name a few. Yet the focus on Piaget and Vygotsky has gained wider popularity for largely historical coincidences of the epistemic market of developmental psychology (about such markets, see Rosa, 1994).

Here we return to the work of Piaget and Vygotsky in a way that reintegrates their ideas. All too often we have observed contemporary researchers claiming that these two developmental thinkers fall on different sides of an individualist–collectivist divide. The construction of this divide is an interesting example of historical myopia in contemporary psychology. It is clear that Vygotsky was not only knowledgeable about Piaget's work (see van der Veer & Valsiner, 1991), but also deeply appreciative of the latter's revolutionary take on human mental development. The differences between Piaget and Vygotsky certainly exist, but these have more to do with their primary foci of interests rather than their belonging to different schools. All too often our reconstructions of psychology's history turn the thinking of particular individual thinkers into representatives of some "school"—usually overlooking the fine-grained details of their actual intellectual efforts.

COMPLEMENTARITY OF PIAGET
AND VYGOTSKY REEXAMINED

Egocentric Speech: Personally Social,
or—The Debate That Never Was

Piaget first dealt with the topic of egocentric speech in his book, *The Language and Thought of the Child* (in French, 1923; in English, Piaget, 1926/1952). In 1934, Vygotsky's *Thinking and Speech* included a chapter (chap. 2—Piaget's theory of child language and thought) written in 1932 as a preface to the Russian edition of the two first books of Piaget—Piaget, 1932). It was a careful—albeit critical—discussion of Piaget's ideas. This was preceded by careful replication efforts of Piaget's investigations and performing a crucial experiment—sometime around 1929—to refute Piaget's claim about the primacy of egocentric speech (van der Veer & Valsiner, 1991). Vygotsky's attitude toward Piaget was always appreciative and critical.

It was only about 25 years later that Piaget commented on Vygotsky's critique, responding to it in a commentary that was published with a 1962 English edition of Vygotsky's *Thought and Language*. Here Piaget was also in an appreciative mood, presenting the supposed controversy between them as a difference of special focus of interest, rather than of basic developmental principles.

Piaget on Egocentric Speech. Piaget (1959) began *The Language and Thought of the Child* by immediately stating the question he wished to address: What is the function of children's talk? Communication would seem to be the obvious answer. It would seem that the child, like the adult, talks to communicate assertions about the world, express emotions and points of view, and get others to act. Piaget questioned this assumption and pointed out that speech seems to serve other functions as well. There is internal speech, which can hardly be considered communicative—at least between persons. More interestingly, there is a form of audible speech that seems to be pleasurable to the speaker, is performed for the speaker's own emotional benefit, and plays no real communicative role. Piaget suggested—and he spent most of the book trying to convince the reader—that most of young children's speech is egocentric; it is noncommunicative speech spoken for the self. According to Piaget (1926/1952), the child is engaging in egocentric speech when

> He does not bother to know to whom he is speaking nor whether he is being listened to. He talks either for himself or for the pleasure of associating anyone who happens to be there with the activity of the moment. This talk is

egocentric, partly because he speaks only about himself, but chiefly because he does not attempt to place himself at the point of view of his hearer. (p. 9)

By analyzing every utterance produced by two boys for about a month during their morning class, Piaget demonstrated that egocentric speech indeed constitutes a large proportion (just under half) of child speech. He arrived at this conclusion based on a classification scheme where the boys' utterances were considered to be egocentric if they were repetitions, part of a monologue, or part of a dual or collective monologue. In contrast, an utterance was considered to be what Piaget called "socialized" if it incorporated adapted information, criticism, commands, requests, or threats, a question or an answer—in other words, speech that reflected that an interlocutor's point of view has been appreciated and taken into account.

Critical to Piaget was the contrast between communicable and noncommunicable thought (i.e., thought can be more or less adapted for dialogue with another person). This is the contrast that distinguished egocentric and socialized speech—the former grounded in directed but noncommunicable thought, and the latter in directed communicable thought. Piaget (1926/1952) considered these two forms of thought to be what he called "two different logics." He was quick to clarify that by "logics" he meant the "sum of habits which the mind adopts in its general conduct of operation" (p. 46). This is certainly an unfortunate lapse in the presentation of a structuralist. It is a common unwarranted assumption that the grand theorists of the past—like Piaget and Vygotsky are considered to be[1]—wrote down ideas that were well groomed and consistent.

Piaget was referring to two different *styles* of thinking. Piaget's use of the notion of logic in his early books follows the lines of James Mark Baldwin's genetic logic. The first of these—communicable thought—makes use of concepts shared by a society. It is thought to be adapted to conventionalized reality, meaning that it is a style of thought that does not assimilate objects to idiosyncratic interpretations, but rather adapts to their objective and consensual features. Communicable thought distinguishes shades of meaning precisely and is easily formulated in precise logical language. In contrast, noncommunicable thought involves idiosyncratic elements such as imagery, analogy, and fantasy and is thereby unadapted to reality. Objects are assimilated to personal viewpoints and interpretations. Although the purpose of communicable thought is understanding, the purpose of noncommunicable thought is satisfying personal desires.

What is clear from reading Piaget's characterization of this style of thought is that it is modeled on the thought that forms the basis for com-

---

[1]See Valsiner (2001) for discussion of Piaget as an empiricist.

munication between two scientists carefully discussing the nature of the physical world. In contrast, his model for noncommunicable (albeit directed) thought seemed to be the self-indulgent, poetic monologue. (Piaget himself united both; see Vidal, 1993).

Vygotsky's Critique. In Vygotsky's (1934/1986) discussion of Piaget's analysis of egocentric speech, he put forward a different interpretation of the phenomenon. In Vygotsky's view, the high proportion of egocentric speech Piaget found in the speech of the young children he studied was most likely an artifact of the particular study. Vygotsky pointed out that the phenomenon of egocentric speech was sensitive to setting. Vygotsky's research group carried out their own experiment in which children participated in similar activities as those in Piaget's study, but in Vygotsky's study certain obstacles or frustrations were introduced that the children had to address (see van der Veer & Valsiner, 1991). Under such conditions, Vygotsky observed that egocentric speech decreased. Explanation for this result entailed the claim that the function of egocentric speech is actually social because it diminishes when the availability of addressees is made complicated (Vygotsky, 1934/1986).

Vygotsky's account of egocentric speech reflects a metatheoretical stance that differs from Piaget's. Vygotsky was primarily interested in the process of development through mental synthesis. Vygotsky was critical of Piaget situating egocentrism developmentally between autism and directed (social) thought and the emphasis Piaget placed on the similarities rather than the differences between egocentric thought and autism. Vygotsky considered a developmental account that viewed an autistic starting point (viewed as not directed to reality) that is eventually superseded by a form of language and thought oriented to reality as unworkable. A developmental starting point that was characterized as a "hallucinatory imagination prompted by the pleasure principle" (Vygotsky, 1934/1986) was, in his view, neither phylogenetically nor ontogenetically viable. The orientation to reality has to be the primary orientation of a viable organism (Vygotsky drew on Bleuler to make this point).

Vygotsky rejected the account of egocentric speech as reflecting an intermediate form of thinking between autistic and socialized directed thought, preferring a functional explanation of the phenomenon. The decrease in egocentric speech when obstacles are presented to a child engaging in playful activity suggested to Vygotsky that this form of speech played an organizing role in the child's activity. This functional (instrumental) role of egocentric speech was supported by an empirical observation:

> An accident that occurred during one of our experiments provides a good illustration of one view in which egocentric speech may alter the course of an

activity: A child of five-and-a-half was drawing a streetcar when the point of his pencil broke. He tried, nevertheless, to finish the circle of the wheel, pressing down on the pencil very hard, but nothing showed on the paper except a deep colorless line. The child muttered to himself "It's broken," put aside the pencil, took watercolors instead, and began drawing a broken streetcar after an accident, continuing to talk to himself from time to time about the change in his picture. (Vygotsky, 1934/1986, p. 31)

In this example, we can discern the instrumental function of egocentric speaking—it entails an audience (in this case, the child) as an instrument of suggestion to reorganize one's own conduct. It becomes clear that the question of egocentric speech here is no longer the issue of having or not having an addressee, but that of playing a specific regulatory role in the child's ongoing experience—whether it occurs in a group of children or in solitude. Egocentric speech is a form of speech that could be considered external thought yet to be internalized.

Adopting this functional view of egocentric speech, Vygotsky rejected Piaget's interpretation of it as a form of speech yet to be socialized. He gave the following alternative developmental account that views the child's use of language as social from the outset:

> We consider that the total development runs as follows: the primary function of speech, in both children and adults, is communication, social contact. The earliest speech of the child is therefore essentially social. But first it is global and multifunctional; later its functions become differentiated. At a certain age the social speech of the child is quite sharply divided into egocentric speech and communicative speech. (We prefer the use of the term communicative for the form of speech that Piaget called socialized, as though it had been something else before becoming social. From our point of view, the two forms, communicative and egocentric, are both social, though their functions differ.) Egocentric speech emerges as the child transfers social, collaborative forms of behavior to the sphere of inner-personal psychic functions. . . . Egocentric speech, splintered off from general social speech, in time leads to inner speech, which serves both autistic and logical thinking. (Vygotsky, 1934/1986, p. 35)

Piaget's Retort. In his comment on Vygotsky's critique, Piaget (1962a) chose to address the criticisms from the perspective of his later work. He organized his retort in terms of what he saw as two different aspects of Vygotsky's critique: egocentrism in general and egocentric speech in particular. Piaget addressed the general issue of egocentrism first, clarifying what he meant by the *cognitive egocentrism* of the young child. In response to Vygotsky's assertion of the primacy of the orientation to reality, Piaget drew a distinction between the tendency of the child toward adaptation to reality and the success of that adaptation. Piaget (1962a) clarified that he agreed with Vygotsky about "the adaptive and functional nature of the activities of the child—and of every human being" (p. 2). However, he pointed out that whereas he saw the extent of the adaptation of the cognitive structures of the young child as limited, Vygotsky displayed an "optimism" regarding that adaptation. Piaget viewed the progressive adaptation of cognitive structures as a decentering, "the perpetual reformulation of previous points of view" (Piaget, 1962a, p. 3), and that cognitive egocentrism (characteristic of the young child, but can still be observed in adults as well) is characterized by the "lack of differentiation between one's own point of view and the other possible ones, and not from an individualism that precedes relations with others" (p. 4).

With regard to egocentric speech, Piaget pointed out that he was in agreement with Vygotsky's analysis of egocentric speech as a developmental transitional point to internalized language, and acknowledged that he did not place enough emphasis on the functional aspect of this form of speech. In turn he criticized Vygotsky for failing to appreciate the young child's inability to *coordinate* viewpoints—the central feature of childhood egocentrism. The following excerpt captures these features of Piaget's response to Vygotsky and also brings out an important difference in what the two theorists meant when they referred to socialized speech:

> In brief, when Vygotsky concludes that the early function of language must be that of global communication and that later speech becomes differentiated into egocentric and communicative proper, I believe I agree with him. But when he maintains that these two linguistic forms are equally socialized and differ only in function, I cannot go along with him because the word *socialization* becomes ambiguous in this context: if an individual A mistakenly believes that an individual B thinks the way A does, and if he does not manage to understand the difference between the two points of view, this is, to be sure, social behavior in the sense that there is contact between the two, but I call such behavior unadapted from the point of view of intellectual cooperation. This point of view is the only aspect of the problem which has concerned me but which does not seem to have interested Vygotsky. (Piaget, 1962a, pp. 7–8)

Piaget's axiom of the developing person striving toward cooperative harmony is in the background of all his theorizing—from his adolescent years (Vidal, 1993) to his later years (Chapman, 1988). It is visible in this difference of view with Vygotsky on what socialized communication is. Piaget—given his background in biological taxonomies—classified conduct (into *adapted* and *unadapted*), whereas Vygotsky—given his original fascination with Hamlet's psychological tension looked at the mismatch of the child's position and that of others (or of a state of affairs in the environment) as the trigger for further development.

The (Unfortunate) Relevance of Translations. So far it seems that the two thinkers were indeed apart in their takes on the ontogeny and functions of egocentric speech. Piaget obviously had only the 1962 translation of *Thinking and Speech* to comment on. Vygotsky's quote (given earlier) reads a bit differently in the Russian original:

> The original function of speech is that of creating a message, social link, impact upon the others around oneself both on behalf of adults and from the side of the child. In this respect, the original speech of the child is purely social ["pervonachal'naia rech rebenka chisto sotsial'naia"]; to call it socialized would be incorrect, since that word is linked with the image of something originally non-social, which becomes social only in the process of its change and development (Vygotsky, 1934/1986, pp. 55–56; translated by J.V.)

It is certainly not the first time that translations of sophisticated theoretical texts between languages created intellectual divides. Vygotsky merely reiterated the basic (Janet's) law of social origins of psychological functions (see Valsiner & van der Veer, 2000). Indeed he refused to assume the objectlike structure of the child (who becomes "socialized" by input from others), and instead retained the emphasis on the active developer assembling one's psychological functions while being social by the nature of the human environment (of other humans, their communication, tools, and signs). This primacy of the active—albeit social in principle—agent is fully consistent with Piaget's focus.

Even this brief presentation of the exchange between Piaget and Vygotsky over the phenomenon of egocentric speech allows us to see that their disagreements can, to a large extent, be seen as differences in emphasis. The two came to study the same phenomenon from different backgrounds and with different basic assumptions. The particular nature of their points of emphasis can be explored by situating their debate over egocentric speech with respect to broader aspects of their developmental theories.

SITUATING THE EGOCENTRIC SPEECH OF PIAGET AND VYGOTSKY

Our contemporary developmental psychology is largely atheoretical and nondevelopmental (Valsiner, 1997, 1998). In fact developmental perspectives have been slowly retreating from what is called *developmental psychology* with only few exceptions (Cairns, Elder, & Costello, 1996; Fischer & Bidell, 1998; Fischer, Yan, & Stewart, 2002; Lyra, 1999; Siegler, 1996). The basic distinction between nondevelopmental and developmental axiomatics can be found in the treatment of ontology—"This is X." The nondevelopmental view treats this statement as pertaining to the inherent quality of "X-ness," which is a stable given at the particular time and place. The developmental viewpoint differs here cardinally—"being X" becomes viewed in terms of "having become X" as well as "potential to become something-else-than X." This amounts to a perspective of historicity. The operative/figurative distinction that has been viewed as a characteristic of Piaget's work maps well onto the developmental/nondevelopmental contrast.

The Operative/Figurative Distinction

Coordinating Piaget and Vygotsky's views on egocentric speech and identifying the complementarity of their frameworks can begin by situating their debate in terms of a central component of each of their theories. Piaget drew a distinction between knowledge as a copy of reality and knowledge that goes beyond being a mere copy and transforms reality. Chapman (1988) referred to this distinction in Piaget's view of knowledge as the distinction between the *figurative* and *operative* aspects of knowledge, respectively. In Piaget's terms (Piaget, 1954, 1962b), this distinction characterizes all aspects of knowledge:

> All knowledge has to do with structures, while affective life provides the energetics, or more precisely, the economics of action. These structures may be figurative, for example, perceptions and mental images, or operative, for example the structures of actions or of operations (in this connection we shall speak of "operational structures" in the proper restrained sense, while "operative" will be used to refer to all external or interiorized actions which precede operations and to actions which attain the operational level). (Piaget, 1969, p. 356)

Thus, *developmental* knowledge is structural *and* dynamic at the same time. Instead of the usual either/or question—is knowledge structural as a given state of affairs (true) or dynamically changing in accordance with situational conditions—Piaget changed the question to that of coordination of the structural and functional facets of knowledge. Thus, it is not surprising that the unity of figurative and operative permeates all the stages of ontogeny of mental functions that Piaget described—from the sensorimotor through to the formal operational period.

Egocentrism of the young child was a characteristic of preoperational thought. Piaget used the term *representation* in this context to mean re-presentation—the evocation of an object in thought without it being present. The development of this capacity coupled with the already coordinated sensorimotor schemes meant that the practical, action-based knowledge that developed during the second year of life could be reformulated on the plane of thought without the actual manipulation of objects. The operative aspect of knowledge at this preoperational stage was the richly coordinated action schemes inherited from the sensorimotor period.

Although representation was necessary for the later development of (concrete) operational thought at about age 7, it imposed a significant (albeit temporary) fixity to knowledge: A mind gradually developing its capacity to represent external reality is not going to be successful at the controlled transformation of that reality (Piaget, 1995). Herein we find the source of the egocentrism of the preoperational period and the specific phenomenon of egocentric speech. It is only as the child acquires a broader repertoire of viewpoints on the same object, and when his viewpoints come up against the opposing perspectives of others, that the conditions for coordinating viewpoints and operational thought are laid down. Thus, the child's thought is decentered; his earlier privileged representations no longer have a distorting influence.

In distinguishing between the figurative and operative aspects of knowledge, Piaget drew a contrast between "anticipations" that derive from the observation of regularities in the world (empirical abstraction) and the "necessary implications" that derive from the coordination of schemes (reflective abstraction). In making this contrast, Piaget distinguished between the kind of knowledge that can derive from external structures and that which requires the individual's own constructive efforts. He expressed this when he stated: "Reality (*le réel*) merely provides regularities which are more or less general but devoid of necessity, which is characteristic of that which is only observable and independent of the models which the subject constructs in the search for reasons" (Piaget, 1986, p. 308). Piaget illustrated the sense of necessity associated with cognitive constructions and the implications that derive from assimilating objects to operative schemes:

> The content of these relations is provided by experience, as too their generality in extension, whilst in intension the subject can grasp the reason for them, which then confers some degree of necessity. For example, at the sensori-motor level, a 10- to 12-month old infant will discover that in pulling a strip of cardboard at the end of which is placed an object which is too far away to be grasped directly, the infant is drawing that object nearer, succeeding in gaining possession of it. If the object is subsequently placed just beyond the cardboard which the infant still pulls, that is because the meaning of the relation "placed upon" is still not yet understood. When, by contrast, the infant uses the cardboard wittingly, we can say that for the infant the situation "placed on" a support implies the possibility of being drawn along, but if (and only if) it is placed "on" the cardboard and not by its side. We shall designate, therefore, such relations by the term "signifying implication" due to the fact that in this case one meaning, such as spatial position, entails another (in this case cinematic use). These relations determine a spe-

cific necessity to the extent that the subject understands their reasons. (Piaget, 1986, p. 306)

Notice his linking implication and necessity with the intensional aspect of categorization. That is, assimilation of an object to a scheme—and its counterpart of accommodation—are constructive acts in that they specify a series of implications regarding the behavior of that object.

As cognitive constructions become more coordinated, richer sets of necessary implications derive from an act of categorization. Piaget's account of the strength of a cognitive structure is essentially formulated in terms of the relationship between the nature of categorization and reasoning. Moreover, underlying Piaget's emphasis on coordination (i.e., transformative, operative knowledge) is an emphasis on the cognitive power associated with assimilating objects to structures rich in implications as opposed to the implicative poverty of figurative representations of the external properties of objects of thought.

Against this background we can see that Piaget's (1926/1952) interpretation of egocentric speech, and his dissatisfaction with Vygotsky's emphasis on its functional connection with inner speech, reflects his emphasis more broadly on development of ever more powerful cognitive constructions. The child's inability to coordinate viewpoints (i.e., the poverty of their cognitive constructions in early childhood) was what Piaget believed Vygotsky did not appreciate in his account of egocentric speech. We see in this Piaget's emphasis on the operative aspect of knowledge.

Vygotsky's interpretation of egocentric speech reflected his commitment to the basic law of sociogenesis of Pierre Janet (see Valsiner & van der Veer, 2000) and what he viewed as the heart of the process of mental development: the internalization of interpsychological structure. Vygotsky conceptualized the process of internalization as constructive and novelty-generating (Lawrence & Valsiner, 1993). Moreover, he viewed the process of internalization as intimately connected with the *construction* of signs and their operative use in structured encounters with the surrounding world (Vygotsky & Luria, 1994). In his view, internalized signs open the door for innovation in the intrapsychological mental system.

Both Piaget and Vygotsky pointed to the construction of the sign as fundamental to the processes of *internalization*, but it is important to distinguish how the two used that term. Although Vygotsky used the term to refer to a process that entailed the creation of signs in both solitary activities (play) and in interaction with others—adults or children, or even with pets—he emphasized that the outcome of the process involved the internalization of "cultural forms of behavior." In Piaget's account of internalization, what is being transferred inward via representation is really the object of thought. The operative schemes that manipulate these objects are already inner implicative schemes of action. Piaget was not interested in the cultural specificity of these objects of thought and the *content* of what is internalized, but rather on how to construct a theory that would account for how a child's operative knowledge is transferred from the external plane of action to internalized mental processes not requiring the support of external structures. Thus, we see a relative emphasis in the views of Vygotsky and Piaget in terms of emphasis on the figurative and operative aspects of knowledge, respectively.

Social Interaction and Its Figurative and Operative Contributions to Thought

Piaget distinguished between the use of the term *social* merely in the sense of "contact between two people" and "intellectual cooperation." The first he was quite happy to grant to egocentric speech, the second he was not. A closer look at how each theorist saw the role of the social in psychological development is in order.

Piaget treated issues of the social in a separate set of essays (Piaget, 1995). He began by giving an independent formulation of the development of logic from a psychological point of view that does not appeal to interpersonal interaction. This he did by describing the transition from operatory sensorimotor knowledge to preoperational thought via representation and, finally, the coordination of viewpoints to achieve a true reversibility of thought. Second, Piaget argued that the development of interpersonal relations (what he referred to as *intellectual socialization*) follows a parallel path from nonsocial, to a fused state of lack of differentiation between the individual and the social, and, finally, to social cooperation with differentiated self and other viewpoints. According to Piaget, these developments parallel one another; they both manifest development toward "the groupements," a formal system of reversible operations. Given this parallel, he raised the problem of explaining the origin of logical operations. Piaget (1995) asked:

> ... does the individual reach equilibrium in the form of the groupement by himself, or is cooperation with others necessary for this to be achieved? Or conversely, does society reach intellectual equilibrium without an internal structuration unique to individual actions? (pp. 153–154)

His answer to this line of questioning focused on two key points. The first involves the possibility of the individual, preoperational child coordinating viewpoints on his own. Piaget (1995) rejected this possibility by stating that, "that would mean, therefore, that one accords the individual the power to make conventions with himself or, in other words, to link present thought with his thought to come, as if it were a matter of different people" (p. 154). An earlier statement in this same essay clarified his position further:

> An operatory groupement is a system of operations with compositions exempt from contradiction, reversible, and leading to the conservation of the totalities envisioned. Now it is clear that thinking jointly with others facilitates non-contradiction. It is much easier to contradict oneself when one thinks only for himself (egocentrism) than when partners are present to recall what one has said previously and what one has agreed upon. (Piaget, 1995, p. 144)

The second point he raised in addressing the issue of the origin of logical operations also dealt with a purely individualist account of the coordination of viewpoints, but dealt with the representational medium through which the viewpoints are realized. He stated:

> Complete reversibility presupposes symbolism, because it is only by reference to the possible evocation of absent objects that the assimilation of things to action schemes and the accommodation of action schemes to things reach permanent equilibrium and thus constitute a reversible mechanism. The symbolism of individual images fluctuates far too much to lead to this result. Language is therefore necessary, thus we come back to social factors. (Piaget, 1995, p. 154)

Three points can be highlighted as the central aspects of Piaget's view of the role of the social in the psychological development of the individual. The first is that there is a clear focus in Piaget's writing on how an individual constructs operational structures. Social factors are highlighted as important components of this constructive process. The nature of these operative structures are not discussed in relation to their social origin. Second, social interaction is seen to *facilitate* the coordination of perspectives as if individual processes could in principle suffice (as if greater processing power would rid the individual of the need for social interaction—a point reminiscent of neo-Piagetian arguments). These two ideas point to an interpretation of the role of the social purely as scaffold with certain formal characteristics (i.e., realizing the groupements in interpersonal interaction) that would enable the individual mind to engage in the necessary processes for constructing operational structures. The third aspect of Piaget's view on the role of the social implicates the figurative aspect of knowledge, but notice that his view again focused on the form of this knowledge as opposed to its content. That is, he suggested that the *conventional* aspect of language as opposed to the *individuality* of images as a representational format is necessary for the kinds of coordinations that would lead to operational thinking. In summary, Piaget backgrounds entirely the *content* of the representations on which the individual's constructive processes operate. What Piaget treated as an unexplored background, Vygotsky treated as his object of investigation.

Two Comparisons. In cultural-historical theory, Vygotsky built on two comparisons. The first of these is a comparison between human and animal psychological functioning, which—interpreted developmentally—led to the thesis that human psychological functioning (in particular, high mental functioning) is qualitatively transformed through the use of symbols. The second was a comparison between "primitive" and modern humans. This contrast generated the claim that the advanced psychological accomplishments of modern societies reflect the effect of the sophisticated symbolic systems developed over historical time. Vygotsky's cultural-historical theory reflects the influence of Engels' dialectical materialism, with its critical point that the specifics of consciousness derive from the nature of materially grounded activities. Moreover, Vygotsky's view that the origins of higher mental functions, apparent in the modern mind, must be traced to cultural history seems to have derived in part from the collective intellectual influence of Durkheim, Lévy-Bruhl, and Thurnwald, including their ethnographic studies of "primitive" peoples and related theoretical claims (van der Veer & Valsiner, 1991).

Although Vygotsky's theorizing clearly incorporated attention to personal constructive processes, these two key comparisons reveal his foregrounding of the structural (i.e., figurative) *specificity* of intrapsychological functioning that derives from the material (especially symbolic) basis of interpsychological functioning.

SUMMARY OF THE EMPHASES OF PIAGET AND VYGOTSKY

Let us distill the various points of emphasis in Piaget's theory as discussed herein into a short series of statements:

1. In characterizing knowledge, we need to distinguish between the structural form of objects of knowledge and the internal representation of that structure (the figurative aspect of knowledge) on the one hand, and the meaningful schemes to which these structures are assimilated on the other. This assimilation amounts to a specification of the object as a type of thing with implications for further action (cognitive or physical) on the object.

2. Cognitive development consists of the progressive coordination of schemes with the result that the cognitive structures formed are increasingly rich in implicational structure, which means that as development proceeds the assimilation of an object to a scheme has increasingly rich implications for action on the object.

3. There are important contributions from the social world within which the individual is embedded. First, a necessary condition for this process of coordination via equilibration to go beyond physical action on objects is the mental evocation of absent objects. This requires representation—specifically, a linguistic form of representation the critical feature of which is its conventional nature. Second, social interaction facilitates the process of coordination.

The vast majority of Piaget's work dealt with Points 1 and 2. The points of emphasis in Vygotsky's theory can in turn be distilled into the following statements:

1. Advanced mental functioning develops largely by transferring inward processes that originate in interaction with others and in the experience with the environment.
2. The interpsychological processes internalized are a semiotic process so we must conceive of the nature of advanced mental functions as semiotically mediated.
3. Because the specifics of these semiotic processes differ culturally and historically, an account of the development of the individual human mind must take into account this specificity.

CONTEMPORARY FRAMEWORKS AND THE OPERATIVE/FIGURATIVE DISTINCTION

What happens when these two components are given equal emphasis? What picture is formed of the process of development? Are novel questions raised? We suggest that keeping the central features of Piaget and Vygotsky's theories in mind and raising such questions would be exceedingly productive for developing richer integrative descriptions and explanations of cognitive developmental phenomena. We do not mean to imply that these questions need to be formulated specifically in terms of Vygotsky's and Piaget's theories or even some hybrid of the two. However, we view much contemporary theorizing as addressing specific aspects of what will ultimately need to be seen as an integrated whole. The legacies of Piaget and Vygotsky and extensions of specific aspects of their work in more recent frameworks have been extensively reviewed (see e.g., Schol-nick, Nelson, Gelman, & Miller, 1999; Wertsch, del Rio, & Alvarez, 1995). The purpose of this final section is not to duplicate those efforts or to pro-vide an alternative reading. Instead we would like to briefly mention some important recent work in light of the distinction between operative and figurative knowledge and then provide a brief discussion of some work carried out within a cognitive linguistic framework that can be viewed as describing how semiotic devices guide the construction of implicative structures. Although not carried out within a developmental framework, this work suggests a way to bridge the figurative and opera-tive emphases in developmental theorizing.

A variety of different approaches to the study of cognitive develop-ment can be seen to echo Piaget's operative emphasis, with its focus on intension and inference. These include (among other approaches): the most extreme form of the domain specificity framework (see e.g., contri-butions to Hirschfeld & Gelman, 1994); an integrated domain-specific, domain-general account (Karmiloff-Smith, 1992); and the neo-Piagetian proposals that we think of cognitive development in terms of central cog-nitive structures (Case, 1992). Although these views depart to varying de-grees from Piaget, they share a common element that, as the prior discus-sion suggested, played an important role in Piaget's theory: the emphasis on the progressive construction of implicational structures that go beyond the representation of external structure.

This research can be contrasted with a branch of research within the sociocultural tradition focusing instead on the characterization of cultural and institutional variation in external structures of social interaction and materially based cognitive practices (e.g., Lave, 1988; Rogoff, 1990, 1997). These authors have argued that learning and knowledge transfer should not be viewed in terms internal to the person, with the power of knowl-edge structures (e.g., concepts, models) characterized in terms of the abstraction of those structures. Instead the material and social embedded-ness and embodied nature of this knowledge means that a characteriza-tion of its growing power through learning must appeal to the history of an individual's participation in cognitive activities. Extension of knowl-edge to new situations will depend on *similarity* to activities in which the individual has previously participated. The rejection of abstraction as a sufficient construct to explain transfer is not a denial of subjectivity. In-deed Lave (1988) commented that "it is a matter of interpretation whether some variant is encompassed by or interrupts routine" (p. 188). According to Lave, theorizing about continuity across activities is possible but is not a matter of prediction based on how abstract the knowledge possessed by an individual is. Instead it is about creating an understanding of the struc-tural and functional characteristics of acting persons in semiotically con-

stituted activities within institutional settings that would motivate particular interpretations.

Granting the rejection of abstraction as an adequate explanatory construct, we suggest that this view begs two questions. First, to what extent
does the researcher's representation of the field of signification (through
semiotic analysis) in a situated activity setting correspond unproblem-
atically to subject interpretations? Second, what are the *necessary, or even
motivated, implications* (from the point of view of the acting subject) of a
particular, semiotically motivated interpretation? The first of these questions amounts to cautioning (see also Budwig, 2003) against the back-
grounding of the subject in the anthropological turn of research on cognition and language (e.g., Hanks, 1996; Lave, 1988; Ochs, 1996). Research
suggesting that contrasting linguistic meaning systems can result in different cognitive categorizations of experience (e.g., Bowerman, 1996) rein-
forces an interest in the characterization of the semiotic characteristics of
activities when cognition and learning are the object of study. However,
the extent and nature of linguistic (or more broadly semiotic) relativity is
an open question (see Gumperz & Levinson, 1996).

At issue here is the transformational processes implicated in the internalization of semiotically mediated interactions. We are dealing here with
the extent to which semiotic systems impact the categorization of experience. To the extent that such a treatment addresses the intensional (as
opposed to the extensional) aspect of categorization we are addressing operative not merely figurative knowledge and we are beginning to address
the role of semiotically based interaction in the construction of implicational structures, thereby bridging the figurative/operative divide. There
is an important role for research addressing the interaction between language and cognition in constructing this bridge. We focus next on an area
of research that is particularly powerful in this respect—cognitive linguistic research on conceptual metaphor and blending. This work goes beyond the role of language in categorization to the role of language (and
other semiotic devices) in guiding inferential patterns and emergent conceptual relations. That is, this work can be seen as contributing to an understanding of how semiotic systems guide the construction of complex
operative knowledge structures.

*Mapping Image-Schematic Inferential Structure and Emergent Con-
structions.* The theory of conceptual metaphor was developed by Mark
Johnson, George Lakoff, Mark Turner, and others (see e.g., Johnson, 1987;
Lakoff, 1990; Lakoff & Johnson, 1980, 1999; Lakoff & Turner, 1989), reflecting a basic commitment of research in cognitive linguistics "to make one's
account of human language accord with what is generally known about
the mind and the brain" (Lakoff, 1990, p. 40). This commitment led to an

attempt to incorporate into linguistics findings in cognitive psychology, among them findings concerning imagery and image-schematic representations. Indeed the importance of image schemas in cognition has been reinforced by linguistic evidence and has led to the formulation of what Lakoff (1990) called the Invariance Hypothesis—a hypothesis central to the cognitive linguistic theory of conceptual metaphor.

The hypothesis is that abstract reason is organized in terms of the inference patterns of image schemas. This hypothesis is based on the identification of broad systematicity in the organization of English according to what Lakoff and Johnson (1980) called *structural metaphors*—implicit in the organization of a vast number of English sentences as knowledge structures (e.g., Argument as war—*He defended his point*; Time is a Limited Resource—*You're wasting time*; and Understanding is Seeing—*I see what you're getting at*). They argued that what grounds the gestaltlike coherence of these structures and what constrains the kinds of mappings between domains of knowledge is a common, generic, multidimensional structure that emerges from our experience. Lakoff (1990) referred to this structure as a generic *event structure* composed of six dimensions: participants, parts, stages, linear sequence, causation, and purpose.

Supporting Lakoff and Johnson's (1980) conclusions concerning the existence of this generic structure, Lakoff and Turner (1989) found that all of the proverbs they studied were organized in terms of this same generic-level structure (a generic-level structure slightly modified from Lakoff & Johnson, 1980). They argued that what are mapped from one domain to another are: causal structure, temporal structure, event shape, purpose structure, modal structure, and linear scales. In turn Lakoff (1990) argued that many of these aspects of event structure are understood metaphorically in terms of image-schematic structures incorporating basic inferential patterns associated with space, motion, and force.

This line of reasoning suggests that a chain of mappings exists—mapping between knowledge structures (e.g., Argument as War) where event structure is mapped and a mapping that suggests that the conceptual components of event structure are construed in terms of image-schematic elements. This led Lakoff (1990) to formulate the Invariance Hypothesis: "that at least some (and perhaps all) abstract reasoning is a metaphorical version of image-based reasoning" (p. 39). Thus, Lakoff's hypothesis is that the relational structure of abstract domains derives from the relational structure constituting image-schematic gestalts involving basic experientially based notions of force, space, and motion.

The grounding in image schemas, of the vast set of metaphorical projections that Johnson, Lakoff, Turner, and others have uncovered, brings this linguistic evidence in agreement with the view that Johnson (1987) expressed concerning the bodily basis of meaning and reason. Indeed he discussed what might be one of the strongest test cases for Lakoff's hypothesis—logical inference. Johnson (1987) argued that patterns of logical inference are grounded in the experientially based inferential patterns of containment.

This research is not developmental. It makes no claims regarding the role that the linguistic manifestation of conceptual metaphor and mapping of inferential structure actually plays in guiding cognitive developmental processes. Indeed the research just cited does not even directly address the psychological reality of the conceptualizations and mappings described. Systematicity in language is cited as indirect evidence for this reality, and there is some more direct experimental evidence to support this (Gibbs, 1994). From a developmental point of view, this work can be seen as having identified semiotic sites that are candidates for analysis as cultural resources that guide the construction of operative knowledge structures. Although these are cultural givens, they must be viewed developmentally as novel constructions utilizing cognitive resources that could potentially lead to novel instances of language use, categorization, and inference. In this sense, if examined developmentally, the appropriation of conceptual metaphor can be seen as an articulation of the emphasis placed by Piaget on the construction of operative structures with Vygotsky's emphasis on the transformative internalization of semiotic mediated interpsychological figurative structures.

Another closely related area of research in cognitive linguistics that can be similarly situated with respect to the skeletal structure outlined earlier is work on blending and conceptual integration (see e.g., Fauconnier, 1997; Fauconnier & Turner, 1996). Within this area of research, linguistic units (or other artifacts) are studied as instructions for the formation of cognitive constructions—that is, instructions for evoking, connecting, and elaborating conceptual structure. These constructions are seen as taking place within a given discourse context. Hence, the details of the discourse context, implied background knowledge, and structures previously evoked in the discourse constitute conceptual resources for the meanings constructed at any given moment in the discourse. At the heart of this view is the construct of a mental space. According to Fauconnier and Turner (1996), "mental spaces are small conceptual packets constructed as we think and talk, for purposes of local understanding and action" (p. 113).

The ways in which mappings are established between spaces is the central topic of this work (Fauconnier, 1997; Fauconnier & Turner; 1996; Turner & Fauconnier, 1995). To illustrate that, consider the following example discussed by Turner and Fauconnier (1995). In 1993, a catamaran sailed from San Francisco to Boston in an attempt to break the record sailing time between these two cities established by a clipper in 1853. At some point during the catamaran's journey, a newspaper reported that "the catamaran was 'barely maintaining a 4.5 day lead' over the clipper" (cited in Turner & Fauconnier, 1995). Turner and Fauconnier commented that the only way "maintaining a lead" could make sense was if the phrase is understood by reference to a blended space in which both the catamaran and the clipper are simultaneously making journey's from San Francisco to Boston.

Fauconnier's (1997) many-space model appeals to four spaces and the mappings between them to account for the construction of blends; two input spaces (in this example, one for each of the 1993 and 1853 runs), a generic space that is structured internally with an abstract schema (e.g., some sailing boat making a run between two cities at some unspecified time), and a blend that is structured by partial input from the two input spaces and the generic space. In this example, both the catamaran and clipper are projected into the blend along with the specifics of the journey. The specific dates are blocked because a space specified with respect to two different times would be internally inconsistent. Only a generic time is projected from the generic space to the blend establishing the simultaneity of the two runs.

An additional aspect of the blend that is crucial to the interpretation of the newspaper report is that the counterfactual space contains relations absent from either input space. The presence of two boats simultaneously on the path between the two cities means that there is a relation of relative position absent from either input. This in turn evokes a counterfactual race frame, with all of the details of a race that that entails (e.g., there can be a winner and a loser, there is a sense of competition, etc.). These details are important for an interpretation of "barely maintaining a 4.5 day lead" in the newspaper report.

A number of key features of blending theory are illustrated by this example. First, blending theory is a generalization beyond the two-domain model of analogical structure mapping (Gentner, 1983, 1989). A key difference that makes it a generalization over the two-domain model is in the nature and directionality of the projections. In Gentner's structure mapping theory, relational structure is projected from a source to a target domain. It is a unidirectional treatment of projections. In contrast, the many-space model at the heart of the theory of blending and conceptual integration allows for projections from multiple input spaces into the blend, which is a conceptual structure constructed online in the context of communication or action. Projections from the different input spaces can be partial and vary in extent, thus accommodating the specific case of the unidirectional mapping in the two-domain model.

Another difference concerns the roles that implicational meaning and emergence play in the two accounts. The structure mapping model focuses on the syntax of mappings. In Fauconnier's (1997) many-space model, implicational meaning is at the heart of the resulting conceptual structure elaborated in the blend. Projections into the blend cannot be separated from the meaning of the entities projected because it is meaning that explains the emergent structure and elaborations from background knowledge. In the example just summarized, the fact that the catamaran and clipper are projected into the same space (allowing for the interpretation that one is ahead of the other) evokes the race frame. That is, a rich set of conceptual entities and relations emerge as the conceptual basis for interpreting the meaning of the newspaper report.

What makes research on blending and conceptual integration interesting in the context of a discussion of cognitive development and its figurative and operative aspects is that the kinds of blends and integration processes discussed in this literature are not just singular creative constructions. Instead they fall into classes of blends and projection patterns closely associated with conventional linguistic units (see e.g., Fauconnier & Sweetser, 1996; Goldberg, 1996). In fact recent developments in blending theory have involved the discussion of processes of conceptual integration in relation to cultural artifacts more generally (see e.g., Fauconnier & Turner, 2002). In this context, cultural artifacts, including linguistic units, are being seen as anchors for creative cognitive constructions. Yet, as is clear given the centrality of emergence in the theory, the external structures of artifacts are seen to constrain but not determine these constructions. Therefore, new generations of artifact users are guided by these external structures. However, creative cognitive processes, and the individual's construction of novel (to him or her) implicational structures, need to be appealed to explain how new generations learn to use these artifacts.

These kinds of analyses of transfer of inferential structure and the construction of cognitively powerful blends point to promising avenues for bridging the operative and figurative emphases of Piaget and Vygotsky, respectively. However, two theoretical leaps are still needed. One is a leap backward to developmental psychology's history to revive the integrative and fundamentally developmental focus of these two theorists (along with others such as Buhler and Cassier) with their close attention to the interrelationships among language, thinking and development. The second leap needed is forward toward an articulation of local analyses of materially based cognition and broader accounts of developing cognitive structures and processes with growing implicative power. Hutchins' (1995) approach to materially and socially distributed cognition articulating three levels of analysis (following Marr)—the computational, algorithmic, and implementational levels—has these characteristics. In addition, the integrative scope of the work of Tomasello (1999) emphasizing the central role of cultural artifacts in development provides a contemporary theoretical lens through which the figurative/operative balance in developmental theorizing may be examined.

REFERENCES

Bowerman, M. (1996). The origins of children's spatial semantic categories: Cognitive versus linguistic determinants. In J. J. Gumperz & S. C. Levinson (Eds.), *Rethinking linguistic relativity* (pp. 145–176). Cambridge, England: Cambridge University Press.

Budwig, N. (2003). The role of language in human development. In K. Connolly & J. Valsiner (Eds.), *Handbook of developmental psychology* (pp. 217–237). London: Sage.

Cairns, R. B., Elder, G. E., & Costello, E. J. (Eds.). (1996). *Developmental science.* New York: Cambridge University Press.

Case, R. (1992). *The mind's staircase.* Hillsdale, NJ: Lawrence Erlbaum Associates.

Chapman, M. (1988). *Constructive evolution: Origins and development of Piaget's thought.* Cambridge, England: Cambridge University Press.

Fauconnier, G. (1997). *Mappings in thought and language.* Cambridge, England: Cambridge University Press.

Fauconnier, G., & Sweetser, E. (Eds.). (1996). *Spaces, worlds and grammar.* Chicago, IL: University of Chicago Press.

Fauconnier, G., & Turner, M. (1996). Blending as a central process of grammar. In A. Goldberg (Ed.), *Conceptual structure, discourse and language* (pp. 113–130). Stanford, CA: CSLI.

Fauconnier, G., & Turner, M. (2002). *The way we think.* New York: Basic Books.

Fischer, K. W., & Bidell, T. R. (1998). Dynamic development of psychological structures in action and thought. In R. M. Lerner (Ed.), & W. Damon (Series Ed.), *Handbook of child psychology: Vol. 1. Theoretical models of human development* (5th ed., pp. 467–561). New York: Wiley.

Fischer, K. W., Yan, Z., & Stewart, J. (2003). Adult cognitive development: Dynamics in the developmental web. In J. Valsiner & K. J. Connolly (Eds.), *Handbook of developmental psychology* (pp. 491–516). London: Sage.

Gentner, D. (1983). Structure-mapping: A theoretical framework for analogy. *Cognitive Science, 7,* 155–170.

Gentner, D. (1989). The mechanisms of analogical learning. In S. Vosniadou & A. Ortony (Eds.), *Similarity and analogical reasoning* (pp. 200–241). Cambridge: Cambridge University Press.

Gibbs, R. W. (1994). *The poetics of mind.* Cambridge: Cambridge University Press.

Goldberg, A. (Ed.). (1996). *Conceptual structure, discourse and language.* Stanford, CA: CSLI.

Gumperz, J. J., & Levinson, S. C. (Eds.). (1996). *Rethinking linguistic relativity.* Cambridge, England: Cambridge University Press.

Hanks, W. F. (1996). *Language and communicative practices.* Boulder, CO: Westview.

Hirschfeld, L. A., & Gelman, S. A. (Eds.). (1994). *Mapping the mind: Domain specificity in cognition and culture.* Cambridge, MA: Cambridge University Press.

Hutchins, E. (1995). *Cognition in the wild.* Cambridge, MA: MIT Press.

Johnson, M. (1987). *The body in the mind.* Chicago, IL: University of Chicago Press.

Karmiloff-Smith, A. (1992). *Beyond modularity.* Cambridge, MA: MIT Press.

Lakoff, G. (1990). The invariance hypothesis: Is abstract reason based on image-schemas? *Cognitive Linguistics, 1*(1), 39–74.

Lakoff, G., & Johnson, M. (1980). *Metaphors we live by.* Chicago, IL: University of Chicago Press.

Lakoff, G., & Johnson, M. (1999). *Philosophy in the flesh.* New York: Basic Books.

Lakoff, G., & Turner, M. (1989). *More than cool reason.* Chicago, IL: University of Chicago Press.

Lave, J. (1988). *Cognition in practice.* Cambridge, England: Cambridge University Press.

Lawrence, J. A., & Valsiner, J. (1993). Conceptual roots of internalization: From transmission to transformation. *Human Development, 36,* 150–167.

Lyra, M. C. D. P. (1999). An excursion into the dynamics of dialogue. *Culture & Psychology, 5,* 4, 477–489.

Ochs, E. (1996). Linguistic resources for socializing humanity. In J. J. Gumperz & S. C. Levinson (Eds.), *Rethinking linguistic relativity* (pp. 407–437). Cambridge, England: Cambridge University Press.

Piaget, J. (1923). *Le langage et la pensee chez l'enfant* [The language and thought of the child]. Neuchatel: Delachaux et Niestle.

Piaget, J. (1932). *Rech i myshlenie rebenka.* Moscow: Gosizdat. [Russian translation of Piaget, 1923, 1924]

Piaget, J. (1952). *The language and thought of the child.* New York: Humanities Press. (Original work published 1926)

Piaget, J. (1954). *The construction of reality in the child.* New York: Basic Books.

Piaget, J. (1959). *The language and thought of the child* (3rd ed.). London: Routledge & Kegan Paul.

Piaget, J. (1962a). Comments. In L. Vygotsky (Ed.), *Thought and language* (pp. 1–14). Cambridge, MA: MIT Press.

Piaget, J. (1962b). *Play, dreams, and imitation in childhood.* New York: Norton.

Piaget, J. (1969). *The mechanisms of perception.* New York: Basic Books.

Piaget, J. (1986). Essay on necessity. *Human Development, 29,* 301–314.

Piaget, J. (1995). *Sociological studies.* New York: Routledge.

Rogoff, B. (1990). *Apprenticeship in thinking.* New York: Oxford University Press.

Rogoff, B. (1997). Evaluating development in the process of participation: Theory, methods and practice building on each other. In E. Amsel & K. A. Renninger (Eds.), *Change and development: Issues in theory, method and application* (pp. 265–286). Hillsdale, NJ: Lawrence Erlbaum Associates.

Rosa, A. (1994). History of psychology as a ground for reflexivity. In A. Rosa & J. Valsiner (Eds.), *Explorations in socio-cultural studies: Vol. 1. Historical and theoretical discourse* (pp. 149–167). Madrid: Fundacion Infancia y Aprendizaje.

Scholnick, E. K., Nelson, K., Gelman, S. A., & Miller, P. H. (1999). *Conceptual development: Piaget's legacy.* Mahwah, NJ: Lawrence Erlbaum Associates.

Siegler, R. (1996). *Emerging minds.* New York: Oxford University Press.

Tomasello, M. (1999). *The cultural origins of human cognition.* Cambridge, MA: Harvard University Press.

Turner, M., & Fauconnier, G. (1995). Conceptual integration and formal expression. *Journal of Metaphor and Symbolic Activity, 10*(3), 183–204.

Valsiner, J. (1997). *Culture and the development of children's action* (2nd ed.). New York: Wiley.

Valsiner, J. (1998). The development of the concept of development: Historical and epistemological perspectives. In W. Damon & R. Lerner (Eds.), *Handbook of child psychology: Theoretical models of human development* (5th ed., Vol. 1, pp. 189–232). New York: Wiley.

Valsiner, J. (2001). Constructive curiosity of the human mind: Participating in Piaget. Introduction to the Transaction Edition of Jean Piaget's *The child's conception of physical causality* (pp. ix–xxii). New Brunswick, NJ: Transaction.

Valsiner, J., & van der Veer, R. (2000). *The social mind: Construction of the idea.* New York: Cambridge University Press.

van der Veer, R., & Valsiner, J. (1991). *Understanding Vygotsky: A quest for synthesis*. Oxford: Basil Blackwell.

Vidal, F. (1993). *Piaget before Piaget*. Cambridge, MA: Harvard University Press.

Vygotsky, L. S. (1962). *Thought and language*. Cambridge, MA: MIT Press.

Vygotsky, L. S. (1982). Myshlenie I rech. In L. Vygotsky (Ed.), *Sobranie sochinenii: Vol. 2. Problemy obshchei psikhologii* (pp. 5–361). Moscow: Pedagogika.

Vygotsky, L. S. (1986). *Thought and language* (2nd ed.). Cambridge, MA: MIT Press. (Original work published 1934)

Vygotsky, L. S., & Luria, A. R. (1994). Tool and symbol in child development. In R. van der Veer & J. Valsiner (Eds.), *The Vygotsky reader* (pp. 99–174). Oxford: Blackwell. (Original manuscript written in 1930)

Wertsch, J. V., del Rio, P., & Alvarez, A. (1995). *Sociocultural studies of mind*. Cambridge, England: Cambridge University Press.

The Social Ontology of Persons

Mark H. Bickhard
Lehigh University

THE SOCIAL ONTOLOGY OF PERSONS

Persons are biological beings who participate in social environments. Is human sociality different from that of insects? Is human sociality different from that of a computer or robot with elaborate rules for social interaction in its program memory? What is the relationship between the biology of humans and the sociality of persons? I argue that persons constitute an emergent ontological level that develops out of the biological and psychological realm, but that is largely social in its own constitution. This requires a characterization of the relationships between the bio/psychological and the social, and of the developmental process of emergence. It also requires a framework for modeling the bio/psychological level that makes any such emergence possible. Neither attachment theory nor information-processing frameworks, for example, will do—the major orientations toward human sociality today make understanding that sociality ultimately impossible. Only an action framework, such as that of Peirce or Piaget,[1] suffices.

---

[1]Piaget (1977/1995) argued that "there are neither individuals as such nor society as such. There are just interindividual relations" (p. 210). The contrast between "individuals as such" and "society as such" is a false opposition, however, and, therefore, the presumed third option "There are just interindividual relations" is incomplete and misleading. The relationships between individuals and social reality are much more complex—and metaphysically deeper—than these options suggest, and the task undertaken in this chapter is to outline a

The discussion proceeds in three general phases: (a) a model of the emergence of social reality, including language, in particular kinds of interaction relations among people; and (b) a model of the sense in which *persons* emerge in individual development as infants, toddlers, and children come to be able to participate in these social realities. The sense in which persons constitute a largely social emergent relative to the biological individual—even extending to the largely social constitution of fundamental issues of normativity and values in life—is a central theme of the discussion. Finally, (c) the dependence of the analysis on an underlying pragmatic or action framework is highlighted: Contemporary alternative frameworks for modeling development cannot satisfactorily address these issues of the social constitution of persons.

INHERENT HUMAN SOCIALITY: ADAPTATION TO ADAPTABILITY

What is it that makes human beings so deeply social? Human beings are highly adapted to some physical specializations, such as tasks involving opposable thumbs and long-distance running, but, above all else, they are adapted to niches requiring adaptability. The ability to handle novelty and complexity, especially temporal complexity, far exceeds that of any other species (Bickhard, 1973/1980a, 1992a). I have argued that the macro-evolutionary sequence of interactive knowing, learning, emotions, and consciousness, of which *Homo sapiens* is the beneficiary, is a sequence of increasing adaptability, increasing ability to handle novelty and complexity (Bickhard, 1973/1980a; Bickhard & D. T. Campbell, in press; Campbell & Bickhard, 1986).

A significant reason for this adaptation to adaptability is likely to be the evolution via positive feedback of social complexity in the origins of the species. As social groups became more complex, the threshold for individuals being able to participate sufficiently to be able to reproduce was increased accordingly. This would raise the level of complexity in future generations, thus increasing the threshold for being able to handle social complexity even further, and so on (Goody, 1995; Humphrey, 1976).[2] Note

model of some of those relationships. In particular, the ontology of persons is itself mostly, though not exclusively, social. Nevertheless, although Piaget was too simplistic in his characterization of the relation between the individual and society, this human social ontology can be modeled only with the general kind of action framework espoused and developed by Piaget.

[2]Such a model, of course, raises the interesting question of why our ancestors took off on this positive feedback trajectory, and not some other species. Certainly various enabling conditions were required, such as second level knowing, both for social complexity in general and language in particular (Campbell & Bickhard, 1986), but other primates share at least

that the complexity of sociality is in strong part a temporal complexity, a complexity of the temporal flow of social processes and interactions.

In being able to process such complexity, human beings simultaneously offer the potentialities of such complexity to each other. The exercise of these abilities can nowhere be so directly encountered as in interactions with others also capable of such complexity—in social interactions. At the core of whatever other advantages are to be derived from human sociality, such as hunting prowess or gathering organization and wisdom, humans are intrinsically social in offering and appreciating the complexity of sociality that only their own species can afford.

THE EMERGENCE OF SOCIAL REALITY: SITUATION CONVENTIONS AND LANGUAGE

The potential for interactive complexity that human beings afford to each other creates a special epistemological problem—how to characterize social situations. A general solution to this problem of characterization, which I call a situation convention, constitutes the basic form of the emergence of social reality out of individual psychology. It is in coming to be able to co-constitutively participate in situation conventions that human beings come to have a social ontology.

In preview, situation conventions constitute a kind of "common understanding" of what the social situation is, and this common understanding constitutes an emergence of a higher level of ontology. Language develops as a system of operators on such social realities, thereby greatly complexifying those realities: Once language has emerged, much of social reality is constituted in potentialities for further language interactions. Such language-generated complexities, however, are elaborations on initial social realities that are not themselves linguistic.

What is the special epistemological problem that humans, and other agents, constitute for each other? A visual scan of a rock is highly informative about what kinds of interactions would be possible with the rock. Rocks are not capable of particularly complex potentialities of interaction. A visual scan of a person, in contrast, leaves open a vast range of interactive possibilities: Is she friend or foe? Is he angry or fearful or happy? Is this an honest person? And so on. The interactive character of a situation

---

rudimentary versions of this. Dunbar (1992, 1993), for example, argues that increased social group size put pressure on means of maintaining social relationships—grooming, for example, is too time and labor intensive for large groups—and early language may have developed to serve this function, thus initiating the complexity feedback. Even if so, this focuses the question on why group size was increasing. It seems plausible that this sociality-intelligence feedback was an evolutionary potentiality waiting to happen, and it was a relatively arbitrary contingency that ancestral *homo sapiens* hit some threshold for it rather than some other species.

involving another person depends strongly on properties and states of that person that are at best only partially discernible.

The complexity of this epistemological problem is greatly enhanced by the fact that the interactive potentialities afforded by another person depend strongly on how that second person construes the interactive potentialities of the first person. If I know that you think that I am angry at you, even if I am not, that has a high relevance to the interactive characterization of the situation involving the two of us. And the same kind of point holds for you with respect to me. The potentialities afforded by the other are in turn dependent on that other's characterization of the potentialities of the first individual—whose potentialities, in turn again, are dependent on how the other is construed. And so on. The epistemological problem of characterizing the other person is symmetrically present for all parties to a situation, and any resolution requires resolution of the reflexivities that are thereby generated.

All parties to such a situation have a common interest in resolving it. All parties have an interest in an accurate interactive characterization of the situation, among many possible such characterizations. Such a problem with a common interest in its resolution is part of the general form of a coordination problem (Schelling, 1963). A coordination problem is one in which there is relative indifference among the parties about which of two or more possible solutions is arrived at (e.g., which side of the road to drive on) just so long as they all arrive at the same one. You and I may be mostly indifferent about which restaurant we meet at for lunch, just so long as we both go to the same one.

A solution to such a coordination problem constitutes a situation convention, a convention about what the situation is (Bickhard, 1980b; Lewis, 1969).[3] Perhaps we always meet on Tuesdays at some particular restaurant for lunch, and the convention of that restaurant on Tuesdays resolves the coordination problem of how to meet for lunch. The convention of driving on the right side of the road resolves the coordination problem of what to do if cars traveling in opposite directions meet on a road.

One important property of conventions is that, although they may be created using language—we might have explicitly agreed to meet at that restaurant on Tuesdays—they can also emerge without explicit agreement. Certainly the conventions of language could not have been created by prior agreement in discussion. An alternative form of the emergence of convention is by precedent and habituation (Berger & Luckmann, 1966;

---

[3]Lewis' model has been strongly criticized (e.g., in Gilbert, 1989). I will not address these criticisms here, except to say that they focus on aspects of Lewis' model that are not carried over into my own in Bickhard (1980a), and the alternative offered seems too narrow. This is a topic that deserves more careful consideration elsewhere.

Lewis, 1969). If we happen to meet at a restaurant one Tuesday and enjoy our conversation, it might occur to us on the following Tuesday that the other person might be at that restaurant again. If we do meet again, and again have an enjoyable conversation, the likelihood of looking forward to meeting the following Tuesday is enhanced. After not very many of such precedent-forming meetings, we will habituate the practice of having lunch at that restaurant on Tuesdays with the expectation of meeting each other there—a convention between us will have emerged—and no discussion about when or where to meet need ever have occurred.

The reflexivities involved in such conventions can yield many kinds of complexity (Bickhard, 1980b; Mehan & Wood, 1975). One kind involves situations in which one party has an interest in creating and maintaining the *appearance* of a symmetry in characterizing the situation, but in reality maintaining an asymmetry. I may be trying to con you, for example, and that depends on keeping you misinformed about what is really going on in our interactions. Another form of complexity arises when one convention modifies another. I may be engaged in a marriage ceremony with someone, but because this is occurring in a play, no state of being married to that person will follow. Such complexities can be of great importance, but they will not be the focus of this discussion.

Of greater relevance for current purposes is the distinction between situation conventions in general, and the special subclass of institutionalized conventions that hold across multiple times and people. Institutionalized conventions can hold between just two people, such as the "lunch on Tuesdays" example above, or across hundreds of millions, such as driving on the right side of the road. They can hold for indefinite periods of time, such as the driving example again, or a convention between two people as part of their relationship, or for shorter periods of time, such as rule created just for this meeting. Non-institutionalized situation conventions, on the other hand, can hold momentarily and ephemerally.

Institutionalized conventions are invoked by indications that are themselves conventionalized as indicators of some particular conventional solution to a coordination problem. These indicators will be themselves stable, such as insignia of rank or traffic signs, or highly iterable, such as recurrent Tuesday lunches or encountering oncoming traffic or invocations of ritual.

This leaves as an apparent mystery the notion of a momentary and ephemeral situation convention: How could something non-recurrent be conventionalized? Certainly conventions established through precedent and habituation must be recurrent. This impression, in fact, is so strong that the original model of convention as solution to a coordination problem limited itself to what I am calling institutionalized conventions, conventions that were manifested in regularities of recurrent behavior (Lewis, 1969).

Institutionalized and Noninstitutionalized Conventions

Institutionalized conventions are invoked by stable or recurrent indicators. These indicators generally evoke some particular convention. Suppose, however, that such indicators were more context dependent in their effects. Suppose that the common understanding of the situation, the situation convention, that they produced among participants when invoked depended on the situation conventional context in which their invocation occurred. In such a case, the particular situation convention produced might never have occurred before, and might be further transformed a moment later by a next invocation of a transforming indicator: An indicator such as a stop sign always invokes the same convention regardless (relatively—emergencies might be an exception) of the context in which they are encountered. A transforming indicator, on the other hand, does not evoke a particular convention per se so much as a conventional *transformation* of the current situation convention into another. A gesture or word that ends a class, for example, transforms the conventions of a class into those of more general social interaction, and might have no clear meaning at all in some other contexts. A deictic, such as "this," or even a proper name, such as "John," will evoke a focus on some object or person, but which object or person will depend fundamentally on the context in which such terms are used. A use of "this" may participate in a discussion of some object that has never been discussed before, and perhaps never will be again, and it may set up a short-term context in which "it" alludes to the focus on that same object a short time later, perhaps in the same sentence (Bickhard & R. L. Campbell, 1992).

Such a moment in the flow of common understanding—in the flow of situation convention creation among participants—would be ephemeral. Such a phenomenon is possible because of the context *de*pendency of situation convention *transformation* rather than the simpler model of context *in*dependent situation convention *invocation*.

I have argued, in fact, that a productive version of such tools for transforming situation conventions is precisely what constitutes language. Language is "a conventional system whereby conventional utterances can be generated that have conventional effects on situation conventions" (Bickhard, 1980b, p. 83). In this view, language is an inherently social phenomenon, not just a cognitive process of transmitting encoded mental contents as in most models of language.

The dominant view of utterances, however, is as encoded mental contents. I do not have space here to rehearse the multifarious flaws in such models, but will instead mention one line of fatal problems. Encodings are real phenomena in the world, with Morse code as an example, but they require interpreters who know or can learn the encoding rules. That is, encodings require that the representational contents involved, the specifications of what a representation is supposed to represent, be already available to the epistemic agent. An encoding can then be defined or learned as carrying that already available content, as standing-in for that already available representation: "..." stands-in for "s" in Morse code, but this works only insofar as "s" is already available.

One consequence of this is that encodings cannot be the foundational form of epistemic access. Encodings are stand-ins for the already represented, not a way in which new representational knowledge can emerge. Encodings are useful because they change the form and perhaps the medium of representation—"..." can be sent over telegraph wires while "s" cannot—not because they are foundational representations. Encodings, therefore, cannot be the foundational form of epistemic access from the mind to the world, as in perception (Bickhard & Richie, 1983), nor from one mind to another, as in language (Bickhard, 1980b).[4]

A superficial counter to this is to posit that all primitive representations are already available innately, and that everything that can be represented at all can be represented by combinations of such innately available representational atoms (Fodor, 1981). The basic logical problem with this stance, aside from its sheer unbelievability, is that it presupposes some process by which *evolution* could create such representations. It gives no model of what that process could be, nor any reason why—given that any such process could exist—it could not be operative in individual learning and development. If it could be operative in individual learning and development, of course, the rationale for needing such an *innate* base of atomic representations evaporates (Bickhard, 1991, 1993).

If such critiques are sound (and this is just one of a great many), then language cannot be of the form standardly assumed. It cannot be the cognitive process of encoding mental contents to then be transmitted for decoding to some other mind or minds. In this standard view, language is only incidentally social—it is a fundamentally cognitive process that can be used for communication. In the alternative outlined, language is intrinsically social—interacting with situation conventions is the fundamental nature of language.

A situation convention is a common understanding of, a solution to the coordination problem of, what sorts of further interactions might be available or expectable in the situation. Language, I am proposing, is itself a productive toolkit for manipulating and influencing the flow of such situation conventions. It follows, then, that a great deal of what a situation af-

---

[4]Contrary to most contemporary models of representation: Cummins (1991, 1996), Dretske (1981, 1988), Fodor (1975, 1981, 1986, 1987, 1990a, 1990b, 1991, 1998), Millikan (1984, 1993), Newell (1980), Newell and Simon (1975, 1987), Vera and Simon (1993), Clark (1993), Haugeland (1991), Rumelhart (1989), Smolensky (1988). See Bickhard (in press), Bickhard and Terveen (1995), and Levine and Bickhard (1999).

fords will be constituted in the potentialities for further interaction of particularly linguistic sort—a great deal of what a situation affords will be constituted in the further conversation that it affords, from lecture, to debate, to argument, to discussion of such-and-such a topic, to intimate exchanges, and so on. A great deal of the ontology of situation conventions is constituted in language potentialities.

I offer situation conventions as the fundamental form of the emergence of social ontology out of individual agent level ontology. This ontology ranges from the momentary common understanding of how to resolve a pronoun in this not yet completed utterance to deeply and complexly institutionalized conventions and processes of government, law, and economics. Language itself has the ontology of being a conventional system, and of being a conventional system that operates on conventions. This recursiveness—language operating on the results of language—and reflexivity—language operating on language itself—generate enormous potential complexity and historicity in social and cultural ontologies.

One example of complexity building on such historicity is the historical emergence of richer and stronger conventional types of human relationships, which permit more complex, large-scale organizations among people. If typifications[5] of human relationships are limited to kinship categories, for example, then the most complex macro-level organization is limited to some sort of *clan* structure. If there is a type of relationship that is based on personal loyalties independent of kinship, then something like *feudal* organizations become possible. If there is a typification of roles that people might occupy as distinct from their occupants, and of relationships among such roles, then *institutional* organizations become possible, whether in church, government, economy, or wherever—which may generate typifications of types of institutions. Bethlehem Steel, for example, is an instance of the type of institution of *corporation*, and such an organizational instance is possible only because of the more general typification of the general type. A particular marriage, for a different level of example, will be an instance of whatever institutional characterizations are available in that society and culture for marriage, and, again, that instance is possible only because of the more general typification available. Similarly, for an example with a different temporal scale, the interactions between customer and check-out clerk play out an institutionalized role relationship thousands of times a day.

In each case, the institutional resources available in the society and culture permit us to characterize both ourselves (e.g., customer) and the other

---

[5]Note that a typification is itself a solution to a coordination problem—the problem of how to socially characterize or categorize the relevant phenomena or conditions. These are of particular importance when the institutionalized characterizations are part of the ontology of what is being characterized (Berger & Luckmann, 1966).

(e.g., check-out clerk), both in immediate interaction and in longer term conditionalized interactive characterizations. Many characteristics of a corporate CEO, for example, may be strongly institutionalized, perhaps even legally so, even though rarely manifest or expected to be manifest—they may be conditional on rare events or circumstances. The responsibilities when declaring corporate bankruptcy, for one example, are conditional and relatively rare.

I have argued that social reality emerges in situation conventions, and that the complexity of human social reality is enormously expanded by the recursiveness and reflexivities of the special meta-convention of language—a conventional system for operating on conventions. The social world is constituted as organizations of institutional forms and their instances, the interactions—largely though not exclusively linguistic—within and among those instances, and as enabled by the conceptual conventions that frame them. These social realities constitute much of the world of the individual, at least as important as the rocks and trees, houses and automobiles, and other physical furniture of the world. I will argue that they constitute much of the normative world of the person as well, and, ultimately, participate in the very ontology of the person.

NORMATIVITY AND VALUES

Situation conventions, thus social realities, involve normative aspects, sometimes powerful normative aspects. They prescribe what one ought to do and feel, what is worthwhile doing and feeling. Such normativities, in turn, are emergent from, ontologically involved in, and function as constraints—and enabling constraints—upon individual level values and actions. In this section, I address these points concerning social normativity, individual normativity, and some of the interrelationships between them.

Social Normativity

One sense in which situation conventions are normative is they involve mutual expectations. After many months of meeting for lunch on Tuesdays, we will have mutual expectations of doing so, and will correspondingly expect there to be some reason for missing a Tuesday lunch, if it is missed, and some reasonable effort to let the other know if a Tuesday is going to be missed. These expectations can be sufficiently strong and taken for granted that we may (tentatively) conclude that some sort of emergency has come up if the other simply fails to show.

If an oncoming car attempts to pass by us on the wrong side of the road, our expectations will be deeply and dangerously violated. The cost of failing to solve this coordination problem can be the loss of one's life, and the strength of the normative force of the convention is correspondingly high.

In general, this form of social normativity arises from the costs and benefits of the convention. Failure of the convention risks the costs of failure of the coordination problem, and whatever else may depend on it.

Another form of social normativity arises when the institutional forms and typifications are *about* normative issues. It may be part of the typification of corporate CEO, for example, not only that there are various multiple responsibilities involved, but also that it is a meaningful and worthwhile aspect of someone's life to aspire to and to undertake such a role. In a different culture, it might be understood that a meaningful and worthwhile form of life to aspire to and undertake is that of a mendicant Buddhist monk. There is a common interest in at least partially characterizing such life choices, or possible such life choices, even for those that I do not—and perhaps would not or could not—choose myself. This is a life-choice level version of the point that I may characterize someone as playing out the role of check-out clerk while I am in the role of customer.

There will be ideologies, of varying degrees of explicitness and elaboration, associated with such normative life possibilities that explain and defend their meaningfulness (Berger & Luckmann, 1966). Such ideologies are involved at this level because issues of ultimate meaningfulness and normativity are at stake, whereas issues in the check-out clerk and customer relationship will generally be more instrumental for all parties involved. Life-choice potentialities address problems of making sense of life, with its vicissitudes and triumphs and ultimate death. There is a common interest involved here in that all parties must characterize each other, at least in general terms, concerning what is taken to be important and what not, and also in that all parties must resolve these issues for themselves in some way or another, and these cultural forms constitute a major resource for attempting to do so.

That is, similar to the case in which the check-out clerk and customer relationship is a typification available to everyone in a relevant culture, and serves as a resource for various ends for all involved, a cultural norm of a form of meaningful life is a typification available to everyone in a relevant culture and serves as a resource for individuals in their own struggles with meaningfulness, self-respect, and other fundamental life issues. There are these parallels in the two forms, but there are also deep dissimilarities. In these two examples, the clerk–customer interaction is momentary, recurrent, and instrumental; the mendicant monk is lifelong, not inherently recurrent, and not instrumental. That the clerk and customer typification is intrinsically a relational interaction is not necessarily a fundamental distinction: being a mendicant monk also requires the participation of others, and is a viable option only in a culture in which the society at large will provide support for such individuals.

The deeper differences are between instrumental and noninstrumental norms. Noninstrumental norms may also involve momentary and recurrent situations: I cannot instrumentally satisfy a norm of feeling kindly toward others, nor can I instrumentally decide to be at peace with the world today. Such norms involve the whole person—they are *about* the whole person—and therefore it is not possible to create the separation that is involved in adopting an instrumental norm for the sake of some other value outside of the norm or goal or value being adopted (Campbell & Bickhard, 1986). If adopted instrumentally, they create versions of the self-contradiction of commanding oneself to be spontaneous (e.g., be spontaneously kind or at peace).

It is reasonably clear how a person makes use of an instrumental possibility offered by his or her culture, such as a purchase at a store, but how is it even conceptually possible to "make use of" a cultural resource for *non*instrumental issues? Doesn't this inherently encounter the self-contradiction just mentioned? Resolving this issue requires a closer look at the individual level ontology of norms and values.

Individual Values

Values are complex phenomena, involving multiple psychological processes: representation, motivation, learning, emotions, language, and levels of knowing. This is not the opportunity to elaborate all of these; I need just enough to be able to make some crucial points about the development of values (Campbell & Bickhard, 1986; Campbell, Christopher, & Bickhard, 2002). To do this, I need to draw out some consequences of the underlying interactive model for processes of learning and development.

The arguments against encodings as foundational hold just as strongly against other forms of epistemic relationships as they do against language being an encoding phenomenon. In particular, perception cannot be a matter of encoding the environment (Bickhard & Richie, 1983), cognition cannot be a matter of manipulating encoding symbols (Bickhard, 1993, 1998, 1999, 2000a, 2002; Bickhard & Terveen, 1995), and, most important for current purposes, learning cannot be a matter of "internalizing" external facts, structures, patterns, skills, or anything else. If our knowledge of the world were in any sense an internalization, a copy, of the world, then we would have to already know the world in order to construct our internal copy of it (Piaget, 1970; a correct insight, in spite of Piaget's own unhelpful use of the notion of internalization).

In general, so long as we think of learning as some version of the signet ring impressing itself into the waxed slate (Aristotle, 1908; Plato, 1892)—in contemporary terminology, *transduction* if at one single time and *induction* if the scratches into the wax are made over time—then we are tempted to think of learning as such a process of the world impressing itself into a passive mind. If representation is emergent in systems of action and interaction, however, as Piaget argued, and as I hold, then there is no temptation to think that the world can impress itself into a mind and create a competent interactive system (Bickhard & Campbell, 1989; Piaget, 1954, 1971, 1977). Encoding and internalization models presume structural homomorphisms between mind and environment; interactive systems have no such homomorphism with the environments that they are competent to interact with. But, if structural homomorphism is not the essence of knowledge and representation, then impression into a passive mind cannot be the process of learning (Bickhard, 1980b).

Instead, mind must be active and constructive, and, barring omniscience, not all of those constructions can be the right ones. Some will fail and must be modified further or discarded and a new try attempted. That is, an action and interaction based model of representation forces a constructivism, and a variation and selection constructivism—an evolutionary epistemology (Bickhard, 1992b, 2002; Bickhard & D. T. Campbell, in press; D. T. Campbell, 1974a; Popper, 1965).

Goal Directedness

An interactive system will, in general, be attempting to satisfy goals. Goals can be simply set points for internal conditions, such as blood sugar level, or they can be complex representations themselves. Goals often involve strong motivation and can also involve emotional stakes and expectations (Bickhard, 2000b), such as the hopes and fears involved in close relationships and careers. At a first level, the satisfiers of goals will be either internal conditions satisfying a set point or external conditions meeting representational criteria. Goals can be instrumental toward other goals, a part of the process of attempting to satisfy some other goal, or they can be more primary and permanent or recurrent, such as a taste for a particular food or music.

Knowing Levels

Human beings, however, are capable of more than one level of knowing (Bickhard, 1978; Campbell & Bickhard, 1986; Piaget, 2001). A first-level interactive system may well have properties that it would be useful for the overall system to be able to represent. For example, there may be one or more particularized instances of a heuristic strategy of doing something three times before giving up and trying another approach to the goal. To be able to represent the commonality among such heuristics—try three times—could help generalize the strategy to new circumstances. Or, for another example, it could be useful to note that various kinds of manipulations of units, such as marbles or pebbles or coins, always permit a reverse manipulation back to the original configuration—unless a unit is added or subtracted. Representing such invariance of number under various manipulations, in fact, has many uses.

Similarly, a second-level system will have properties that might be useful to be able to represent from a third level. An example might be to be able to represent a space of possibilities of configuration in an experiment so as to make sure that all such possibilities are accounted for (Bickhard, 1978; Campbell & Bickhard, 1986).

For current purposes, however, the important kind of phenomenon is that of higher level goals. Goals at higher knowing levels will be about the organization and process at lower levels, or they can be about the entire system. Insofar as such goals are not just momentarily instrumental toward others, insofar as they are primary (at the highest, noninstrumental, level), they will constitute values about the organization and process that constitutes the person. Again, as at lower levels, they can involve potentially strong motivational and emotional aspects and expectations.

Such values may be explicit and articulable, or they may be implicit in various kinds of phenomena and circumstances that make us uneasy or for which we are vigilant. There can also be complex interactions. For one example, suppose I have an articulable value of being safe, but that certain social situations do not feel safe to me because they threaten to expose some feared weakness or inadequacy. That fear itself may be implicit, presupposed, in many other stances toward life and ways of being that I have grown up with. And it may be of extreme difficulty for me to try to examine all of this because examining it is already acknowledging the weakness and inadequacy that I fear. That way lies psychopathology (Bickhard, 1989; Bickhard & Christopher, 1994; Christopher & Bickhard, 1994).

My current focus, however, is how values develop, and, ultimately, how that development can make use of socially and culturally available resources. Values must be constructed in some sort of evolutionary epistemological process, similarly to everything else in the interactive system. Internally, values will be constructed with respect to organizations and processes at a lower level. Those lower level phenomena will be what the higher level value representation is constructed to represent. Those lower level phenomena, then, will tend to constitute satisfiers of the newly constructed value. The lower level phenomena, however, do not fully determine the higher level value—there may be many kinds of values that a particular way of being could be a satisfier of, and any single value constructed on the basis of that lower level way of being in effect "unfolds" one of those values that previously had been implicit in the lower way of being. Such unfolding, however, makes that formerly implicit value now explicit, and it may be found to be in conflict with other values or with other ways of being at the lower levels. This kind of value conflict, and processes and attempts to remove it, can generate its own important tendencies and motivations toward further development.

The selection pressures involved in the construction of a new value are not limited to the internal milieu being unfolded. They will include external criteria. It is not possible to construct the value of being the toughest kid on the playground if there are no playgrounds and the concept is simply not available in your culture. On the other hand, in attempting the construction of a value unfolding some sense of wanting respect, if playgrounds are a part of your world and being tough seems recommended as a way of being respected, then such a construction becomes quite feasible.

Here we find the general answer to the question of how cultural resources can play a fundamental role in the development of even noninstrumental values in the individual. Development is a quasi-evolutionary process. It makes use of what is available, and cultural resources constitute a crucially important part of what is available. A quasi-evolutionary process will tend to explore possibilities that are available to it, including possibilities in the external social and cultural world. Even insofar as the search for values, or the reflective analysis and potential modification of values, is deliberate and itself conscious, social possibilities that do not exist cannot be explored, and conceptual possibilities that are not culturally made available are unlikely to be created.

Cultural resources, then, even those constituting underlying fundamentally valued ways of life, frame the possibilities that the individual can explore in their own development and in their search for an acceptable way of being. Society frames the possibilities for the core of personal identity.

Relationships

Another important aspect of sociality is to be found in longer term institutionalized relationships among two or a few people—friendships, social groups, intimate relationships, marriage. The primary significance of such relationships that I wish to focus on here is that, while some deep values can be lived in relationship to society at large—perhaps the monk and the professional would be two kinds of examples—other values have to do with more individuated forms of relating. I can be kind to (or more powerful than) a stranger in a moment of interaction, but I can be a worthwhile spouse or a successful parent (or an ultimately triumphant tyrant) only over much longer times. More simply, some values are about what we do, while others have to do with who we are and with our biographies as we attempt to live and make sense of them. Some of the deepest of such bio-graphical values have their realm of development in such long-term relationships.

Yet even here we find the fundamental role of society and culture. What counts as a successful friendship or marriage, and what kinds of friendship or marriage I might be able to find a partner for, are strongly constrained by the society and its resources that I live in. It is difficult today for a man to be a successful lord, benefactor, and protector of the household in the sense in which it might have been in the 19th century. It is difficult to even want to do so—the cultural and conceptual resources have changed (though clearly various vestigial remnants are to be found).[6]

ONTOLOGICALLY SOCIAL PERSONS

An infant is a socially tuned biological creature with marvelous capacity for development into a participant in, and co-creator of, social realities. As the infant develops, the ability to interact with the physical world and the world of abstractions, such as numbers, increases enormously, but the social aspect of interaction occupies an ever greater portion of overall interactive capabilities. The individual becomes a language user and a generating member of conversations, social hierarchies, role relationships, institutionalized relationships, friendships, intimate partnerships, collegial relationships and those of superiors and subordinates, and so on. The infant becomes a social being; a social and cultural being, a person, emerges in the development of the infant.

The notion of emergence is appropriate here (Bickhard, 2000c; R. J. Campbell & Bickhard, in preparation). In infancy we begin as primarily biological creatures with a superlative openness to social development. In adulthood, the biology is different, but not massively so. Instead what has most changed between infancy and adulthood is the emergence of an entirely new kind of being, one who participates in society and culture and history. And the person, in so participating, participates in the emergent creation of society in turn. Nonaggregative novel properties, myriads of them, appear in the emergence of the social person, and, further, we find

---

[6]Something akin to the unfolding process occurs in social and cultural evolution as well as in individual development. For example, the evolution of what counts as a successful professional, a successful spouse, and a successful parent, have no grand designer ensuring that they remain in some kind of integrated coherence. They will unfold over time in ways that can be divergent and can create on a social level conflicts that are akin to those found in the unfolding of values in the individual. Clearly, however, neither the quasi-evolutionary process of social development per se nor the social processes that react to the conflicts of such divergence, will be the same as in the individual.

major and widespread examples of downward causation (D. T. Campbell, 1974b, 1990) such as building houses and highways and high-speed Internet systems.[7]

The person, then, as distinct from the biological body, is strongly social in his or her ontology. The person is constituted in the multiple ways of being social that that individual has developed in that society and culture and historical time. To re-iterate, this is largely an ontology of language processes: of discussions, lectures, arguments, commands, sympathies, jokes, rituals, and so on and on. The ontology of the person is massively social, which, in turn, is massively an ontology of language.

Ontological Hermeneutics

This social ontology of persons is convergent with the notions of ontological hermeneutics (Bickhard, 1992c; Campbell & Bickhard, 1986; Gadamer, 1975, 1976). It differs, however, in that the interactive social ontology of persons is an emergent ontology, not an ontology that purports to capture the totality of human ontology. It is emergent in the biological and psychological development of an individual who, however massively social, is not entirely social in his or her being.

This point is important not only as a comparison of theories, but also for its potential implications regarding, for example, human ethics. If human ontology is entirely social, if language constitutes the boundaries of my world, then it may be that to violate the ethics embedded in my culture is to in some sense violate my own being. This frames a powerful model of ethics that is open to the ontological hermeneuticist who finds human ontology to be entirely social, but it also forces the conclusion that no principles of ethics have valid application beyond the boundaries of the cultural tradition in which they were formed. There is no valid ethical reasoning to be done by someone in the West European tradition about Aztec human sacrifice or tribal female "circumcision."

In contrast, the interactive model accounts for the massive social ontology of persons, but embeds that in a universal ontology of biological beings open to and with inherent interests in sociality, and with particular biological and psychology capacities, such as the knowing levels, that participate and make possible that emergence of the ontologically social person. In such a view, language does not define the horizons of life. It is at least possible that there are universals of intrinsic social and individual interest in the nature of all persons, regardless of culture. If so, violations of

---

[7]Downward causation is the causal influence of higher levels of organization on the dynamics of lower levels. It is often taken as the benchmark of genuine emergence (Bickhard, 2000c; Campbell & Bickhard, in preparation).

such interests would constitute violations of the intrinsic nature of being for anyone—they would be candidates for trans-cultural kinds of ethical failures. Making a case for particular such universals would require extensive discussion beyond what I provide here, but one general theme of such a discussion (though not the only one) would be that the inherent social openness of human beings involves an inherent interest in individual flourishing with respect to that sociality, and ways of being that violate that interest thereby violate an inherent aspect of one's being. It seems plausible, for example, that developing into the kind of person who enjoys torturing others inherently constitutes a failure to be a full human person, no matter what the culture may contain. This model does not give any kind of perspective of objective certainty. Instead, it provides an ontological framework that permits defeasible explorations of trans-cultural ethical issues and reflections.[8]

A META-THEORETICAL POINT

The model outlined of the social ontology of the person is conceptually dependent on the underlying model of persons as interactive systems. It is the openness of the infant to the development of special kinds of social interactions that permits the emergence of a co-creating participant in such social realities. Similarly, it is the underlying interactive ontology that makes sense of there being a genuine emergence involved in this development: an emergence of a novel, massively downward causing, new level of interaction.

This is in contrast to the theoretical resources available in other frameworks. Attachment theory, for example, addresses human social development with some powerful research programs (Bowlby, 1969; Sroufe, 1984, 1995). Attachment theory, however, has largely grown out of an underlying object relations theory. But the sociality of people in object relations theory is a matter of the existence of innate energies or affects that are devoted to motivating, to pushing, interactions with others (Bickhard,

---

[8]This framework makes much more sense when examined from a character or virtue ethical perspective than from any kind of individual action or duty perspective. If the most basic failures are failures of being a person, of character, then a virtue ethics is almost forced. Note that such failures are with respect to an inherent ontology of persons, not failures to meet some contingent innate criteria. That is, such moral constraints could not be fundamentally different without human beings being ontologically no longer human. Gene-based "morality," in contrast, is contingent on evolutionary history, and could be quite different if selection pressures had been different or if the actual selection pressures had produced a different evolutionary response. Gene-based "morality" may not be arbitrary in the sense that evolutionary reasons might be found to explain it, but it is arbitrary relative to human ontology.

1992a). This is a functional sociality, but it is not an ontological sociality of the person. It is a sociality of actions only, genetically induced, much like the sociality of social insects, but with more scope for learning involved. The sociality of insects is inherent in the genome, not in the ontology of the individual insect. Human beings are socially open as infants, but their sociality is not genetically fixed (Berger & Luckmann, 1966). It develops as a culture sensitive ontological emergent over many years.

Similarly, information-processing models, which dominate contemporary models of cognition, provide no resources for understanding human ontology as being intrinsically and emergently social. The data banks of an information-processing system may or may not contain a great deal of information about interacting with other people. In either case, however, nothing about the information-processing system itself is changed. Human beings as information processors can process social information alongside of nonsocial information, but there is nothing special about that information qua information, and certainly no ontological emergence in consequence of storing it in the data (Bickhard, 1995).[9]

The presuppositions of major theoretical orientations today make understanding human social ontology impossible. Modeling human social ontology, then, is not independent of framework or grounding theories. It requires an action or interaction based model—one in the general pragmatic tradition of Peirce and Piaget. Conversely, it seems abundantly clear that human beings *are* largely social in their basic being, so any framework that precludes accounting for that ontological sociality is thereby undermined.

CONCLUSIONS

Humans are ontologically social. They are constituted in important respects out of the resources available in their cultures and social environments. This social ontology is emergent in the development in the individual of the ability to co-constitutively participate in social realities, in situation and institutionalized conventions. These influences are deepest in their framing of the issues and possibilities of what constitutes meaningful and successful ways of being in one's life and one's relationships.

---

[9]Furthermore, the motivation for interacting socially is utterly opaque from such a perspective. There should be no more reason to interact social than non-socially from the perspective of such a model, except perhaps insofar as basic biological rewards are found or needs met. Such a conception of relating as being driven solely by food and sex was characteristic of early psychoanalytic theorizing, and was one of the sources of the multiple ad-hoc additions to psychoanalytic theory, including object relations theory, made over the ensuing decades—such a model was simply too divergent from reality for even analysts to overlook (Bickhard, 1992a).

Accounting for such phenomena requires being able to account for the emergence of such a social ontology in individual social development. Neither the sociality of innate energies or affects in object relations theory, nor the sociality of massive social data in an information processor's data banks can account for such emergence. It requires a pragmatic account, in which the person *is* his or her way of interacting in the world. Given such an integration of person and action, as there emerge special social realities to interact with and as the individual becomes someone who can participate in such interactions, a further emergence occurs: The individual ontologically becomes a social, cultural, person. Only a Piagetian-style, action-based, pragmatist model can begin to account for the full complexities involved.

ACKNOWLEDGMENTS

Thanks are due to Richard Campbell, Robert Campbell, and John Christopher for helpful comments on an earlier draft of this chapter, and to the editors, Jeremy Carpendale and Ulrich Mueller, for useful suggestions on the penultimate draft.

REFERENCES

Aristotle. (1908). De Anima (On the soul). In W. D. Ross (Ed.), *The works of Aristotle* (pp. 424a 17–22). Oxford, England: Clarendon.

Berger, P. L., & Luckmann, T. (1966). *The social construction of reality.* New York: Doubleday.

Bickhard, M. H. (1978). The nature of developmental stages. *Human Development, 21,* 217–233.

Bickhard, M. H. (1980a). A model of developmental and psychological processes. *Genetic Psychology Monographs, 102,* 61–116. Taken from Bickhard, M. H. (1973). *A model of developmental and psychological processes.* PhD Dissertation, University of Chicago.

Bickhard, M. H. (1980b). *Cognition, convention, and communication.* New York: Praeger.

Bickhard, M. H. (1989). The nature of psychopathology. In L. Simek-Downing (Ed.), *International psychotherapy: Theories, research, and cross-cultural implications* (pp. 115–140). Westport, CT: Praeger.

Bickhard, M. H. (1991). The import of Fodor's anti-constructivist argument. In Les Steffe (Ed.), *Epistemological foundations of mathematical experience* (pp. 14–25). New York: Springer-Verlag.

Bickhard, M. H. (1992a). Scaffolding and self scaffolding: Central aspects of development. In L. T. Winegar & J. Valsiner (Eds.), *Children's development within social contexts: Research and methodology* (pp. 33–52). Hillsdale, NJ: Lawrence Erlbaum Associates.

Bickhard, M. H. (1992b). Piaget on Variation and Selection Models: Structuralism, logical necessity, and interactivism. In L. Smith (Ed.), *Jean Piaget: Critical assessments.* New York: Routledge.

Bickhard, M. H. (1992c). How does the environment affect the person? In L. T. Winegar & J. Valsiner (Eds.), *Children's development within social contexts: Metatheory and theory* (pp. 63–92). Hillsdale, NJ: Lawrence Erlbaum Associates.

Bickhard, M. H. (1993). Representational content in humans and machines. *Journal of Experimental and Theoretical Artificial Intelligence, 5,* 285–333.

Bickhard, M. H. (1995). World mirroring versus world making: There's gotta be a better way. In L. Steffe & J. Gale (Eds.), *Constructivism in education* (pp. 229–267). Hillsdale, NJ: Lawrence Erlbaum Associates.

Bickhard, M. H. (1998). Levels of representationality. *Journal of Experimental and Theoretical Artificial Intelligence, 10*(2), 179–215.

Bickhard, M. H. (1999). Interaction and representation. *Theory & Psychology, 9*(4), 435–458.

Bickhard, M. H. (2000a). Information and representation in autonomous agents. *Journal of Cognitive Systems Research, 1,* 65–75. http://www.elsevier.nl.

Bickhard, M. H. (2000b). Motivation and emotion: An interactive process model. In R. D. Ellis & N. Newton (Eds.), *The caldron of consciousness* (pp. 161–178). Amsterdam: J. Benjamins.

Bickhard, M. H. (2000c). Emergence. In P. B. Andersen, C. Emmeche, N. O. Finnemann, & P. V. Christiansen (Eds.), *Downward causation* (pp. 322–348). Aarhus, Denmark: University of Aarhus Press.

Bickhard, M. H. (2002). Critical principles: On the negative side of rationality. *New Ideas in Psychology, 20,* 1–34.

Bickhard, M. H. (in press). The dynamic emergence of representation. In H. Clapin, P. Staines, & P. Slezak (Eds.), *Representation in mind: New approaches to mental representation.* Amsterdam: Elsevier.

Bickhard, M. H., & Campbell, D. T. (in press). Variations in variation and selection: The ubiquity of the variation-and-selective-retention ratchet in emergent organizational complexity. *Foundations of Science.*

Bickhard, M. H., & Campbell, R. L. (1989). Interactivism and genetic epistemology. *Archives de Psychologie, 57*(221), 99–121.

Bickhard, M. H., & Campbell, R. L. (1992). Some foundational questions concerning language studies: With a focus on categorial grammars and model theoretic possible worlds semantics. *Journal of Pragmatics, 17*(5/6), 401–433.

Bickhard, M. H., & Christopher, J. C. (1994). The influence of early experience on personality development. *New Ideas in Psychology, 12*(3), 229–252.

Bickhard, M. H., & Richie, D. M. (1983). *On the nature of representation: A case study of James Gibson's theory of perception.* New York: Praeger.

Bickhard, M. H., & Terveen, L. (1995). *Foundational issues in artificial intelligence and cognitive science: Impasse and solution.* New York: Elsevier Scientific.

Bowlby, J. (1969). *Attachment.* New York: Basic.

Campbell, D. T. (1974a). Evolutionary epistemology. In P. A. Schilpp (Ed.), *The philosophy of Karl Popper* (pp. 413–463). LaSalle, IL: Open Court.

Campbell, D. T. (1974b). "Downward Causation" in hierarchically organized biological systems. In F. J. Ayala & T. Dobzhansky (Eds.), *Studies in the philosophy of biology* (pp. 179–186). Berkeley, CA: University of California Press.

Campbell, D. T. (1990). Levels of organization, downward causation, and the selection-theory approach to evolutionary epistemology. In G. Greenberg & E. Tobach (Eds.), *Theories of the evolution of knowing* (pp. 1–17). Hillsdale, NJ: Lawrence Erlbaum Associates.

Campbell, R. J., & Bickhard, M. H. (in preparation). Physicalism: Particulars and configurations.

Campbell, R. L., & Bickhard, M. H. (1986). *Knowing levels and developmental stages.* Contributions to Human Development. Basel, Switzerland: Karger.

Campbell, R. L., Christopher, J. C., & Bickhard, M. H. (2002). Self and values: An interactivist foundation for moral development. *Theory and Psychology, 12*(6), 795–823.

Christopher, J. C., & Bickhard, M. H. (1994). The persistence of basic mistakes: Re-exploring psychopathology in individual psychology. *Journal of Individual Psychology, 50*, 223–231.

Clark, A. (1993). *Associative engines.* Cambridge, MA: MIT Press.

Cummins, R. (1991). *Meaning and mental representation.* Cambridge, MA: MIT Press.

Cummins, R. (1996). *Representations, targets, and attitudes.* Cambridge, MA: MIT Press.

Dretske, F. I. (1981). *Knowledge and the flow of information.* Cambridge, MA: MIT Press.

Dretske, F. I. (1988). *Explaining behavior.* Cambridge, MA: MIT Press.

Dunbar, R. I. M. (1992). Neocortex size as a constraint on group size in primates. *Journal of Human Evolution, 20*, 469–493.

Dunbar, R. I. M. (1993). Coevolution of neocortical size, group size and language in humans. *Behavioral and Brain Sciences, 16*, 681–735.

Fodor, J. A. (1975). *The language of thought.* New York: Crowell.

Fodor, J. A. (1981). The present status of the innateness controversy. In J. Fodor (Ed.), *RePresentations* (pp. 257–316). Cambridge, MA: MIT Press.

Fodor, J. A. (1986). Why paramecia don't have mental representations. In P. A. French, T. E. Uehling, & H. K. Wettstein (Eds.), *Midwest studies in philosophy X: Studies in the philosophy of mind* (pp. 3–23). Minneapolis, MN: University of Minnesota Press.

Fodor, J. A. (1987). *Psychosemantics.* Cambridge, MA: MIT Press.

Fodor, J. A. (1990a). *A theory of content.* Cambridge, MA: MIT Press.

Fodor, J. A. (1990b). Information and representation. In P. P. Hanson (Ed.), *Information, language, and cognition* (pp. 175–190). Vancouver: University of British Columbia Press.

Fodor, J. A. (1991). Replies. In B. Loewer & G. Rey (Eds.), *Meaning in mind: Fodor and his critics* (pp. 255–319). Oxford: Blackwell.

Fodor, J. A. (1998). *Concepts: Where cognitive science went wrong.* London: Oxford University Press.

Gadamer, H.-G. (1975). *Truth and method.* New York: Continuum.

Gadamer, H.-G. (1976). *Philosophical hermeneutics.* Berkeley: University of California Press.

Gilbert, M. (1989). *On social facts.* Princeton, NJ: Princeton University Press.

Goody, E. N. (1995). *Social intelligence and interaction.* London: Cambridge University Press.

Haugeland, J. (1991). Representational genera. In W. Ramsey, S. P. Stich, & D. E. Rumelhart (Eds.), *Philosophy and connectionist theory* (pp. 61–89). Hillsdale, NJ: Lawrence Erlbaum Associates.

Humphrey, N. K. (1976). The social function of intellect. In P. P. G. Bateson & R. A. Hinde (Eds.), *Growing points in ethology* (pp. 303–317). London: Cambridge University Press.

Levine, A., & Bickhard, M. H. (1999). Concepts: Where Fodor went wrong. *Philosophical Psychology, 12*(1), 5–23.

Lewis, D. K. (1969). *Convention.* Cambridge, MA: Harvard University Press.

Mehan, H., & Wood, H. (1975). *The reality of ethnomethodology.* New York: Wiley.

Millikan, R. G. (1984). *Language, thought, and other biological categories.* Cambridge, MA: MIT Press.

Millikan, R. G. (1993). *White queen psychology and other essays for Alice.* Cambridge, MA: MIT Press.

Newell, A. (1980). Physical symbol systems. *Cognitive Science, 4*, 135–183.

Newell, A., & Simon, H. A. (1975). Computer science as empirical inquiry: Symbols and search. In (1987). *ACM Turing Award Lectures: The First Twenty Years, 1966–1985* (pp. 287–313). New York: ACM Press; Reading, MA: Addison-Wesley.

Newell, A., & Simon, H. A. (1987). Postscript: Reflections on the Tenth Turing Award Lecture: Computer Science as Empirical Inquiry—Symbols and Search. In *ACM Turing Award Lectures: The First Twenty Years, 1966–1985* (pp. 314–317). New York: ACM Press; Reading, MA: Addison-Wesley.

Piaget, J. (1954). *The construction of reality in the child.* New York: Basic.

Piaget, J. (1970). *Genetic epistemology.* New York: Columbia.

Piaget, J. (1971). *Biology and knowledge*. Chicago: University of Chicago Press.

Piaget, J. (1977). The role of action in the development of thinking. In W. F. Overton & J. M. Gallagher (Eds.), *Knowledge and development: Vol. 1* (pp. 17–42). New York: Plenum.

Piaget, J. (1995). *Sociological studies*. London: Routledge.

Piaget, J. (2001). *Studies in reflecting abstraction* (Robert L. Campbell, Ed. & Trans.). Hove, England: Psychology Press.

Plato. (1892). Theaetetus. In B. Jowett (Ed. & Trans.), *The Dialogues of Plato, Vol. IV* (p. 191). Oxford, England: Clarendon.

Popper, K. (1965). *Conjectures and refutations*. New York: Harper & Row.

Rumelhart, D. E. (1989). The architecture of mind: A connectionist approach. In M. I. Posner (Ed.), *Foundations of cognitive science* (pp. 133–160). Cambridge, MA: MIT Press.

Schelling, T. C. (1963). *The strategy of conflict*. New York: Oxford University Press.

Smolensky, P. (1988). On the proper treatment of connectionism. *Behavioral and Brain Sciences, 11*, 1–74.

Sroufe, L. A. (1984). The organization of emotional development. In K. R. Scherer & P. Ekman (Eds.), *Approaches to emotion* (pp. 109–128). Hillsdale, NJ: Lawrence Erlbaum Associates.

Sroufe, L. A. (1995). *Emotional development*. London: Cambridge University Press.

Vera, A. H., & Simon, H. A. (1993). Situated action: A symbolic interpretation. *Cognitive Science, 17*(1), 7–48.

7

The Development and Overcoming of "Universal Pragmatics" in Piaget's Thinking

Rainer Döbert
Social Science Research Center, Berlin

Students of the humanities who have dealt with Piaget have repeatedly tried to play the early Piaget against the late Piaget (e.g., Furth, 1987; Habermas, 1981, 1983; Miller, 1986). The reason is that sociological considerations in Piaget's early writings seem to play a greater role than they do in the publications beginning with, say, *Biology and Knowledge* (1967/ 1971). The complaint of sociologists is usually that this deemphasis of sociological concerns in Piaget's thinking represents an *unlearning*—a loss of significant insights—and therefore must be reversed.

A different approach would be to check at least whether the "deemphasis of sociological concerns" is not purely contingent in nature (coinciding with the fact that Piaget only once had a chair in sociology). It is rarely considered whether the deemphasis of sociological concerns occurred at the deep structure of his theory. One might even ask whether this deemphasis rests on an insight that moves beyond current dichotomies such as individualistic-social, monologic-dialogic, or monologic-discursive. According to this antithetical supposition, Piaget would have undergone a learning process. The plausibility of this interpretation is suggested by the fact that the considerations in *Erkenntnistheorie der Wissenschaften vom Menschen* (1970/1973)—that is, after *Biology and Knowledge*—readily integrated the sociological thoughts of the young Piaget. Moreover, the third French edition of *Sociological Studies* (*Ètude Sociologiques*, 1977) contained absolutely no disclaimers with respect to his former ideas. Despite *Biology and Knowledge* (1967/1971) and the "unsocio-

logical" *Equilibration of Cognitive Structures* (1975), Piaget's sociological
treaties continued to be seen as thoroughly acceptable. Only their theoretical status seems to have changed.

Therefore, it makes sense to take a detailed look at what Piaget imagined the relation between psychology and sociology to be and what
changes can be found in his position. The objective is to demonstrate that
Piaget (a) tried out a number of models of interaction between person-
related and social factors, including models dominating contemporary
discussion about the foundations of rationality (e.g., universal pragmatics
as exemplified by the work of Habermas); and (b) as he advanced to reconstructing the operative deep structure of thinking, recognized that it is
completely irrelevant from a structural perspective whether one analyzes
the rational coordination of actions in terms of individual or social processes. Against this background, efforts to reevaluate the young Piaget appear in a new light. To show this I examine some stages of the development of Piaget's thought as reflected in his *Moral Judgement of the Child,
Exchange of Qualitative Values, Social Life and Logic*, culminating in his final
position of an identity of social and individual structures. Using this position as a yardstick, Miller's theory of collective learning processes (1986) is
assessed. In a final section, the functions of intellectual exchange within an
encompassing theory of procedural rationality are delineated.

FLUCTUATIONS IN *THE MORAL JUDGMENT OF THE CHILD* (1932/1962)

This early study by Piaget is justifiably considered a prime example of the
period when he was still thinking sociologically. It contains formulations
that seem to suggest a reduction of rationality and logic to the social dimension. It is stated that "free discussion between individuals" (Piaget,
1932/1962, p. 90), or cooperation, is "the one determining factor in the formation of the rational elements in ethics and in logic" (p. 91). For that reason, the child is able to "dissociate custom from the rational ideal" (p. 72)
only after the transition to free cooperation has been made. "For it is of the
essence of cooperation as opposed to social constraint that, side by side
with the body of provisional opinion which exists in fact, it allows for an
ideal of what is right functionally implied in the very mechanism of discussion and reciprocity" (pp. 72–73). In the context of play, this characteristic means, for example, that the child takes the rules actually governing a
game of marbles and measures them by the "spirit of the game" (p. 73),
which "is nothing more or less than the spirit of reciprocity" (p. 73). These
are risky formulations because a case of sociological reductionism is in
fact involved. I say *risky formulations* because one can easily find a sociological interpretation only for the aspect of equal opportunity that charac-

terizes the spirit of the game ("excessive individual differences" [p. 73] are to be avoided). Difficulties for this interpretation arise, however, when it is pointed out that "difficult games [are preferred] because they are more 'interesting' " (p. 74) and that it is a matter of skill. Skill at playing marbles is not a social competence any more than building a tower or being able to shoot well. The difficulty of the game depends on the distance from which the marbles have to be hit, on their relative massiveness, and the like. Certainly all these factors are inherent not in the social spirit of reciprocity, but rather in the physical nature of the situation. Taking a closer look, one would hardly want to follow the sociological or discursive reductionism discernible in these passages quoted from Piaget.

In any case, one can say at least one thing: Not even in *The Moral Judgment of the Child* did Piaget stick to this extreme position, in which the substantive dimension is reduced to the social dimension. He could not stick to it, because the sensorimotor phase acquires a specific rationality that can be touched only superficially by social factors (Piaget, 1932/1962). Hence, the motor rule develops through an interplay of accommodation and assimilation—sustained by a "desire for a form of exercise which takes account of the particular object being handled" (p. 87). Evidently, learning processes in the substantive dimension are at stake. Therein lies the rationality of the motor rule. This rationality is initially overlain by and apt to be threatened by the intervention of social factors—namely, by authority and language. To Piaget (and in Anglo-Saxon empiricist tradition), language is not *the* bulwark of truth that it represents in the standard stereotype of German humanism; it is at least just as much the bulwark of *blindness*. For one thing, the child at first adopts social patterns of interpretation blindly. With the transition to autonomous cooperation, a kind of return to the objective rationality of the motor phase takes place: "The 11-year-old player has rediscovered the schema of experimental legality and rational regularity practised by the baby" (p. 100). However, the schema has been transformed. Whereas motor intelligence is constantly threatened by incursions from imagination and needs, the intelligence of the 11-year-old child is subject to the norms of reciprocity—in other words, that intelligence is socially controlled. The interplay of social interaction and substantive experiences in dealing with objects is thus conceived of in terms of a control hierarchy—a thought not implying the *generation* of the object. Social cooperation purifies motor intelligence of the sprinklings of egocentric fantasies. Thus cleansed, motor intelligence becomes the substance of socialized reason: "The motor being and the social being are one. Harmony is achieved by the union of reason and nature" (p. 100). Mark his words: reason and nature.

This second model—let us say a moderate sociological one—exists alongside the reductionist model, with Piaget leaving open how the decision between the competing or complementary (generation plus control) models would have to be made. "Whether cooperation is an effect or a cause of reason, or both, reason requires cooperation in so far as being rational consists in 'situating oneself' so as to submit the individual to the universal" (Piaget, 1932/1962, p. 107). Hence, "at least control, and perhaps more" is the concluding position taken in *The Moral Judgment of the Child*. The question is how to reach a clarification. One answer seems evident: definitely not by juxtaposing global formulations such as cooperation, discussion, discourse, reason, and nature. If any progress is to be made toward an explication of the relationship between valid knowledge and the social process, one has to go into details. Between interaction and substantive appropriateness a transfer can exist only at the formal, structural level. For that reason, it is necessary to identify the operative deep structure of interaction to see which structural contributions can arise from that side.

By way of explanation, a brief comment on Piaget's concept of structure is in order. Like most sociological concepts of structure, it is shaped by the notions of constancy and equilibrium. Yet equilibrium is not static because living systems must always actively produce and defend it by means of actions or operations. If these operations are optimally coordinated, the actor can steer toward any earlier state of affairs from one instance to the next. That is, he or she can maintain equilibrium. The constitutive ensemble of coordinated operations compose structure in Piaget's sense. For instance, series of numbers are structured if one knows how to handle the operations $+$, $-$, $\times$, $\div$, and $=$ appropriately. One then operates on the basis of a logical group or grouping, whereby composability, associativity, reversibility, identity, and tautology have to be fulfilled. Set theory is an example no doubt familiar to the reader. The hypothesis that equilibrium and reversibility can be established only if grouplike structures form in discrete fields of action marked Piaget's thinking early on (at least by 1942), though he was not immediately able to substantiate this hypothesis empirically. In *The Moral Judgment of the Child*, Piaget did not treat this level of reconstruction of rational equilibration at all yet. Systems of moral or interactive operations were not discussed in the book. That level was not a focus until his later sociological writings, which are examined in the following.

THE EXCHANGE OF QUALITATIVE VALUES

Approaches to a structural reconstruction of interaction are found in Piaget's (1941/1995a) "Essay on the Theory of Qualitative Values in Static ("Synchronic") Sociology," from which it can be gathered that Piaget had to begin by groping on the surface of phenomena. I say *on the surface of phenomena* because this article was dominated by the concept of equilibrium. He inferred grouplike operations from the existence of an equilibrium more than he identified and analyzed the relevant operations in their interplay.

Piaget assumed that a society can be understood only if one studied its obligatory rules, its conventional symbols, and the exchange of goods or quantifiable and nonquantifiable (qualitative) values (knowledge, political leadership, entertainment, etc.). In this article, he was concerned with the exchange of qualitative values. He broke down its structure by adopting from the field of economics a generalized schema of equilibrated exchange through which "equality of final utilities" (1941/1995a, p. 106) is attained. Two equations apply to this equilibrated exchange:

Equation I:

$$(r_a = s_b) + (s_b = t_b) + (t_b = v_a) = (v_a = r_a), \text{ with}$$

r_a being the action of a in the service of b,

s_b being the satisfaction that b draws from a's action,

t_b being the action that b owes a (virtual), and

$v_a = b$'s esteem for a (virtual).

The acquired esteem (rights, resources) is converted and, if there is equilibrium, thereby becomes subject to Equation II:

$$(v_a = t_b) + (t_b = r_b) + (r_b = s_a) = (s_a = v_a).$$

The two equations basically say something very plain: If a does something for me, I draw satisfaction that calls for reciprocation and makes me esteem a, so in response I am prepared to do something of equal worth for him. If both equations are satisfied and if a minimal hierarchy of shared, collective preferences can be assumed, social systems can preserve and reproduce themselves. However, the equilibrium thereby achieved is extraordinarily unstable because the constancy of the values is continuously endangered (Piaget, 1941/1995a) by forgetfulness, vested interest, inflation or deflation of values, and the like.

Therefore, real equilibrium does not yet exist within this purely factual exchange. That is why "groupings of reversible substitutions" (Piaget, 1941/1995a, p. 122)—coordinated operations—did not yet enter the discussion in connection with these simple exchange processes. Because of the notorious instability of exchange processes, all societies have mechanisms specialized in conservation: norms whose general function consists in the "conservation of values" (Piaget, 1941/1995a, p. 129). Norms thus provide for stability and guarantee equilibrium. The obvious thing to do, then, is to seek structures of action in the processes of norm-building as such, and that is what Piaget attempted. It is quite useful to take a brief look at this variant of Piaget's thinking because it illustrates that Piaget had considerable difficulty in his early writings when it came to actually apprehending the operative deep structure of thinking and acting—which he clearly conjectured to be group structure in the logical sense—in real-world interaction.

Exchange values can be conserved through moral or legal norms. In the case of legal norms, the corresponding mechanism is simple enough. Through operations of acknowledging (*reconnaissance*) and enacting (*édiction*) (Piaget, 1941/1995a), the virtual exchange values v and t are transformed into rights and obligations (codified or uncodified). Morality accomplishes conservation by way of operations that coordinate the means and ends (i.e., the actions r and the satisfactions s) in selfless perspective—in other words, through " 'the reciprocal substitution of scales' or 'the reciprocal substitution of means and ends, s_b becoming an end for a and r_a a value in itself for b" (Piaget 1941/1995a, p. 116).

To explain the stabilizing function of norms, Piaget then used the two previously cited equations describing equilibrium of simple exchange (Equation I = morality; Equation II = law). Just how inadequately the structural components of law and morality are spelled out in this way is shown best in the case of law, although Piaget (1941/1995a) actually found it easy "to constitute a complete logic of legal values" (p. 126). One need only interpret Equation II properly. In

$$(v_a = t_b) + (t_b = r_b) + (r_b = s_a) = (s_a = v_a),$$

v_a is a's right to enact norms,

t_b is b's obligation to meet the norms,

r_b is the corresponding action that b takes, and

s_a is a's satisfaction at the fact that the norms are met.

In a word, if b acknowledges and meets a's norms, then normative equilibrium exists, and that equilibrium, as such, must evidence a group structure. The structure (group) is manifestly inferred from the function (stabilization) without relevant aspects of structure being identified.

Can things really be that simple? Indeed, inconsistencies accumulated during this phase of Piaget's thinking:

1. The operations of enacting and acknowledging only define the realm of law, just as the "substitution . . . of scales" (1941/1995a, p. 127)

only defines the realm of morality. This basis does not enable one to make out which legal and moral rules to acknowledge. Yet all legal and moral development then falls through the theoretical sieve because that development consists precisely in replacing particular moral notions or laws with better ones.

2. This flaw is connected with the fact that during this period Piaget (1941/1995a) often discussed the function of norms by illustrating it with individual rules such as lying and promising. The operative structure of moral consciousness would thus fully exist with the first orientation to a moral rule—that is, at about 5 years of age. Making norm systems logical and systematizing them would, accordingly, not be a focus of theory building. This position was untenable because Piaget's own theory held that isolated action schemas are all too susceptible to egocentrism. Consequently, Piaget (1950/1995b) later saw the operative group structure embodied only in rule systems: "A system of legal rules is the very model of a set of social interactions having acquired the structure of an operatory grouping" (p. 61).

3. According to Piaget (1941/1995a), morality is subdivided into "morality of duty" and a "morality of reciprocity" (p. 121), with the former being said to derive from unilateral respect and the latter from reciprocal respect. The former is heteronomous, whereas the latter is autonomous. Both subdivisions of morality, however, are normatively stabilized through obligation, so both must be said to have a group structure. In them the values are integrated "in a set of 'groupings' of reversible substitutions, some asymmetrical . . . and the others symmetrical . . . , but all formally analogous to the logical 'groupings' themselves" (Piaget, 1941/1995a, p. 121). However, heteronomous morality is adhered to blindly without insight. It almost stands for irrationality, certainly not for rationality, which is embodied in structured intelligence.

4. The problem raised earlier can be illustrated from yet another angle. Spontaneous exchange is also associated with states of equilibrium—without normative stabilization. These states of equilibrium should therefore also evidence grouplike structures. Piaget (1950/1995b) reasoned in precisely this way in "Explanation in Sociology" when he described equilibrated exchange as the embodiment of a group characterized by composability ($AB = BC = AC$, where AB means A is exchanged for B) and associativity, an inverse ($AB = BA$), and the condition that "the product $AB \_ BA$ is either identity or null" (p. 66). This group already exists before normative stabilization. Normative stabilization only fixates the group, so to speak, by adding obligation, a mere regulation, to each transaction. It is not immediately apparent whether a new group structure ensues in the process or precisely what its components are.

In summary, the difficulties mentioned earlier may suggest that Piaget was having considerable trouble identifying the operative basis of interactions at the time he published the "Essay on the Theory of Qualitative Values in Static ('Synchronic') sociology" (1941), and that subsequent revisions were to be expected. Nonetheless, he had a fundamental intuition that he never abandoned—namely, that he had to look in every area of action for groupings that are "formally analogous to the logical 'groupings' themselves" (p. 121). Formal analogy is therefore the point of departure for modeling the relation between social and logical structures. Yet this hypothesis is comparatively weak because there need not be any interaction between the structures of social action and the forms of logic. During this period, social interaction is neither necessary nor sufficient for rationality and logic.

SOCIAL LIFE AND LOGIC

A stronger approach was offered in the article entitled "Logical Operations and Social Life" (Piaget, 1945/1995d). By and large, the article was an attempt to clarify the relationships between the purely individual and social factors of mental development. Although Piaget had commented on this topic many times, he considered it fruitful to renew the discussion because he had meanwhile learned more about the operational structure of logic. He hoped that "the operatory interpretation of [the logical] fact, far from complicating the relationships between reason, individual intelligence, and social life, appears to simplify the terms of the debate in an important way" (p. 134).

It is clear that the individual components are not derived simply from the social components because the primal forms of intelligence, as noted earlier, can be made out in the presocial, sensorimotor phase—at the level of action. Actions must be coordinated, and logic only formulates "the final equilibrated form of actions toward which all sensory-motor and mental evolution tends" (Piaget, 1945/1995d, p. 142). Of course this form of equilibrium is again the grouping. The question is whether the individual could arrive at this organizational form alone or whether the intervention of social factors is essential. One circumstance supporting the latter hypothesis is that cognitive and sociocognitive development run largely in parallel, but this parallelism is nothing more than an external indicator. To interpret this indicator, one must realize that interactions are actually only sets of actions—actions not on nature, but rather on other actors. If these actions are to be brought into equilibrium, they must attain the state of "composable and reversible systems" (1945/1995d, p. 145) as well. That is, they must also acquire group structure. Then they can promote the development of intelligence too: "Individuals' actions on one another, . . . only create a logic on the express condition that they themselves acquire a form of equilibrium analogous to the structure whose laws may be defined at the end-point of the development of individual actions" (1945/1995d, p. 146).

To create (*créer*) is a strong formulation that can be read in terms of constitution (generation) theory. Piaget also used verbs such as *end* (*aboutir*; Piaget, 1945/1995d) and *lead to* (*entraîner*) to capture the effects that the social process has on the origin of logical thinking. All these points readily lend themselves to a reductionist reading in terms of a sociologism. Yet that is precisely what Piaget wanted to avoid—just as much as he wanted to avoid the strict individualist positions. These global formulations are therefore elusive.

To move forward, Piaget analyzed the structure of intellectual exchange, which is also an exchange of qualitative values. For that reason, the equilibrium equations presented previously can be used in this context as well. They only have to be interpreted properly—namely, as an exchange of sentences that can be accepted or rejected. The terms of the equations assume the following meanings:

r_a is the utterance of a sentence (true or false).

s_b is b's acceptance (or rejection) of this sentence.

t_b is b's duty to abide by the acceptance or rejection.

v_a is the value that this engagement bestows upon r_a (valid).

If these meanings are inserted into the equilibrium equations, the result is, as Chapman (1986) quite correctly noted, basically a variant of universal pragmatics *sensu* Habermas. It deals with the presuppositions and validity claims that speakers universally and inevitably make when they engage in a discourse (basically equal rights to utter speech acts like asserting, disputing, etc., in a spirit of truthfulness). As a brief example of Piaget's variant only, $(s_a = s_b)$ means that a utters a sentence that b accepts, and $(s_b = t_b)$ means that b feels an obligation to abide by this acceptance and hence to forgo contradictions. Further, $(t_b = v_a)$ attributes sentence s_a a value (validity) that prompts a to conserve his or her statement as identical, and so forth. The most important thing is that Equations I and II, when interpreted in this manner, imply equilibrium of intellectual exchange only if a and b respect the full reciprocity of the right to speak—that is, if they are absolutely equally warranted (and equally competent) interlocutors (Piaget, 1945/1995d). Constraint provides for an unstable equilibrium at best—one that is bound to break down if b, whose opinions have depended on a, "begins to think for himself, that is, it ends with social differentiation" (p. 150). Intellectual exchange in this case is thus described as the equally warranted utterance of speech acts expressing assertion and agreement or—as people are fond of putting it today without adding an iota to Piaget—as free discourse.

It remains to be shown that this cooperative speaking does in fact evidence the traits of reversible operational systems characteristic of groupings, and in that regard Piaget went beyond "qualitative values". He pointed out that it is necessary to produce correspondence between sentences, which can be conceived of as operations. He added that the absence of contradiction results directly from the reversibility of thinking and, in intellectual exchange, cannot simply be understood as an indicator of equilibrium as far as the thinking of the individual goes. Rather, the absence of contradiction is achieved as a normative, social rule. The same is true of the identity principle, which becomes a real rule only through social exchange: "The 'principle of identity' only constitutes a rule by virtue of exchanges. In individual thought, identity is the product of direct operations composed with inverse ones" (1945/1995d, p. 153).

Piaget (1945/1995d) concluded from all these observations that this form of intellectual exchange "necessarily takes the form of a system of reciprocal operations and consequently of *groupements*" (p. 151). However, he did not infer that logic would reduce to interactional logic in the sense, say, that a complete transfer of social group structures to the individual logic of operations would occur. The two components make appeal to one another, but have to be differentiated as discrete components, although there is a direct transfer as concerns identity and the absence of contradiction. Formal analogy between individual and social structures still prevailed as a model. Indeed the question addressed in "Logical Operations and Social Life" (1945/1995d) is based on the central supposition that the difference between the system references individual and social is insurmountable. That was to change.

Something else was to change as well, and the changes were already becoming apparent in theoretical bottlenecks. Piaget, with his construct of universal pragmatics, remained stuck largely on the surface of social processes: Asserting and agreeing can be observed directly. The two equations ostensibly describing equilibrated intellectual exchange contained nothing other than acts of asserting and agreeing and postulates of conserving these acts as acts. Therefore, the theory was completely tied to the level of what was empirically observable. Explanatory, theoretical constructs could not be accommodated anywhere. Not that Piaget would have failed to sense that there were other things still awaiting explanation. For example, he wrote that consensus between *a* and *b* could come about only "through a convergence between *a* and *b* concerning the facts invoked by *a* and recognized by *b*" (Piaget, 1945/1995d, p. 151). How and under which conditions this convergence is actually produced cannot be described with the pragmatic model of intellectual cooperation. Its terminology captures only the results of thinking: consensus and dissent. The definitive shape of a social phenomenon—in this case, consensus on xy—cannot be explained with speech acts per se any more than with the previously cited phenomena of obligation as such or with the enactment of and compliance with legal norms.

This shortcoming is linked directly to another. In the social dimension of speech (i.e., pragmatics), it is impossible to determine whether a social arrangement is rational or substantively appropriate. Delusional consensus is not a rare historical phenomenon. Piaget also sought to avoid reducing the substantive dimension merely to the social dimension. Referring to Durkheim, he definitely meant it critically when he wrote: "Thus, truth reduces to what everyone agrees to" (Piaget, 1945/1995d, p. 135). The substantive dimension, however, falls right through the coarse mesh of the terminology used in universal pragmatics and thereby generates paradoxes. In a later article, "Explanation in Sociology," Piaget (1950/1995b) pointed out that a formally and thoroughly rationalized legal system with operative group structure can justify the worst abuses because it conserves the wrong content. This possibility also pertains to formal logic, where "systems of propositions which are formally correct but false in their content" (1950/1995b, p. 61) can conserve the greatest nonsense. However, as long as one does not leave the ground of universal pragmatics, full reversibility of such delusional cases must be acknowledged because the rules of contradiction and identity are respected: formally coherent reversible nonsense. Within the theory, solely on the basis of equal rights to speak, nothing can be learned about material truth, development of science, and social evolution. This point became clearer to Piaget and led him to increasingly revise his earlier thought.

THE IDENTITY OF STRUCTURES

Since the appearance of *The Psychology of Intelligence* (Piaget, 1947/1950), a variant of the relationship between intra- and interindividual structures has been emerging—one that points beyond a merely formal analogy and proposes that the corresponding structures are identical. According to this variant, even an isolated subject would have to organize his thinking into grouplike structures if he wanted to think "in an orderly way." He would have to bring his sequential mental states into a kind of interaction that would justify speaking of a " 'society' between his different 'selves' " (1947/1950, p. 164), with the interrelations between the individual selves involved conforming to the logic of grouping. "The laws of grouping constitute general forms of equilibrium which express both the equilibrium of interindividual interaction and that of the operations of which every socialized individual is capable when he reasons internally in terms of his most personal and original ideas" (1947/1950, p. 165). When individual action reaches the level of operative structures, the discrete actions become combinable and can be transformed in many different ways, and that is precisely what makes it possible to link them with the actions of others as well (Piaget, 1950/1995b). At one level—the interplay of operations—it does not matter whether I have to associate action x with my own action y or with somebody else's action y_. For that reason, Piaget's writings from then on contain innumerable formulations disaffirming the relevance of the distinction between inter- and intraindividual. He spoke instead of "one and the same over-arching process" (1950/1995b, p. 89). Cooperation and grouped operations are said to be "one and the same reality viewed from two different standpoints" (1950/1995b, p. 89) because there are not two different kinds of equilibration of actions and because actions directed toward objects and actions directed toward other persons are inseparably linked (1950/1995b).

One can easily and plausibly illustrate this argument with the example of cooperative bridge building, the operative structure of which Piaget tried to analyze. The actors cooperate by seeking each other's corresponding, reciprocal, or complementary operations (bridge piers of the same shape, with opposite incline, with banks of different heights and at different elevations; Piaget, 1950/1995b). Virtually nothing else can happen if both bridge piers are built by one person because the same actions by one and the same person have to be joined to arrive at the same result. What is true for actions is also true for the logic of propositions, about which Piaget (1950/1995b) said: "The logic of propositions is therefore by its very nature a system of exchanges, and whether the exchanged propositions are those of internal dialogue or of distinct persons does not matter" (p. 90).

It is no different in the moral sphere. If I want to use a given store of resources for two of my needs, I have to be able to divide by two; the same holds true if one of the needs is felt by one person and the other need by a different person. When it comes to reconstructing the operative structures of action—that is, to the level of competence theory—a monologic–dialogic difference does not exist. Hence, *cooperation* was written by Piaget as *co-operation* so that the word's appearance would underscore the idea that society builds on identical structuring activity just as the coordinated actions of individuals do. With a measure of self-satisfaction, Piaget (1960/1995e) thus wrote: "At that level, to wonder whether it is intra-personal operations that engender interpersonal cooperations or vice versa is analogous to wondering what came first, the chicken or the egg" (p. 294). This position is exactly the one taken in *Erkenntnistheorie der Wissenschaften vom Menschen* (1970/1973):

> In the final analysis, one comes to a necessary convergence of the "most general" forms of both social interaction and the coordination of individual actions. Better said, we are talking about two inseparable aspects of one and the same reality: ... It therefore appears pretty senseless to want to play a social and an individual logic off against each other. (p. 141; translation from German)

This position seems unassailable to me because the thought experiment presented before (two workers or one constructing a bridge) can be carried out at any time in its inter- and intraindividual variants. The living work of the artisan is divided up in the transition to manufacturing and distributed to a collective. Yet the individual tasks must still be coordinated just as in the intraindividual case. *First*, you bore a hole, *then* you put in a screw. If I look at a familiar mountain landscape first from one side and then from the opposite side, I face the same problem of coordination as when a partner describes his view from the opposite side, and so forth. Such is the basic situation to begin with. It states that logic coordinates actions and thoughts, period, regardless of whether the reference system is individual or social.

If these basic facts may be regarded as correct, it seems that assertions about a deemphasis of sociological aspects in Piaget's late work are tenable only in a superficial sense. None of Piaget's examples is of a sociological nature, but it takes little more than an intellectual twist to introduce sociological components into the equilibrium model. The discontinuities that compel the actor to improve his present structures need not arise from his own experience, needs, and so forth. Instead each discontinuity can be generated or triggered socially. In terms of structural theory, system reference (individual or social) makes absolutely no difference. Hence, if the same old sociological story of monologization is brought up again, the suspicion arises that one has not made the effort to think through Piaget's theory down to the level of operative structures.

Drawing on competence theory to overcome this polarity between individual and social logic, Piaget left the level of directly observable disputing and agreeing (speech act theory). Consensus is not created by establishing norms or equal rights to speak per se. These factors can just as well be a condition of the possibility for dissent, as when actors do not manage to coordinate the content of their statements into a logical group. Consensus is then no longer directly an embodiment of groupings. Rather it is explained by the nonobservable, ordered interplay of operations behind the semantics of the uttered sentences: "To a certain relation established from A's viewpoint there corresponds, after interaction, such and such a relation from B's viewpoint. . . . These correspondences are what, for each proposition stated by A or B, *determine* the agreement (or, in the case of non-correspondence, the disagreement) of the parties" (Piaget, 1947/ 1950, p. 165; italics added). For example, if the person facing me says "right," I have to think "left" to respond in a coordinated way. At that point, the focus of interest is no longer on relations between speech acts as such, but rather on relations between semantics. True, the old schema from exchange theory is used in "Explanation in Sociology" (1950/1995b), but Piaget reinterpreted it, emphasizing semantics partly by pointing out that the consensus between interlocutors necessarily adopts one of three forms: (a) "one-to-one correspondence between two isomorphic series of propositions," (b) "agreement about a common truth . . . which justifies the different points of view" (symmetry), or (c) "addition between complementary sets" (p. 93). The level of universal pragmatics in theory building is thereby overcome—for good reason as shown before. Agreeing and disputing, consensus and dissent henceforth surface only as dependent variables or observable events that are to be explained by means of the theoretical constructs of operative intelligence.

In summary, a few preliminary conclusions may be drawn. Although Piaget's *Moral Judgment of the Child* aimed for a reductionist sociological variant of the relationship between logic and social process, the existence of motoric rationality simultaneously forced him to acknowledge the extrasocial roots of rationality. He wanted to strengthen the extrasocial at least with social phenomena, drawing primarily on structural affinities/similarity between social interaction and substantive logic. He tried to underline the group character of normatively stabilized interaction as a formal analogue of logical groupings. He also experimented with universal pragmatics. Neither variant led very far, nor did either of them go beyond affinities between structures that had to be fundamentally differentiated. In the end, there seemed to be an utterly individualized logic. I say *seemed* because in reality something quite different had occurred: Monologic logic was imbued with a thoroughly sociological dimension in the sense that it could be assigned an interindividual interpretation at any time. In this regard it was neutral. That is why Piaget could go ahead and take the intraindividual perspective to its conclusion, as in *Equilibration of Cognitive Structures* (1975), without having to retract any of his sociological tenets. In terms of competence theory, the transition from the intra- to the interindividual perspective amounted to a minimal problem of translation.

COLLECTIVE LEARNING PROCESSES WITH MILLER

It is against this background that one should see one more recent attempt to emphasize the sociological dimension of Piaget—namely, Miller's (1986) *Kollektive Lernprozesse (Collective Learning Processes)*. Given the extensive discussions about "Piaget and Sociology" (see the literature references in Habermas, 1981; Miller, 1986), I selected the contribution by Miller because his attempt to put Piaget's theory into a dialogic context drew on Habermas' (1981) precepts, which are particularly influential in the German scene, and because Miller made an effort to substantiate his arguments empirically. To that extent, Miller's work represents one of the few direct empirical tests of Habermas' theory. The book contains an abundance of valuable observations and elaborations on the state of sociological research that this article cannot give due attention. It also contains a fundamental error—namely, the assertion that Piaget's theory of intellectual exchange should be interpreted from the perspective of universal pragmatics.

Let us turn briefly to Miller's theoretical repertoire. The concept of argumentation is of focal concern: "An *argumentation* consists of a sequence of utterances made by different speakers" (Miller, 1986, p. 163). It "is successful if those participating in it succeed in developing a shared argument[.] . . . In the process, the pros and cons typical of an argumentation play a fundamental role" (pp. 225–226). It is impossible to overlook them: "Argumentations are spatiotemporal, empirically perceivable events" (p. 224). In the logic of argumentation, a.o. rules of transition must be specified—namely, rules of transition between utterances. They are understandable as conditions of an ideal speech situation and encompass a generalization principle, an objectivity principle, and a truth principle. For example, the principle of generalization reads as follows: "In an argumentation, a statement is not justified until it has been converted into something collectively valid by means of what is collectively valid" (p. 235). In concrete terms: a's utterance is disputed by b's utterance; b's utterance is challenged by c and not upheld, so a prevails, for a no longer provokes contradiction, and everyone agrees. All that is universal pragmatics.

These instruments provide thin conceptual cover because *pragmatics* refers to the informationally impoverished dimension of speech in which the diversity of the operative processing of experiences cannot be fully represented in its diversity. There is agreement and rejection, all in all very little—in any case not enough to understand developmental progress and mental functioning. To show this it is useful to take a closer look at one of Miller's empirical studies.

In that experiment, Miller (1986) confronted a group of 3-year-olds and a group of 5-year-olds with a beam scale in individual and group tests to elicit argumentations and predictions. A beam scale is a kind of seesaw on which units of weight can be hung at regular intervals from the fulcrum. In the test, the experimenter first locked the scale's beam in place, distributed the weights along it, and then asked the children to indicate whether they thought the beam would remain straight or whether its right or left arm would sink after the scale's lock was released. Correct predictions are come to by multiplying the weight by the distance from the fulcrum, a two-dimensional scheme marking the upshot of development. Miller's age groups are far off from this upshot, and this has implications for their capacity to argue with one another.

On the whole, one could describe the behavior of the 3-year-olds as being focused primarily on the parameter of weight, but the group discussion was able to stress the parameter of distance as well, to which the children then veer completely. Quotation marks must enclose the expression *group discussion* because children of this age do not usually discuss, but rather state a thesis ("to the right"), acknowledge the antithesis ("to the left"), and then settle on one of the two sides without providing a rationale. The two parameters are never considered simultaneously; one immediately extinguishes the other. It is all exactly what one would expect on the basis of Piaget's theory. The knowledge of 3-year-olds is still largely "action knowledge"—that is, not yet controlled by reflection. It is egocentric knowledge in the sense that it is influenced little by any notion that others could see something else. It is also unidimensional because the child simply does not have cognitive schemas for dealing with two dimensions and must therefore "cognitively suppress" surplus information (Piaget, 1975/1976, pp. 69–75).

These obstacles are in part eliminated among the 5-year-olds. Knowing that both dimensions are relevant, they keep them in mind and argumentatively play them against each other. They only have trouble calculating distance and weight accurately because they cannot construct the exact formula. This is about how the traditional Piagetian description of Miller's results would look. Explication of the universal pragmatic manifestations of the children's cognitive competencies is generally dispensed with because the developmental obstacle is assumed to lie elsewhere. When new schemas have been acquired, there is no longer a problem with the corresponding asserting and disputing.

To highlight the relevance of the pragmatic dimension, Miller had to coat this customary presentation of his experimental results in the rhetoric of contradicting and agreeing. A small segment of his qualitative data may serve as a test of the relative success of this strategy.

The discussion of the 5-year-olds relevant here deals with a particular arrangement of the weights on the beam scale. On the left arm, three weights hung immediately next to the fulcrum; on the right arm, one weight was placed at twice the distance from the fulcrum. It was difficult for the children to predict the beam's behavior. At first they sang out balance. Miller intervened with the question of whether everyone thought balance. Daniel then pointed out the greater number of weights and chose "to the left." Annette countered with, "Oh, Daniel, that one [on the right] is further away from the middle. But—it's going down [on the right]." Andrea intervened with, "Even so, balance!!", and so forth. Daniel finally joined them: "Robert, choose 'balance.' Look. Here [on the left] are three [weights], here is one, but it is further . . ." (Miller, 1986, p. 183). The cogency of the traditional Piagetian description should be obvious. Miller paraphrased the events in part as follows:

> Daniel does not dispute . . . that the statement expressed with Annette's contribution is empirically correct; in other words, he does not dispute the *empirical tenability* of Annette's statement but rather its *explanatory relevance* for a successful response to the question of the argumentation. (p. 184)

Both theoretical concepts are defined as follows: "The criterion of *empirical tenability* refers to the question of the acceptability of an argument's statements. The criterion of explanatory relevance refers to the question of the acceptability of transitions between an argument's statements" (p. 188). The differentiation between these two constructs is said to mark the developmental progress of 5-year-olds compared with the younger ones: They can accept an opposing argument and still maintain their own positions. How is this theoretical description to be assessed?

It would be idle to dispute that the cited interaction sequence can indeed be described in this manner because the description is far too close to the factual sequence of events to be challenged. The theoretical concepts do not refer to any unobservable variable. Daniel did not dispute Annette's observation, only her conclusion—one *sees* that.

Yet the constructs do not make plausible what actually could go on in the minds of the children as they try to solve the problem at hand (predicting the behavior of the beam scale). After all this problem does not occur in Miller's terminology. *Empirical tenability* and *explanatory relevance* are terms without any substantive information about the world (of beam scales). The point is to make it comprehensible why the 5-year-olds have no need to dispute the empirical tenability of their peers' observations to come up with different conclusions. In this respect, the customary Piagetian description of the matter at hand works: *Because* Daniel operates with a two-dimensional schema, he can concede Anette's observation without having to draw her conclusion. The conditions that make Miller's distinctions possible lie behind the tangible phenomena; they lie in the area of—or better, behind—semantics.

In addition, his constructs do not capture the children's relevant developmental advances. Even younger children are able to distinguish empirical tenability from explanatory relevance. "You don't really know," said little Jana (3) to defend her dissenting opinion. In so doing she need not cast doubt on the opposing side's rationale ("because that one is up front") (Miller, 1986, p. 172). Hana argued in exactly the same way against Dirk. Dirk chose "to the left," Hana countered with "to the right," Dirk legitimated his prediction by pointing out the weight ("because that's higher"), and Hana wriggled out of the trap with, "You don't know that at all." Because the children in the experiments also produced many incorrect solutions, Hana's rejoinder is completely rational. It disputes the explanatory relevance of a statement without needing to cast doubt on its empirical tenability: Granted, that side is higher, but do we really know what the consequence is? Thus, universal pragmatics seems not to be successful in reconstructing developmental progress.

Do all these deficits come as a complete surprise? Hardly if one keeps in mind that the pragmatic dimension of language is not the collecting tank of our knowledge about the social and physical worlds; hardly if one keeps in mind that we break through to the interplay of operations only when we study the organization of this knowledge. In this respect, I do not consider it a coincidence that the topic of operations received comparatively scant attention in Miller's book. Its lack of prominence reinforced the sociologism, for as shown earlier, it is only at the level of operative reconstructions that the polarity between the social and individual vanishes—as a mere difference in content. That is why I conclude that the shift to pragmatics turns the state of the discussion back more than 50 years.

THE MEANING OF COOPERATION
AND INTELLECTUAL EXCHANGE
FOR A THEORY OF STRUCTURAL LEARNING:
PROCEDURAL RATIONALITY

To avoid misunderstandings, this chapter concludes with a few words explaining why interaction and free discussion should play an essential role in any comprehensive theory of the development of cognitive and practical competencies. If we humans were gods, this formulation of the statement would be untenable because we would have no problems with performance and would not have to work tediously up to more complex knowledge. Yet we do have performance problems, and what Piaget has to say about the importance of free, intellectual cooperation leaves little doubt that its relevance is to be sought *there*. Cooperation is a "procedure

of a purely formal nature . . . exclusively a method. . . . The commitments
. . . which I undertake by virtue of cooperation lead me I know not where.
These commitments are thus formal and not material" (Piaget, 1928/
1995c, p. 208). If one cannot know where each intellectual exchange leads,
it must be completely idle to take the universal pragmatic presuppositions
of "undominated discourse" and rub them against each other with infinite
patience in Habermasian manner, hoping to glean from them something
about individual or collective structural development. They contain nothing of structure, but they are the stage that provides a favorable milieu for
the performance of development dramas.

These presuppositions are medium, engine, and important control
mechanism in the development of operative structures because they coun-
teract individual shortcomings and temptations—temptations to be satisfied with less than the cognitive optimum in the substantive dimension.
To give some examples:

- Because partners in a discourse cannot know where a given line of
reasoning will lead, and because they do not always see through the implications of their own statements, they are frequently tempted to violate
the principles of identity and contradiction. This tendency is countered by
the socially generated normative quality of these principles.

- Interests and cognitive limitations often lead the individual to suppress relevant dimensions of a specific issue. Such malfunctions are corrected because what is suppressed is objectively and intractably present in
the form of other persons.

- Egocentric projections are rejected, meaning that the individual need
not construct the negations of his or her own arguments.

- Orientations, experiences, and needs are differentially distributed in
society. In the social realm, the individual thus comes under the pressure
of increased complexity, which can be coped with only through structural
learning. Monofactorial, monofunctional arrangements have virtually no
chance of survival.

- Ready-made ways to coordinate are socially accumulated and need
not be reinvented in each case. One is confronted by them and must only
see through their meaning and functioning—an accomplishment usually
managed more quickly than inventing. The interaction also generates
pressure for accelerated appropriation.

- Intellectual exchange appears to favor incremental solutions at which
the individual alone would not arrive. The data provided by Miller (1986)
contain an instructive example. Discussing Kohlberg's Heinz dilemma (in
which a person breaks into a drug store to steal vital medicine), children
hit on the thought of two break-ins—to minimize the damage to the drug-

gist—and perfect this double break-in into a serial robbery. They had a good, collective idea.

Given what Piaget said about intellectual cooperation, however, it also becomes clear that this learning mechanism demands a great deal of the individuals involved. People have to be resilient, oriented to substantive matters, and competent so they can resist the perfidious group pressure under which cooperation can slip into coercion (group think) at any time. Often the individual is able to resist only by invoking the substantive dimension—namely, superior insight. An appropriate procedural theory of rationality would thus have to operate in the triangle delineated by the individual, the substantive dimension, and the social dimension. In other words, cognitively able and autonomous subjects agree on the issue, and this social performance forces them to restructure their competencies neither monologically nor dialogically, but rather just logically.

REFERENCES

Chapman, M. (1986). The structure of exchange: Piaget's sociological theory. *Human Development, 29,* 181–194.

Furth, H. P. (1987). *Wissen als Leidenschaft* [Knowledge as desire]. New York: Columbia University Press.

Habermas, J. (1981). *Theorie des kommunikativen Handelns* [Theory of communicative action] (2 vols). Frankfurt am Main: Suhrkamp.

Habermas, J. (1983). *Moralbewußtsein und kommunikatives Handeln* [Moral consciousness and communicative action]. Frankfurt am Main: Suhrkamp.

Miller, M. (1986). *Kollektive Lernprozesse* [Collective learning processes]. Frankfurt am Main: Suhrkamp.

Piaget, J. (1950). *The psychology of intelligence* (M. Percy & D. E. Berlyne, Trans.). London: Routledge & Kegan Paul. (Original work published 1947)

Piaget, J. (1962). *The moral judgment of the child* (M. Gabain, Trans.). New York: Collier. (Original work published 1932)

Piaget, J. (1971). *Biology and knowledge: An essay on the relations between organic regulations and cognitive processes* (B. Walsh, Trans). Chicago and Edinburgh: University of Chicago Press. (Original work published 1967)

Piaget, J. (1973). *Erkenntnistheorie der Wissenschaften vom Menschen* [Theory of knowledge for the sciences of man] (E. Höhnisch, Trans.). Frankfurt am Main: Ullstein. (Original work published 1970)

Piaget, J. (1976). *L'équilibration des structures cognitives.* Paris: Presses Universitaires de France.

Piaget, J. (1977). *Ètude Sociologiques* (3rd ed.). Geneva: Librairie DROZ. (Original work published 1965)

Piaget, J. (1995a). Essay on the theory of qualitative values in static ("synchronic") sociology (W. Mays, Trans.). In J. Piaget (Ed.), *Sociological studies* (pp. 97–133). London: Routledge. (Original work published 1941)

Piaget, J. (1995b). Explanation in sociology (C. Sherrard, Trans.). In J. Piaget (Ed.), *Sociological studies* (pp. 39–96). London: Routledge. (Original work published 1950)

Piaget, J. (1995c). Genetic logic and sociology (R. Kitchener, Trans.). In J. Piaget (Ed.), *Sociological studies* (pp. 184–214). London: Routledge. (Original work published 1928)

Piaget, J. (1995d). Logical operations and social life (T. Brown & M. Gribetz, Trans.). In J. Piaget (Ed.), *Sociological studies* (pp. 134–157). London: Routledge. (Original work published 1945)

Piaget, J. (1995e). Problems of the social psychology of childhood (T. Brown, Trans.). In J. Piaget (Ed.), *Sociological studies* (pp. 287–318). London: Routledge. (Original work published 1960)

A Bridge too Far: On the Relations Between Moral and Secular Reasoning

Bryan W. Sokol
Simon Fraser University

Michael J. Chandler
University of British Columbia

> *Whenever you find yourself on the side of the majority, it is time to pause and reflect.*
>
> —Mark Twain (*Notebook*, 1904)

INTRODUCTION: "TWO OF EVERY SORT SHALT THOU BRING"

Way back then, when deep *structures* and general *stages* of reasoning were the talk of the town, and references to *domain* this or *modular* that were still few and far between—way back, say, a short quarter century ago—any call for the construction of new bridges (e.g., Baird & Sokol, in press; Chandler, Sokol, & Wainryb, 2000) between the literatures on children's folk conceptions of mental life and their moral reasoning competence would have struck many as superfluous at best. Like Noah's calls to prepare for the great flood, no one would have seen the need. Why work to bridge two "domains" that are already joined at the hip? As matters stood then, children's epistemic and moral lives, although seen to be manifestly different in content, were nevertheless generally understood to be only phenotypically different expressions of one and the same underlying thing. One need only look to Kohlberg's work (e.g., 1981, 1984) or the early writings of Piaget (1932/1965), on which Kohlberg's ideas were founded, to catch a backward glimpse of what was then a widely held system of beliefs about the structural dependence, and so conceptual inseparability, of these two facets of children's thinking—two reputedly different faces of the same coin. Piaget (1932/1965, 1954/1981) is particularly noted for his claims that the same underlying form of equilibrium and formal structures were central to both children's intellectual and moral reasoning development. His famous analogy, "logic is the morality of thought just as morality is the logic of action" (Piaget, 1932/1965, p. 398), was recited like a mantra among mid-20th-century novitiates to Piaget's ecclesiastical order. Stripping this same notion of most of its rhetorical flair, Kohlberg similarly argued, and many argued with him, that "justice operations of reciprocity and equality parallel operations of reciprocity and equality in the logico-mathematical domain" (Colby & Kohlberg, 1987, p. 12). Such claims led many to conclude, as Kohlberg had, that "logical . . . operations are built into the definitions of the moral stages" (Colby & Kohlberg, 1987, p. 12) or, more simply, logic and morality are "dual aspects of one and the same thing" (Kitchener, 1981, p. 262). The fact that, way back then, just about everyone was echoing this same sentiment does not make it right of course, nor, just as important, does it now make it entirely wrong.

That was then. Now with the crest of Piaget's and Kohlberg's popularity having past half a diurnal cycle ago, the tide of contemporary research, especially in the cognitive-developmental literature, is running strongly in a more functional and typically more neo-nativist direction, and we are newly awash in a flotsam of modules and jetsam of content-specific domains (see e.g., Hirschfeld & Gelman, 1994). Contained in this rising flood are various domain-specific theories of number (Wynn, 1995), biology (Springer & Keil, 1989), selves (Moshman, 1998), physics (Spelke, 1991), and even food (Rozin, 1990)—to name just a few—that threaten to overspill the once common ground and submerge more classical accounts, leaving the separate islands of research concerned with children's conceptions of mind and morality isolated and in need of some new connective efforts to rejoin them. That is, all the necessary or structural or co-constitutive relationships that were once assumed to be automatically in place have long since been effectively washed away, and new calls to build new bridges over these troubled waters seem like good, even unifying, ideas. Those who had previously felt on solid footing, standing pat on a place that once ran unbroken between the moral and epistemic, now feel at risk of being swept along by a building current of evidence brought out by more modular-minded researchers who commonly count moral and epistemic development as merely two more domains in a seemingly arbitrary sea of increasingly discrete mental modules.

Although we aim to distance ourselves from this modular majority, we—like they—have found our own personal efforts to learn about children's moral and cognitive development (e.g., Chandler, Sokol, & Hallett,

2001) strangely alienated and (despite our own persistent commitments to what we later describe as a grand narrative of some description) in need of some sort of bridging. Like many of our once land-locked colleagues, we too have come to understand that what we once casually assumed to be the conceptual high ground now appears as intertidal at best and in need of some serious diking up. In short, we have found ourselves strung out awkwardly with both feet off the ground, caught between a modular majority whose views we do not entirely support and a growing apprehension that the theoretical ground beneath our feet is less than solid. Rather, it now appears that cognitive and moral life are not as seamlessly connected as older and easier aphorisms about the logic of this and that once led us to comfortably assume. Like Noah, we believe that the downpour of new evidence concerning (in our case) the distinctiveness of certain moral and epistemic domains is real evidence that will not dry up quickly. As such if one wishes to get from here to there in this contemporary deluge, some real connective links seem required. It seems we must gather up our ideas two by two and link them together—not just at the *algorithmic level* of more functional relations, but also at the seabed level of their topographical or formal *design features* (Marr, 1982). Like Mark Twain, we have seen the modular majority and it looks uncommonly like ourselves. Evidently, it is time to pause and reflect.

Exactly what we hope to reflect on is how to stay afloat in what amounts to a rising tide of new evidence that is all in favor of domain specificity, without being forced to conclude that it is water all the way down or that there is no common bedrock whatsoever beneath the surface layer of divisiveness that makes everything look singular and one off. From the perspective we are trying to float, then, what first needs to be accomplished, if we are to keep our heads above water, is to find ways to keep clear of not only a raft of misconceptions currently careening about regarding the older, so-called *domain-general* understanding of children's epistemic and moral development, but also of the serious prospect of being blind-sided by all of the loose facts issuing out of the modularity side of what Flanagan (1991) called the unity–modularity antinomy. The way we plan to attempt all this is by taking up a form of levels analysis (Chandler, Lalonde, & Sokol, 2000; Chandler & Sokol, in press), which is meant to distinguish between *formal* and *functional* kinds of explanations. In doing all this, we attempt to sort through some of what we take to be the common misreadings of Piaget's notion of structure and, more particularly, his carefully articulated view of how epistemic and moral forms of knowledge can be both separate and the same. By the end, it will hopefully be clear that the best way to rejoin the currently isolated literatures on children's theories of mind and moral development is not so much about the job of building bridges as it is about draining the swamps of

confusion that work to obscure connections already present. We mean to
go about this reclamation effort in three easy steps or parts.

PART I: "WHAT THEREFORE GOD HATH JOINED
TOGETHER, LET NO MAN PUT ASUNDER"

It is commonly said that we are living through an era of increasing specialization—an era that, as it plays itself out in cognitive psychology, is increasingly disapproving of older domain-general accounts of the sort
frequently associated with Piaget. General is out and content-specific domains and mental modules are in. In such up-to-date quarters, abstract
notions of *formal logics* and *structures d'ensemble* are now regularly seen as
the antediluvian and largely forgettable parts of our collective past—an
allegedly darker time when the scales had not yet fallen from our eyes—
before we had come to recognize as distinct what clearer vision has now
revealed to be separate. Such sentiments are especially afoot in the areas
of both children's theories of mind and are easily read into contemporary
research dealing with the "domains" of sociomoral development.

The prevailing double vision of those espousing a "theory-theory" account of young people's changing conceptions of mental life (e.g., Gopnik
& Wellman, 1994) is, for example, now widely considered to be at least
twice as revealing as Piaget's presumably more myopic view. This contrast has been made especially explicit by Wellman and Gelman (1998),
who argued that, ". . . in their construal of cognitive structures . . . theory-
theory proposals are quite unlike Piaget's . . . there is no insistence on domain-general logical stages that are independent of specific contents.
Rather, theories are domain-specific, content-full structures that are
shaped by the acquisition of knowledge in the domain itself" (pp.
559–560; see also Wellman & Gelman, 1992). Similarly, in Gelman and
Baillergeon's (1983) much rehearsed refutation of Piaget's theory of cognitive development, they concluded that the child "works out concepts in
separate domains without using the kinds of integrative structures that
would be required by a general stage theory" (p. 214). The bulk of Piaget's
work, on this account, has grown increasingly out of step with the march-
ing orders of most contemporary theory theorists. It is no wonder then
that, in our fashion-conscious professional world, a growing contingent of
researchers invested in the study of children's developing conceptions of
mental life concur with Gopnik (1993) that "almost all of Piaget's substantive claims about the child's conception of the mind have turned out to be
wrong" (p. 14) and we have finally seen "the collapse of classical Piagetian
theory" (Meltzoff, 1999, p. 252).

Although such bold claims, we contend, better serve to astound than to engage serious debate, there is little doubt that contemporary dissatisfaction with all claims of domain generality, and particularly Piaget's sympathies in this regard, is running high and stretches well beyond the rhetorical extravagances practiced by some theory theorists. In much the same way, related patricidal grumblings can also be heard from many contributors to the literature on children's sociomoral development. Although there are good reasons to believe that words like *domain specificity* have rather different meanings in the theories of mind and moral development literatures, theorists of sociomoral development, no less than their more coldly cognitive counterparts, have generally come to doubt that their subject matter can be usefully painted using Piaget's or Kohlberg's broad brush strokes.

The work of Turiel (e.g., 1979, 1983a, 1983b, 1998, 2002) and his colleagues (e.g., Turiel & Davidson, 1986; Turiel, Hildebrandt, & Wainryb, 1991; Turiel, Killen, & Helwig, 1987) provides what is perhaps the best known of such domain-specific accounts (for a comprehensive review, see Turiel, 1998). Although when addressing matters that are unarguably moral (i.e., clear matters of justice and fairness) these authors write and reason in ways that are generally consonant with a common reading of Piaget, they are equally committed to driving a wedge between strictly moral concerns, on the one hand, and more conventional considerations, on the other—matters that are said to be too frequently and too casually bracketed together into a single developmental story. Here the separate domain of social conventions, for example, is not understood to be a subspecies of morality per se, but rather designates different concerns that, although perhaps evaluative and prescriptive in character, nevertheless lay outside of the orbit of the strictly moral. Young people's maturing conceptions of such conventional matters are argued to follow a different developmental trajectory from that characteristic of morality and to be subject to contextual and cultural variations not evident in the strictly moral domain. As such domain theories found in the moral arena do not, as is commonly the case with more modularist theories of cognitive or epistemic development, begin as an all-out attempt to debunk Piaget. They do, however, generally group together Piaget (or at least the "early" Piaget) with Kohlberg and others who, on their evidence, have injudiciously treated distinct moral, conventional, and prudential matters as being all of one piece. For instance, Turiel et al. (1991) argued quite forcefully that their "position of domain specificity stands in contrast with 'global' approaches" (p. 3), in general, and with Piaget's (1932/1965) *Moral Judgment of the Child*, in particular, as a global or generalist position that is said to "characterize moral development as a series of progressive differentiations" (Turiel et al., 1991, p. 4) from a broader and initially undifferentiated common cognitive matrix.

In many respects, Turiel (1979) can be seen as one of the early harbingers of other more recent accounts, suggesting almost a quarter of a century ago that, ". . . individuals develop [distinctive] conceptual frameworks or 'theories' which serve to *structure* social phenomena" (p. 100). Although such claims generally avoid presuming the existence of some fanciful neural architecture made up of purpose-built mental modules so common in theory-theory speak (see Turiel, Hildebrandt, & Wainryb, 1991), they nevertheless insist that a proper understanding of children's conceptions of the social realm must be parsed into several distinct domains of knowledge (Turiel and associates argued for no less than three: the *personal* or prudential, *societal* or social-conventional, and *moral*). Anything short of such divisions, it is argued, would fail to make adequate sense of the often contradictory, multifaceted, and asynchronous developmental patterns that are now so well documented in children's and adults' reasoning about the social world (Turiel & Davidson, 1986). Domain-general accounts, from this view, simply fail to make adequate provision for the unwieldy facts of sociocognitive development.

On some readings efforts such as these of Turiel and his colleagues to distinguish between different domains of prescriptivity are best viewed as a helpful threshing operation that serves to separate the moral *wheat* from conventional *chaff*. Others (e.g., Glassman & Zan, 1995; Lourenço, 2002, 2003; Rest, Narvaez, Bebeau, & Thoma, 1999) see in such efforts the seeds of nativism and the risk of costing the study of morality its proper developmental credentials. Whatever one's position on this controversy—and here we remain agnostic—it has grown increasingly clear that there are important tensions between so-called "theories of the grand design" and advocates of more domain-specific alternatives—tensions that cannot be resolved, we mean to argue, unless or until some of the conceptual roots that support such competing views are better exposed.

As a first stab in this direction, we mean to promote the idea that many of the invisible roots of contemporary, domain-specific accounts run straight to the heart of contemporary poststructuralist or postmodern thinking (Chandler, 1997). This case is most clearly made in reference to current modularist views in the area of cognitive and epistemic development. Here the opposition between domain-specific and domain-general views in psychology mirrors, in many important respects, a similar debate in contemporary philosophical circles where relatively new-on-the-ground postmodernist arguments—favoring contextually rich and situation-specific notions of the human condition—are pitted against more modernist explanations or so-called *grand narratives* (Lyotard, 1979). That is, because of their subsumptive ambitions, any and all domain-general views tend to be discounted by their critics as just-so stories or secularized versions of tales of divine providence (Chandler, 1997; Chandler, Lalonde, & Sokol, 2000).

Domain-specific accounts of moral development, although not as straightforwardly postmodern as their theory-theory counterparts, nevertheless build their own distinct platform using some of the same planks. The most explicit of these shared parts is a common commitment to seeing multiples where others have seen only singularities. Turiel and coworkers, for example, are critical of the "globalist" assertions and emphasis on "core cognitive structures" (Turiel, 1983b, p. 67) that they find in both Kohlberg's theory and Piaget's early writings. On their alternative view, multiple aspects of children's sociomoral functioning demonstrate distinct developmental trajectories and delimited domains of knowledge that should not be regarded as *structurally* interdependent, but only as *informationally* related (see e.g., Turiel, 1979, p. 102). Although they in fact credit their position to Piaget's later writings (e.g., Piaget's [1964/1967] *Six Psychological Studies*) and even consider it to be in close alignment with contemporary currents of the Piagetian enterprise, their unyielding emphasis on "domains" and "separate developmental sequences" (Turiel, 1983b, pp. 74–75), when juxtaposed with recent modularist moves in the theories-of-mind literature, are easily swept together as instances of one and the same postmodern expression that "all grand narratives are dead" (Lyotard, 1979). Regardless of whether exactly the same sentiments toward Piaget are shared by both domain theorists of moral development and theory theorists of mind (and clearly they are not), when viewed from afar they all appear to fall onto the same side of the unity–modularity antinomy that currently divides the field.

The pendulum swing in the study of cognitive and moral development from abstract, general, and modern, on the one hand, to the contextual, domain-specific, and postmodern, on the other—that is, from a broad view of structure to a narrower view—is not an isolated event and is perhaps best seen as a much broader "habit," as Nietzsche (1988) put it, "of seeing opposites," than as the inevitable consequence of any fair reading of the available evidence. Rather, as we mean to argue, the present clash between domain-general and domain-specific frameworks, especially as this debate has played out with regard to cognitive structures, is a debate that need not have happened, but did, all because of a kind of category mistake that collapses the distinction between formal analyses, or abstract claims about logical and necessary relationships, and more functional explanations that deal primarily with causal and empirical relationships between mental structures. Further, even if it were true that opposing domain-general and domain-specific theories formed our only two alterna-tives, it would still be a mistake to cast Piaget and his theory as the para-digm instance of all things general and global. Far from holding down an extreme corner of this debate, Piaget actually provided the possibility of a third way (or *tertium quid*; see Smith, 1993) that allows for the negotiation of a middle ground between the extremes of the present either/or polemic in which the general and specific are too often portrayed in mutually ex-clusive terms. To make any kind of explanatory headway in this direction, however, something more must first be said about the often ambiguous meaning of the term *structure* and its various usages in descriptions of how mental and moral life might relate.

PART II: "I BEHELD THE EARTH, AND, LO, IT WAS WITHOUT FORM"

In view of the fact that much of 20th-century developmental psychology was given over to still unfinished debates about what has or should be meant by talk of mental structures, there is no hope of detailing, let alone arbitrating, such disagreements here. One way to understand all of these still contentious claims, however, is to cut them in half by distinguishing between what we call *functional*, or antecedent-consequence accounts, on the one hand, and *formalist* or *reconstructive* (Habermas, 1979) accounts, on the other. Drawing on this distinction, what can be said with reasonable confidence is that, at least for some of these contenders (i.e., the func-tionalists), talk of mental structures is typically invoked as a way to point to presumptive hidden causes of manifest behavior, whereas others (i.e., the formalists) have aimed to explicate or elucidate patterned relations seen to obtain between events.

Structures of the first sort are earmarked here as *functional* in character to bring out the fact that they are meant to explain why a range of phenotypically diverse behaviors might arrive more or less simulta-neously on the ontological scene by regarding them all as children of a common parent (Chandler, 1991). That is, by these lights, particular fami-lies of concrete actions are seen as the mechanical consequence (or effects) of the inner workings of some common, but invisible, material structure or hidden mechanism situated within the black box of the mind—mecha-nisms that, working in conjunction with local circumstances and con-straints, literally produce what happens next. On such accounts, structure stands apart from and behind manifest behaviors while forming part of a broad causal nexus that functions to put into practice the actions that we, as behavioral scientists, actually record.

By contrast, descriptions of structures of the second and more reconstructive sort that we have labeled *formalistic* is not antecedent-consequence talk about presumptive empirical relations of cause and effect, but is meant instead to mark out or elucidate constitutive relations of identification—relations that hold between wholes and parts, or tokens and types—that, once specified, give new and more unified interpretive meanings to the otherwise seemingly disparate behaviors in question. They aim to do this not by specifying what mechanically causes what, but by explicating the kind or type of individual we are presumably dealing with—someone who could be more or less counted on to behave in the future in ways that are consistent with the characterization on offer. This reconstructive process is seen to involve a kind of boot strapping that takes the form of sifting imaginatively through events and *abductively abstracting* (Peirce, 1931) formal or logical relations that are thought to mark family resemblances or patterned relations between actions whose like-mindedness might otherwise go unnoticed. As such, structures of this formalistic sort are part of the taxonomy of action and are not meant to reference anything outside of such actions. On this reading, "structures" are not reified entities operating (functioning) behind the back of concrete actions, but represent instead epistemic tools employed by researchers, and sometimes by their research subjects, to imaginatively organize features of human lives. Although formal structures, by this way of reckoning, do not actually cause anything, or at least not in any traditional mechanical sense, they are nevertheless understood by many (e.g., Chandler, 1991; Dennett, 1987; Hanson, 1958; Marr, 1982; Overton, 1998) to represent a necessary part of what is a full complement of explanatory tools in the sciences, in general, and the developmental sciences, in particular.

The immediate use to which we mean to put this functionalist–formalist distinction is as a tool in our own efforts to better sort out what Piaget and others have said, and presumably meant, about the relation between mental and moral life, in general, and the question of domain specificity, in particular. The most appropriate place to open this bid for greater clarity is with still one more candidate exegesis of what Piaget really meant by talk of *structures*, moral and otherwise.

According to Chapman (1988),

> Piaget's use of the term "structure" is characterized by a certain ambiguity. On the one hand, "structure" may refer to *formal* properties of a certain type of thinking. . . . On the other hand, Piaget believed that cognitive structures of this kind possess a *functional* reality. . . . Thus, when Piaget described two different performances as examples of the "same" structure, he could have been saying merely that they have the same formal properties, or he could have been making the stronger statement that they are the observable manifestations of the same functional organization. (p. 343; italics added)

Although all of this is perhaps important, and lends some potential le-
gitimacy to both functional and formalistic readings of Piaget's work, it
amounts to more of a restatement of the problem than a solution. Still, it
does serve as a caution to those who are perhaps too quick to pick and
choose among their favorite Piagetian bits and pieces in an effort to add
borrowed authority to their claims—especially those who, in Chapman's
(1988) words, recklessly "assimilated Piaget's structural-stage theory to
their own functionalist approach" (p. 363). Among those who stand accused of such reckless handling is, somewhat ironically, Kohlberg (see
Carpendale, 2000; Youniss & Damon, 1992), whose work on children's
moral development is commonly seen to have otherwise done more for
the Piagetian cause in North America than any other (Lapsley, 1996).

Kohlberg is said to be guilty of having employed an exclusively functionalist reading of Piaget's formulation of structure, and particularly his
account of general stages in cognitive development, as stepping stones to
the conclusion that children's thinking in one content area, such as their
reasoning about the physical world, is necessarily functionally related to
their reasoning in other areas, such as morality, all because they are both
regarded as equivalent effects of the same common causal structure. On
this view, which is the familiar domain-general interpretation of Piaget's
theory, both physical and moral reasoning are understood as borrowing
from a single underlying cognitive architecture that, when brought to bear
on problems in one or the other content area, should (all other things being equal) generate similarly organized judgments. According to this
functional reading, any evident changes in one area of reasoning should
be reflected automatically in all others because each is thought to be
grounded in a single operative structure.

It was precisely this logic that led Kohlberg to formulate his famous
"necessary-but-not-sufficient" hypothesis (Colby & Kohlberg, 1987, p. 13),
in which progress in children's physical reasoning (e.g., from preoperational to concrete-operational thinking) is seen as a necessary conceptual
prerequisite to attaining higher levels of moral reasoning. If one were to accept Kohlberg's more functionalistic reading of Piaget, it follows that the
question of how children's intellectual or conceptual development relates
to moral reasoning is to be answered in straightforward causal terms. Just
as obviously, and on the same reading, if available evidence proves that
there are important disjunctures between different sectors of children's
moral and secular deliberations, such evidence could be viewed as an important disconfirmation of any functionalist, domain-general view. There
are, however, good reasons to be suspicious of such functionalist answers.

One of the strongest cautions against such exclusively functionalist interpretations of Piaget's theory comes again from Chapman (1988), who
argued that just because "Piaget recognized the same formal structure to

characterize thinking in different areas of content does not imply that these areas are united in any single functional totality" (p. 346). There is in fact little to suggest that Piaget subscribed to any such *unity thesis* (Flanagan, 1991) in his attempts to order the many varieties of children's thinking, moral or otherwise. In fact, not only does Piaget's work fail to fit such a domain-general description, but so too does the work of most others.[1] It seems pure lain instances of what could be called domain-general accounts of cognition exist primarily in textbooks.

Important, for our argument, functional accounts, with their antecedent-consequence structure, do not exhaust the ways that distinctive forms of moral and secular reasoning might relate. In addition to, or in the place of, such *functional unities*, there are also *formal analogies* (Chapman, 1988, pp. 343–346), of which Piaget's "logic is the morality of thought" mantra can be read as a prime example. On this reading, the relationship between logic and morality is rooted in the common organizing principle that Piaget claimed could be seen as running through both individual and social activities (see Smith, 1995), and not, as is widely assumed, as a result of causal linkages between the two. That is, the "general logic" that Piaget (1965/1995) argued is "common to both social and individual actions" (p. 94)—the so-called *structure* that joins children's sociomoral and private-epistemic lives—is not, as he reminded us, "a logic in itself" or any other material entity that serves some causal or "legislative" function. Rather, it merely represents a "form of equilibrium immanent in . . . these actions themselves" (Piaget, 1965/1995, p. 94). It should be clear from the foregoing that Piaget is speaking of a formalistic concept—an idealized principle of equilibrium—that, although giving common meaning to parallel processes, is not the same as insisting they are functionally one and the same (see Kitchener, 1981).

Still as Piaget's own theory would seem to predict, contemporary developmentalists as a whole, and the majority of those caught up in talk of domains in particular, have been quick to assimilate his formalistic views to their own more functional schemas of understanding. That is, despite numerous reminders (e.g., Brown, 1988; Chandler, 1991; Chapman, 1988; Overton, 1991) or direct warnings (Flavell, 1962) to hold "in abeyance [our] habitual ways of looking at things" (p. 16) and to be generally prepared, when reading Piaget's theory, to face "epistemological concerns foreign to [our] experience . . . [and] methods different from those we would [commonly] espouse," there remains, as Lourenço (2001) recently observed, a collective "tendency to reify and convert into functional enti-

---

[1]For a rare counterexample, see Anderson (1983), who claimed explicitly that "all the higher cognitive processes, such as memory, language, problem solving, imagery, deduction, and induction, are manifestations of the same underlying system" (p. 1).

ties what at its best is simple descriptive metaphors" (p. 98). This bad habit of transforming all talk of structure into functional structures and causal entities—or as Lourenço (2001) would say, "to equate analogies to homologies" (p. 107)—has led to countless misreadings of Piaget's work, not the least of which has been to think that abstract and theoretical conceptions of structure were ever imagined by him to exist apart from practical activity or just plain action in general.

PART III: "AND THE THIRD DAY HE SHALL RISE AGAIN"

In an attempt to distance themselves from functionalist readings of mental structures that seem to inevitably veer toward the more static and disembodied, and to better capture instead the dynamism of Piaget's view, a number of scholars (e.g., Boesch, 1984; Chapman, 1988; Kitchener, 1985; Overton, 1998; Smith, 1995; Youniss, 1978, 1981) have shifted their attention away from an exploration of structures to "*action* as the [primary] unit of analysis" (Smith, 1995, p. 12; italics added). They do so, they are quick to stress, on the grounds that Piaget was never a structuralist in the functionalist terms just outlined. Rather he was first and foremost an action theorist—or as Boesch (1984) qualified, "the main action theorist in development[al] psychology" (p. 173). Both of these claims need some serious defending.

Although at times maddeningly ambiguous, Piaget (1932/1965) was uncharacteristically clear in his rejection of any view that treats structure like a static, ready-made mechanism that "straightaway organizes the contents of consciousness" or allows it to serve as a disembodied "principle from which concrete actions can be deduced" (p. 399). As such children's reasoning is not, at least on Piaget's view, what Kohlberg and many others have proposed: "the application of a logical rule to derive a solution" (Carpendale, 2000, p. 187). Such a reified or static view of mental logic, it is argued, puts the functionalist cart before the actionable horse. Instead the logic or structure that Piaget evokes necessarily remains embedded in the action sequence itself—that is, it comes neither before nor after, but during action. Structure is, as Piaget said (1932/1965), "implied in the functioning at work" (p. 399) and so cannot be separated from the content out of which it emerges or the activities of which it is a part. Rather than driving a wedge between individuals' thoughts and actions, Piaget never imagined that conceptual structures preceded children's actions (and therefore caused them). Rather such structures are always "immanent" in action. The notion that "thought becomes abstract by becoming *disengaged* from particular actions" (Youniss, 1978, p. 239; italics added), and that such free-floating structures then go on to cause behavior, is in fact quite foreign to Piaget's view.

Taking up such an action perspective, as we encourage here, promises to avoid many of the fundamental confusions surrounding Piaget's complicated views of structure. Specifically, by putting action in the interpretive driver's seat, we are now in a better position to steer clear of the functionalist tendency to reify cognitive structures and transform them all into causal mechanical entities. Moreover, action also helps us clarify the often-murky relations between form and content in Piaget's theory. If, as Chapman (1988) argued, form and content are seen by Piaget to be inseparable, with "structure . . . immanent in the content structured" (p. 346), and, if structure is "implied in the functioning at work," as Piaget (1932/1965, p. 399) tried to make clear, then to argue, as functional theorists often do, that form or structure governs particular content-laden actions ends up amounting to the paradoxical claim that structure causes itself.

As potentially helpful as all of this may seem to be by your standard action theorist, some would regard attempts to rub out all references to the notion of structure, and simply replace them with action terms, as the equivalent of jumping from frying pan to fire. That is, despite the good things to say in its favor, the notion of *action* alone does not solve all our conceptual problems. This is because, as Dewey pointed out more than half a century ago (Dewey & Bentley, 1949/1960; see also Garrison, 2001; Handy, 1973), the concept of action, much like the notion of structure, also has two different meanings—meanings that change as easily as attaching the seemingly benign prefixes of *inter* and *trans*. Of these two, *inter*action has the deepest functionalist roots. As Meacham (1977) pointed out: "Interaction assumes elements can be located and described independently of one another . . . [and that] each element acts causally upon the others within some organization" (p. 264). The counterpart notion of *trans*action, by contrast, has an altogether more formalistic set of connotations and generally refers to the idealized spaces in between such material elements. That is, the so-called *individual elements* in a transactional relationship do not exist independently from each other, but are, as Meacham (1977) claimed, "derived as secondary categories within the transactional system" (p. 264). He went on to take up the transactional activity of buyer and seller as a metaphoric means to illustrate this symbiotic union. The "activity of exchange," he argued, once it is assumed as primary, serves to define and distinguish the separate elements of buyer and seller. Without such an assumption of activity, *buyer* and *seller* would cease to be meaningful terms.[2]

---

[2]Although buyers and sellers are useful here to clarify the meaning of transactional models, Sameroff and Chandler (1975) provided a more developmental example in which *infants* and *caregivers* are the two terms being defined in a relational network.

There is growing consensus (e.g., Kitchener, 1985, 1996; Riegel & Mea-cham, 1978), at least as it applies to Piaget's theory, that references to *action* are primarily of this transactional, as opposed to interactional, variety. The "ultimately real" for Piaget, as Kitchener (1996) suggests, "are the basic transactions between individuals, or between individual and environment" (p. 245), not one or the other of these terms in isolation. Indeed one of the more radical upshots of this view is that "there are simply no separate, enduring entities independent of their relations" (Kitchener, 1985, p. 287). For this reason, Youniss (1978, 1980, 1981, 1987) and his colleagues (Davidson & Youniss, 1995; Youniss & Damon, 1992) began to reinterpret Piaget's views on children's social development, in general, and his (1932/1965) volume *Moral Judgment of the Child*, in particular, from what Furth (1969) first described as a *relational* framework (see also Overton, 1998), in which "self and other as isolated entities are denied in favor of relations" (Youniss, 1978, p. 245).

A central assumption on this more relational reading of Piaget is that "forms of interactions [sic] constitute social existence" (Youniss, 1981, p. 192). As such, "if there is a logic [or structure] in social or moral thought," according to Youniss (1978, p. 238), it cannot be found in the abstract grouping of disembodied mental principles (i.e., in so-called *stages* of reasoning) as Kohlberg and so many others have subsequently come to accept. Rather, such logical structure must be located in the *relations* or *systems of relations* in which children actually engage.

This line of reasoning has led those who adopt such a relational view to re-read Piaget's descriptions of children's heteronomous and autonomous forms of morality, not as hard and fast developmental *stages* as Kohlberg and others would have it, but as "simultaneous but separate spheres" (Youniss & Damon, 1992, p. 275) of patterned activity in children's social lives. More specifically, the alternative view that Youniss and his colleagues have worked to float "builds a systematic case for two streams of development" (Youniss & Damon, 1992, p. 270)—streams that take their distinct forms from either the *unilateral* authority relations that children have with parents and other adults or from more cooperative *reciprocal* relations they establish with members of their own peer group. Viewed in these terms, the actual degrees of separation dividing such accounts of unilateral and reciprocal prescriptive relations, on the one hand, and the moral and conventional areas promoted by domain theorists, on the other, become small to vanishing. This is all the more the case because, as Wright (1982) pointed out, Piaget's position is "a good deal more complex" than a simple shift from unilateral "this" to reciprocal "that" (see also Nucci, chap. 10, this volume). Rather, Piaget generally saw these two contrasting modes of relating to others as providing only idealized anchor points on a densely populated continuum of intermediate relational forms. None of the points on this continuum, as Piaget (1932/1965) remarked, stands entirely on its own: "constraint is never unadulterated . . . and conversely cooperation is never absolutely pure" (p. 84). Still as Piaget would have it, young children's relationships are, at first, more often dominated by authority figures of some kind, and so early forms of moral reasoning tend to reflect (although are certainly not wedded to) a heteronomic bent of rigidity and blind obedience to the letter of the law. As the balance of children's relationships shift to include more and more friendships with peers and other cooperative activities, their value system becomes more autonomous and begins to reflect a flexible stance toward the negotiation of rules that better fit the spirit of fairness and justice. All this suggests, as Fowler (1998) described, that "for Piaget, advances in moral thought should not be solely attributed to qualitative advances in domain general thought," but rather to "a shift in the locus of knowledge construction from the world of adult/child relations to peer relations" (p. 285).

What is especially remarkable about all this talk of action-based, relational perspectives of Piaget's work, and particularly the alternative impression it provides of the *Moral Judgment of the Child* (1932/1965), is not only the significant shift of emphases it encourages from the internal and private cognitive structures of children to the more social and dynamic patterns of transactional activity seen to constitute their social lives. Nor is it merely a new appreciation that, whatever else Kohlberg might have done to promote a Piagetian look at moral development, he almost certainly distorted the original meaning of Piaget's words to fit his own brand of structuralism, effectively turning "Piaget's proposed developmental relation on its head" (Youniss & Damon, 1992, p. 277; see also Wright, 1982) by focusing not on children's practical activities and relationships, but almost exclusively on what Piaget (1932/1965, p. 174ff.) derisively argued was a more alienated form of "theoretical knowledge." No, neither of these, although important, is it.

Rather, what is especially remarkable here is that by choosing, on good authority, to: (a) read Piaget's structural claims as more formalistic than functional; (b) restore action to its original place of centrality in his theory; and (c) clarify the fundamental differences between *trans*actions versus *inter*actions, one can actually succeed in these three easy steps to not only resurrect the notion of action-based structures in their intended social-relational context, but to also promote an alternative reading of the *Moral Judgment of the Child* (1932/1965) that actively supports, rather than competes with, domain-specific accounts of moral development. That is, armed now with the suggestion that Piaget was actually aiming to capture "two [distinct] streams" in children's construction of the social world, and with the idea that, despite their opposing currents, both heteronomous and autonomous valuation strategies can exist "simultaneously" in the child's mind and even be expressed at "a very early age" (Youniss & Damon, 1992, p. 276), we seem to arrive at a conceptual place that makes room for all the compelling evidence in support of domain specificity without imagining that the only road to accomplishing all of this is one that bypasses Piaget's otherwise remarkable theoretical insights. In support of this alternative strategy, it is noteworthy that, although Turiel and his colleagues do not typically feature the existence of different relationships per se as a means to account for the differential patterns in which children construct their social and moral knowledge, they clearly explain that different social "objects" have a distinct impact on this constructive process. For instance, central to Turiel's own claim about the development of distinct domains of knowledge is the notion that ". . . interactions with fundamentally different types of objects should result in the formation of distinct conceptual frameworks" (Turiel, 1979, p. 108) and, even more pointedly, that ". . . the constellation of social interactions associated with moral events . . . differ from that associated with events of a conventional nature" (Turiel, 1983a, p. 44). At least in our own view such a re-reading of Piaget's theory offers a better alternative than the module-bedecked, neo-nativist path currently pursued by many contemporary theory theorists.

Of course there is always the possibility that some in the "habit of seeing opposites" will try to push these issues too far and perhaps begin to imagine that Piaget was somehow a modular theorist in disguise or was, after all, a closet postmodern thinker. Such a pendulum swing from one side to the other of the various antinomies we have worked to detail would hardly do justice to Piaget's rich and carefully articulated views. Nor is such an about face necessary if the hierarchical system of formal and functional levels of analysis we have offered are seen as complementary as opposed to conflicting viewpoints. Be this as it may, what we can say with some confidence is that as long as the only choices offered are those between the general and particular—a Hobson's choice between disconnected islands of pure structure and pedestrian practice—there will always be bridges needing to be built, and they will always prove to be a bridge too far.

REFERENCES

Anderson, J. (1983). *The architecture of cognition*. Cambridge: Harvard University Press.
Baird, J. A., & Sokol, B. W. (Eds.). (in press). *Mind, morals, and action: The interface between children's theories of mind and socio-moral development*. San Francisco: Jossey-Bass.
Boesch, E. E. (1984). The development of affective schemata. *Human Development, 27,* 173–182.
Brown, T. (1988). Ships in the night: Piaget and American cognitive science. *Human Development, 31,* 60–64.

Carpendale, J. I. M. (2000). Kohlberg and Piaget on stages of moral reasoning. *Developmental Review, 20,* 181–205.

Chandler, M. J. (1991). Alternative readings of the competence-performance relation. In M. Chandler & M. Chapman (Eds.), *Criteria for competence: Controversies in the conceptualization and assessment of children's abilities* (pp. 5–18). Hillsdale, NJ: Lawrence Erlbaum Associates.

Chandler, M. J. (1997). Stumping for progress in a post-modern world. In K. A. Renninger & E. Amsel (Eds.), *Change and development: Issues of theory, method, and application* (pp. 1–26). Mahwah, NJ: Lawrence Erlbaum Associates.

Chandler, M. J., Lalonde, C. E., & Sokol, B. W. (2000). Continuities of selfhood in the face of radical developmental and cultural change. In L. P. Nucci, G. B. Saxe, & E. Turiel (Eds.), *Culture, thought, and development* (pp. 65–84). Mahwah, NJ: Lawrence Erlbaum Associates.

Chandler, M. J., & Sokol, B. W. (2003). Level this, level that: The place of culture in the construction of the self. In C. Raeff & J. Benson (Eds.), *Social and cognitive development in the context of individual, social, and cultural processes* (pp. 191–216).

Chandler, M. J., & Sokol, B. W. (in press). Level this, level that: The place of culture in the construction of the self. In C. Raeff & J. B. Benson (Eds.), *Culture and development: Essays in honor of Ina Uzgiris.* New York: Routledge.

Chandler, M. J., Sokol, B. W., & Hallett, D. (2001). Moral responsibility and the interpretive turn: Children's changing conceptions of truth and rightness. In B. F. Malle, L. J. Moses, & D. A. Baldwin (Eds.), *Intentions and intentionality: Foundations of social cognition* (pp. 345–365). Cambridge: MIT Press.

Chandler, M. J., Sokol, B. W., & Wainryb, C. (2000). Beliefs about truth and beliefs about rightness. *Child Development, 71,* 91–97.

Chapman, M. (1988). *Constructive evolution: Origins and development of Piaget's thought.* Cambridge, England: Cambridge University Press.

Colby, A., & Kohlberg, L. (1987). *The measurement of moral judgment: Vol. 1. Theoretical foundations and research validation.* New York: Cambridge University Press.

Davidson, P., & Youniss, J. (1995). Moral development and social construction. In W. M. Kurtines & J. L. Gewirtz (Eds.), *Moral development: An introduction* (pp. 289–310). Boston: Allyn & Bacon.

Dennett, D. C. (1987). *The intentional stance.* Cambridge, MA: MIT Press.

Dewey, J., & Bentley, A. F. (1960). *Knowing and the known.* Boston: Beacon. (Original work published 1949)

Flanagan, O. (1991). *The science of the mind* (2nd ed.). Cambridge, MA: MIT Press.

Flavell, J. H. (1962). Historical and bibliographic note. In W. Kessen & C. Kuhlman (Eds.), *Thought in the young child* (Vol. 27). *Monographs of the Society for Research in Child Development,* Serial No. 83.

Fowler, R. C. (1998). Limiting the domain account of early moral judgment by challenging its critique of Piaget. *Merrill-Palmer Quarterly, 44,* 263–292.

Furth, H. G. (1969). *Piaget and knowledge: Theoretical foundations.* Englewood Cliffs, NJ: Prentice-Hall.

Garrison, J. (2001). An introduction to Dewey's theory of functional "trans-action": An alternative paradigm for activity theory. *Mind, Culture, and Activity, 8,* 275–296.

Gelman, R., & Baillergeon, R. (1983). A review of some Piagetian concepts. In J. H. Flavell & E. M. Markman (Eds.), *Handbook of child psychology* (pp. 167–230). New York: Wiley.

Glassman, M., & Zan, B. (1995). Moral activity and domain theory: An alternative interpretation of research with young children. *Developmental Review, 15,* 434–457.

Gopnik, A. (1993). How we know our minds: The illusion of first-person knowledge of intentionality. *Behavioral & Brain Sciences, 16,* 1–14.

Gopnik, A., & Wellman, H. M. (1994). The theory theory. In L. A. Hirschfeld & S. A. Gelman (Eds.), *Mapping the mind: Domain specificity in cognition and culture* (pp. 257–293). Cambridge, England: Cambridge University Press.

Habermas, J. (1979). *Communication and the evolution of society*. Boston: Beacon.

Handy, R. (1973). The Dewey–Bentley transactional procedures of inquiry. *Psychological Record, 23*, 305–317.

Hanson, N. R. (1958). *Patterns of discovery*. New York: Cambridge University Press.

Hirschfeld, L. A., & Gelman, S. A. (1994). Toward a topography of mind: An introduction to domain specificity. In L. A. Hirschfeld & S. A. Gelman (Eds.), *Mapping the mind: Domain specificity in cognition and culture* (pp. 3–35). Cambridge, England: Cambridge University Press.

Kitchener, R. F. (1981). Piaget's social psychology. *Journal for the Theory of Social Behavior, 11*, 253–277.

Kitchener, R. F. (1985). Holistic structuralism, elementarism, and Piaget's theory of "relationalism." *Human Development, 28*, 281–294.

Kitchener, R. F. (1996). The nature of the social for Piaget and Vygotsky. *Human Development, 39*, 243–249.

Kohlberg, L. (1981). *The philosophy of moral development: Moral stages and the idea of justice (Essays on Moral Development, Vol. 1)*. San Francisco: Harper & Row.

Kohlberg, L. (1984). *The psychology of moral development: The nature and validity of moral stages (Essays on Moral Development, Vol. 2)*. San Francisco: Harper & Row.

Lapsley, D. K. (1996). *Moral psychology*. Boulder, CO: Westview.

Lourenço, O. (2001). The danger of words: A Wittgensteinian lesson for developmentalists. *New Ideas in Psychology, 19*, 89–115.

Lourenço, O. (2002, August). *Ten capital sins in Turiel's domain approach*. Paper presented at the 17th biennial meeting of The International Society for the Study of Behavioural Development, Ottawa, Canada.

Lourenço, O. (2003). Making sense of Turiel's dispute with Kohlberg: The case of the child's moral competence. *New Ideas in Psychology, 21*, 43–68.

Lyotard, J. F. (1979). *The postmodern condition: A report on knowledge*. Minneapolis: University of Minnesota Press.

Marr, D. (1982). *Vision: A computational investigation into the human representation and processing of visual information*. New York: W. H. Freeman.

Meacham, J. (1977). A transactional model of remembering. In N. Datan & H. W. Reese (Eds.), *Life-span developmental psychology: Dialectical perspectives on experimental research* (pp. 261–284). New York: Academic.

Meltzoff, A. (1999). Origins of theory of mind, cognition and communication. *Journal of Communication Disorders, 32*, 251–269.

Moshman, D. (1998). Identity as a theory of oneself. *The Genetic Epistemologist, 26*(3), 1–9.

Nietzsche, F. (1988). *A Nietzsche reader* (R. J. Hollingdale, Ed.). London: Penguin.

Overton, W. F. (1991). Competence, procedures, and hardware: Conceptual and empirical consideration. In M. Chandler & M. Chapman (Eds.), *Criteria for competence: Controversies in the conceptualization and assessment of children's abilities* (pp. 19–42). Hillsdale, NJ: Lawrence Erlbaum Associates.

Overton, W. F. (1998). Developmental psychology: Philosophy, concepts, and methodology. In W. Damon (Series Ed.) & R. M. Lerner (Vol. Ed.), *The handbook of child psychology: Vol. 1. Theoretical models of human development* (5th ed., pp. 107–188). New York: Wiley.

Peirce, C. (1931). *Collected papers of Charles Sanders Peirce* (C. Hartshorne & P. Weiss, Eds.). Cambridge, MA: Harvard University Press.

Piaget, J. (1965). *The moral judgment of the child* (M. Gabain, Trans.). New York: The Free Press. (Original work published 1932)

Piaget, J. (1967). *Six psychological studies*. New York: Vintage. (Original work published 1964)

Piaget, J. (1981). *Intelligence and affectivity*. Palo Alto, CA: Annual Review. (Original work published 1954)

Piaget, J. (1995). *Sociological studies*. London: Routledge. (Original work published 1965)

Rest, J., Narvaez, D., Bebeau, M. J., & Thoma, S. J. (1999). *Postconventional moral thinking: A neo-Kohlbergian approach.* Mahwah, NJ: Lawrence Erlbaum Associates.

Riegel, K. F., & Meacham, J. A. (1978). Dialectics, transaction, and Piaget's theory. In L. A. Pervin & M. Lewis (Eds.), *Perspectives in interactional psychology* (pp. 23–47). New York: Plenum.

Rozin, P. (1990). Development in the food domain. *Developmental Psychology, 26,* 555–562.

Sameroff, A. J., & Chandler, M. J. (1975). Reproductive risk and the continuum of caretaking causality. In F. D. Horowitz (Ed.), *Review of child development research* (Vol. 4, pp. 187–244). Chicago: University of Chicago Press.

Smith, L. (1993). *Necessary knowledge: Piagetian perspectives on constructivism.* Hove, England: Lawrence Erlbaum Associates.

Smith, L. (1995). Introduction to Piaget's *Sociological Studies.* In L. Smith (Ed.), *Sociological studies* (pp. 1–22). London: Routledge.

Spelke, E. S. (1991). Physical knowledge in infancy. In S. Carey & R. Gelman (Eds.), *The epigenesis of mind: Essays on biology and cognition* (pp. 133–169). Hillsdale, NJ: Lawrence Erlbaum Associates.

Springer, K., & Keil, F. C. (1989). On the development of biologically specific beliefs: The case of inheritance. *Child Development, 60,* 637–648.

Turiel, E. (1979). Distinct conceptual and developmental domains: Social convention and morality. In H. E. Howe & C. B. Keasey (Eds.), *Nebraska Symposium on Motivation, 1977: Social Cognitive Development* (Vol. 25, pp. 77–116). Lincoln: University of Nebraska Press.

Turiel, E. (1983a). *The development of social knowledge: Morality and convention.* Cambridge: Cambridge University Press.

Turiel, E. (1983b). Domains and categories in social-cognitive development. In W. F. Overton (Ed.), *The relationship between social and cognitive development* (pp. 53–89). Hillsdale, NJ: Lawrence Erlbaum Associates.

Turiel, E. (1998). The development of morality. In W. Damon (Series Ed.) and N. Eisenberg (Vol. Ed.), *The handbook of child psychology: Vol. 3. Social, emotional, and personality development* (5th ed., pp. 863–932). New York: Wiley.

Turiel, E. (2002). *The culture of morality: Social development, context, and conflict.* Cambridge: Cambridge University Press.

Turiel, E., & Davidson, P. (1986). Heterogeneity, inconsistency, and asynchrony in the development of cognitive structures. In I. Levin (Ed.), *Stage and structure: Reopening the debate* (pp. 106–143). Norword, NJ: Ablex.

Turiel, E., Hildebrandt, C., & Wainryb, C. (1991). Judging social issues: Difficulties, inconsistencies, and consistencies. *Monographs of the Society for Research in Child Development,* Vol. 56 (Serial 224).

Turiel, E., Killen, M., & Helwig, C. C. (1987). Morality: Its structure, functions, and vagaries. In J. Kagan & S. Lamb (Eds.), *The emergence of moral concepts in young children* (pp. 155–244). Chicago: University of Chicago Press.

Twain, M. (1935). *Notebook* (prepared by A. B. Paine). New York: Harper.

Wellman, H. M., & Gelman, S. A. (1992). Cognitive development: Foundational theories of core domains. *Annual Review of Psychology, 43,* 337–375.

Wellman, H. M., & Gelman, S. A. (1998). Knowledge acquisition in foundational domains. In W. Damon (Series Ed.) & D. Kuhn & R. Siegler (Vol. Eds.), *The handbook of child psychology: Vol. 2. Cognition, perception and language* (5th ed., pp. 523–573). New York: Wiley.

Wright, D. (1982). Piaget's theory of moral development. In S. Modgil & C. Modgil (Eds.), *Jean Piaget: Consensus and controversy* (pp. 207–217). London: Holt, Rinehart, & Winston.

Wynn, K. (1995). Infants possess a system of numerical knowledge. *Current Directions in Psychological Science, 4,* 172–177.

Youniss, J. (1978). Dialectical theory and Piaget on social knowledge. *Human Development, 21,* 234–247.

Youniss, J. (1980). *Parents and peers in social development*. Chicago: University of Chicago Press.

Youniss, J. (1981). A revised interpretation of Piaget (1932). In I. E. Sigel, D. M. Brodzinsky, & R. M. Golinkoff (Eds.), *New directions in Piagetian theory and practice* (pp. 191–201). Hillsdale, NJ: Lawrence Erlbaum Associates.

Youniss, J. (1987). Social construction and moral development: Update and expansion of an idea. In W. M. Kurtines & J. L. Gewirtz (Eds.), *Moral development through social interaction* (pp. 131–148). New York: Wiley.

Youniss, J., & Damon, W. (1992). Social construction in Piaget's theory. In H. Beilin & P. Pufall (Eds.), *Piaget's theory: Prospects and possibilities* (pp. 267–286). Hillsdale, NJ: Lawrence Erlbaum Associates.

Developmental Epistemology and Education

Leslie Smith
Lancaster University

Several distinctions cut across the argument in this chapter. One concerns individual and social contributions to cognitive development (Chapman, 1999). Another deals with causal and normative contributions to cognitive development (Bickhard, 2002). Underlying both is the ambiguity of "cognitive development." What I address in this chapter are some of the key features of a unitary framework combining individual and social contributions in a jointly causal and normative account. The argument is in two steps. One deals with development in psychology and epistemology. The proposal is for a developmental epistemology that is distinctive in two ways: (a) both individual and social elements are co-instantiated in a process of knowing, and (b) this process is empirical with both causal and normative elements. The other step deals with education interpreted through this framework. Learning through teaching is a paradigm case of social interaction. So the second step is to show how the general framework fits this paradigm case.

DEVELOPMENTAL PSYCHOLOGY AND DEVELOPMENTAL EPISTEMOLOGY

The terms *cognitive* and *development* are ubiquitous in the titles of well-known books (e.g., Flavell, Miller, & Miller, 1993; Piaget, 1985; cf. Lourenço & Machado, 1996). However, there is ambiguity here. Children's minds develop under different causal conditions. Knowledge develops on the basis of normative reason. A unitary account should deal with both (Smith, 2003). In fact research in developmental psychology has been preoccupied with the former without parity of regard for the latter. This preoccupation was not lost on Piaget (1963) in his Foreword to Flavell's commentary. There continues to be a significant omission with no unitary interpretation of causality and normativity in most accounts (cf. Bickhard, 2002; Brown, 1996). In this section, I propose some principles for a reconciling framework covering both the causal basis of children's development and the normative basis of the development of knowledge.

Developmental Psychology and Epistemology

The discussion in this section is in two parts. One marks out a reconciling framework. The other sets out a general argument for developmental epistemology.

Reconciling Interpretation. There is an elegant view under which the difference between psychology and epistemology is exclusive (they are polar opposites) and exhaustive (there is no mediator). Psychology deals with causal origins. Epistemology deals with normative grounds. Reichenbach (1961) dubbed this the "two contexts" of knowledge—a context of discovery in causal psychology and a context of justification in logic. The assumption is that logic is the normative (formal) science of truth with epistemology regarded as a similarly normative discipline. These contexts are interpreted to be mutually exclusive and collectively exhaustive and provide a basis for the *genetic fallacy* (Sainsbury, 1991). This fallacy is committed when an account about the origin (discovery) of knowledge in psychology is presented as an account of the truth of what is known (justification). Thus are causal and normative disciplines independent.

This elegant view exacts a price. Psychology could not—and not merely does not—have anything to say about the legitimation (justification) of human knowledge. If Reichenbach is right, psychology is simply irrelevant. This is a high price to pay for elegance. A key assumption has been made that the distinction psychology–logic maps onto the distinction empirical–normative. This assumption can be challenged. It is worth checking out an alternative view under which causal psychology (CP) and normative epistemology (NE) are exclusive opposites. One is empirical, the other normative. But they are not exhaustive. There is a mediator in developmental epistemology (DE) directed on causal and normative facts. Facts are facts. They are empirical, observable, and testable. They can be scientifically investigated. DE is similar to CP: Both are empirical disciplines. Yet not all facts are causal in that normative facts are noncausal facts. DE is similar to NE: Both deal with norms, but in different ways. NE is the formal study of norms, whereas DE deals with normative facts, which are instantiations of the norms (values) invoked by human agents. Norms have both individual and cultural instantiations and as such are central to human minds in action in social worlds. Normative facts amount to the actual use made by human agents of the norms at their disposal. These uses include initial access to norms, their constitution, and the formation of better norms. DE strictly requires CP in an account of initial access. Yet DE goes beyond CP in also dealing with the actual constitution of a norm along with the development of better norms. This is a normative, and not merely a causal, process. The use of norms amounts to development as the advance from "the causal to the logical" (Piaget, 1995, p. 51). Under this reconciling interpretation, there is a trichotomy, not just a dichotomy. In short, DE has a dual focus on both causal and normative facts and as such is a *tertium quid* or third alternative (Piaget, 1923; see Smith, 1993, p. 36). This position differs from Reichenbach's position in three ways. First, it accepts that the distinction between psychology and logic is exclusive, but denies that it is exhaustive. DE is an empirical discipline (Smith, 2003). Second, it requires a contribution from CP that makes a necessary, but not sufficient, contribution to an account of the development of knowledge (Smith, 1999b). Third, it opens up a new ontology of normative facts. So DE is also a normative discipline (Smith, 2002b).

General Argument. Here is a general argument for this reconciling interpretation:

1. Human knowledge has an empirical origin.
2. Knowledge has normative properties.
3. Knowledge develops.
   therefore
4. Developmental mechanisms have both empirical and normative properties.

Premise 1 states that human knowledge is empirically mediated. This leaves open the specific character of any psychological mediation through either of the two main "lines of development"—in the genome and in the culture (Vygotsky, 1994). This premise is also compatible with Kant's (1933, B1) distinction between experience as "début" and as "derivation." Human knowledge starts with experience at the outset of life, but it is not thereby due to (derived from) experience. The latter requires a "third line." An example would be Piaget's (1985) model of the construction of knowledge through equilibration. Nonmediated knowledge (i.e., knowledge possessed in the absence of its prior acquisition) is ruled out by Premise 1, which requires human knowledge to have an empirical origin. An analogy might help here. Suppose Jo and Sam have a brown tan. This similarity can be due to a causal difference—Jo's sun-tan and Sam's artificial tan (Mele, 1995). Two otherwise identical coins can differ in their normative origin, one being legal tender and the other an illegal counterfeit (Searle, 1999). So it is with the process of knowing generative of true knowledge. The difference between an epistemic process and product was regarded as causal by Bruner (1966), but as normative by Piaget (1950, p. 13). This marks off CP and DE, respectively.

Premise 2 states that knowledge has normative properties. It is through a process of knowing that these norms are used by the knower and these uses are normative facts. All norms are such that, "by a subject's recognising them as valid, they become 'normative facts' " (Piaget, 1966). This is because they are facts "in experience permitting the observation that subject such-and-such considers him- or herself to be obligated by a norm, irrespective of its validity from the observer's point of view" (Piaget, 1950, p. 30). Normative facts are "imperative rules whose origin is in social interactions of all kinds, and which act causally, in their turn, in the context of individual interactions" (Piaget, 1995, p. 69). Notice three points here. One is that this interpretation of *normative facts* means that they have both empirical and normative properties (Smith, 2003). Second, normative facts are empirical without being reducible to causal facts (Smith, 2002b). Third, normative facts not only augment the stock of developmental problems in ontogenesis, but also function in developmental mechanisms. Through their historical use, norms have a future (Smith, 2002a).

Using an autonomy, entailment, intersubjectivity, objectivity, universality (AEIOU) framework, five normative properties of knowledge are reviewed in Table 9.1 using simple examples of mathematical knowledge. This quintet is exemplary rather than comprehensive, in that there is a general class of similar norms covering all human experience. The outstanding problems in each case concerns sequences and mechanism in virtue of which these developmental advances are made.

Premise 3 states that knowledge develops. This is a normative claim which is different from Premise 2. The term *development* implies that the outcome is better than the origin. In this context, *better* means epistemically better in much the way it means morally better in moral contexts. In the ontogenesis of knowledge, the evidence is clear cut (Damon, 1998). If reasoning on the selection task is typical, there is no evidence that infants can succeed, some evidence that children can do so under specifiable conditions, and quite a lot of evidence about adolescents' understanding (Johnson-Laird, 1999).

TABLE 9.1
AEIOU Framework

Variable	Description
Autonomy (Piaget, 1995, p. 60)	• Obedience to reason, which is neither anarchic nor heteronomous • Reasoning because of rules, not reasoning in line with rules • Knowing by reasoned assent, not compliant acceptance • From heteronomy to autonomy
Equality/Entailment (Piaget, 1986, p. 312)	• Knowing "what has to be," knowing what could not be otherwise • Truth with no exceptions because there could not be any • Inference from truth (p) to necessity (p) is a modal fallacy • From empirical to necessary knowledge
Intersubjectivity (Piaget, 1949, p. 2)	• What is known is self-identical (one and the same thing) and so common ground • Different thinkers can know the same thing, which is potentially open to us all • Knowing what is common ground, not just claiming to know • From subjective thinking to intersubjective thought
Objectivity (Piaget, 1971a, p. 35)	• Knowing what is true (*ergo* is not false) • Truths can be known and believed, falsehoods can be believed but not known • Acknowledging as true, not just making a correct response • From subjective thinking to objective truth
Universality (Piaget, 1952, p. 3)	• Knowing what is always the case • Generalization in mathematics and science • Understanding a universal in one context, not transfer over several contexts • From particular knowledge to the universalization of knowledge

Note. From Smith (1999b, 2002a, 2002b, 2003)
Indicative Examples:
- two plus two makes four (*1984*, Orwell, 1949)
- 2 does not "make" 4 but its meaning "implies" that $2 + 2 = 4'$ (Piaget, 1971a)
- $3 + 4 = 7$ (Kant, 1933)
- $(3 + 4 = 7) \Rightarrow (3 \times 4 = 12)$ (Grize, 1963)
- if you drop equality from arithmetic, there's almost nothing left (Frege, 1979)
- necessity is what could not be otherwise (*De Interpretatione*, 18b Aristotle, 1987)
- inference from n to $n + 1$ is a creative ascent to universality (Poincaré, 1905)

Conclusion 4 is entailed by Premises 1 to 3. To make the same point, anyone who is inclined to deny conclusion 4 is rationally required to deny one or more of Premises 1 to 3. Premise 1 points to there being a mechanism by which human knowledge arises, and an account of this mechanism would be empirical. Conclusion 4 covers there being an empirical mechanism. Premises 2 and 3 point to there being a normative element in the development of knowledge. Conclusion 4 covers this as well. What is distinctive about this conclusion is this dual requirement, a developmental mechanism with both empirical and normative elements. Thus, conclusion 4 is substantive because it goes beyond each of the three premises taken severally.

Developmental psychologists with an interest in cognitive development in CP alone could remain content with Premise 1, regarding Premise 2 with indifference. Equally, developmental epistemologists with interests in DE alone could remain content with Premise 2, ignoring the demands of Premise 1. This is the ambiguity over the term *cognitive development* in that each strategy taken independently is incomplete. Something more is required, which leads to the next section.

Unit of Analysis as Act of Judgment

The argument in the previous section has two implications. One is that the unit of analysis in DE should be both causal and normative. The other concerns developmental explanations, which once again should combine causality and normativity. This second implication is discussed elsewhere (Smith, 2002b, 2003). The rest of this section deals with the first implication.

An act of judgment fits the implication that a unit of analysis should combine causal and normative properties. This proposal has its basis in Frege's normative epistemology, augmented by Piaget's developmental epistemology (Smith, 1999a, 1999b). Any such *act* always has a causal origin for investigation in empirical psychology. Any such *judgment* is based as well on normative criteria in virtue of which it is legitimated. It is this dual requirement for both causal and normative elements that make DE distinctive. This proposal is compatible with Piaget's (1950; cf. Ferrari et al., 2001) hypothesis according to which knowledge is an interaction between a knowing subject and an object (S–O interaction), such that the interaction is not external to that subject, but rather is an "interaction remaining interior to the subject" (p. 338). An interaction would be external if a knowing subject were in interaction with a physical object or another person in the actual world—pebbles and people are different from the person counting them. An interaction would be internal (remain interior) if that object were an intentional object (Searle, 1999). This can be brought out in two ways—one about responses and the other about reasoning.

Responses are central in psychological tasks. A correct response can be due to causal processes. The respondent is likely to know neither which processes nor what contribution they make to the formation of that response, whether correct or incorrect. Psychologists state that, methodologically, it is "practically worthless" to ask people to use introspection as reliable evidence of the processes influencing their own behavior (Eysenck & Keane, 2000, p. 4). In psychological models of representational redescription, responses can be made (a) without conscious access and verbal report, (b) with conscious access but without verbal report, or (c) with both (Karmiloff-Smith, 1992). These psychological claims may be causally sound, but they miss the normative point in DE. The formation of knowledge is not merely a causal process. Epistemic formation includes causal access. It also includes normative constitution and development. Here's why. First, Plato (1956) argued that intellectual search would have to be unsuccessful in the absence of all prior conceptions of its object. A causal process devoid of normative properties would be vulnerable in exactly this way just because knowledge is defined through its normative properties. A paradigm case is that knowledge entails (not causes) the truth of what is known (Moser, 1995). This in turn requires relations of necessitation covering equality and entailment (Sainsbury, 1991). A psychological individual devoid of normativity would be epistemically blind and so incapable of recognizing objectivity and necessity. Second, a psychologically reliable process interpreted exclusively through a causal model can lead to error (Frege, 1979). The cases are well known in psychological research directed on misperception, "false" memory, and misunderstanding (Eyenck & Keane, 2000). A psychologically reliable process can fit the local contingencies of a particular context or cultural niche without due regard for universality of understanding (Feldman, 1995). This means that both the intersubjectivity and universality of knowledge would be sacrificed. Third, there are levels of epistemic excellence in much the way that there are levels of moral goodness. Aristotle (1987, *NE*, 1144b, 26–27) pointed out that it is one thing to make a moral response in accord with a moral rule and something else again to do so in virtue of that rule (cf. Kant, 1966, sect. 390). Autonomy would be—in principle and not merely in fact—out of reach of anyone who did things merely in extrinsic accordance with psychological laws without ever doing them because of their intrinsic value.

Acts of judgment have a causal origin for investigation in CP directed on responses. But this is a necessary, not sufficient, condition. What is also required is a contribution from DE about how agents use historically available norms to control their own reasoning generative of novel knowledge in the future. This is where reasoning fits in covering "the deep relations which link action to reason" (Piaget, 1925, p. 209). Reasoning is an action—something that an agent knows how to do (Piaget, 1967). This is a commitment to a "logic of action," not to a "mental logic" (Johnson-Laird, 1999). "The primordial question is to know what are the child's available resources (*disponibilités*)" (Piaget, 1998, p. 26). The task of providing evidence about what "was actually at the subject's disposal (is) a question of fact" (Piaget, 1977, p. 5; my amended translation). Actions have normative, and not merely causal, properties in that any "action necessarily deforms the ideal in virtue of its mixture of fact and norm" (Piaget, 1918, p. 116). Reasoning has its origin in causal contexts, but reasoning also has reasons or grounds. These grounds are not causes external to the agent. If grounds or reasons are causes internal to the agent, that is another matter. It misses the point to say that agents have an incomplete realization of the causal processes of their own reasoning. Much nearer the mark is the development in realization in becoming aware of more grounds and reasons (cf. Piaget's *prise de conscience*; cited in Ferrari et al., 2001). Presented with any actual reasoning, the investigator in DE should do two things. One is to ascertain the grounds on which it should be based. The other is to ascertain which grounds are actually used by the reasoner. These are normative facts such as those in the AEIOU framework.

EDUCATION AND DEVELOPMENTAL EPISTEMOLOGY

Although education was not the principal concern in Piaget's research program, it was explicitly included in it (Smith, 1997). Piaget had a distinctive account of education. This account was dependent on his DE. My discussion deals with ten questions. The common belief is that each leads to an affirmative answer in the context of Piaget's account (i.e., "Yes, this fits Piaget's account which is thereby open to objection"). My discussion of some of these questions elsewhere amounts to a countercase (Smith, 1993, 2001, 2002a). This countercase generates negative answers to the same ten question (i.e., "No—this is not Piaget's educational account at all"). This countercase is dependent on the earlier argument for DE in an earlier section.

Q&A on Education, Teaching, Assessment, Learning

Question 1: Is Piaget's account of education well understood?

Not so. During a 50-year period, Piaget expressly denied that his position on education was that set out in the otherwise astute commentaries due to Susan Isaacs (Piaget, 1931, p. 138), Lev Vygotsky (Piaget, 2000, p. 251), and Jean-Paul Bringuier (Piaget, 1980, p. 129).

Question 2: Is Piaget's account of education exclusively individualistic?

This question assumes an exclusive interpretation of the "individual–social" distinction in the earlier section. Its basis is Piaget's (1970, p. 721) discussion of a solitary child counting pebbles in a physical world devoid of culture and without a teacher in sight. This case is regarded as a paradigm case of cognitive development, which is then generalized to cover all pedagogical interactions in Piaget's educational account. All of these interactions are with objects S-O, such as physical pebbles, and none is with subjects S-S, such as teachers and parents. Culture and context are just not in this frame at all. The inference is that this is a travesty that requires the rejection of Piaget's educational account generative of the travesty. This argument has many sponsors (Smith, 2002a, 2002b). Yet it is flawed. It ignores a main point implied five pages earlier in the same paper that "this obviously does not mean the teacher should not devise experimental situations to facilitate the pupil's invention" (Piaget, 1970, p. 715). Second, Piaget was never committed to a "cult of the individual" (Mays & Smith, 2001) nor even to cultural individualism in that "society no more knows how to create reason than does the individual" (Piaget, 1995, p. 227), still less to a view of development as an "all-or-none" advance (Chandler, 2001). Third, his educational credo was elegantly summarized in this way: "Each individual is led to think and re-think the system of collective notions" (Piaget, 1995, p. 76). Collective notions are cultural for transmission by social agencies (parents, teachers, peers). Rethinking them is in the best tradition of "education for intellectual freedom" (Piaget, 1998, p. 162).

Question 3: Is education defined by Piaget as a learner–teacher interaction?

This question arises as a presumed lacuna in Piaget's account, which is reckoned to say next to nothing about learner–teacher interactions (cf. Bransford et al., 2001). Yet this is to miss the main plot. *Education* was defined by Piaget (1971b, p. 137) as an interaction between learners and values. The values in question are those values invoked by teachers in their culture. The task of teachers is to contribute to learners' value formation. Notice that values are *intrinsic* to this definition, whereas teachers are *instrumental* in selecting which values these are and then assisting in their formation. That is why the answer to Question 3 is "no." First, Piaget's definition covers all values without stipulating "the" values of education. Thus, it covers such different values as those of the Boy Scouts (Piaget, 1998, p. 50) and the contrary values of the Hitler Youth (Piaget, 1995, p. 25). Intellectual values are included, such as the values in the school curriculum—history, art, and mathematics (see Piaget, 1998). All values have normative, rather than causal, properties because they lay down what is and is not valuable, and so bear on human preferences about what is good, right, true, and so on, whether in itself or in relation to alternatives. Taken together, this means that an educational interaction directed on value formation is a sociocultural—not a merely physical—interaction in Piaget's account (*pace* Cole & Wertsch, 1996). Whereas Plato (1956) gave a negative answer to the question "Can moral values be taught?", Piaget's answer would be, "Yes—teaching can be successful just in case it is based on construction."

Question 4: In Piaget's account, isn't teaching unnecessary in that children develop regardless of whether they go to school?

Bryant (1995) regarded the independence of schooling and development as a defect of Piaget's account. Using a different argument, Case (1999) had a comparable view, but matters are not so clear cut. *Development* can be used in a wide and narrow sense. In its wide sense, development amounts to the whole of experience. In its narrow sense, development amounts to schooling.

The narrow sense was invoked by Piaget (1976, p. 23) in remarking that all education is an acceleration. The initial construction of knowledge may take centuries, yet its reconstruction routinely occurs during schooling because "ideas which have been painfully 'invented' by the greatest geniuses (have) become, not merely accessible, but even easy and obvious, to schoolchildren" (Piaget, 1995, p. 37). This is the reconstruction of knowledge when children are "led to think a collective notion." Notice this term *led* with its implication that this is a contribution made by teaching. As such this is the basis of the negative reply to Question 4, in that schooling was regarded by Piaget as a historically based necessity in "our" societies.

Even so teaching is not necessary if the wide sense of development is at issue. This is clear in Piaget's analysis of a crucial thought experiment independently analyzed by Vygotsky (1994; see Smith, 2002b). The thought experiment concerns a society of exact contemporaries, such as a society of children of the same age. The point about such a society is that it is *causally* abnormal. There are no previous generations as guardians of past cultural knowledge and practices, no intergenerational transmission from one generation to the next. The absence of social agency from a "zone of proximal development" is a causal difference. Notice that this absence was recognized by Piaget (1995) to result in profound differences—differences arising from the absence of social assistance in knowledge transmission. Piaget's point was that development would be *difficult,* but not *impossible*—difficult in view of this abnormal causal context, but not impossible because the normative problem remains the same. This normative problem is the problem normally faced by any individual in value formation in the pursuit of better knowledge, and this fits the epistemological position set out above.

Question 5: If all learning is "spontaneous" in Piaget's account, is teaching "a waste of time"?

Piaget's (1952, ch. 3–4) commitment to "spontaneity" was required by his distinction between "provoked-spontaneous" learning. The implication is that teaching is either ineffective or redundant—a failure if "too early," futile if "too late." Either way teaching "drops out." Yet this question embodies two conflations. One concerns (a) *spontaneous,* which can have a social meaning due to oneself alone, not to anyone else, or an epistemological meaning autonomous. The second conflation concerns (b) *teaching,* in that Question 5 invokes a quantifier (*all, some, none*) without any indication as to which.

Taking (b), Question 5 could mean that all, some, or no teaching is a "waste of time." The first and last of these can be ruled out. The claim *no teaching is a waste of time* implies that *all teaching is successful.* All the educational evidence shows it to be false (Stigler & Hiebert, 1999). Alternatively, the claim could mean *all teaching is a waste of time.* This is equivalent to *no teaching is successful.* Yet this will not do either because some teaching is successful (Reynolds & Farrell, 1996). So the implied quantifier is that *some teaching is a waste of time.* This is compatible with the claim that *some teaching is successful.* This was expressly admitted by Piaget (2000, p. 251): Knowledge can be successfully transmitted by teaching.

Applying this plausible conclusion to (a) rules out its social meaning: Plainly if some learning is due to teaching, this cannot be nonsocial. Thus, (a) concerns the epistemological meaning *autonomy.* Piaget's (1995) argument was that, "language, family and school education, and the set of other 'institutions' . . . exert pressure on the individual during his entire life" (p. 217). This pressure can be causal. One example is social training due to conditioning (Mele, 1995). Another is cultural conformity due to "normative pressure" (von Wright, 1983). In such cases successful learning would not thereby be autonomous. The argument is not that sociocultural forces should be eliminated. This is impossible. Rather, the argument is that if heteronomous learning, which is causal, is to be superseded, a normative advance must be made to autonomy. At issue here is the question left open earlier about the advance from the causal to the normative. The question Piaget asked was: If sociocultural pressure is ubiquitous as it is efficacious, how can learning be autonomous? The key difference was stated to be this:

It is not by knowing the Pythagorean theorem that the free exercise of a person's reason will be assured. Rather, it is assured by having rediscovered that there is such a theorem and how to prove it. The aim of intellectual education is not to know how to repeat or to conserve ready-made truths (a truth that is parroted is only a half-truth). It is in learning to gain the truth by oneself at the risk of losing a lot of time and of going through all the roundabout ways that are inherent in real activity. (Piaget, 1976, p. 106; my amended translation)

Interpreted in this way, autonomous learning can be a "spontaneous" consequence of teaching without being an effect—and thereby a nonspontaneous outcome—of teaching. This is why the answer to Question 5 is "no". The general issue underlying this answer concerns the formation of values such as autonomy. This issue resurfaces in Question 10.

Question 6: Isn't assessment in terms of Piaget's stages educationally irrelevant?

This question is ambiguous by lumping together distinct assessment functions (Goldstein, 1991). Its scope is restricted in Question 6 to diagnostic assessment, and the answer is "no". Formative and summative assessment are considered in Questions 7 and 8. First, Piagetian stages are levels. Any level can be viewed by analogy with a contour line on a map. Contours are hierarchically related as well as invariant to terrain, climate, and itinerary (Smith, 2002b). Notice that developmental levels are educationally acceptable at least in the National Curriculum (2001) in England where the main school subjects are defined in terms of hierarchical levels. In Piaget's account, these are levels of epistemic interaction (i.e., levels of individual or collective knowing). This fits the definition of *education* under Question 3. They are not levels "in the child," nor are they age related other than as indicators (not criteria) of developmental level (Smith, 1993, sect. 20). Second, the earlier argument was that the formation of the epistemological values in the AEIOU framework was expected to take place through a series of such levels. School-based education is typically concerned with progression in knowledge by reference to these epistemic values. Third, it is widely accepted that diagnostic assessment is as important in education as it is poorly implemented under classroom conditions (Black, 1998). Yet it is precisely its potential utility as a diagnostic tool in educational settings that makes Piagetian assessment invaluable (Ginsburg, 1997).

Question 7: Formative assessment—there's a big lacuna in Piaget's account here?

This question is important just because teaching is expected to make a contribution to learning through formative or dynamic assessment (Black

& Wiliam, 1998; Shephard, 2000). This apparent omission from Piaget's account continues to be a prime motivational factor behind social constructivism in education (Torrance & Pryor, 1998). Yet this omission is apparent, not real. There is a creative contribution from teaching in Piaget's account: "A teacher creates a learning context which evokes a spontaneous elaboration of the part of the learner" (Piaget, 2000, p. 252). The difference between "creating learning" and "creating a context for learning" is an important difference. It is here invoked by Piaget and is comparable to the view stated by Vygotsky (1994, p. 366). In Piaget's (1973) account, this means that the teacher is less "a person who gives 'lessons' and is rather someone who organises situations that will give rise to curiosity and solution-seeking in the child, and who will support such behaviour by means of appropriate arrangements" (p. 85). This is because "the role of *the teacher becomes central* as the animator of discussions *in consequence of having been the instigator*, within each child, of the taking of possession of that remarkable power of intellectual construction which is manifest in all genuine activity" (1998, p. 191; italics added). Piaget (1998, pp. 48, 144–46, 178, 181, 194, 228, 263) repeatedly observed that too little empirical investigation had been carried out in "educational science."

Question 8: Criterion-referenced assessment—this too is missing?

Assessment is norm referenced when scores are interpreted in terms of standardized performances of other individuals in a specified population. Notice that this is a descriptive—not a value-laden—use of *norm*, which is different than the use of *normative* in an earlier section and Question 3. The naturalistic fallacy is committed if the factual norm is used to infer a value-laden norm (Smith, 2003). By contrast, assessment is criterion referenced when scores of any individual are interpreted in terms of some external criterion (Black, 1998; DES, 1988). Evidence of reliable scaling based on Piagetian levels can be found in both national (Bond, 1997) and international (Shayer et al., 1988) studies. This means that these levels could provide a basis for criterion referencing in education, and so the answer to Question 8 is "no."

Question 9: Does Piaget's account of teaching require individualized learning?

Peer learning can be productive in human development (Hogan & Tudge, 1999), education (Galton et al., 1999), or both (Shayer, 1997). These commentators imply that this fits Vygotsky's—but not Piaget's—account. So their implied answer imputed to Piaget in Question 9 is "yes." Yet this is contradicted by Piaget's commitment to group learning in the classroom.

This means that the answer to Question 9 is "no." This was explicit in Piaget's (1998) support for "active learning in schools," which *necessarily presupposes collaboration in work*" (pp. 45–46; italics added). His contention was that "group work is in principle more 'active' than purely individual work" (p. 158). It was also combined with two further hypotheses—one that "the group develops the intellectual independence of its members" (p. 159) and the other that "weak and lazy pupils, far from being abandoned to their lot, are stimulated and obligated by the group" (p. 166). Implicated in group learning is "the method of self-government consisting in attributing to pupils a share in the responsibility for scholarly discipline" (Piaget, 1998, p. 167). Piaget interpreted this as "rediscovery by oneself" (p. 46) as well as being "a process of social education, aiming—like all of the others—to teach individuals how to escape from their egocentrism so as to collaborate between themselves and to submit to shared rules" (p. 128). Notice that "rediscovery" takes place in the social context of the group, the success of which amounts to the individualization of knowledge. This individualization is normative, covering both poles of the "individual–social" continuum.

Question 10: Is Piaget's account of school learning based solely on equilibration?

Equilibration was long regarded by Piaget (1918, 1985) as a central developmental mechanism. Ginsburg (1981) argued that its further elaboration was a prerequisite of its use in education. There is an apparent dilemma here. Either equilibration is a central developmental mechanism or it is not. If it is, Piaget's account is undermined because this construct seems to be a failure both formally and empirically. If it is not a developmental mechanism, there is nothing left in that account to explain progress in education. The counterargument is that this dilemma is open to challenge. Piaget's (1985) model of equilibration is incomplete. True, what is presented is neither a formal nor a testable model (Smith, 2002b; but see Müller et al., 1999). Even so the model is intelligible (Smith, 2003) and even admitted to be the only available model dealing with both causality and normativity in the development of knowledge (Brown, 1996, 2002). Equilibration is reckoned to work interdependently with—not independently of—factors at work in the "two lines" (genome, culture). This means that the working of equilibration is internal, not external, to genetic and cultural factors in virtue of the actual use made of norms in causal settings. For Piaget (1995) "human knowledge is *essentially* collective and social life *constitutes* an essential factor in the creation and growth of knowledge, both pre-scientific and scientific" (p. 30). Notice that this is a constitutive (normative), not a causal, claim. Further, this is linked to the epistemic framework above. Autonomy is involved as "real autonomy in the classroom" (Piaget, 1998, p. 167). In school learning, Piaget's (1971a) proposal was that children should not do what they want. Rather, they should want to do what they do. A learner should be a free agent, but should not have free license (Piaget, 1998, pp. 213, 259). Autonomy is not anarchy because rational thought and self-indulgent thinking are not the same thing (1998, p. 165). Intersubjectivity is involved if different individuals make common reference to their shared knowledge by the use of a cognitive structure, which is both "collective and individual" (1995, p. 94). An example is knowing the necessity or objectivity of the Pythagorean theorem on rational, not just cultural, grounds. Universality is involved in that the essential task of pedagogy is "to lead the child from the individual to the universal (where) this ascent from the individual to the universal corresponds to the very processes of the child's intellectual and moral development" (Piaget, 1998, p. 81). Equilibration is a construct that covers both the causal origin of knowing and its normative legitimation in these five cases of advance "from the causal to the normative" (Piaget, 1995, p. 51).

Education and Reasoning

Under Question 2, it was noticed that Piaget's credo at the end of World War II was "education for intellectual freedom." In the same discussion, Piaget (1998) specifically noted that "it is *necessary to teach* children to think" (p. 163; italics added). This is an instructional prescription. It refutes the default view according to which Piagetian pedagogy is teaching-free. This prescription predates recent proposals about teaching directed on reasoning as the 4th R of schooling (Resnick, 1987) or the thinking curriculum (Coles, 1993). Rousseau (1974) regarded childhood as *the sleep of reason*. This useful analogy leads to the question, "How do children wake up?" This question is partly causal and partly normative—*reason* is a value-laden term. One proposal is "by reasoning," in that reasoning based on reasons leads to reason (Moshman, 1994).

The phenomena here are not in doubt. Reasoning can lead to compliance devoid of conscious recognition. "We adhere to our old customs for the universe to be conserved" (Piaget, 1998, pp. 110–111). Reasoning can also lead to compliance with recognition. An example is Winston Smith in Room 101 who was asked how many fingers are on a human hand and then causally brought to change his mind from "Four" to "Five" (Orwell, 1983, p. 215). Reasoning can lead to rational assent. An example is Luther's stance in nailing his theses to the door—"Here I stand—I can't do otherwise." What is wanted is an interpretation of development and education that is explanatory of the range of outcomes through the reasoning that is contributory to them. Piaget's account invoked in response to Question 10 aspires to do exactly that.

CONCLUSION

The main question in this chapter concerned whether the "individual–social" distinction was exclusive or inclusive. I have set out an argument for an inclusive interpretation with its basis in developmental epistemology dealing with the empirical development of knowledge, notably during childhood. The central proposal was for an act of judgment to be the unit of analysis with both causal and normative properties. This unit of analysis has the capacity to deal with normative facts about the access to, constitution of, and development in norms by individual agents in the causal contexts of sociocultural worlds. An AEIOU framework was used to set out five paradigm examples of epistemic norms. It should be complemented by an interpretation in developmental psychology about causal facts. The causal origin of human knowledge is a natural necessity, but it is not sufficient. The interpretation proposed here sets out a reconciling research program in two respects. One is a single framework with both individual and social instantiations. The other is its capacity to augment the stock of developmental problems—notably about the advance from the causal to the normative. A main implication is that the development of human reasoning can be adequately explained only through a mechanism that is both causal and normative.

Education was accepted in UNESCO (Piaget, 1976) to be about the universal right to education (i.e., the right of each and every individual in any decent society). Education is also centrally concerned with the value formation of individuals in sociocultural contexts. A review of Piaget's account of education based on developmental epistemology covered three principal aspects of education: teaching, assessment, and learning. It was argued that the implied answers to "standard" questions about alleged deficiencies in all three aspects were open to challenge and even refutation. Piaget's proposals about teaching creative learning contexts, formative assessment through group learning, and learning as self-government are notable. They are also in line with proposals for a developmental mechanism about normative advance from causal origins such as the AEIOU framework.

In short, teaching makes a successful contribution to learning in virtue of the access to, constitution of, and development in epistemic and other norms. As such this amounts to the application in a particular case (education) of a general framework about "cognitive development" as developmental epistemology with both individual and social instantiations. Both this general epistemic framework and this educational application have their basis in Piaget's model.

REFERENCES

Aristotle. (1987). *A new Aristotle reader*. Oxford: Blackwell.

Bickhard, M. (2003). Biological emergence of representation. In T. Brown & L. Smith (Eds.), *Reductionism and the development of knowledge* (pp. 105–131). Mahwah, NJ: Lawrence Erlbaum Associates.

Black, P. (1998). Learning, league tables and assessment. *Oxford Review of Education, 24,* 57–68.

Black, P., & Wiliam, D. (1998). Assessment and classroom learning. *Assessment in Education, 5,* 7–74.

Bond, T. (1997). Measuring development: Examples from Piaget theory. In L. Smith, J. Dockrell, & P. Tomlinson (Eds.), *Piaget, Vygotsky, and beyond* (pp. 167–182). London: Routledge.

Bransford, J. D., Brown, A. L., & Cocking, R. R. (2001). *How people learn: Brain, mind, experience and school*. Washington, DC: National Academy Press.

Brown, T. (1996). Values, knowledge, and Piaget. In E. Reed, E. Turiel, & T. Brown (Eds.), *Values and knowledge* (pp. 137–170). Mahwah, NJ: Lawrence Erlbaum Associates.

Brown, T. (2003). Reductionism and the circle of the sciences. In T. Brown & L. Smith (Eds.), *Reductionism and the development of knowledge* (pp. 3–26). Mahwah, NJ: Lawrence Erlbaum Associates.

Bruner, J. (1966). *Toward a theory of instruction*. Cambridge, MA: Harvard University Press.

Bruner, J. (2000). Piaget et Vygotsky: Célébrons la divergence. In O. Houdé & C. Meljac (Eds.), *L'esprit piagétien*. Paris: Presses Universitaires de France.

Bryant, P. (1995). Children and arithmetic. In L. Smith (Ed.), *Critical readings on Piaget* (pp. 312–346). London: Routledge.

Case, R. (1999). Conceptual development in the child and in the field: A personal view of the Piagetian legacy. In E. Scholnick, K. Nelson, S. Gelman, & P. Miller (Eds.), *Conceptual development: Piaget's legacy* (pp. 23–52). Mahwah, NJ: Lawrence Erlbaum Associates.

Chandler, M. (2001). Perspective taking in the aftermath of the theory-theory and the collapse of the social role-taking literature. In A. Tryphon & J. Vonèche (Eds.), *Working with Piaget: Essays in honour of Bärbel Inhelder* (pp. 39–64). Hove: Psychology Press.

Chapman, M. (1999). Constructivism and the problem of reality. *Journal of Applied Developmental Psychology, 20,* 31–43.

Cole, M., & Wertsch, J. (1996). Beyond the individual-social antinomy in discussions of Piaget and Vygotsky. *Human Development, 39,* 250–256.

Coles, M. (1993). Teaching thinking. *Educational Psychology, 13,* 333–344.

Damon, W. (1998). *Handbook of child psychology* (5th ed.). New York: Wiley.

DES. (1988). *Task group on assessment and testing: A report*. London: HMSO.

Eysenck, M., & Keane, M. (2000). *Cognitive psychology: A student's handbook* (4th ed.). Hove: Psychology Press.

Feldman, D. (1995). Learning and development in nonuniversal theory. *Human Development, 38,* 315–321.

Ferrari, M., Pinard, A., & Runions, K. (2001). Piaget's framework for a scientific study of consciousness. *Human Development, 44,* 195–213.

Flavell, J., Miller, P., & Miller, S. (1993). *Cognitive development* (3rd ed.). Englewood Cliffs, NJ: Prentice-Hall.

Frege, G. (1979). *Posthumous papers*. Oxford: Blackwell.

Galton, M., Hargreaves, L., Comber, C., Wall, D., & Pell, A. (1999). *Inside the primary classroom 20 years on*. London: Routledge.

Ginsburg, H. (1981). Piaget and education. In L. Smith (Ed.), *Jean Piaget: Critical assessments* (Vol. 3, pp. 354–370). London: Routledge.

Ginsburg, H. (1997). *Entering the child's mind*. Cambridge: Cambridge University Press.

Goldstein, H. (1991). *Assessment in schools*. London: Institute for Public Policy.

Grize, J.-B. (1963). Des groupements à l'algèbre de Boole. In L. Apostel, J.-B. Grize, S. Papert, & J. Piaget (Eds.), *La filiation des structures* (pp. 25–64). Paris: Presses Universitaires de France.

Hogan, D., & Tudge, J. (1999). Implications for Vygotsky's theory of peer learning. In A. O'Donnell & A. King (Eds.), *Cognitive perspectives on peer learning*. Mahwah, NJ: Lawrence Erlbaum Associates.

Johnson-Laird, P. (1999). Deductive reasoning. *Annual Review of Psychology, 50,* 109–135.

Kant, I. (1933). *Critique of pure reason* (2nd ed.). London: Macmillan.

Kant, I. (1966). *Groundwork of the metaphysics of morals*. In H. Paton (Ed.), *The moral law* (pp. 51–135). London: Hutchinson.

Karmiloff-Smith, A. (1992). *Beyond modularity: A developmental perspective on cognitive science*. Cambridge, MA: MIT Press.

Lourenço, O., & Machado, A. (1996). In defense of Piaget's theory: A reply to 10 common criticisms. *Psychological Review, 103,* 143–164.

Mays, W., & Smith, L. (2001). Harré on Piaget's *Sociological Studies*. *New Ideas in Psychology, 19,* 221–236.

Mele, A. (1995). *Autonomous agents: From self-control to autonomy*. New York: Oxford University Press.

Moser, P. (1995). Epistemology. In R. Audi (Ed.), *The Cambridge dictionary of philosophy* (pp. 233–238). Cambridge: Cambridge University Press.

Moshman, D. (1994). Reason, reasons and reasoning. *Theory and Psychology, 4,* 245–260.

Müller, U., Sokol, B., & Overton, W. (1999). Developmental sequences in class reasoning and propositional reasoning. *Journal of Experimental Child Psychology, 74,* 69–106.

National Curriculum. (2001). http://www.nc.uk.net/home.html.

Office for Standards in Education (Ofsted). (1999). *Primary education 1994–98.* London: HMSO.

Orwell, G. (1983). *Nineteen eighty-four*. London: Penguin.

Piaget, J. (1918). *Recherche* [Search]. Lausanne: La Concorde.

Piaget, J. (1923). La psychologie des valeurs religieuses [Psychology of religious values]. In Association Chrétienne d'Etudiants de la Suisse Romande (Ed.), *Sainte-Croix 1922* (pp. 38–82).

Piaget, J. (1925). Psychologie et critique de la connaissance [Psychology and knowledge critique]. *Archives de Psychologie, 19,* 193–210.

Piaget, J. (1931). Le développement intellectuelle chez les jeunes enfants [Intellectual development in young children]. *Mind, 40,* 137–160.

Piaget, J. (1949). *Traité de logique* [Treatise on logic]. Paris: Colin.

Piaget, J. (1950). *Introduction à l'épistémologie génétique: Vol. 1. La pensée mathématique* [Introduction to genetic epistemology: Vol. 1. Mathematical thought]. Paris: Presses Universitaires de France.

Piaget, J. (1952). *The child's conception of number*. London: Routledge & Kegan Paul.

Piaget, J. (1963). Foreword. In J. Flavell (Ed.), *The developmental psychology of Jean Piaget* (pp. vii–ix). New York: Van Nostrand.

Piaget, J. (1966). Part II. In E. Beth & J. Piaget (Eds.), *Mathematical epistemology and psychology* (pp. 131–304). Dordrecht: Reidel.

Piaget, J. (1967). *Logique et connaissance scientifique* [Logic and scientific knowledge]. Paris: Gallimard.

Piaget, J. (1970). Piaget's theory. In P. Mussen (Ed.), *Handbook of child psychology* (3rd ed., pp. 703–732). New York: Wiley.

Piaget, J. (1971a). *Biology and knowledge.* Edinburgh: Edinburgh University Press.

Piaget, J. (1971b). *Science of education and the psychology of the child.* London: Longman.

Piaget, J. (1973). Comments on mathematical education. In A. Howson (Ed.), *Developments in mathematical education* (pp. 79–87). Cambridge: Cambridge University Press.

Piaget, J. (1976). *To understand is to invent.* London: Penguin.

Piaget, J. (1977). *Psychology and epistemology.* London: Penguin.

Piaget, J. (1980). In J.-C. Bringuier (Ed.), *Conversations with Jean Piaget* (pp. 1–143). Chicago: University of Chicago Press.

Piaget, J. (1985). *The equilibration of cognitive structures: The central problem of intellectual development.* Chicago: University of Chicago Press.

Piaget, J. (1986). Essay on necessity. *Human Development, 29*, 301–314.

Piaget, J. (1995). *Sociological studies.* London: Routledge.

Piaget, J. (1998). *De la pédagogie* [On pedagogy]. Paris: Odile Jacob.

Piaget, J. (2000). Commentary on Vygotsky. *New Ideas in Psychology, 18*, 241–59.

Piaget, J. (2001). *Studies in reflective abstraction.* Hove: Psychology Press.

Plato. (1956). *Meno.* London: Penguin Books.

Poincaré, H. (1905). *Science and hypothesis.* London: The Walter Scott.

Reichenbach, H. (1961). *Experience and prediction: An analysis of the foundations and the structure of knowledge.* Chicago: University of Chicago Press.

Resnick, L. (1987). *Education and thinking.* Washington: National Academy Press.

Reynolds, D., & Farrell, S. (1996). *Worlds apart.* London: HMSO.

Rousseau, J.-J. (1974). *Emile.* London: Dent.

Sainsbury, M. (1991). *Logical forms.* Oxford: Blackwell.

Searle, J. (1999). *Mind, language and society.* London: Weidenfeld & Nicolson.

Shayer, M. (1997). Piaget and Vygotsky. In L. Smith, J. Dockrell, & P. Tomlinson (Eds.), *Piaget, Vygotsky and beyond* (pp. 36–59). London: Routledge.

Shayer, M., Demetriou, A., & Pervez, M. (1988). The structure and scaling of concrete operational thought: Three studies in four countries. *Genetic, Social and General Psychology Monographs, 114*, 309–375.

Shephard, L. (2000). The role of assessment in a learning culture. *Educational Researcher, 29*(7), 4–14.

Smith, L. (1993). *Necessary knowledge.* Hove: Lawrence Erlbaum Associates.

Smith, L. (1997). Jean Piaget. In N. Sheehy & A. Chapman (Eds.), *The biographical dictionary of psychology* (pp. 447–452). London: Routledge.

Smith, L. (1999a). What Piaget learned from Frege. *Developmental Review, 19*, 133–153.

Smith, L. (1999b). Epistemological principles for developmental psychology in Frege and Piaget. *New Ideas in Psychology, 17*, 83–117, 137–147.

Smith, L. (2001). Jean Piaget. In J. A. Palmer (Ed.), *50 Modern thinkers on education: From Piaget to the present* (pp. 37–44). London: Routledge.

Smith, L. (2002a). *Reasoning by mathematical induction in children's arithmetic.* Oxford: Pergamon.

Smith, L. (2002b). Piaget's model. In U. Goswami (Ed.), *Handbook of cognitive development* (pp. 515–537). Oxford: Blackwell.

Smith, L. (2003). From epistemology to psychology in the development of knowledge. In T. Brown & L. Smith (Eds.), *Reductionism and the development of knowledge* (pp. 201–228). Mahwah, NJ: Lawrence Erlbaum Associates.

Stigler, J., & Hiebert, J. (1999). *The teaching gap*. New York: The Free Press.
Torrance, H., & Pryor, J. (1998). *Investigating formative assessment*. Milton Keynes: Open University Press.
von Wright, G. H. (1983). *Practical reason*. Oxford: Blackwell.
Vygotsky, L. (1994). *A Vygotsky reader*. Oxford: Blackwell.

Social Interaction and the Construction of Moral and Social Knowledge

Larry Nucci
University of Illinois at Chicago

The contemporary study of moral development began with Piaget's (1932) classic studies of children playing the game of marbles. Piaget's assumption at the time was that one could best understand a young child's emerging morality through observation of their indigenous rule-governed activities. By watching children playing a game transmitted and enacted by the children, one could observe the emergence of normative collective social knowledge within individual children prior to their ability to reconstruct normative understandings at the level of consciousness (the verbal level). In essence, for Piaget, the structures of moral understanding, as in the case of all operative knowledge, begin at the level of activity (Piaget & Inhelder, 1964). Through reflective abstraction, activities are transformed into cognitive operations and self-reflective knowledge (consciousness). In the moral plane, the negotiation of normative regulation and social relations eventually result in the *logic of social interactions* and an awareness of moral principles.

For Piaget this process of moral socialization was not simply an acquisition of prepackaged cultural messages, but rather the active renegotiation of social relations and the gradual reworking of one's fundamental conceptions of self and other in reciprocal interaction. Thus, Piaget (1932) characterized the emergence of morality in young children as a revolution taking place at two levels. At the cognitive level, the child was described by Piaget (1932) as shifting from a period of egocentrism (in which the child conflates his or her own perceptions and wishes with those of others) to a phase of perspectivism or decentration (in which the child is able to differentiate and coordinate his or her own perspective with those of others). In addition to this global cognitive shift, the child's morality was thought by Piaget to reflect a revolution in social relations from a heteronomous respect for authority and norms to an autonomous orientation based on mutual respect and reciprocity. Piaget (1932) also speculated that this shift in moral orientation rested on the child's social interactions with peers of equal social power, and that moral growth was hindered by the inherently asymmetrical power relations between children and adults. As a consequence, Piaget recommended that parents reduce their power in relation to children as a way to support their move toward moral autonomy.

Subsequent work on children's moral and social growth has affirmed Piaget's emphasis on the child's social interactions for the construction of social knowledge, but has altered our view of how morality and social experience are related. In particular, Piaget's dichotomy between adult–child social interactions and child–child interactions, and his mapping of those asymmetries in social relations onto heteronomous and autonomous child morality, have been replaced with a more heterogeneous view of social interactions within both sets of relations and resulting social cognitions (Turiel, 1998). Piaget (1932) also recognized that social relations cannot be characterized as entirely heteronomous or autonomous and that elements of each are at work in social relations throughout development. However, he viewed these as competing moral orientations that function in terms of degree of influence, rather than elements of parallel social cognitive frameworks. Thus, for Piaget, one or another moral orientation is in ascendance at different points in development (i.e., heteronomy in early childhood; autonomy in later periods). The more recent work covered in this chapter finds that issues of authority, norms, reciprocity, justice, and autonomy coexist in the social interactions between children and adults as well as among peers. Moreover, these differential patterns of social interaction are associated with notions of morality, convention, authority, and personal autonomy, which emerge as differentiated conceptual systems in early childhood (Nucci, 2001; Turiel, 1983, 1998).

The discussion of these issues begins with a presentation of the social interactions associated with the child's construction of concepts of morality and social convention. This section looks at research on child–child interactions followed by work examining adult responses to children's moral and conventional transgressions. Issues of childhood autonomy are further explored in the subsequent section, which presents research on parent–child interactions around issues within the personal domain. We conclude the review of social interactions and sociomoral development with work that has examined the nature of adolescent–parent conflict.

This final section further illustrates that differential patterns of social interaction are associated with the construction of moral, social, and personal conceptual frameworks.

SOCIAL INTERACTIONS AND THE CONSTRUCTION OF MORAL AND CONVENTIONAL CONCEPTS

Within the social sphere, Piaget's basic view that moral knowledge rests on an underlying framework of reciprocity and fairness has been affirmed in studies of children's moral judgments (Damon, 1977; Turiel, 1998). However, we have also learned that young children's concepts of morality are distinct from their notions of the arbitrary conventions established by social groups and authority (Turiel, 1978, 1983). Preschool-age children tend to treat moral issues, such as theft of someone's personal goods or harm to another person, as wrong irrespective of the presence or absence of a governing rule, and they base these judgments on the effects that such actions have on the welfare of others. In contrast, young children's judgments about conventions such as whether to refer to an adult by a title and surname are dependent on the presence of a governing rule. Contrary to the intuitions that led Piaget to study children's games as a way to learn about their moral thinking, morality appears to be constructed out of patterns of social interaction that are distinct from the social interactions associated with conventions and consensually established norms such as game rules. The initial studies that explored the social interactions associated with the construction of moral and conventional concepts looked at patterns of interaction in the context of social transgressions. By focusing on naturally occurring transgressions, the investigators were able to be certain that a given norm was in effect. In addition, the exchanges that took place around transgressions were thought to entail a sort of social grammar in which children negotiate, test, employ, and clarify social norms (Much & Shweder, 1978). Finally, children's responses to one another's transgressions have also been viewed as efforts to repair the social fabric (Sedlak & Walton, 1982) and negotiate social responsibility.

Patterns of Peer Interaction

The general picture that has emerged from these studies is nicely illustrated in the following set of peer exchanges first reported in Nucci and Nucci (1982a, 1982b) and since presented in a number of sources—most recently Nucci (2001). Children in these examples range in age from 8 to 12 years. However, similar patterns have been reported for children as young as age 3. Findings with young children are discussed in more detail later.

Social Convention

1. *A boy and a girl are sitting together on the grass, away from the other children,* tying their shoes. Another boy (2) sings out to them, "Bobby and Alison sittin' in a tree, K-I-S-S-I-N-G," etc.

2. A girl (1) *is sucking on a piece of grass.* Girl (2) says to girl (3), "That's what she does, she sucks on weeds and spits them out." Girl (3) says, "Gross!" Girl (2) says, "That's disgusting!" Girl (1) then places the piece of grass down and ceases placing grass in her mouth.

Moral

1. *Two boys* (1 and 2) *are throwing sand at a smaller boy* (3). Boy 3 says, "Dammit-you got it in my eyes. It hurts like hell. Next time I'm gonna kick your heads in." Boy (1) says to boy (2), "Hey, did you hear that? Next time he's gonna kick our heads in." They both laugh and throw more sand in the face of boy (3). Boy (3) then spits at boy (1) and runs away.

2. *Two boys have forcibly taken a sled away from a younger boy and are playing with it.* A girl who was watching says to the boys, "Hey, give it back a-holes. That's really even odds, the two of you against one little kid." The girl then pulls the sled away from one of the older boys, pushes him to the ground, and hands the sled back to the younger boy. He takes the sled and the incident ends.

What is illustrated in these four actual playground events is that children respond to issues of morality in ways that center around the effects of the actions, whereas the responses to convention are focused on the normative status of the acts as not in keeping with "the done thing." In the case of moral events, children experience such issues as victims as well as perpetrators or third-person observers. The transgression (such as hitting, stealing, or damaging property) is followed by peer statements of injury or loss, and/or evaluations of the act as unjust or hurtful. Generally, these reactions have a high degree of emotion. In the case of very young children, the reaction may consist solely of crying. In addition, children tend to avenge moral transgressions or avert further actions through attempts at retaliation. Rarely do children respond to a moral transgression by referring to a rule. Young children often attempt to involve adults as mediators or as a form of retaliation. As discussed below, the tendency to involve adults in moral disputes steadily decreases with age.

Peer reactions to transgression are, in turn, generally followed by transgressor responses. For the most part, these reactions either attempt to repair social relations (a) through direct apology for the act, (b) by efforts at restitution, or (c) by simple cessation of the behavior. Or they attempt to explain or excuse the act by (a) claiming that it was justifiable retribution for a prior harm ("You hit me first"), (b) claiming that no harm was intended, or (c) claiming that no substantial harm or injustice resulted from the act ("Oh, you're all right. I just tapped you"). Transgressor reactions in a minority of cases (see moral example 1) also include derision of the respondent and/or continued engagement in the transgression. This last form of reaction, however, is more common in the context of conventional events.

In contrast with the pattern of interactions observed in moral events, peer interactions involving breaches of convention tend to arouse relatively little emotion and focus on the normative status of the acts. The transgression (such as engaging in counter sex-role behavior, violating dress norms, or using an improper form of greeting) is followed by peer responses focusing on social norms and social expectations. Respondents state governing rules, evaluate the acts as odd or disruptive, and attempt to achieve conformity through ridicule (see conventional example 1). Transgressor reactions to these peer responses include attempts to conform through compliance with the norm or defense of their conduct through challenges of the rule ("We don't have to do that. Who made up that dumb rule?"). Finally, because conventions achieve their force through social consensus and/or imposition by authority, transgressors sometimes react to peer respondents by challenging their authority to uphold the norm ("You're not my mother") or ignoring the respondent and continuing to engage in the behavior.

These patterns of child response to transgression have been observed in emergent form among toddlers (Dunn & Munn, 1985, 1987; Dunn & Slomkowski, 1992; Smetana, 1984, 1989a, 1989b) and preschool children in home and school contexts (Much & Shweder, 1978; Nucci & Weber, 1995; Nucci & Turiel, 1978; Ross, 1996). Beginning in toddlerhood, children respond to violations of moral transgressions generally as victims. Their responses indicate that they have experienced such acts as hurtful. In turn their reactions provide information to peer transgressors about the hurtful effects of the actions. Very young children generally do not respond to violations of conventions. This finding is not surprising in that conventional acts are not prescriptive. By preschool, however, children begin to respond to peer violations of generally held conventions, such as dresses for girls and not boys, but do not as yet respond to peer violations of conventions particular to the school setting (e.g., norms regarding classroom cleanup), which are left to the adults to worry about (Nucci, Turiel, & Encarnacion-Gawrych, 1983).

Patterns of Adult Response to Transgression

As described at the start of the chapter, Piaget (1932) stressed that the unavoidable disparity in power between children and adults creates an inescapable climate of moral heteronomy. This power differential so colored adult–child interactions in Piaget's depiction that he minimized the proactive role that adults might play in helping children focus on the intrinsic elements of moral interactions. However, when researchers have looked more carefully at adult–child interactions, they have uncovered that the pattern of adult responses to children's transgressions is also different by domain rather than solely focused on compliance to social norms. Adult responses to moral transgressions complement those of children and often follow them in time (Smetana, 1984). Mothers of toddlers provide social messages focusing on the hurtful effects of moral transgressions and also attempt to persuade children to engage in prosocial behaviors and share or "be nice" (Gralinski & Kopp, 1993). As children grow older, these adult responses become more elaborated: Children are provided more explicit social messages regarding the harmful impact of their actions and are asked by teachers and parents to consider the perspective of the other person ("Mary, how do you feel when people lie to you?") and reflect on their own motivations for acting as the did ("Why did you do that?").

Adult responses to convention also complement those of children. Mothers' responses to toddlers' violations of convention generally focus on commands to cease the behavior and less frequently include statements that address the conventional features of the acts (e.g., the underlying rules, the disorder caused by the action; Smetana, 1984). As children develop, mothers and teachers provide more comprehensive statements regarding the underlying social rules and social expectations.

By elementary school, adult feedback about violations of convention take the form of direct rule statements or reminders of rules and expectations ("Raise your hand before talking") or statements labeling the transgressions as unruly, disorderly ("Its getting too noisy in here"), unmannerly ("Chew with your mouth closed. Where are your manners?"), inappropriate for the context ("Dan, those ripped jeans are okay for play, but not for school"), and generally inconsistent with conventional expectations ("That's not the way for a Hawthorne student to act." "Susan, act your age"). In early adolescence, as children begin to struggle with the functions and meaning of conventions within the larger social order, adult messages to children sometimes contain explanations of these more abstract connections.

In summary, the pattern of adult responses to moral and conventional events complements those of children. Interestingly, however, the relative proportion of child transgressions involving adult or child respondents differs by domain. Here some of Piaget's (1932) assumptions and insights appear to be borne out. Adults respond less often to children's moral transgressions than do other children. Conversely, adults are more likely than children to respond to violations of conventions. For example, a study of 2- and 3-year-old children's social interactions (Smetana, 1989a) reported that conflicts with peers occurred primarily over issues of possessions, rights, taking turns, aggression, and unkindness (all moral issues), whereas children's conflicts with mothers occurred primarily over manners and politeness, rules of the house, and cultural norms (all conventional issues). Similar findings were reported for somewhat older (3- and 4-year-old) children in a study looking at naturally occurring events in the home (Nucci & Weber, 1995). This study found that the majority of children's moral events took place in free-play settings and involved feedback from children more often than from the mothers. Violations of convention, in contrast, were more generally responded to by mothers than by young children.

These patterns also carry over to school settings. Children are more likely than teachers to respond to other children's moral transgressions, whereas teachers are the primary respondents to violations of school convention (Nucci & Nucci, 1982b; Nucci & Turiel, 1978). These findings are consistent with the view that children's moral understandings develop primarily out of peer interactions (Damon, 1977; Piaget, 1932).

Part of the explanation of the differences in rate of responding to moral transgressions is due to the fact that moral transgressions often take place and are resolved out of the view of parents or teachers. However, this factor alone does not account for the rate with which parents and teachers engage in responses to children's moral transgressions. It also seems that adults and children both prefer to allow children to resolve their own moral disputes—a trend that increases as children get older. For example, one study reported that parental responses to children's moral events increase during toddlerhood, whereas adult intervention appears to decrease from preschool years to middle childhood (Gralinski & Kopp, 1993). Similarly, it has been found that the rate of teacher responses to children's moral transgressions at school gradually decreases from Grades 3 to 5 and by Grade 7 is so infrequent that the researchers were unable to apply statistical analyses to the patterns of adult response (Nucci & Nucci, 1982b). For their part, preschool-age children would rather work out conflicts on their own without adult intervention as the preferred means to resolve moral disputes (Killen & Turiel, 1991), and beginning in middle childhood children gradually ask for less help from adults in resolving moral conflicts (Nucci & Nucci, 1982a, 1982b).

These trends say nothing about the importance or effectiveness of adult as opposed to peer responses to moral issues. However, these findings are consistent with the characterization of morality as emerging out of intrinsic features of social interactions—features that are accessible even to young children. These findings sit in contrast with traditional views of children as the passive recipients of adult morality. However, the arbitrary nature and relative opaqueness of conventions may explain why children are less likely than adults to respond to social convention. Although young children do respond to violations of peer conventions of dress, speech, and play patterns (Corsaro, 1985; Killen, 1989; Nucci & Nucci, 1982a; Nucci, Turiel, & Encarnacion-Gawrych, 1983), it is not until middle childhood that children respond to peer breaches of the norms of adult-structured institutions such as school (Nucci & Nucci, 1982b). The emergence of such peer responses with age may be related to developmental changes in children's conceptions of the social organizational functions of convention. In any case, the important point is to recognize that children's constructions of their notions of morality, and of the conventions of society, are emerging out of different aspects of their social experiences.

SOCIAL INTERACTIONS AND THE PERSONAL

Concurrent with their efforts to navigate the moral and normative constraints of the social world, children also actively seek to carve out a zone of personal prerogative and privacy (Nucci, 1977, 1996). These are actions or concerns that the child considers to pertain primarily to him or herself, and therefore to be outside of the area of justifiable social regulation (Nucci, 1996). Although there is considerable cultural variation in what specific things are considered personal, allowance for some area of personal choice appears to be culturally universal. Within American culture, actions that children and adults tend to treat as personal include the content of an individual's correspondence and self-expressive creative works, recreational activities, choice of friends or intimates, and actions that focus on the state of one's own body (Nucci, 1981; Nucci, Guerra, & Lee, 1991; Smetana, 1982; Smetana, Bridgeman, & Turiel, 1983). It has been hypothesized that individuals attempt to control a personal domain of actions to maintain personal integrity, agency, and individuality (Nucci, 1996). Thus, there is a certain amount of dynamic tension between what the individual is motivated to assert as within his or her sphere of the personal and what the social group (such as the family) and culture define as within the shared behaviors defined by custom and convention.

Social Interactions Between Adults and Young Children

Studies exploring the early patterns of family interaction associated with moral, conventional, and personal events have uncovered distinctive patterns associated with actions in each domain. The patterns associated with moral and conventional issues were described earlier. What seems to set them apart from the interactions surrounding the construction of the personal is the degree to which personal issues engender resistance and negotiation between adults and children. Interaction patterns between parents and young children were initially explored in an observational study (Nucci & Weber, 1995) of the at-home interactions between 20 middle-class suburban mothers and their 3- or 4-year-old children. The parenting styles of the mothers fell within what Baumrind (1971) described as authoritative parenting. These mothers had a set of firmly established behavioral expectations, but were flexible in their disciplining of children.

Pairs of mothers and children were observed during four activity periods over a span of 3 days. Among the things discovered was that mothers almost never negotiated with children regarding moral, conventional, or prudential forms of conduct. In contrast, nearly one quarter of the observed interactions around personal issues involved negotiation and concession on the part of the mothers. The degree to which negotiations took place in the context of mixed events was also interesting. A mixed event is one in which there is overlap among the domain characteristics of the action. Over 90% of the observed mixed events involved overlap between conventions or prudential concerns about the child's safety with the personal domain. Mothers engaged in negotiation with their children about such mixed events about half of the time. This type of interaction over a mixed issue is illustrated in the following.

Mother: Evan, it's your last day of nursery school. Why don't you wear your nursery sweatshirt?

Child: I don't want to wear that one.

Mother: This is the last day of nursery school, that's why we wear it. You want to wear that one?

Child: Another one.

Mother: Are you going to get it, or should I?

Child: I will. First I got to get a shirt.

Mother: [Goes to the child's dresser and starts picking out shirts.] This one? This one? Do you know which one you have in mind? Here, this is a new one.

Child: No, it's too big.

Mother: Oh, Evan, just wear one, and when you get home, you can
            pick whatever you want, and I won't even help you. [Child
            puts on shirt.]

This case presents a conflict between a dress convention (wearing a particular shirt on the last day of school) and the child's view that dress is a personal choice. The mother acknowledges the child's resistance and attempts to negotiate, finally offering the child a free choice once school is over. This example illustrates several things. For one, the mother provided direct information to the child about the convention in question: "This is the last day of nursery school, that's why we wear it." At the same time, she displayed an interest in fostering the child's autonomy and decision making around the issue. The child's resistance, which conveyed his personal interest, was not simply cut off, but was guided by the mother who linked it to his autonomy: "Are you going to get it, or should I? . . . You can pick whatever you, want, and I won't even help you." In the end, there is compromise. The child got to choose, but within a more general conventional demand (enforced by the mother) that he wear a shirt.

The verbal exchange engaged in by the mother and child in the prior example illustrates that the mothers in this study acted in ways that indicated an understanding that children should have areas of discretion and personal control. The excerpt also illustrates ways in which children, through their resistance, provided mothers with information about their desires and needs for personal choice. Analyses of the children's responses show that assertions of prerogative and personal choice did not occur to the same degree across all forms of social interaction, but were disproportionately associated with events involving personal issues. Assertions of prerogative and choice comprised 88% of children's responses in the context of mixed events and 98% of their responses in the case of predominantly personal events. In contrast, such responses comprised less than 10% of children's statements in the context of moral or prudential events and about 25% of their responses to conventional events. These behavioral measures indicate that middle-class preschool-age children are able to distinguish between the personal and matters of social regulation. Interviews conducted with the children revealed that they viewed personal, but not moral or conventional, behaviors as ones that should be up to the self and not the mother to decide.

This (Nucci & Weber, 1995) observational study also provided evidence that middle-class mothers provide children areas of personal choice without requiring a process of negotiation. Mothers generally do not explicitly tell young children that a particular behavior is something that is a matter of the child's personal choice. When they do give such explicit statements, they look like the following discussion between a mother and her daughter over the girl's hair style.

> *Mother*:   If you want, we can get your hair cut. It's your choice.
> *Child*:   I only want it that long—down to here. [Child points to where she wants her hair cut.]

More typically, the social messages mothers directed to children about personal issues were in the indirect form of offered choices such as illustrated in the following exchange.

> *Mother*:   You need to decide what you want to wear to school today.
> *Child*:   [Open a drawer.] Pants. Pants. Pants.
> *Mother*:   Have you decided what to wear today?
> *Child*:   I wear these.
> *Mother*:   Okay, that's a good choice.
> *Mother*:   How would you like your hair today?
> *Child*:   Down. [Child stands by the bed, and her mother carefully combs her hair.]

In the prior interaction, the mother, through a set of offered choices, conveys the idea that dress and hairstyle are matters for the child to decide. The child might then infer that such behavior is personal. Through both direct and indirect forms of communication, mothers show a willingness to provide children areas of personal discretion. The fact that mothers are more likely to tell children what to do in the context of moral, conventional, and prudential behaviors than in the context of personal ones is an indication that mothers view the former as issues in which the child needs to accommodate to specific external social demands and meanings, whereas the personal issues are for the child to interpret and control.

In summary, mothers displayed systematic differences in their responses to children as a function of whether the issues in question were ones within the child's personal domain. The study also provided evidence that children play an active role in relation to their mothers and provide feedback in the form of requests and resistances to their mothers that afford mothers information regarding the child's claims to areas of personal control. This feedback is not simply a generalized resistance to adult authority (Brehm & Brehm, 1981; Kuczinski et al., 1987), but a limited set of claims to choice over a personal sphere. This is most evident in cases of mixed events and suggests that mothers open to their children's feedback have direct access to information about their own children's needs for a personal domain. This work on the personal also indicates that Piaget's (1932) assumption about the unilateral direction of adult–child relations was something of an oversimplification. Children and parents are both involved in establishing an equilibrium between areas of social/moral regulation and areas of the child's discretion and autonomy. Children are not responding to parents as wholly heteronomous, but actively resist parental power and authority on issues they feel are outside the legitimate sphere of parental control.

As already stated, the child's construction of the personal is not accomplished solely at the individual level, but through reciprocal interaction between the child and members of society. For this to occur, there must also be some understanding on the part of adults that children should be accorded an area of personal discretion. We have already seen evidence of this in the observations of mother–child interactions. Similar interaction patterns occur in preschool settings, although the degree of adult–child negotiation is less than at home (Killen & Smetana, 1999). More direct evidence of adult appreciation of the need for a personal zone among young children was obtained in an interview study with middle- and working-class mothers of young children conducted within the same community and a neighboring suburb as in the Nucci and Weber study (Nucci & Smetana, 1996).

The interview focused on the mothers' views of whether and around what sorts of issues children should be given decision-making authority and around which issues mothers should exert their authority. They were asked to explain how they determined which behaviors to leave up to their children and why they allowed or encouraged children to determine those things for themselves. Mothers were also asked about their sense of what issues generated conflicts between themselves and their children, how these conflicts were resolved, and what role they saw themselves playing in those mother–child exchanges.

All of the mothers interviewed in this study supported the notion that children 4 to 7 years of age should be allowed choice over some things and that children should be allowed to hold their own opinions. Mothers justified allowing children to exercise choice on the grounds that decision making fostered competence and allowing children to hold opinions of their own fostered development of the child's agency and self-esteem. Thus, these mothers appeared to value permitting their children areas of freedom to foster their personal development and autonomy. However, mothers placed boundaries around actions they left up to children to determine. Mothers stated that their children were allowed to exercise choice over such personal issues as play activities, playmates, amount and type of food, and choice of clothes. Nevertheless, mothers stated that they placed limits on children's actions when they went counter to family or societal conventions and when they posed risks to the child or others.

In addition to limiting children's activities when they conflicted with conventional, moral, or prudential considerations, mothers stated that they occasionally limited their children's activities in the areas they had stated they allowed children to determine or control. As we saw in the observational study (Nucci & Weber, 1995), mother–child conflicts over these personal issues often resulted in compromise by the mother. In their interviews (Nucci & Smetana, 1996), mothers expressed a willingness to compromise over such issues to support the child's agency, self-esteem, and competence. Mothers viewed themselves as acting rationally and pragmatically in response to their perceptions of the child's personal competence and the risks a given act posed to the child. In the context of mother–child disagreements, mothers tended to see themselves primarily as educators and less often as controllers or nurturers.

When placed together with the results of at-home observations (Nucci & Weber, 1995), these interviews with mothers provide an integrated portrait of how mothers and preschool-age children establish and foster the emergence of the child's autonomy and sense of a personal domain of privacy and choice. The picture that emerges is not one of across-the-board struggle and conflict, but rather of a shared and differentiated worldview in which autonomy and choice coexist with obedience and conformity to common norms and rational moral and prudential constraints. Those conflicts that do arise are not random in nature, but generally fall within the range of issues at the edge of the child's personal domain and what the mother views as matters of social convention or the child's safety.

Adolescent–Parent Conflicts

Smetana's (1989b) work on adolescent–parent conflicts indicates that similar child resistance to adult control over personal issues continues and increases as children grow up. Research with older children and adolescents has indicated that they view adults as retaining authority over moral issues (Smetana, 1989b; Smetana, Braeges, & Yau, 1991; Smetana, Yau, Restrepo, & Braeges, 1991). Moreover, adolescents view parents as having a duty or obligation to regulate moral behavior and see themselves as obliged to obey parental moral rules (Smetana, Killen, & Turiel, 1991). Accordingly, the Smetana group found that moral issues are an infrequent source of conflict in adolescent–parent relationships. Adolescents also typically believe that parents have a duty or obligation to regulate the conventions within the family (Smetana & Asquith, 1994). However, the endorsement of obedience to convention appears to decline with age. A similar pattern appears to hold for prudential matters that touch on issues of the adolescent's health or safety. Younger adolescents (under the age of 15) generally maintain that parents have the authority and obligation to regulate behaviors that impinge on the adolescent's safety or well-being (Tisak, 1986). As they grow older, however, adolescents tend to view such issues of personal welfare as falling within their own sphere of responsibility and personal jurisdiction (Smetana & Asquith, 1994).

As might be expected, adolescent–parent conflicts generally arise in the context of these areas of change. Conflicts tend to occur over issues parents perceive as important to the conventions that serve to organize and structure family and household organization and that adolescents see as interfering in their personal lives. The kinds of issues that generate most conflicts in American households are such things as preferences for TV programs or music, spending decisions (e.g., whether to spend allowance money on games), appearance (dress, makeup), activities (time spent talking on the phone), schedules (bedtimes, curfews), and where the adolescent is permitted to go without seeking specific parental permission (Smetana & Asquith, 1994). Parents justify their perspective by appealing to family or cultural norms, parental authority, the adolescent's role-related responsibilities in the family (e.g., clean up room, mow the lawn, etc.), need for politeness and manners, and perceived social cost of adolescent nonconformity (e.g., parents' embarrassment, concern about others' misperceptions of the child). Adolescents, in turn, understand but reject their parents' social-conventional interpretations of disputes and appeal instead to exercising or maintaining personal jurisdiction (Smetana, 1989b; Smetana, Brages, & Yau, 1991).

Far fewer family disputes arise over issues that concern risks to the adolescent's health or safety. This is because such prudential issues have an objective quality to them that is obvious to both parties. Nevertheless, the tendency of adolescents to engage in risk taking and to believe in their own invulnerability is a potential source of aggravation and alarm to parents. In the case of prudential issues, there is a self-evident overlap between the parents' role as nurturer and protector and the adolescent's position as "master of his(her) own house." Matters of personal safety are by definition self-referential, and parents of adolescents often find themselves in the position of shaking their heads as they watch their offspring engage in relatively harmless, but foolish actions (e.g., going to school without headgear in subzero winter weather) emblematic of their children's desire to take control of their own lives.

For the most part, such issues are conflict-free because most adolescents do not engage in high-risk behaviors. In other cases, however, adolescents do make foolish choices with long-term negative consequences. One measure of personal maturity is the degree to which one can make intelligent cost–benefit analyses of behaviors such as drug use, which may bring momentary pleasure, but long-term damage to the user. Studies of adolescent concepts of drug use have reported a strong relationship between self-reported drug use and the tendency to see the behavior as simply a matter of personal choice (Nucci, Guerra, & Lee, 1991). Adolescents who are not involved in drug use tend to see such behavior as wrong because of the potential harm such behavior can cause to oneself. In addition, high drug users are much more likely than low drug users to endorse themselves, rather than parents or others, as having legitimate authority over decisions to engage in drug use (Nucci et al., 1991). However, even when adolescents view prudential issues such as drug and alcohol use as legitimately regulated by parents or teachers, adolescents view parents as having significantly less authority over these issues than their parents do (Smetana & Asquith, 1994).

The general pattern that emerges from this work on adolescent–parent relations is that there is a gradual increase in the range of issues that adolescents assume as matters of personal choice rather than subject to parental authority. Parents generally lag behind in their recognition of areas within which adolescents should have decision making, but nonetheless give adolescents a wider degree of freedom than they give to younger children (Nucci et al., 1996; Smetana & Asquith, 1994). This shift is also accompanied by a degree of adolescent–parent conflict. Smetana (1995) recently pooled the data from her series of studies on adolescent–parent conflict to examine the overall patterns that emerge within normal families. Her analysis looked at over 300 families and included findings from her work with Chinese adolescents and parents in Hong Kong. In her report, Smetana (1995) noted that in addition to her own findings of prototypical and in some cases intense adolescent–parent conflicts within her Hong Kong families, anthropological accounts of adolescent–parent conflicts in 160 cultures provide evidence that such conflicts are widespread (Schlegel & Barry, 1991). Smetana's work included observations of family interactions as well as interviews with individual family members.

On the basis of a statistical procedure called *cluster analysis,* Smetana identified three basic patterns of dealing with adolescent–parent conflict. The most prevalent pattern, labeled *frequent squabblers,* is one in which adolescents and parents engage in frequent, low-intensity conflicts over everyday details of family life. A second, smaller group comprised the *placid* families, who reported rare conflicts and whose conflicts were of low or moderate intensity. The third group, labeled *tumultuous* families, had frequent conflicts (although fewer than squabblers) that were very intense.

In terms of parenting patterns, these three family patterns did not differ in their rate of regulation of moral, conventional, or prudential issues. The differences that emerged were over the regulation of multifaceted and personal issues. *Tumultuous* and *squabbling* families had more rules than placid families over multifaceted issues. Parents from *tumultuous* families were more likely to be divorced or remarried and had lower socioeconomic status (SES) than other parents. Parents in *tumultuous* families were more authoritarian, had more rules, were more restrictive of their adolescents' personal jurisdiction, and were less likely to engage in compromise or negotiation than either of the other two family types. In these families, parents felt more of an obligation to regulate personal issues and were less likely to view personal issues as within the adolescents' jurisdiction. Smetana (1995, 1996) concluded that these families appeared to intrude more deeply than is developmentally or culturally appropriate in their adolescents' personal domains. In other work, we have found that parental overintrusion into adolescents' personal area is associated with symptoms of depression and hostility in children (Hasebe, Nucci, & Nucci, 2001).

Placid families reported fewer conflicts, but were not conflict-free. These tended to be higher SES families in which parents were professionally employed. They engaged in more joint decision making than did other parents, were less restrictive, and were rated by their children as higher in warmth.

Squabbling families were in many ways similar to *placid* families in their willingness to engage in negotiation and compromise with their adolescent children. Like the *placid* families, they displayed more warmth than the parents in *tumultuous* families. Relative to *placid* families, however, *frequent squabblers* tended to use a greater number of social-conventional rationales.

These findings indicate that a certain degree of adolescent–parent conflict is to be expected and most likely reflects the normal process of realignment between parents and children as children move toward adult status. What is important and of interest is that this realignment is not in the form of an across-the-board negotiation of all moral and societal values, but the specific adjustment of locus of responsibility for decision making in the personal domain. This shift is not an invention of liberal parenting or Western democratic culture, but a basic part of human development. Research studies conducted with African-American (Smetana & Gaines, 1999; Trosper, 2001); Brazilian (Lins-Dyer & Nucci, 2000; Nucci, Camino, & Sapiro, 1996); Chinese (Xu, 2000; Yau & Smetana, 1994), and Japanese (Hasebe, Nucci, & Nucci 2001) children, adolescents, and parents have reported similar domain-related patterns of social interaction.

CONCLUSIONS

The basic thesis of this chapter is that the child's construction of moral concepts and social norms emerges out of qualitatively differing patterns of social interaction that correspond to moral, conventional, and personal domains of social knowledge. In other places, we have addressed the ways in which these basic knowledge systems are applied to the interpretation of complex social situations in which elements from more than one domain are involved (Nucci, 2001; Turiel, 1998). Evidence from a combination of observational and interview studies indicates that the child's moral and social growth is not a matter of reconstructing at an individual level the norms maintained by the culture or its socializing agents (Mantovani, 2000). Although children's social interactions generally involve discourse, they are not engaged in such discourse solely for the purpose of understanding the values of older members of the culture. This becomes quite clear when we examine the nature of social interactions and corresponding concepts around issues children and adolescents treat as personal. Social interactions about personal issues often involve resistance and negotiation in which the adult, rather than the child, makes the greater adjustment. However, such instances of resistance generally do not characterize the nature of social interactions between children and adults around moral or conventional issues. Thus, we cannot simply view the social interactions of children in terms of resistance and gradual accommodation to norms of society. The picture that has emerged is one of heterogeneity that corresponds to facets of the moral, normative, and personal social realms of children and adults. Rather than dividing up into a binary set of relations as Piaget proposed, the social worlds of both children and adults are multifaceted and structured by similar basic forms of social interaction having to do with moral issues of fairness and welfare, conventions and customs, and personal matters of choice, privacy, and autonomy.

REFERENCES

Baumrind, D. (1971). Current patterns of parental authority. *Developmental Psychology Monographs*, 4(1, Part 2).

Brehm, S. S., & Brehm, J. W. (1981). *Psychological reaction: A theory of freedom and control*. New York: Academic Press.

Corsaro, W. (1985). *Peer culture in the early years*. Norwood, NJ: Ablex.

Damon, W. (1977). *The social world of the child*. San Francisco: Jossey-Bass.

Dunn, J., & Munn, P. (1987). The development of justifications in disputes. *Developmental Psychology*, 23, 791–798.

Dunn, J., & Slomkowski, C. (1992). Conflict and the development of social understanding. In C. U. Schantz & W. W. Hartup (Eds.), *Conflict in childhood and development* (pp. 70–92). Cambridge, England: Cambridge University Press.

Gralinski, H., & Kopp, C. (1993). Everyday rules for behavior: Mothers' requests to young children. *Developmental Psychology*, 29, 573–584.

Hasebe, Y., Nucci, L., & Nucci, M. (2001). *Parental control of the personal domain and adolescent symptoms of psychopathology: A cross-national study in the U.S. and Japan*. Unpublished manuscript, Western Illinois University, Macomb, IL.

Killen, M. (1989). Context, conflict and coordination in early social development. In L. T. Winegar (Ed.), *Social interaction and the development of children's understanding* (pp. 114–136). Norwood, NJ: Ablex.

Killen, M., & Smetana, J. (1999). Social interactions in preschool classrooms and the development of young children's conceptions of the personal. *Child Development, 70,* 486–501.

Killen, M., & Turiel, E. (1991). Conflict resolution in preschool social interactions. *Early Education and Development, 2,* 240–255.

Kuczinski, L., Kochanska, G., Radke-Yarrow, M., & Girnius Brown, O. (1987). A developmental interpretation of young children's non-compliance. *Developmental Psychology, 23*(6), 799–806.

Lins-Dyer, T., & Nucci, L. (2000, April). *The impact of social class on daily life decisions of mothers and daughters in northeastern Brazil.* Paper presented at the biennial meeting of the Society for Research on Adolescence.

Mantovani, G. (2000). *Exploring borders: Understanding culture and psychology.* London: Routledge.

Much, N., & Shweder, R. A. (1978). Speaking of rules: The analysis of culture in breach. In W. Damon (Ed.), *New directions for child development: Vol. 2. Moral development* (pp. 19–39). San Francisco: Jossey-Bass.

Nucci, L. (1977). *Social development: Personal, conventional, and moral concepts.* Unpublished doctoral dissertation, University of California, Santa Cruz.

Nucci, L. (1981). Conceptions of personal issues: A domain distinct from moral or societal concepts. *Child Development, 52,* 114–121.

Nucci, L. (1996). Morality and the personal sphere of actions. In E. Reed, E. Turiel, & T. Brown (Eds.), *Values and knowledge* (pp. 41–60). Hillsdale, NJ: Lawrence Erlbaum Associates.

Nucci, L. (2001). *Education in the moral domain.* Cambridge, England: Cambridge University Press.

Nucci, L., Camino, C., & Sapiro, C. (1996). Social class effects on Northeastern Brazilian children's conceptions of areas of personal choice and social regulation. *Child Development, 67,* 1223–1242.

Nucci, L., Guerra, N., & Lee, J. Y. (1991). Adolescent judgments of the personal, prudential, and normative aspects of drug usage. *Developmental Psychology, 27,* 841–848.

Nucci, L., & Nucci, M. S. (1982a). Children's responses to moral and social-conventional transgressions in free-play settings. *Child Development, 53,* 1337–1342.

Nucci, L., & Nucci M. S. (1982b). Children's social interactions in the context of moral and conventional transgressions. *Child Development, 53,* 403–412.

Nucci, L., & Smetana, J. (1996). Mothers' concepts of young children's areas of personal freedom. *Child Development, 67,* 1870–1886.

Nucci, L., & Turiel, E. (1978). Social interactions and the development of social concepts in pre-school children. *Child Development, 49,* 400–407.

Nucci, L., Turiel, E., & Encarnacion-Gawrych, G. (1983). Children's social interactions and social concepts in the Virgin Islands. *Journal of Cross-Cultural Psychology, 14,* 469–487.

Nucci, L., & Weber, E. K. (1995). Social interactions in the home and the development of young children's conceptions within the personal domain. *Child Development, 66,* 1438–1452.

Piaget, J. (1932). *The moral judgment of the child.* New York: The Free Press.

Piaget, J., & Inhelder, B. (1964). *The early growth of logic in the child.* New York: Norton.

Ross, H. (1996). Negotiating principles of entitlement in sibling property disputes. *Developmental Psychology, 32,* 90–101.

Schlegel, A., & Barry, H. III. (1991). *Adolescence: An anthropological inquiry.* New York: The Free Press.

Sedlak, A., & Walton, M. D. (1982). Sequencing in social repair: A Markov grammar of children's discourse about transgressions. *Developmental Review, 2*, 305–329.

Smetana, J. G. (1982). *Concepts of self and morality: Women's reasoning about abortion.* New York: Praeger.

Smetana, J. G. (1984). Toddlers' social interactions in the context of moral and conventional transgressions in the home. *Developmental Psychology, 25*, 1767–1776.

Smetana, J. (1989a). Toddler's social interactions in the context of moral and conventional transgressions in the home. *Developmental Psychology, 25*, 499–508.

Smetana, J. (1989b). Adolescents' and parents' reasoning about actual family conflict. *Child Development, 60*, 1052–1067.

Smetana, J. G. (1995). Conflict and coordination in adolescent–parent relationships. In S. Shulman (Ed.), *Close relationships and socioemotional development* (pp. 155–184). Norwood, NJ: Ablex.

Smetana, J. G. (1996). Adolescent–parent conflict: Implications for adaptive and maladaptive development. In D. Cicchetti & S. L. Toth (Eds.), *Rochester Symposium on Developmental Psychopathology: Vol. VII. Adolescence opportunities and challenges* (pp. 1–46). Rochester, NY: University of Rochester Press.

Smetana, J., & Asquith, P. (1994). Adolescents' and parents' conceptions of parental and adolescent autonomy. *Child Development, 65*, 1147–1162.

Smetana, J., Braeges, J. L., & Yau, J. (1991). Doing what you say and saying what you do: Reasoning about adolescent–parent conflict in interviews and interactions. *Journal of Adolescent Research, 6*, 276–295.

Smetana, J. G., Bridgeman, D., & Turiel, E. (1983). Differentiation of domains and prosocial behavior. In D. Bridgeman (Ed.), *The nature of prosocial development: Interdisciplinary theories and strategies* (pp. 163–183). New York: Academic Press.

Smetana, J., & Gaines, C. (1999). Adolescent–parent conflict in middle-class African American families. *Child Development, 70*, 1447–1463.

Smetana, J., Killen, M., & Turiel, E. (1991). Children's reasoning about interpersonal and moral conflicts. *Child Development, 62*, 629–644.

Smetana, J., Yau, J., Restropo, A., & Breages, J. (1991). Adolescent–parent conflict in married and divorced families. *Developmental Psychology, 27*, 1000–1010.

Tisak, M. (1986). Child's conception of parental authority. *Child Development, 57*, 166–176.

Trosper, T. (2001). *African-American middle class family: Parenting strategies for children's transgressions.* Unpublished doctoral dissertation, University of Illinois at Chicago.

Turiel, E. (1978). The development of concepts of social structure: Social convention. In J. Glick & K. A. Clarke-Stewart (Eds.), *The development of social understanding* (pp. 25–107). New York: Gardner.

Turiel, E. (1983). *The development of social knowledge: Morality and convention.* Cambridge, England: Cambridge University Press.

Turiel, E. (1998). The development of morality. In W. Damon (Ed.), *Handbook of child psychology: Vol. 3. Social, emotional, and personality development* (5th ed., pp. 863–932). New York: Academic Press.

Xu, F. (2000). *Chinese children's and mothers' concepts regarding morality, social convention, and children's personal autonomy.* Unpublished doctoral dissertation, University of Illinois at Chicago.

Yau, J., & Smetana, J. G. (1994). *Adolescent–parent conflict among Chinese adolescents in Hong Kong.* Unpublished manuscript, University of Hong Kong.

From Joint Activity to Joint Attention: A Relational Approach to Social Development in Infancy

Ulrich Müller
Pennsylvania State University

Jeremy I. M. Carpendale
Simon Fraser University

In the last decade, there has been growing interest in the onset and development of social behaviors in infancy, such as joint attention, and the developmental relation between joint attention and communicative behaviors (Carpenter, Nagell, & Tomasello, 1998; Corkum & Moore, 1995; Morissette, Ricard, & Décarie, 1995). Empirical research has identified a number of behavioral changes beginning at about 9 months that appear to reflect a new level in infants' social understanding. For example, around 10 months of age, infants begin to follow the pointing gesture of another person (Carpenter et al., 1998; Morissette et al., 1995), and they engage in social referencing behaviors (i.e., they display the tendency to look toward their parents and use their parents' emotional expression when faced with ambiguous situations; Walden & Ogan, 1988). The ability to coordinate attention with others is essential for the emergence of communicative behaviors and social referencing, is a prerequisite for language acquisition, and makes further social and cognitive development possible.

Although there is widespread agreement that important changes in social behaviors occur at the end of the first year of life, there is considerable controversy over the interpretation of these changes. According to a rich interpretation, the emergence of communicative gestures and social referencing is taken to indicate that infants have acquired the abilities to view other persons as being psychologically related to the world and to impute mental states to self and others (Bretherton, 1991; Legerstee, 1998). Specifically, Tomasello (1999) argued that the discovery of the mental state of intentionality in self and other persons underlies the changes in social behaviors at the end of the first year of life.

According to a lean interpretation, the onset of joint attention and communicative behaviors does not require that we attribute to infants an understanding that others engage in psychological relations with objects (Corkum & Moore, 1995). Rather, these social behaviors merely indicate that infants "have coordinated representations of others' activities with certain expectancies about their own instrumental actions in relation to objects" (Moore & Corkum, 1994, pp. 368–369).

In this chapter, we suggest that the controversy over the interpretation of social behaviors in infancy is influenced by largely unrecognized theoretical models and frameworks (Jopling, 1993). We discuss two such frameworks—individualist and relational—and we show that these frameworks present widely divergent ways of conceptualizing social development. We argue that the individualist framework encounters a variety of conceptual problems, and we suggest that the relational framework is better suited to explain social development. Finally, we use the development of gaze following as an example to outline the approach to social development from the perspective of the relational model.

EPISTEMOLOGICAL APPROACHES TO SOCIAL DEVELOPMENT: I. THE INDIVIDUALIST FRAMEWORK

A key characteristic of the individualist framework is that social relations are considered to be internal cognitive-perceptual processes within the private mental sphere of each individual. Consequently, the individualist framework begins with the first-person perspective and considers social relations and knowledge of other minds as inferential and derivative from the inspection of one's own mind. According to the individualistic framework, "we always begin by taking ourselves as the touchstone of whether others can be said to house a mind. The knowledge of other minds is parasitic on our knowledge of our own mind" (Jopling, 1993, p. 291).

To derive the knowledge of other minds from one's own mind, philosophers (e.g., Russell, 1921) have traditionally employed the analogical argument. Dilthey (1989) succinctly formulated the conceptual structure of the analogical argument in terms of the following syllogism:

Major Premise: A specific bodily process B has as its correlate or antecedent a specific psychic process A. (Whenever B appears, it has A as its antecedent.)

Minor Premise: A bodily process b contained in my present perception is similar to the bodily process B.

Conclusion: The affinity between b and B allows us to posit a psychic state a, similar to A, as the antecedent or correlate of b. (pp. 388–389)

The use of the analogical argument to derive knowledge of other minds becomes necessary because the individualist framework makes two basic assumptions about the workings of the mind. The first assumption is that knowledge of one's own mind is private and immediate, whereas knowledge of other minds is inferential and mediated (Hacker, 1990). The second assumption is that a hiatus exists between the inner (mind, mental states such as intentionality) and outer (behavior), and that the only link between inner and outer is an external, causal relation. Consequently, the outer is viewed as a barricade behind which the inner is hidden (ter Hark, 1990; Wilkerson, 2000).

These assumptions can be traced back to Descartes' fundamental ontological dualism between mind and body. As is well known, Descartes (1641/1960, p. 132) argued that the mind (*res cogitans*) must be strictly distinguished from the physical, spatially extended world (*res extensa*). For Descartes, the human body belongs like all other bodies to *res extensa*—a plenum of matter driven by mechanical forces. Ultimately, the body is nothing but a machine that, in a mysterious way, is controlled by the mind (Descartes, 1972, p. 141). However, if behavior simply consists of the mechanical movements of the body (i.e., movements in space), how can we possibly know of other minds? Descartes (1641/1960, p. 89) argued that our knowledge of other minds is indirect and mediated by judgments. This proposal prepares the ground for the analogical argument.

The Cartesian picture of the mind has a strong influence on contemporary approaches to social development. Contemporary developmental psychologists view mental states such as intentionality lying behind and being separate from body movements (e.g., Legerstee, 1998; Wellman & Philipps, 2001, pp. 126–127). For example, Meltzoff, Gopnik, and Repacholi (1999) claimed that "our sensory experience of other people tells us about their movements in space but does not tell us directly about their mental states" (p. 17). Moreover, in contemporary approaches to social development, the relationship between mental states such as intentionality and actions is pervasively viewed as an external, causal relation (e.g., Wellman & Phillips, 2001, p. 138; Zeedyk, 1996; for exceptions, see Frye, 1991; Wilkerson, 1999, 2000).

Furthermore, a common argument in contemporary theories is that infants' knowledge of other minds is derived from knowledge of their own mind, and the analogical inference is used to explain how infants arrive at an understanding of other minds (e.g., Meltzoff & Brooks, 2001; Tomasello, 1999). For example, according to Meltzoff and colleagues (Meltzoff et al., 1999; Meltzoff & Brooks, 2001), the innately given ability to form abstract and cross-modal representations allows infants to detect equivalences between the observed actions of other persons and the proprioceptive experience of their own actions. As a consequence, infants recognize the fundamental similarity between self and other, share bodily states with the other, and interpret the other person's act as "like me" (Meltzoff et al., 1999, pp. 34–35). Because infants can readily act like others and realize that others can act like them, this sharing of behavioral states allows a

> foothold for infants attributing like mental states to others. We envision a three-step developmental sequence: (a) When I perform that bodily act I have such and such a phenomenal experience, (b) I recognize that others perform the same type of bodily acts as me, (c) the other is sharing my behavioral state; ergo, perhaps the other is having the same phenomenal experience. (Meltzoff et al., 1999, p. 35)

CRITICISM OF THE INDIVIDUALIST FRAMEWORK

The individualist framework and its Cartesian tenets have repeatedly been criticized (e.g., Hacker, 1990; ter Hark, 1990). In the following, we focus on the criticism that has been directed against the analogical argument.

The analogical argument has been criticized for a variety of reasons (Scheler, 1913/1954). First, it has been argued that the analogical argument is artificial and does not correspond with the experience that we have in our everyday encounters with other people (Jopling, 1993; Wittgenstein, 1982, para. 767). Second, the ability to match their own proprioceptively experienced actions to the visually experienced actions of others does not allow infants to infer the similarity between their own experience and the experience of other people because infants' own living body is experienced from within, whereas another person's body is experienced from the outside (Merleau-Ponty, 1960/1964; Scheler, 1913/1954). As Soffer (1999) pointed out, to establish a similarity between one's own bodily experience and another person's bodily experience, the ego must be able to take an external perspective on its experience: "It is not my body as experienced by *me* that might resemble the body of the other, rather it is my body as would be viewed by the other that would resemble the other's body as viewed by me" (p. 155; italics original). In addition, to make the analogical inference, infants must be capable of some sort of counterfactual reasoning because they must model someone else's feelings on the basis of feelings that they, at that moment, do not have. Although this is ultimately an empirical question, it is doubtful that young infants are capable of either taking an external perspective on their own experience or counterfactual reasoning.

Third, it is not clear what could serve as the criterion for determining that another person feels and experiences the same thing that I do (Wittgenstein, 1958, para. 350). To establish sameness or identity, an independent criterion must be introduced; the criterion cannot be one of the terms for which identity is being established. However, the analogical argument uses one of the terms (ego) for which identity is being established as the criterion. Thus, the analogical argument cannot explain how ego determines that alter is having the same experience.

Fourth and finally, Scheler (1913/1954) and Lipps (1907) showed that analogical reasoning cannot, for logical reasons, lead to the notion of other, let alone the notion of other minds. Rather, the analogical inference can only lead to the conclusion that, "There is another of my psychic states again" (Lipps, 1907, p. 708; our translation). The notion of alter ego is illicitly introduced into the conclusion due to the equivocal use of the word *ego*. In the analogical argument, the word *ego* indiscriminately refers to both my ego and the alter ego, thereby eliminating the fundamental difference between ego and alter ego, which is exactly what the argument is meant to explain. Scheler (1913/1954) concluded that the analogical argument would be logically correct only if it implied that "*it is my own self that is present here as well—and not some other and alien self*" (pp. 240–241; italics original). It is important to realize that this is a criticism of the claim that the original acquisition of the notion of alter ego is derived from analogical reasoning. Scheler (1913/1954) did not deny that we do make analogical inferences on occasion. However, analogical reasoning cannot account for the original acquisition of the notion of other, but rather presupposes it. To address the fundamental problems encountered by the individualistic framework, we turn to the relational framework.

EPISTEMOLOGICAL APPROACHES TO SOCIAL DEVELOPMENT: II. THE RELATIONAL FRAMEWORK

The basic tenet of the relational framework is that the self always already lives within a social world and is always already immersed in relations with others. These relations are not established in the mind of the individual, but in common space through interaction and dialogue in the course of which the partners respond to each others' actions and coordinate as well as pattern each others' activities. Neither self nor other are primary. Rather self and other are sustained by particular interactive relations, and it is within and through these relations that concepts of self and other evolve (Baldwin, 1897; Jopling, 1993; Overton, 1998).

As a consequence, from the perspective of the relational framework, the development of social understanding is conceived of in a way that is diametrically opposed to that of the individualist framework. The individualist perspective conceives of the development of social understanding as proceeding from the inside out (i.e., the results of individual information processing are applied to external objects, which sometimes happen to be people particularly if their pattern of behavior corresponds to the pattern of behavior that infants display). By contrast, the relational perspective conceives of the development of social understanding as proceeding from the outside in (i.e., social relations are first established in interactions with other people and only later are these relations internalized).

In many respects, the position endorsed by Piaget (1977/1995) in his *Sociological Studies* is a relational position. There Piaget contrasted the relational position with individual and collectivist positions and suggested that "the substantialist language of whole and parts ought to be replaced by a language based on relations between individuals or individuals in groups" (Piaget, 1977/1995, p. 210). For Piaget, then, neither individual nor group is primary, but rather the interactions between individuals. Furthermore, Piaget rejected the division of intelligence into two independent worlds—the world of intrapersonal, individual cognition, and the world of interpersonal, social cognition. Because the interactions and cooperations established between individuals are subject to the same kinds of combinations and transformations as are intraindividual operations, both tend toward the same form of equilibrium, which consists in the construction of reversible systems of relations. Both individual and interpersonal intelligence are two inseparable aspects of the same reality: "The internal operations of the individual and the interpersonal coordination of points of view constitute a single and the same reality, at once intellectual and social" (Piaget, 1977/1995, p. 307).

The relational framework also rejects the Cartesian assumption that the inner is something private and hidden behind and only externally related to the outer. According to the relational framework, inner and outer are intrinsically related, and the outer is expressive of the inner:

> It is *in* the blush that we perceive shame, *in* the laughter joy. To say that "our only initial datum is the body" is completely erroneous. This is true only for the doctor or the scientist, i.e., for man in so far as he abstracts artificially from the expressive phenomena. (Scheler, 1913/1954, p. 10)

Similarly, when we notice that a person is ashamed, we do not talk either about the behavior or the state of mind in isolation of each other. Rather, we talk "about the one *via* the other" (Wittgenstein, 1958, p. 179). The language games of the inner and the outer are intermeshed and penetrate each other, with outer behavior serving as the criterion for the ascription of inner mental states (Hacker, 1990; Wittgenstein, 1980, para. 292, para. 1066–1076). The intrinsic connection between mental states and outer expression is nicely captured by Wittgenstein's (1958) aphorism that "the human body is the best picture of the human soul" (p. 178).

The relation between inner and outer is thus an internal, implicative, not an external, causal relation. Mental states do not cause behavior. Rather mental states such as intentions are logically connected with behavior and cannot be identified independently of the behavior of which they are expressive (Greve, 2001; von Wright, 1971). In the next section, we elaborate the developmental implications of the relational framework, and we demonstrate its fertility by analyzing the development of gaze following from a relational perspective.

CONSIDERING THE STARTING POINT IN ACCOUNTS OF SOCIAL DEVELOPMENT IN INFANCY

Examining the starting point in developmental theories is important because "starting points have a tendency to haunt us all the way through to our theoretical conclusions" (Jopling, 1993, p. 290). From a relational framework, the starting point for development is a state of relative undifferentiation between subject and object and inner and outer (Baldwin, 1906; Piaget, 1937/1954). From birth, infants are intrinsically directed toward the environment, and the relation between subject and world is from the beginning charged with meaning (Piaget, 1936/1963, 1965/1971). However, initially infants do not differentiate between their actions and the objects on which these actions bear because each action constitutes an undifferentiated whole and establishes an immediate relation between body and objects (Piaget, 1970/1972). As a consequence, experience is immediate in the sense that infants cannot distance themselves from their lived body. Rather, the lived body is the sole point of reference—the dynamic center on which experience converges (Piaget, 1937/1954, 1970/1972).

Piaget (1945/1962) described this starting point as "egocentrism . . . the failure to distinguish between the subjective and the objective" (p. 285), and he conceived of the infant as being "the centre of the universe—but a centre that is unaware of itself" (Piaget, 1970/1972, p. 21). The concept of egocentrism also applies to social understanding. According to Piaget (1962/2000), social egocentrism "stems from non-differentiation between one's own and other possible points of view and not at all from an individualism which precedes relations with other people . . ." (p. 244). It constitutes a serious misunderstanding to interpret these characterizations as implying that infants are initially asocial, "autistic" beings (e.g., Meltzoff & Brooks, 2001, p. 172). Clearly, infants live in and are affected by the social world from birth (Piaget, 1977/1995, p. 278), but they do not initially differentiate the directedness of other persons from their own directedness. Rather infant and other person form an "undifferentiated group life" (Merleau-Ponty, 1964, p. 119). At this developmental level, infant and caregiver may share knowledge without the infant being aware of the fact that knowledge is shared (Baldwin, 1906; Moore & Corkum, 1994). If intersubjectivity is ascribed to this early relationship between infant and caregiver, it must be kept in mind that this ascription occurs from the outside point of view of another observer and does not appropriately characterize the infant's point of view (see Baldwin, 1906, pp. 138–144).

Recently, the view that infants start from a position of relative undifferentiation between self and other has been seriously challenged (Legerstee, 1998; Rochat & Striano, 1999; Trevarthen & Aitken, 2001). The findings that newborns respond differently to external and self-administered stimulation (Rochat & Hespos, 1997), that 2-month-old infants react differently to social and nonsocial stimuli (e.g., Legerstee, Corter, & Kienapple, 1990), and that infants engage in finely attuned emotional exchanges with others (Trevarthen & Aitken, 2001) are cited as empirical evidence for the presence of self–other differentiation at birth or in early infancy. In these studies, infants' discrimination between and differential responding to different types of stimuli constitutes the basis for inferences about their level of social understanding and self-understanding. However, discrimination or differential responding do not enable us to determine whether the meaning of the discrimination is grasped. A different reaction to two different stimuli indicates only that each stimulus is followed by one specific reaction, which could be quite independent of the other and might have nothing to do with the other (Straus, 1932/1963). Thus, there is no reason to attribute reflective self-awareness and explicit differentiation between self- and other-directedness to infants on the basis of differential responding (Case, 1991; Soffer, 1999).

In the context of the finely attuned interchanges that are characteristic of the early interactions between infant and caregiver, the other person is likely experienced as complementary to infants' needs and expectations. Clearly, against the backdrop of this tightly interlocked, undifferentiated self–other system, the other is differentiated from "the rest of the environment and cannot be treated as one 'object' among many" (Soffer, 1999, p. 154). However, if we assumed that infants are able to explicitly differentiate themselves from other persons, it would be difficult to explain a number of developmental phenomena. For example, young infants react to distress responses of others with distress responses themselves (Bischof-

Köhler, 1989; Hoffman, 1991; Piaget, 1945/1962, Obs. 2). These responses are due to contagion (i.e., the distress cues from another person are confounded with unpleasant feelings that are aroused in the self; Hoffman, 1991). Thus, contagion is due to a lack of differentiation between self and other. By contrast, when infants are about 18 months old, they respond to distress cues of another person by trying to console the other person (Bischof-Köhler, 1989; Zahn-Waxler, Radke-Yarrow, Wagner, & Chapman, 1992). These empathic responses must be based on some rudimentary differentiation between the other person's directedness and infants' own directedness because infants' responses are more appropriate to the other person's situation than to their own situation (Hoffman, 1991).

Taking the lack of differentiation between self- and other-directedness and inner and outer as a starting position for an account of social development has four important implications. First, if initially infants do not differentiate between inner and outer, mental and bodily aspects of behavior, then the task of understanding the other person's mental states, emotions, and directedness (i.e., intentionality) is radically transformed. Because the inner and outer are not differentiated, infants do not interpret mental states, intentionality, and emotions as lying behind their behavioral expressions. Rather behavioral expressions disclose their meanings first in interpersonal bodily engagement. This point was nicely captured by Merleau-Ponty (1964):

> If I am a consciousness turned toward things, I can meet in things the actions of another and find in them meaning, because they are themes of possible activity for my own body. . . . At first, the child imitates not persons but conducts. The problem of knowing how conduct can be transferred from another to me is infinitely less difficult to solve than the problem of knowing how I can represent to myself a psyche that is radically foreign to me. (p. 117)

Consequently, from a relational perspective, it is unnecessary to stipulate that to understand another person's emotions and attentional directedness infants must construct a 'theory' about unobservable, hidden entities (Butterworth & Jarrett, 1991; Hobson, 1993; Wilkerson, 1999).

Second, from a relational perspective, social development is not conceived of as a process in the course of which infants make the transition from a behaviorist toward an intentionalistic understanding of others. Because from birth infants are intentional and directed beings (Piaget, 1965/1971; Zelazo, 1996), they endow all events, including the behaviors of others, with a directedness. However, initially they do not differentiate their own from another person's directedness (Soffer, 1999, p. 160). Consequently, from a relational perspective, the problem faced by infants is not primarily one of establishing similarity to the other. Rather, their major task is to "break up" this initial lack of differentiation (Soffer, 1999, p. 157).

Third, social development is not an all-or-none process. Rather, social development is a gradual process that consists of a sequence of levels that characterize increasing differentiation and integration between self- and other-directedness. The task of any account of social development is thus identifying the organization of each developmental level and describing the processes that lead to the developmental transformations.

Fourth, from a relational perspective, development is conceived of as a process of decentration. This process was masterfully described in Piaget's (1937/1954, 1945/1962, 1936/1963) books on sensorimotor development in infancy. Key to Piaget's description is the intrinsically relational nature of subject and world: As infants differentiate and coordinate their action schemes, they construct increasingly complex spatial, causal, and temporal relations between objects in the world (Piaget, 1936/1963, p. 211). The "more numerous the links that are established among the schemata of assimilation, the less it remains centered on the subjectivity of the assimilating subject" (Piaget, 1937/1954, p. xi). Applied to social development this means that developmental psychologists must study how infants in interactions with others construct more complex relations among themselves, other persons, and objects, and thereby gradually differentiate and integrate self- and other-directedness.

In the following, we show that social development in infancy follows the same process of decentration and that this process involves the construction of more complex relations among self, other, and objects. This process is initially a consequence of embodied, practical interactions, in which the projects of the infant meet resistance of other people (Soffer, 1999) or in which new projects are developed in the course of discovering interesting results in the context of interactions (Moore & Corkum, 1994; Piaget, 1975/1985). We use the development of gaze following to show that the construction of more complex relations between others and objects leads to the differentiation between self- and other-directedness. We suggest that social development is thus part and parcel of overall cognitive development in infancy and does not constitute a separate line of development. Further, we adopt Piaget's theory of sensorimotor development to identify and analyze different levels of gaze following.

SENSORIMOTOR ANALYSIS OF GAZE OF FOLLOWING

Gaze following is crucial to joint attention. *Joint attention* is commonly defined as the ability to follow another person's gaze. Conceptually, joint attention occurs when two individuals simultaneously attend to each other and some third object. When infants understand that another person's attentional directedness is independent of their own attentional directedness, they have mastered a practical concept that does not apply to the physical world. However, gaze following also involves more general aspects of cognition such as the understanding of spatial relations (Morissette et al., 1995). We suggest that the understanding of both other directedness and spatial relations are, to some extent, interdependent and both involve the construction of increasingly complex relations between other persons and objects. Furthermore, using Piaget's theory of sensorimotor development as a framework, we propose that these relations are constructed through the differentiation and coordination of action (including perception) schemes. In the course of this process, the experience of and interactions with other persons lose their immediacy, others becomes autonomous centers of activity, and infants learn to differentiate between self- and other-directedness. We identify and describe different levels in the development of gaze following during the first 18 months of life.

Before reviewing and analyzing the data on gaze following, a brief note on the experimental procedures by means of which gaze following is established is in order. In gaze following studies, infants generally watch an adult turn his or her head toward a target object. Gaze following is taken to be established when infants follow the adult's turn and direct their gaze toward the same object as the adult. However, scoring criteria for gaze following vary considerably across studies. For example, in a study by Deák and colleagues (Deák, Flom, & Pick, 2000), very liberal scoring criteria were used: The time infants looked at the area around the target location (as indicated by the adult's focus of attention) was compared to the looking time averaged across three distractor locations; whether infants looked first to the target location was not taken into consideration. By contrast, in other studies (e.g., Morissette et al., 1995), more conservative scoring criteria were used: Infants' gazes at exactly the correct location were compared with all other responses combined (i.e., incorrect looks, no gaze, gaze at other person), and only infants' first looks were taken into consideration. It is not surprising that different scoring criteria yield different results. Ideally studies should report results that are generated through the use of different criteria (e.g., D'Entremont, 2000). Procedural differences (e.g., presence or absence of objects, manner in which directedness is displayed) and differences in the materials employed further contribute to the variability in the empirical literature on gaze following.

Level 1 (2–4 months): Primary Circular Reactions

Convincing empirical evidence for gaze following has been provided for infants as young as 3 months of age. When infants that age are confronted with an adult who turns her head to one of two close targets within the infants' visual field, they move their eyes significantly more often in the direction of the correct target than the incorrect target (D'Entremont, 2000; D'Entremont, Hains, & Muir, 1997). When the target objects are moving or when the target objects are farther away, however, 3-month-olds do not reliably follow the head turn of the adult (D'Entremont, 2000). Instead, when the target objects are more distant, infants do not move their eyes and keep on looking at the adult's head. This finding suggests that unless 3-month-olds' attention is attracted by a peripheral stimulus, they have a difficult time disengaging their attention from the central stimulus (i.e., the adult's head; D'Entremont, 2000; see also Butcher, Kalverboer, & Geuze, 2000; Hood, Willen, & Driver, 1998). Around 4 months of age, infants' attention can also be cued in the direction of an adult's eye movements (Farroni, Johnson, Brockbank, & Simion, 2000; Hood et al., 1998). Directed motion plays an essential part in this cueing effect: When the motion of the pupils is not visible and infants are only exposed to the final direction of the gaze, the cueing effect of the eyes disappears (Farroni et al., 2000).

These observations are in general agreement with Piaget's (1936/1963) concept of *primary circular reactions,* which lead to the fusion of heterogenous schemes that apply to different features of the environment (Piaget, 1936/1963, pp. 61–62, 142–143, 231; Piaget, 1985, p. 73). As a consequence, infants develop simple expectations by incorporating into familiar schemes new features that function as signals (Piaget, 1936/1963, pp. 193–194, 248). These signals are fused with the infants' immediate activity (Piaget, 1936/1963, pp. 194, 284), and objects are experienced as direct extension of the previous action. This is why infants' search for objects only extends the previous action (Piaget, 1937/1954, Obs. 4, 5). Infants are able to track moving objects within their visual field (Piaget, 1937/1954, Obs. 2, 5; 1936/1963, Obs. 28–31), but objects leaving the visual field are only rediscovered if they are within the extension of the "accommodation movement immediately preceding" (Piaget, 1937/1954, p. 110).

Applied to gaze following, this means that infants are able to track another person's head turn or eye direction, which function as signals for interesting sights. Tracking involves the continuation of the perceptual accommodation movement, which is triggered by movements of the components of the face. Tracking the movements of components of another person's face may have its origin in the imitation of head movements (Piaget, 1945/1962, pp. 11–14); in the course of imitation, the other person's movement may become a signal for interesting sights.

At this level, however, tracking is limited to the immediate visual field; because perceptual activity is not dissociated from its immediate object, it only occurs when a peripheral object is available to facilitate disengagement of attention from the central stimulus. The ability to more flexibly engage and disengage visual attention may, in turn, gradually emerge due to the practice of visual schemes, which in the third month leads to the abilities to alternate glances and visually compare objects (Piaget, 1936/1963, Obs. 35). Infants also do not understand that objects move along trajectories that are independent of themselves, nor do they understand other persons as autonomous centers of activity that establish relations with the world that are independent of infants' relations. Rather, the interactions with other persons are immediate in the sense that they are dyadic and do not involve objects (Adamson & Bakeman, 1991). Others are not used as intermediaries. Consequently, they have not been objectified and are not yet endowed with permanence (e.g., Bell, 1970; Jackson, Campos, & Fischer, 1978).

Level 2 (5–8 months): Secondary Circular Reactions

Six-month-old infants look more frequently in the direction of the adult's head turn than in the incorrect direction as long as targets are presented within their visual field (Butterworth & Jarrett, 1991). Still, gaze-following abilities in 6-month-olds are limited in a number of respects. First, they have problems turning toward targets that are either farther away or moving (D'Entremont, 2000). However, in contrast to 3-month-olds, 6-month-olds no longer fail to disengage attention from the central stimulus, but rather turn to the incorrect target. This type of error suggests that they are not tracking the adult head movement as it occurs, but rather use the direction of the movement as a cue to search for interesting events (Butterworth & Jarrett, 1991; D'Entremont, 2000).

A second limitation of gaze following at this age is that 6- to 7-month-old infants cannot be trained to turn their head in response to interesting events outside their visual field when the occurrence of these events is contingent on the head turn of another person (Corkum & Moore, 1995). Rather, infants perseverate (i.e., they gaze in one direction only; Corkum & Moore, 1995). The third limitation of infants' gaze following is that when two objects are displayed on the same side, they identify the target object only if it is the first object along their scan path (Butterworth & Jarrett, 1991).

How can these gaze-following behaviors be understood from the perspective of sensorimotor development? Piaget described infants' behavior at this age in terms of secondary circular reactions, which consist of the reapplication of action schemes that produced interesting results (Piaget, 1936/1963). Because secondary circular reactions simply reproduce a result discovered by chance, the schemes used in the reproduction constitute "a global and indissoluble totality" (Piaget, 1936/1963, p. 238). Means are barely differentiated from ends, relations between objects are used but not analyzed, and infants are not able to comprehend more than one object at a time (Piaget, 1937/1954, p. 131; 1963, p. 232). Although infants show foresight that is related to things (Piaget, 1936/1963), the indicators involved in foresight are not independent of infants' actions (Piaget, 1936/1963, Obs. 109).

During the period of secondary circular reactions, spatial relations are centered on the infant ("subjective group"; see Piaget, 1937/1954). Subjective groups are due to the fact that infants can only rediscover their own positions relative to objects and do not yet relate objects to each other. Therefore, infants conceive of objects' positions as being relative to their actions and not as relative to their actual displacements in common and objective space (Piaget, 1937/1954, p. 121). As a consequence, infants do not differentiate between displacements of their actions and displacements of objects, and their search for objects that leave their visual field is limited to tracking movements that continue those tracking movements that were initiated while the moving object was still within their visual field (Piaget, 1937/1954, p. 168, Obs. 95; see also Churcher & Scaife, 1982).

The characteristics of secondary circular reactions explain some features of infants' gaze-following abilities. The abilities to process one object at a time and use a cue as an indicator for the appearance of interesting events explains why infants at this level can use the head turn of another person as an orienting signal that specifies the direction for the infant to look for an interesting event. However, infants do not re-orientate their visual attention to follow another person's gaze to an object outside of their visual field (Butterworth & Jarrett, 1991; Corkum & Moore, 1998) because they are unable to understand the relation between two objects. This is why infants perseverate in training studies (Corkum & Moore, 1995): They look in the same direction in successive trials because they simply reapply the action that led to an interesting result. Infants' behavior at this age also shows that they do not understand that another person can establish spatial relations to objects that are independent of their own spatial relations. For that reason, they look at the first object along their scan path independently of where another person is looking. Because their practical concept of space is still subjective, infants act as if their visual space were shared by others (Butterworth, 1995; Butterworth & Jarrett, 1991). In following the gaze of another person, their attention is captured by the first salient object (D'Entremont, 2000); if no salient or distinctive objects are available, they have difficulties disengaging their attention from the adult's head (Morrisette et al., 1995). Thus, the structure of the environment "completes for the infant the communicative function of the adult's signal" (Butterworth & Grover, 1990, p. 611). The structure of the environment leads to de facto shared meaning without infants being aware of sharing meaning (Butterworth, 1995; Corkum & Moore, 1995).

Level 3 (8–12 months): Coordination
of Secondary Circular Reactions

When they are about 8 months old, infants can be trained to follow a head turn toward a target outside their visual field when the target follows contingently on the head turn (Moore & Corkum, 1998). By 12 months, infants do not require training any longer; they spontaneously follow the head turn of another person (Corkum & Moore, 1998; Lempers, 1979). The movement of the adult's head seems to play an important role in gaze following because 8- to 9-month-old infants who can be trained to follow a dynamic head turn cannot be trained to follow a static head orientation toward a target (Moore, Angelopoulos, & Bennett, 1997). Even at 12 months of age, only 50% of infants spontaneously follow a static head orientation (Lempers, 1979). Until they are 12 months old, infants cannot identify the target of the adult's gaze when the target is the second object along their scan path (Butterworth & Jarrett, 1991; Morissette et al., 1995).

Piaget (1936/1963) termed the period of sensorimotor development between the ages of 8 and 12 months *coordination of secondary circular reactions*. During this period, infants break up the global action schemes of the previous period and flexibly apply them to new situations in new combinations. Means and ends become differentiated, resulting in the coordination of two separate schemes and subordination of one scheme (means, transitional scheme) to the other scheme (end). Infants process and establish relations between two objects simultaneously: "Two objects are distinguished from one another, and are, henceforth, placed in interrelation" (Piaget, 1936/1963, p. 233; see also Case, 1991; Sugarman, 1984). For example, when Jacqueline at 10 months grasps Piaget's hand, places it against a swinging doll that she is not able to set into motion herself, and exerts pressure on Piaget's index finger so that he puts the doll into motion (Piaget, 1936/1963, Obs. 127; see also Piaget, 1937/1954, Obs. 141–144), the two objects (hand, doll) remain distinct and are still reciprocally coordinated.

The ability to construct means–end relations has repercussions for infants' understanding of signs, causality, and space. With respect to signs, infants become capable of detaching cues ("indicators") from their circular reactions and foreseeing events "conceived of being independent and connected with the activity of the object" (Piaget, 1936/1963, p. 248). With respect to causality, infants start to attribute independent powers to another person such that the body of another person becomes a partly independent source of causal activity. As a consequence, infants act on someone else's body, not as on inert matter that is merely extending their own action but by releasing the activity of the other body through a discreet pressure (e.g., a mere touch; see Piaget, 1937/1954, p. 262). Thus, infants transfer efficacy to an intermediary (Piaget, 1937/1954, p. 264) that is conceived of as being capable of producing the desired result. However, another person's activity still remains partly dependent on the child's activity.

With respect to space, simple reversible spatial groups emerge (Piaget, 1937/1954, pp. 154, 162). For example, infants slowly move their heads from Position A to another B and from B back again to A to study various perspectives of an object (Piaget, 1937/1954, Obs. 88–91). However, the spatial groups at this level remain midway between subjective and objective groups because infants cannot yet understand relations that are completely independent of their actions. The infant "does not yet recognize positions and displacements as being relative to one another, but only as relative to himself" (Piaget, 1937/1954, p. 183). The lack of understanding relations as being relative to objects is apparent in the A-not-B error: Infants search for an object at a location where they previously found the object and not at the location where they saw the object disappear (Piaget, 1937/1954, Obs. 39–45). "The object screen is therefore not considered by the child as something with which the hidden object is in relationship: the screen is still perceived as relative to the subject and not as relative to the object" (Piaget, 1937/1954, p. 192).

The emergence of the ability to establish spatial relations between objects explains why infants follow another person's gaze when the gaze is directed toward a target outside their visual field. Given the results from training studies (Corkum & Moore, 1995, 1998), it is likely that gaze following to targets outside the visual field is initially used as a procedure to make interesting events last and head movement is necessary to trigger gaze following. Furthermore, a necessary condition for infants' learning to follow the gaze of another person to targets outside their visual field appears to be that both target object and another person's head are connected within infants' visual space. For example, infants will turn their head in response to another person's head turn to a degree that the other person's head remains in the periphery of their visual field. If a target appears to the other side of their peripheral visual field, infants will latch onto this target, but will terminate their gaze-following behavior if no target appears in their peripheral visual field (Butterworth & Cochran, 1980).

Eventually, however, infants become capable of using the other person's head turn as an indicator, and they also come to establish spatial relations between another person and the object even in the absence of movement cues (Moore et al., 1997). It is difficult to determine whether 12-month-olds already understand that the other person has a directedness toward objects that is completely independent of their own directedness. Their limited understanding of other persons as autonomous centers of activity suggests that the understanding of the directedness of other persons retains a subjective quality. Using conservative scoring criteria, 12-month-old infants are not able to follow the gaze of another person if the target of the other person's attention is not the first object along their scan path (Morisette et al., 1995) and their ability to following another person's gaze in the absence of a target remains fragile (Corkum & Moore, 1995). These findings suggest that infants do not construct spatial relations between another person and objects that are relative to the other person and not relative to themselves.

Level 4 (12–18 months): Tertiary Circular Reactions

At around 15 months, infants learn to follow the adult's head turn to objects outside their visual field even when targets are absent (Corkum & Moore, 1995). This finding indicates that infants understand that the other person's directedness is independent of their own directedness. Furthermore, between 12 and 18 months, infants increasingly learn to localize the target of adults' attention correctly even when the target is not the first along their scan path and they must ignore the first object along their scan path (Butterworth & Jarrett, 1991; Deák et al., 2000; Morrisette et al., 1995). Using conservative scoring criteria, infants still fail to search for items located behind them (Butterworth & Jarrett, 1991), and they encounter some difficulties even at 15 months to locate a target when it is the second object along their scan path and relatively far away from their midline (Morisette et al., 1995).

Piaget (1936/1963) described the period from 12 to 18 months in terms of tertiary circular reactions. Infants now systematically vary their actions to discover new properties of objects. Furthermore, infants try out different means to accomplish a goal, thereby successively adjusting means and goals and flexibly moving from means to goal and from goal to means (Müller, Sokol, & Overton, 1998). Both kinds of behavior patterns lead infants to increasingly detach the object from their actions and construct relations that are relative to objects and no longer relative to themselves. As a consequence, another person becomes an autonomous center of activity (Piaget, 1937/1954, p. 276, Obs. 152).

With respect to space, infants start to discover and use complex interrelations among objects (Piaget, 1937/1954). For example, infants start to search for objects placed behind themselves and other people (Piaget, 1937/1954, Obs. 104–105). Infants also start to construct objective groups of spatial displacements that coordinate spatial relations among locations. For example, infants move from Location A to location B, then from Location B to Location C, and from Location C back to Location A (Piaget, 1937/1954, Obs. 117).

The acquisition of objective spatial groups explains why infants start to direct their gaze toward a target even if it is not the first along their scan path and why they become capable of locating a target behind their back. Initially, the determination of another person's gaze in these situations may be inaccurate and may follow a process of gradual readjustment as infants flexibly put the adult's directedness in relation to the possible target objects. Furthermore, the understanding of other persons as autonomous centers of activity explains why infants come to understand that the other person's directedness is independent of their own directedness.

Level 5 (18 months): Operational Coordination

At 18 months, infants' search for targets located behind them becomes more successful (Deák et al., 2000, exp. 2) particularly when their visual field is empty of targets (Butterworth & Jarrett, 1991). Moreover, 18-month-old infants do not look at an object A that is in the direction of an adult's head turn if the adult's line of sight contains a barrier that obstructs the view of A. Instead, 18-month-olds look inside the barrier. However, if the barrier contains a window, infants will look at the object A (Butler et al., 2000). By contrast, 15-month-olds' looking behavior does not differ in situations that contain either a barrier with window or a barrier without window. Thus, it is only after 18 months that infants understand that screens can function as visual obstructions to looking (Butler et al., 2000). Finally, 18-month-old infants begin to use eye movement as a cue to locate targets outside their visual fields even when eye movements are not accompanied by head movements (Butterworth & Jarrett, 1991; Corkum & Moore, 1995; Moore & Corkum, 1998).

At this developmental level, infants start to successively coordinate two types of relations (Müller et al., 1998). For example, infants become capable of exhaustively grouping two types of objects. They first sort one type of object and then switch to sorting the other type of object (Sugarman, 1983). Successive grouping of objects into two different sets involves a flexible shift from one similarity relation to another similarity relation. Successive coordination of two relations is also found in spatial cognition. For example, Piaget (1937/1954, Obs. 123) observed that when Jacqueline's ball rolled too far under a bed to be reached from the side at which it disappeared, she walked around the bed and retrieved the ball from the other side of the bed. In this example, Jacqueline must have been capable of successively evaluating the position of the ball with respect to both sides of the bed.

Successive coordination of two spatial relations is required for the understanding that an occluder can obstruct another person's gaze toward a target. In this case, infants must be able to understand the other person in relation to two objects (A, the occluder; B, the target). At 15 months, infants still appear to be incapable of coordinating two spatial relations.

Infants' use of eye movement as cues may also be based on the successive coordination of relations. The understanding of eye movements as cues for another person's directedness involves the understanding that eyes are actively directed at and receptively related to objects (Plessner, 1976). That is, by 18 months infants come to understand that when another person is moving her eyes she is not only directed toward objects, but also receives an interesting sight. This interpretation is consistent with the findings that embarrassment (Lewis, Sullivan, Stranger, & Weiss, 1989) and mirror self-recognition (e.g., Bischof-Köhler, 1989) also emerge at around 18 months. We suggest that the coordination of the active (looking) and passive receptive (being looked at) function of the eyes is a prerequisite for both the emergence of embarrassment and mirror self-recognition. If this interpretation is correct, infants would have developed some rudimentary understanding of visual attention at around 18 months (see also Moore & Corkum, 1998).

CONCLUSION

We have suggested that approaches to social development in infancy can be characterized in terms of two epistemological frameworks: individualist and relational. Although many contemporary approaches are based on the individualist framework, we have pointed out fundamental problems with this framework, justifying the consideration of a relational approach. We have elaborated such an approach by drawing on Piaget's theory of sensori-motor development and using the development of gaze following as an example. From a relational perspective, social development is a process of gradual decentration that starts from a point of undifferentiation among self, other, and object and leads to the increasing differentiation between and coordination of infants' own attentional directedness and other persons' attentional directedness toward objects. To the extent that infants construct more complex relations between other persons and objects, other persons become autonomous agents who have an independent attentional focus. As a result, infants come to grasp another person's referential intent, which provides the foundation for language learning. Linguistic communication, in turn, further transforms children's social understanding.

From the relational perspective, the infant's understanding of the physical world, such as spatial relations, is intertwined with their developing social understanding. The construction of relations between other persons and objects is essential for the process of decentration because it leads to the breaking of the immediacy of the initial relationship between an infant and another person. As shown elsewhere (Müller & Carpendale, 2000), a relational, sensorimotor analysis can also be fruitfully applied to the development of interactions between infants and caregivers. These interactions gradually lead to increasingly complex types of coordination between infants' and other persons' actions and result in infants acquiring the ability to view themselves as the recipient of another person's action and to take an external, reflective perspective on themselves. However, the fact that similar structures are found in different areas of development should not be misunderstood as implying that a general cognitive structure is applied to different areas. The particular structural relations must be constructed in each area anew. Although physical and social cognition are partly intertwined, there are enough differences between interactions with persons and interactions with objects to make the issue of whether there is any developmental synchrony across areas a largely empirical enterprise. However, if our analysis is correct, the development of physical as well as social cognition obeys the same developmental principle: In both areas development proceeds from an initial lack of differentiation and coordination to increasing differentiation and coordination. Developmental synchronies between physical and social cognition may thus be due to the fact that the same type of developmental process is operative in both domains.

Finally, we would like to point out that the relational approach as presented here shares many features with Case's (1991) neo-Piagetian theory and the theory of joint attention as developed by Moore and Corkum (1994; Corkum & Moore, 1995). From a relational perspective, what is crucial for social development is not the discovery of some mental entity such as intention, but rather the construction of increasingly complex relations among the infant's actions, the other person's actions, and objects. It is in the context of practical interactions that explicit notions of self and other arise. Hence, the construction of a "theory of mind" presupposes and is based on unreflective practical interactions at the sensorimotor level.

ACKNOWLEDGMENTS

We thank Chris Moore and Tim Racine for comments on an earlier draft of this chapter. The preparation of this chapter was supported by a Social Sciences and Humanities Research Council of Canada operating grant to the second author.

REFERENCES

Adamson, L. B., & Bakeman, R. (1991). The development of shared attention during infancy. *Annals of Child Development, 8*, 1–41.

Baldwin, J. M. (1897). *Social and ethical interpretations in mental development.* New York: Macmillan.

Baldwin, J. M. (1906). *Thought and things* (Vol. 1). New York: Arno.

Bell, S. (1970). The development of the concept of the object and its relationship to infant–mother attachment. *Child Development, 41,* 291–312.

Bischof-Köhler, D. (1989). *Spiegelbild und empathie* [Mirror image and empathy]. Bern: Huber.

Bretherton, I. (1991). Intentional communication and the development of an understanding of mind. In D. Frye & C. Moore (Eds.), *Children's theories of mind: Mental states and social understanding* (pp. 49–75). Hillsdale, NJ: Lawrence Erlbaum Associates.

Butcher, P. R., Kalverboer, A. F., & Geuze, R. H. (2000). Infants' shifts of gaze from a central to a peripheral stimulus: A longitudinal study of development between 6 and 26 weeks. *Infant Behavior & Development, 23,* 3–21.

Butler, S. C., Caron, A. J., & Brooks, R. (2000). Infant understanding of the referential nature of looking. *Journal of Cognition and Development, 1,* 359–377.

Butterworth, G. (1995). Origins of mind in perception and action. In C. Moore & P. Dunham (Eds.), *Joint attention: Its origins and role in development* (pp. 29–40). Hillsdale, NJ: Lawrence Erlbaum Associates.

Butterworth, G., & Cochran, E. (1980). Towards a mechanism of joint visual attention in human infancy. *International Journal of Behavioral Development, 3,* 253–272.

Butterworth, G., & Grover, L. (1990). Joint visual attention, manual pointing, and preverbal communication in human infancy. In M. Jeannerod (Ed.), *Attention and performance XIII* (pp. 605–624). Hillsdale, NJ: Lawrence Erlbaum Associates.

Butterworth, G., & Jarrett, N. (1991). What minds have in common is space: Spatial mechanisms serving joint visual attention in infancy. *British Journal of Developmental Psychology, 9,* 55–72.

Carpenter, M., Nagell, K., & Tomasello, M. (1998). Social cognition, joint attention, and communicative competence from 9 to 15 months of age. *Monographs of the Society for Research in Child Development, 63* (Serial No. 255).

Case, R. (1991). Stages in the development of the young child's first sense of self. *Developmental Review, 11,* 210–230.

Churcher, J., & Scaife, M. (1982). How infants see the point. In G. Butterworth & P. Light (Eds.), *Social cognition: Studies of the development of understanding* (pp. 110–136). Chicago, IL: Chicago University Press.

Corkum, V., & Moore, V. (1995). Development of joint visual attention in infants. In C. Moore & P. Dunham (Eds.), *Joint attention: Its origins and role in development* (pp. 61–83). Hillsdale, NJ: Lawrence Erlbaum Associates.

Corkum, V., & Moore, V. (1998). The origins of joint visual attention in infants. *Developmental Psychology, 34,* 28–38.

Deák, G., Flom, R. A., & Pick, A. D. (2000). Effects of gesture and target on 12- and target on 12- and 18-month-olds' joint visual attention to objects in front of or behind them. *Developmental Psychology, 36,* 511–523.

D'Entremont, B. (2000). A perceptual-attentional explanation of gaze-following in 3- and 6-month-olds. *Developmental Science, 3,* 302–311.

D'Entremont, B., Hains, S. M. J., & Muir, D. W. (1997). A demonstration of gaze following in 3- to 6-month-olds. *Infant Behavior and Development, 20,* 569–572.

Descartes, R. (1960). The meditations concerning first philosophy. In R. Descartes (Ed.), *Discourse on method and meditations* (pp. 67–141). Indianapolis, IN: Bobbs-Merrill Educational Publishing. (Original work published 1641)

Descartes, R. (1972). *Treatise on man.* Cambridge, MA: Harvard University Press.

Dilthey, W. (1989). *Selected works: Vol. 1. Introduction to the human sciences* (R. A. Makkreel & F. Rodi, Eds.). Princeton, NJ: Princeton University Press.

Farroni, T., Johnson, M. H., Brockbank, M., & Simion, F. (2000). Infants' use of gaze direction to cue attention: The importance of perceived motion. *Visual Cognition, 7,* 705–718.

Frye, D. (1991). The origins of intention in infancy. In D. Frye & C. Moore (Eds.), *Children's theories of mind: Mental states and social understanding* (pp. 15–38). Hillsdale, NJ: Lawrence Erlbaum Associates.

Greve, W. (2001). Traps and gaps in action explanation: Theoretical problems of a psychology of human action. *Psychological Review, 108,* 435–451.

Hacker, P. M. S. (1990). *Wittgenstein, meaning, and mind.* London: Blackwell.

Hobson, R. P. (1993). *Autism and the development of mind.* Hove, England: Lawrence Erlbaum Associates.

Hoffman, M. L. (1991). Empathy, social cognition, and moral action. In W. M. Kurtines & J. L. Gewirtz (Eds.), *Handbook of moral behavior and development: Vol. 1. Theory* (pp. 275–301). Hillsdale, NJ: Lawrence Erlbaum Associates.

Hood, B. M., Willen, J. D., & Driver, J. (1998). Adult's eyes trigger shifts of visual attention in human infants. *Psychological Science, 9,* 131–134.

Jackson, E., Campos, J. J., & Fischer, K. W. (1978). The question of decalage between object permanence and person permanence. *Developmental Psychology, 14,* 1–10.

Jopling, D. (1993). Cognitive science, other minds, and the philosophy of dialogue. In U. Neisser (Ed.), *The perceived self* (pp. 290–309). Cambridge, MA: MIT Press.

Legerstee, M. (1998). Mental and bodily awareness in infancy: Consciousness of self-existence. *Journal of Consciousness Studies, 5,* 627–644.

Legerstee, M., Corter, C., & Kienapple, K. (1990). Hand, arm, and facial actions of young infants to a social and nonsocial stimulus. *Child Development, 61,* 774–784.

Lempers, J. D. (1979). Young children's production and comprehension of nonverbal deictic behaviors. *The Journal of Genetic Psychology, 135,* 93–102.

Lewis, M., Sullivan, M. W., Stranger, C., & Weiss, M. (1989). Self-development and self-conscious emotions. *Child Development, 60,* 146–156.

Lipps, T. (1907). Das Wissen von fremden Ichen [The knowledge of alter egos]. *Psychologische Untersuchungen, 1,* 694–722.

Meltzoff, A. N., & Brooks, R. (2001). "Like me" as a building block for understanding other minds: Bodily acts, attention, and intention. In B. F. Malle, L. J. Moses, & D. A. Baldwin (Eds.), *Intentions and intentionality* (pp. 171–191). Cambridge, MA: MIT Press.

Meltzoff, A. N., Gopnik, A., & Repacholi, B. M. (1999). Toddlers' understanding of intentions, desires, and emotions: Explorations of the dark ages. In P. D. Zelazo, J. W. Astington, & D. R. Olson (Eds.), *Developing theories of intention* (pp. 17–41). Mahwah, NJ: Lawrence Erlbaum Associates.

Merleau-Ponty, M. (1964). The child's relations with others. In M. Merleau-Ponty (Ed.), *The primacy of perception* (pp. 96–155). Evanston, IL: Northwestern Press. (Original work published 1960)

Moore, C., Angelopoulos, M., & Bennett, P. (1997). The role of movement in the development of joint visual attention. *Infant Behavior and Development, 20,* 83–92.

Moore, C., & Corkum, V. (1994). Social understanding at the end of the first year of life. *Developmental Review, 14,* 349–372.

Moore, C., & Corkum, V. (1998). Infant gaze following based on eye direction. *British Journal of Developmental Psychology, 16,* 495–503.

Morissette, P., Ricard, M., & Décarie, T. G. (1995). Joint visual attention and pointing in infancy: A longitudinal study of comprehension. *British Journal of Developmental Psychology, 13,* 163–175.

Müller, U., & Carpendale, J. I. M. (2000). The role of social interaction in Piaget's theory: Language for social cooperation and social cooperation for language. *New Ideas in Psychology, 18,* 139–156.

Müller, U., Sokol, B., & Overton, W. F. (1998). Reframing a constructivist model of the development of mental representation: The role of higher-order operations. *Developmental Review, 8*, 155–201.

Overton, W. F. (1998). Relational-developmental theory: A psychological perspective. In D. Görlitz, H. J. Harloff, G. Mey, & J. Valsiner (Eds.), *Children, cities, and psychological theories* (pp. 315–335). Berlin: Walter de Gruyter.

Piaget, J. (1954). *The construction of reality in the child.* New York: Basic Books. (Original work published 1937)

Piaget, J. (1962). *Play, dreams and imitation in childhood.* New York: Norton. (Original work published 1945)

Piaget, J. (1963). *The origins of intelligence in children.* New York: W. W. Norton. (Original work published 1936)

Piaget, J. (1971). *Insights and illusions of philosophy.* New York: The World Publishing Company. (Original work published 1965)

Piaget, J. (1972). *The principles of genetic epistemology.* New York: Basic Books. (Original work published 1970)

Piaget, J. (1985). *The equilibration of cognitive structures* (T. Brown & K. J. Thampy, Trans.). Chicago, IL: The University of Chicago Press. (Original work published 1975)

Piaget, J. (1995). *Sociological studies.* London: Routledge. (Original work published 1977)

Piaget, J. (2000). Commentary on Vygotsky's criticism of language and thought of the child and judgement and reasoning in the child. *New Ideas in Psychology, 18*, 241–260. (Original work published 1962)

Plessner, H. (1976). *Die Frage nach der Conditio Humana* [The quest for the human condition]. Frankfurt am Main: Suhrkamp.

Rochat, P., & Hespos, S. J. (1997). Differential rooting response by neonates: Evidence for an early sense of self. *Early Development & Parenting, 6*, 105–112.

Rochat, P., & Striano, T. (1999). Social-cognitive development in the first year. In P. Rochat (Ed.), *Early social cognition: Understanding others in the first months of life* (pp. 3–34). Mahwah, NJ: Lawrence Erlbaum Associates.

Russell, B. (1921). *The analysis of mind.* London: Allen & Unwin.

Scheler, M. (1954). *The nature of sympathy* (P. Heath, Trans.). Hamden, CT: Archon. (Original work published 1913)

Soffer, G. (1999). The other as alter ego: A genetic approach. *Husserl Studies, 15*, 151–166.

Straus, E. (1963). *The primary world of senses* (2nd ed.; J. Needleman, Trans.). New York: The Free Press of Glencoe. (Original work published 1932)

Sugarman, S. (1983). *Children's early thought: Developments in classification.* Cambridge, MA: Cambridge University Press.

Sugarman, S. (1984). The development of preverbal communication. In R. L. Schiefelbusch (Ed.), *The acquisition of communicative competence* (pp. 23–67). Baltimore: University Park Press.

ter Hark, M. (1990). *Beyond the inner and the outer.* Dordrecht: Kluwer.

Tomasello, M. (1999). *The cultural origins of human cognition.* Cambridge, MA: Harvard University Press.

Trevarthen, C., & Aitken, K. J. (2001). Infant intersubjectivity: Research, theory, and clinical applications. *Journal of Child Psychology and Psychiatry, 42*, 3–48.

Walden, T., & Ogan, T. (1988). The development of social referencing. *Child Development, 59*, 1230–1240.

Wellman, H. M., & Phillips, A. T. (2001). Developing intentional understandings. In B. F. Malle, L. J. Moses, & D. A. Baldwin (Eds.), *Intentions and intentionality* (pp. 125–148). Cambridge, MA: MIT Press.

Wilkerson, W. S. (1999). From bodily motion to bodily intentions: The perception of bodily activity. *Philosophical Psychology, 12*, 61–77.

Wilkerson, W. S. (2000). Knowledge of self, knowledge of others, error, and the place of consciousness. *Continental Philosophy Review, 33,* 27–42.

Wittgenstein, L. (1958). *Philosophical investigations.* Oxford: Blackwell.

Wittgenstein, L. (1980). *Remarks on the philosophy of psychology: Vol. 1.* Chicago: The University of Chicago Press.

Wittgenstein, L. (1982). *Last writings on the philosophy of psychology: Vol. 1.* Chicago: University of Chicago Press.

Wright, G. H. von (1971). *Explanation and understanding.* Ithaca, NY: Cornell University Press.

Zahn-Waxler, C., Radke-Yarrow, M., Wagner, E., & Chapman, M. (1992). Development of concern for others. *Developmental Psychology, 28,* 126–136.

Zeedyk, M. S. (1996). Developmental accounts of intentionality: Toward integration. *Developmental Review, 16,* 416–461.

Zelazo, P. D. (1996). Towards a characterization of minimal consciousness. *New Ideas in Psychology, 14,* 63–80.

12

Piaget's Theory and Children's Development of Prosocial Behavior: The Force of Negation

Orlando Lourenço
University of Lisbon–Portugal

Since the translation of Piaget's (1965/1995) *Sociological Studies* in 1995, it is clear that the widespread belief that Piaget's theory is inherently individualistic and leaves no room for the role of the social in development is misleading at its best, nonsensical at its worst. Even authors who have identified some problems in Piaget's sociological theory (see Carpendale & Müller, chaps. 1 and 11, this volume) acknowledge that the essays included in his *Sociological Studies* demonstrate the continuity of his interest in the social dimension of development.

However, instead of arguing in favor of the existence of a social dimension in Piaget's theory, I follow a different track in this chapter. Specifically, I argue that some of Piaget's key cognitive concepts may help us understand the development of certain social behaviors. A case in point is prosocial behavior or "voluntary behavior intended to benefit another" (Eisenberg & Fabes, 1998, p. 701). This chapter shows, both theoretically and empirically, that Piaget's (1974) concepts of affirmation and negation and his ideas on costs and gains involved in children's centrations and operations (Piaget, 1957) are of much value in helping us understand empirical phenomena of children's development of prosocial behavior. These Piagetian concepts shed some light on the finding that as children get older, and specifically during the latter half of the first decade of life, "there is increasing evidence of altruistic concern and related prosocial action" (Eisenberg & Fabes, 1998, p. 746; see also Krebs, 1970; Underwood & Moore, 1982).

The chapter is in four parts. First, I briefly summarize extant accounts of children's development of prosocial behavior, and I discuss the main ideas that lie at the heart of the Piagetian perspective advocated here (see also Lourenço, 1990, 1993a, 1994a). In the second part, I present diverse findings that provide support for the Piagetian framework as a viable explanation of children's development of prosocial behavior. The findings show that (a) as children get older they increasingly think of prosocial acts in terms of negation and gain construction rather than in terms of affirmation and cost perception; (b) there is a relation between children's tendency to conceptualize prosocial acts in terms of gain construction and the development of coordination of affirmations and negations in a Piagetian sense; and (c) there is a relation between children's tendency to construct gain in prosocial acts and their prosocial behavior. Next, I elaborate on some strengths and limitations of the Piagetian perspective explored here and, in the process, suggest topics for further research within this framework. Finally, I summarize the main ideas explored in this chapter and consider their implications for the debate on the role of the social in Piaget's theory.

WHAT DEVELOPS IN CHILDREN'S DEVELOPMENT OF PROSOCIAL BEHAVIOR?

Older children's tendency to share "more and more generously than younger ones" (Underwood & Moore, 1982, p. 27) has been explained from different theoretical perspectives (for review see Bryan, 1975; Eisenberg & Fabes, 1998). According to the *normative approach* (Berkowitz, 1972), older children are generally more prosocial than younger children because they have learned a norm of social responsibility or a norm dictating sharing goods with needy others. Appealing as this approach may be, it raises some problems. First, to invoke the existence of norms to explain the occurrence of certain social behaviors risks being "nothing more than giving *ad hoc* explanations for results that we could not have predicted in advance" (Darley & Latané, 1970, p. 2). Second, the normative approach does not really explain how norms develop in the first place. Third, some studies (e.g., Solomon, Ali, Kfir, Houlihan, & Yaeger, 1972) found that the verbal statement of the norm dictating giving goods to needy persons was not correlated with age, which shows that older children's altruism may not be dependent on such a norm.

According to the behavior-freeze hypothesis, younger children are less prosocial than older ones because they "are timid within the experimental situation and too frightened to initiate a charitable action" (Bryan, 1975, p. 164). However, there is no evidence in the developmental literature suggesting such freezing in younger children. Indeed the opposite seems to be the case (Shantz, 1983). Furthermore, some studies on the influence of warmth in children's donations have shown that when prosocial behavior involves self-denial (e.g., donations), children are more likely to be prosocial after experiencing a *cold* rather than a *warm* relationship with the experimenter (Weissbrod, 1980).

Another explanation of the correlation between age and altruism suggests that the value of the goods to be donated changes as children get older. According to this cost model (Dovidio, 1984), younger children are less prosocial than their older counterparts because the goods to be donated or shared are of more value to them. Although cost matters in prosocial behavior (Barnett, Thompson, & Schroff, 1987), a problem with the cost model is that age is seen as a criterion rather than an indicator for developmental changes. In other words, increasing age is treated as if it always implied less perception of cost. As a consequence, psychological processes that are involved in less perception of cost with increasing age are not considered.

According to the cognitive developmental theory (e.g., Bar-Tal, Raviv, & Leiser, 1980), the increase of generosity with age is mainly due to children's growing capacities of decentration and perspective taking (Eisenberg & Miller, 1987). Although the increase of prosocial behavior may be associated with the child's ability to take the perspective of another person, some studies show that the availability of a particular level of perspective-taking skills does not guarantee that a child will act in a prosocial way (Severy & Davis, 1971). This seems to imply that cognitive decentration may not have sufficient motivational power to engage prosocial behavior, which questions the idea that children's development of prosocial behavior simply represents a movement from centration or self-oriented propensity to decentration or others-oriented perspective taking. From the preceding considerations, it is clear that we are far from a thorough understanding of children's development of prosocial behavior and there is still room for the Piagetian perspective explored in this chapter.

Two models that Piaget used at different stages of his career to account for the child's transition from preoperational to operational thought are relevant for thinking about the child's prosocial development. The first model is, to some extent, influenced by game theory (Piaget, 1957). This model has a functionalist orientation because it emphasizes costs and gains. The second model describes developmental stages in terms of the relations between affirmations and negations in the course of development (Piaget, 1974). This model was developed in the context of the equilibration theory (Piaget, 1975/1985) and has a more structural orientation.

In 1957, Piaget argued that young children's judgments and justifications on many tasks involve low cost but also small gain. That is, children's centrations are simple in terms of coordination of actions, low cost, but they are also not very productive in terms of correct judgments and operational justifications, small, if any, gain. In contrast, children's operations, as is the case when the child coordinates density and space on a conservation number task, are more complex in terms of coordination of actions, dimensions, or perspectives. As such they represent a "behavior of equilibrium which is, at the same time, more *costly* and more *productive*" (Piaget, 1957, p. 58; italics added).

Some years later, this relatively functional cost–gain model gave way to a more structural model, which characterizes young children's thought by a "disequilibrium between affirmations and negations, with the former having more 'weight' than the latter . . ." (Piaget, 1974, p. 5). This occurs because

> the positive [or more visible] characteristics of objects, actions or operations are given directly as observable, whereas the negative [or less visible] characteristics imply, in different degrees, inferential mechanisms related to the possible results of action, or the anticipated properties of an object, or the oppositions in relation to other objects. (p. 17)

As development proceeds, children become capable of coordinating affirmation and negation—that is, of going beyond the more concrete, perceptual, and salient aspects involved in all intellectual situations and social interactions (see Piaget, 1974; Müller, Sokol, & Overton, 1999).

Applied to children's development of prosocial behavior, the integration of these two Piagetian models leads to the idea that younger children's tendency to be less prosocial than older children is partly due to the young child's propensity to think of prosocial acts more in terms of cost and affirmation (cost perception) than in terms of gain and negation (gain construction). If the anticipation of costs obviously involved in prosocial acts is relatively simple and therefore akin to a Piagetian affirmation, the anticipation of possible gains—mainly psychological or moral—is more difficult cognitively and therefore akin to a Piagetian negation.

Several predictions can be derived from this Piagetian proposal. First, with increasing age children should be more likely to think of prosocial acts in terms of gain construction than cost perception. Second, this change should appear not only in cross-sectional studies, but also in longitudinal ones. Third, this developmental change should occur in relatively different cultural contexts. Fourth, children's ability to construct gain in prosocial acts should correlate positively with their capacity to coordinate affirmations and negations on Piagetian affirmation/negation tasks. Fifth, the child's ability to construct gain in prosocial acts should be positively associated with their prosocial behavior. I address these predictions in the rest of this chapter.

THE COST-PERCEPTION/GAIN-CONSTRUCTION
PERSPECTIVE: EMPIRICAL FINDINGS

In the following, data from several studies that tested the Piagetian approach to prosocial development are presented. Generally, (a) these data involved the same number of boys and girls at each age level; (b) the data for male and female are combined because no statistically significant sex differences were found; (c) most of the data refer to children from middle- to upper middle-class Portuguese families; and (d) although figures for statistical analyses are not reported, the findings were always statistically significant using appropriate statistical tests (e.g., chi-square; nonparametric Spearman rank correlations; Kruskal–Wallis analysis of variance [ANOVA]). Most of the results summarized here have been described elsewhere in greater detail (e.g., Lourenço, 1990, 1993a, 1993b, 1994a).

Cross-Sectional Study

The sample of the cross-sectional study consisted of 90 children: 30 six-year-olds, 30 eight-year-olds, and 30 eleven-year-olds. All children listened to a story (i.e., a prosocial dilemma) with an altruistic character and a nonaltruistic character. The altruistic character was a child who decided to comfort a needy child instead of going to a party; the nonaltruistic character did the opposite. The critical question that was asked after children had listened to the story was which character has gained more at the end of the story and why (for further details, see Lourenço, 1990).

Choice of the altruistic character was coded as a *gain-construction* response and choice of the nonaltruistic character as a *cost-perception* response. As Table 12.1 shows, 6-year-olds tended to view the prosocial act in terms of cost perception, 11-year-olds in terms of gain construction, and 8-year-olds almost equally tended to view the act in terms of gain construction and cost perception.

As for children's reasons, cost-perception responses were justified with material gain for the nonaltruistic character (e.g., "she gained more be-

TABLE 12.1
Frequency of Cost-Perception/Gain-Construction
Responses as a Function of Age

Response Category	6-year-olds	8-year-olds	11-year-olds
Cost perception	25 (83.3)	13 (43.3)	1 (3.33)
Gain construction	5 (16.7)	17 (56.7)	29 (96.7)
Total	30 (100)	30 (100)	30 (100)

Note. Numbers in parentheses are percentages.

cause she went to the party"), whereas gain-construction responses were justified with gain for the prosocial character. This youngest group considered the gain of the prosocial character as a material gain (e.g., "she gained more because the needy child will reciprocate the favor on another occasion"). By contrast, the two groups of older children considered the gain of the prosocial character as psychological or moral gain (e.g., "she gained more because her schoolmate became a good friend," psychological gain; "she gained more because she helped her schoolmate and did a right thing," moral gain).

The findings from this cross-sectional study are consistent with the Piagetian approach because they support one of its main predictions—namely, that with increasing age children are more likely to think of prosocial acts in terms of gain construction than cost perception.

Longitudinal Study

Although cross-sectional differences between different age groups provide empirical support for developmental hypotheses, they would receive even more support from longitudinal studies that showed directional changes within the individual. The longitudinal study presented here covers a 4-year period in which children's cost-perception/gain-construction competence was assessed at three different times: T1, T2, and T3. At T1 the sample consisted of the 30 six-year-olds who were also involved in the cross-sectional study described earlier. This sample was observed 2 years later (T2) when children were 8-year-olds and again 4 years after (T3) when they were 10- to 11-year-olds (Lourenço, 1993a, 1993b). Because 10 children were lost during the study (6 from T1 to T2 and 4 from T2 to T3), complete longitudinal data for only 20 children are available. Children's cost-perception/gain-construction responses were assessed with the prosocial dilemma and methodology mentioned previously.

Table 12.2 presents the frequency of children's cost-perception/gain-construction responses over time. The analysis of the data shows that in the 4-year interval the initial cost-perception responses became gain-construction responses, whereas no initial gain-construction response reversed to cost perception. This pattern held for all but one child. Additional longitudinal data (not reported) reveal that this developmental sequence is also found when children from other cohorts are used and when cost-perception/gain-construction responses are assessed with other prosocial dilemmas (e.g., sharing, helping, and donating; see Lourenço, 1993a, 1994a).

Taken together these longitudinal data strengthen the Piagetian approach presented here, and they are consistent with the cross-sectional findings reported earlier. The child's increasing ability to think of pro-

TABLE 12.2
Frequency of Types of Change in Children's
Initial Responses in a 4-Year Period

Response Category	T1*	From T1 to T2			From T2 to T3		
		Up**	Equal	Down	Up	Equal	Down
Cost perception	17	9	8	—	7	1	—
	(85)	(52.9)	(47.1)		(87.5)	(12.5)	
Gain construction	3	—	3	0	—	12	0
	(15)		(100)			(100)	

*T1 = 1988; T2 = 1990; T3 = 1992.
**Up = change from cost perception to gain construction; Down = change from gain construction to cost perception; Equal = no change.

social acts in terms of gain construction occurs at the individual level, and therefore seems to be a truly developmental phenomenon.

Cross-Cultural Study

Developmental hypotheses should be valid across relatively different cultural contexts. The cross-cultural study reported next consisted of a sample of 90 African children equally divided by three age levels: 5- to 6-year-olds, 7- to 8-year-olds, and 10- to 11-year-olds. Children were from Cape Verde, an ex-Portuguese colony that became independent in the mid-1970s. Some children were interviewed in Portuguese, but most were interviewed in their native language—Crioulo.

Children's cost-perception/gain-construction responses were assessed using four prosocial dilemmas: helping, sharing, comforting, and donating (Lourenço, 1992). These dilemmas also involved two characters: one altruistic and one egoistic. The data presented here, however, refer only to children's answers and justifications on what is considered to be a direct cost-perception/gain-construction assessment (i.e., "Which character ended by gaining more at the end of the story and why?").

Table 12.3 shows that these African children picked cost-perception/gain-construction responses according to a pattern similar to that of their European (Portuguese) counterparts. Despite some variation across prosocial dilemmas, 5- to 6-year-olds tended to give cost-perceptions responses, 10- to 11-year-olds tended to give gain-construction responses, and children at intermediate age levels fell in between these groups. The children's justifications for their cost-perception/gain-construction responses were consistent with their initial options.

Taken together these cross-cultural results provide further support for the Piagetian approach to the development of prosocial behavior because they show that the child's growing ability to think of prosocial acts in

TABLE 12.3
Frequency of African Children's Cost-Perception/Gain-Construction
Responses as a Function of Age and Prosocial Dilemma

Age Level* (years)	Helping		Sharing		Comforting		Donating	
	Cost-per	Gain-con	Cost-per	Gain-con	Cost-per	Gain-con	Cost-per	Gain-con
	**							
5–6	24	6	17	13	17	13	23	7
7–8	15	15	7	23	9	21	19	11
10–11	10	20	2	28	5	25	7	23

*N = 30 for each age level.
** = Cost-per = Cost-perception responses; Gain-con = Gain-construction responses.

terms of gain construction emerges in different cultural contexts. In other words, because it appears in different cultural contexts, children's growing ability to conceptualize prosocial acts in terms of gain construction seems to be more a result from a continuous interaction with the social milieu, a developmental phenomenon, than a result from a particular type of experience, a learning phenomenon.

Children's Gain-Construction Competence and Affirmation/Negation Coordination

According to the Piagetian approach, the anticipation of costs involved in a prosocial act is relatively simple and therefore akin to a Piagetian affirmation, whereas the anticipation of possible gains (mainly psychological or moral) is more difficult cognitively and therefore akin to a Piagetian negation. Consequently, children's performance on cost-perception/gain-construction tasks should correlate positively with their performance on Piagetian, affirmation/negation tasks. Next I present a study that examined this prediction in a sample of 24 six-year-olds, 24 eight-year-olds, and 24 eleven-year-olds (see also Lourenço, 1993a, 1994a). The sample is a subsample of the cross-sectional study described earlier.

Children's ability to construct gain in prosocial acts was assessed by taking into account their direct and indirect cost-perception/gain-construction responses on the prosocial dilemma described previously (i.e., comforting a needy child vs. going to a party). The direct cost-perception/gain-construction question asks the child which character (altruistic or egoistic) had gained more at end of the story and why. The indirect question asks the child to indicate which character felt happier and more pleased at the end of the story and why. Once again the child's choice of the altruistic character was considered a gain-construction response and the choice of the egoistic character a cost-perception response. For the sake of simplicity, *no-gain* responses mean that the child picked the cost-perception alternative twice (i.e., on both direct and indirect questions), *double-gain* responses mean that she picked the gain-construction alternative twice, and *single-gain* responses mean that she picked the gain-construction alternative only once.

Children's affirmation/negation coordination was assessed by their performance on a Piagetian affirmation/negation task. The task consists of a simple transfer of n elements from one collection to another (see Piaget, 1974). First, the child is asked to make two (parallel) rows with "the same thing" of elements (i.e., six fruit gums) in each row. The child is then told that one row is her row and the other row is the experimenter's row. Next the experimenter covers his collection and asks the child to transfer one (or two or more) fruit gum from her row to his collection. Then the experimenter asks the child the critical question: "How many more gums have I got than you and why?" When children predict a difference of n instead of $2n$ elements, the experimenter uncovers his collection and asks the child to explain the difference of $2n$ instead of n elements between the collections.

Piaget's clinical method was used throughout the task. (For a detailed analysis of this method see Piaget, 1926). The child's performance was classified as Level 0, 1, 2, or 3. A response was scored at *Level 0* if the child answered the critical question in absolute rather than relative terms (e.g., "Now you've got seven." Experimenter: "Can you remember what I asked you?" Child: "Yes, how many gums there are now in your row"). Responses at Level 0 showed no understanding of the nature of the task. A response was scored at *Level 1* if the child understood the critical question, but predicted a difference of n elements between the collections. Moreover, at this level the child does not answer correctly even when confronted with the disconfirmation of her initial prediction (e.g., "You said before that now I have one more gum than you, but if you look at my row you will see that I have two more gums than you. Why is that?" Child: "Yes! When your row was covered, you added another gum to your collection without me noticing it"). Thus, a child at Level 1 had no understanding of negation. Responses were scored at *Level 2* if the child started to give a wrong prediction, but answered correctly after being probed during the task (e.g., "I said before that you've got one more gum than me, but now I can see that you've two more because when I gave you one of mine I took it away from my collection, and one plus one are two, not one"). A child at Level 2 was thus capable of coordinating affirmation and negation after feedback (empirical coordination). A response was scored at *Level 3* if, from the beginning of the task, the child provided appropriate reasons to justify her spontaneous predictions. A child at Level 3 was thus able to logically coordinate affirmation and negation.

TABLE 12.4
Frequency of Children's Different Responses on the
Cost-Perception/Gain-Construction and Affirmation/Negation Tasks

Age Level (years)*	Cost-Perception/Gain-Construction Task			Affirmation/Negation Task			
	No gain	Single gain	Double gain	Level 0	Level 1	Level 2	Level 3
6	18	6	0	20	4	0	0
8	6	10	8	0	21	3	0
11	0	4	20	0	10	11	3

*N = 24 for each age level.

Three aspects of the data summarized in Table 12.4 are particularly relevant to the Piagetian approach. First, children's understanding of negation or the coordination between affirmations and negations increases
strongly with age—a result consistent with Piaget's (1974) findings. Second, the increment in children's gain-construction competence is revealed
by direct and indirect assessments, which is consistent with the cross-
sectional and longitudinal data reported before. Third, children's gain-
construction competence was positively correlated with their ability to coordinate affirmations and negations. In the oldest age group, none of the
20 children who gave double-gain responses scored at Level 0, whereas
the children who scored at Level 3 always gave double-gain responses. In
the intermediate age group, all of the 18 children who gave single- or double-gain responses scored at Level 0. Finally, in the youngest age group,
the great majority of children who gave no-gain responses also scored at
Level 0.

To summarize, the correlational data are consistent with the idea that
concepts from Piaget's theory shed light on the development of prosocial
behavior. Specifically, the findings show that children's affirmation/ne-
gation coordination was positively related to their capacity to construct
gain in prosocial acts.

Children's Gain-Construction Competence and Their Prosocial Behavior

For the Piagetian approach to be a viable explanation of children's development of prosocial behavior, one has to show that children's competence
to construct gain in prosocial acts is positively related to their prosocial
behavior. In the following, data pertinent to this issue are presented. The
data come from a new sample of 90 children equally divided into three
age levels: 30 five- to six-year-olds, 30 seven- to eight-year-olds, and 30
ten- to eleven-year-olds (Lourenço, 1994a, 1994b).

Children's competence to construct gain in prosocial acts was assessed by taking into account their direct and indirect cost-perception/gain-construction responses to four prosocial dilemmas: sharing, donating, helping, and comforting. Children's gain-construction scores could range from 8 to 0. They received a score of 8 if gain-construction responses were given to both the direct and indirect questions of each dilemma (i.e., two questions times four dilemmas). They received a score 0 if cost-perception responses were given throughout. Subsequently, three categories (groups) were created by classifying gain-construction as *low* (from 0 to 3), *middle* (4), and *high* (from 5 to 8).

Children's prosocial behavior was assessed by their donations to anonymous schoolmates in an opportunity-to-donate situation often used to study children's altruistic or prosocial behavior (e.g., Bar-Tal et al., 1980). After completing the cost-perception/gain-construction tasks mentioned earlier, the child received six fruit gums for her participation in the study. She was then told that she might keep all of them or donate some and keep some for herself. The experimenter emphasized that none of the child's teachers and colleagues would come to know about her donations. Then the experimenter left the room. When the child returned to the classroom, the experimenter determined how many fruit gums had been added to the donation box in the experimental room.

As Table 12.5 shows, the number of children who donated at least one of their fruit gums increased significantly with age, which is consistent with the general finding that "altruism increases with age" (Krebs, 1970, p. 290). More important, nonparametric Spearman rank correlations showed that children's gain-construction scores were positively correlated with their altruistic behavior. Overall, nonaltruistic children had lower gain-construction scores, whereas altruistic children had higher gain-construction scores. This pattern was also found when children's

TABLE 12.5
Number of Altruistic and Egoistic Children
as a Function of Age and Gain-Construction Scores

Gain-Scores	Age Level (years)*					
	5–6		7–8		10–11	
	Altruistic	Egoistic	Altruistic	Egoistic	Altruistic	Egoistic
Low**	2	17	2	7	0	2
Middle	3	2	4	2	1	0
High	5	1	12	3	25	2

*N = 30 for each age level.
**Low gain: from 0 to 3; middle gain: 4; high gain: from 5 to 8.

gain-construction scores were correlated with their mean donation in the opportunity-to-donate situation (see Lourenço, 1993a, 1994a).

In summary, the correlation between children's prosocial behavior and their competence to construct gain in prosocial acts is consistent with the idea that the development of prosocial behavior can be addressed from a Piagetian perspective. Specifically, the findings support the prediction that children's gain-construction competence is positively associated with their prosocial behavior.

STRENGTHS, LIMITATIONS, AND BEYOND

The data presented previously suggest that the Piagetian perspective provides a viable account of the development of prosocial behavior. Thus, some of Piaget's cognitive concepts and operations help us understand the development of a specific type of social behavior (i.e., prosocial behavior). By implication, his theory has the potential to illuminate our thinking about social development even when it does not appeal directly to social concepts.

The cost-perception/gain-construction perspective has other noteworthy aspects. First, this perspective articulates functional and structural features in children's development of prosocial behavior. It is clear that the cost–gain dimension influences all prosocial behaviors (see Eisenberg & Fabes, 1998). Costs and gains in prosocial behavior, however, have been conceived more in terms of function than structure. In other words, when costs and gains are considered in prosocial behavior, they are generally regarded as determinants that influence such a behavior regardless of one's cognitive and developmental capacities. The Piagetian approach integrates both—structure and function—and goes beyond just functionalist accounts. According to the Piagetian approach, more than given directly as observable, gains in prosocial behavior are constructed on the basis of structural and developmental processes (e.g., coordination of affirmation and negation).

Second, to date researchers have been interested in one's normative conceptions of prosocial reasoning—why people say that we should or should not be prosocial in certain situations (Jackson & Tisak, 2001). Eisenberg's (1982) categories of prosocial reasoning (e.g., stereotypic reasoning, "I should help because it is the decent thing to do"; approval-oriented reasoning, "I should help because my friends will think I did the right think"; needs-oriented reasoning, "I should help because the girl really needs help"; abstract internalized reasoning, "I should help because I am often touched by things that I see happen"; see Carlo, Eisenberg, & Knight, 1992, p. 337) are a case in point. The Piagetian approach suggests that non-normative conceptions of prosocial reasoning, such as those perceived or construed by people to shed light on their own and others' prosocial acts, may play a role in determining such acts. In this vein, a further topic of research would be to investigate whether children's cost-perceptions/gain-constructions in prosocial acts turn out to be more predictive of their prosocial behavior than children's normative conceptions of prosocial reasoning as conceptualized by Eisenberg (1982).

Third, attempting to conceptualize children's development of prosocial behavior in terms of cost-perception/gain-construction enables us to overcome, to some extent, the endless altruism–egoism debate (see *Psychological Inquiry*, 1991). As Dovidio (1991) pointed out, "both altruistic and egoistic motives can exist within a single organism" (p. 126). This is consistent with the idea that children construct gains in acts that in their very nature seem to imply only sacrifice for the self. It is also in accord with Overton's relational perspective (see chap. 2) of the individual-social antinomy.

Fourth, the idea that the development of prosocial behavior constitutes a movement from cost perception (and centration) to gain construction (and compensation) has implications for the promotion of prosocial behavior in children. For example, a previous study found that children become more altruistic when they are taught to construct material, psychological, and moral gain through social-cognitive conflicts (Lourenço, 1997). Specifically, after being confronted with several gain-construction responses displayed by older children on diverse prosocial dilemmas, younger children changed their initial cost perceptions into gain constructions and exhibited more prosocial behavior in the opportunity-to-donate situation described previously.

Finally, ongoing research (Lourenço, 2003) suggests that the cost-perception/gain-construction perspective may help us understand two types of findings reported in the literature on children's antisocial behavior. The first finding is that "physically aggressive behavior, even among rejected children, tends to decline as children become older" (Crick & Ladd, 1990, p. 614). The second finding is that, compared with their nonaggressive peers, aggressive children are more likely to anticipate from their antisocial acts more positive outcomes and fewer negative consequences (Perry, Perry, & Rasmussen, 1986). In antisocial acts, however, the anticipation of possible gains seems easier than the anticipation of possible costs. This means that, if applied to the child's development of antisocial behavior, the cost-perception/gain-construction hypothesis regarding prosocial behavior becomes a gain-perception/cost-construction hypothesis. That is, one may think that the decline of physically aggressive behavior among older (and more developed) children is partly due to their greater ability to see antisocial acts more in terms of physical, psychological, and moral cost, a type of a Piagetian negation, than in terms of material gain, a type of a Piagetian affirmation. This possibility, which remains to be explored, also speaks to the existence of a social dimension in Piaget's theory.

Although the findings mentioned throughout this chapter support the Piagetian perspective, they should be interpreted cautiously. First, these findings are not critical results because they were not obtained in studies designed to test all the alternative explanations of children's development of prosocial behavior. Therefore, one might object that some of findings mentioned throughout the chapter could also be explained in terms of these explanations.

One might also object that the Piagetian approach to the development of prosocial behavior is too rational (i.e., that children's prosocial behavior can be motivated by immediate affective rewards of an empathic nature and not merely by cognitive constructions of gain; Batson, 1990; Eisenberg & Miller, 1987). Moreover, although children's gain-construction competence was found to be positively and significantly associated with a measure of prosocial behavior, the association was only moderate, which is consistent with the widespread idea that children's prosocial behavior is multiply determined (Hampson, 1981).

In addition, the reported associations are correlational and do not suggest any causal direction between cognition and prosocial development. It should be noted, however, that the claim is not that previous explanations of children's development of prosocial behavior are wrong and that the Piagetian account explored in this chapter constitutes the best account of the development of prosocial behavior.

Furthermore, conceptualizing cost perception as a Piagetian affirmation and gain construction as a Piagetian negation might not be evident to everyone. However, for Piaget (1985), an affirmation is an observable and a negation is an inference based on the coordination of actions. Thus, from the perspective of Piaget's theory, it is reasonable to consider the understanding of possible (psychological and moral) gains in prosocial acts as requiring mainly construction, inference, and coordination of actions and the understanding of the obvious costs in such acts as requiring mainly perception and direct observation.

It could also be objected that the reported correlations between children' s gain-construction competence and their prosocial behavior are based on simple and contrived measures of such competencies and behaviors. The same could perhaps be said of children's ability to construct a more complex concept of negation. In this respect, further studies designed to include other cost-perception/gain-construction tasks (e.g., real prosocial dilemmas), other affirmation-negation tasks (see Piaget, 1974), and other measures of children's prosocial behavior (e.g., naturalistic studies) would certainly be important to strengthen or challenge the Piagetian approach espoused here.

CONCLUSIONS

The discussion of the role of the social in Piaget's theory is generally restricted to Piaget's explicit contribution to the various levels in which we can relate the individual and the social. As most chapters of this volume cogently show, this is an excellent means to elaborate on some of Piaget's insights and problematic thoughts on the matter. In this chapter, however, I followed a different and less traveled road. The case for the existence of a social dimension in Piaget's theory can also be made by showing the heuristic value of some of his cognitive concepts. I illustrated the relevance of Piaget's theory for considering social development by showing its potential in helping us understand the development of prosocial behavior in children. Moreover, Piaget's influence on social cognition in general (Shantz, 1983) and on Kohlberg's (1984) work in particular (see Carpendale, 2000) also testify, albeit indirectly, on behalf of the relevance of his theory for thinking about social development. Indeed it would be ironic if an inherently individualistic theory could inspire a myriad of studies devoted to the analysis of social cognition and behavior.

In the first part of this chapter, I discussed the issue of what develops in children's development of prosocial behavior. In the process, I elaborated the distinctive features of a Piagetian, affirmation/negation or cost-perception/gain-construction perspective. In the second part, I presented cross-sectional, longitudinal, cross-cultural, and correlational data that are consistent with the two main propositions of the Piagetian perspective: With increasing age children become more likely to think of prosocial acts in terms of material, psychological, and moral gain than in terms of material cost, and this increasing ability seems to be positively related to children's capacity to understand negation in a more complex way as well as to their prosocial behavior. In the third part, I sketched some further applications of the Piagetian approach to the development of prosocial behavior. For example, its potential to help us understand certain aspects of children's antisocial behavior may be seen as one of its positive features.

All in all, the possibility of framing children's development of prosocial (and perhaps antisocial) behavior in terms of Piagetian cognitive concepts shows that even if it is true that Piaget's sociological imagination has significant limitations, both in principle and in practice, it is also true that, as Chapman (1992) remarked, his theory has, both in principle and in practice, potentials that "are still insufficiently assimilated or accommodated to in development psychology" (p. 39). This chapter provides an example of how we may start to explore these potentials.

ACKNOWLEDGMENT

The writing of this chapter was supported by funding from FCT (Portuguese Foundation for Science and Technology). I am grateful to the editors for helpful comments on an earlier version of the manuscript.

REFERENCES

Bar-Tal, D., Raviv, A., & Leiser, T. (1980). The development of altruistic behavior: Empirical evidence. *Developmental Psychology, 16,* 516–525.

Barnett, M., Thompson, S., & Schroff, J. (1987). Reasons for not helping. *Journal of Genetic Psychology, 148,* 489–498.

Batson, C. (1990). How social an animal? The human capacity for caring. *American Psychologist, 45,* 336–346.

Berkowitz, L. (1972). Social norms, feelings, and other factors affecting helping behavior and altruism. In L. Berkowitz (Ed.), *Advances in experimental social psychology* (pp. 63–108). New York: Academic Press.

Bryan, J. (1975). Children's cooperation and helping behaviors. In E. Hetherington (Ed.), *Review of child development* (pp. 127–181). Chicago: University of Chicago Press.

Carlo, G., Eisenberg, N., & Knight, G. (1992). An objective measure of adolescents' prosocial moral reasoning. *Journal of Research on Adolescence, 2,* 331–349.

Carpendale, J. (2000). Kohlberg and Piaget on stages and moral reasoning. *Developmental Review, 20,* 181–205.

Chapman, M. (1992). Equilibration and the dialectics of organization. In H. Beilin & P. Pufall (Eds.), *Piaget's theory: Prospects and possibilities* (pp. 39–59). Hillsdale, NJ: Lawrence Erlbaum Associates.

Crick, N., & Ladd, G. (1990). Children's perceptions of the outcomes of social exchanges: Do the ends justify being mean? *Developmental Psychology, 26,* 612–620.

Darley, J., & Latané, B. (1970). Norms and normative behavior: Field studies of social interdependence. In J. Macaulay & L. Berkowitz (Eds.), *Altruism and helping behavior* (pp. 83–101). New York: Academic Press.

Dovidio, J. (1984). Helping behavior and altruism. An empirical and conceptual overview. In L. Berkowitz (Ed.), *Advances in experimental child psychology* (pp. 362–427). New York: Academic Press.

Dovidio, J. (1991). Commentaries: The empathy-altruism hypothesis: Paradigm and promise. *Psychological Inquiry, 2,* 126–128.

Eisenberg, N. (1982). The development of reasoning regarding prosocial behavior. In N. Eisenberg (Ed.), *The development of prosocial behavior* (pp. 219–249). New York: Academic.

Eisenberg, N., & Fabes, R. (1998). Prosocial development. In W. Damon (Series Ed.), & N. Eisenberg (Ed.), *Handbook of child psychology: Vol. 3. Social, emotional, and personality development* (pp. 701–778). New York: Wiley.

Eisenberg, N., & Miller, P. (1987). The relation of empathy to prosocial and related behaviors. *Psychological Bulletin, 101,* 91–119.

Hampson, R. (1981). Helping behavior in children: A person-situation model. *Developmental Review, 1,* 93–112.

Jackson, M., & Tisak, M. (2001). Is prosocial behavior a good thing. Developmental changes in children's evaluations of helping, sharing, cooperating, and comforting. *British Journal of Developmental Psychology, 19,* 349–367.

Kohlberg, L. (1984). *Essays on moral development: Vol. 2. The psychology of moral development: Moral stages, their nature and validity.* San Francisco: Harper & Row.

Krebs, D. (1970). Altruism: An examination of the concept and a review of the literature. *Psychological Bulletin, 73,* 258–302.

Lourenço, O. (1990). From cost-perception to gain-construction: Toward a Piagetian explanation of the development of altruism in children. *International Journal of Behavioral Development, 13,* 119–132.

Lourenço, O. (1992). Para uma explicação Piagetiana do aumento do altruísmo na criança: Alguns dados interculturais [Toward a Piagetian explanation of children's development of altruism: Some cross-cultural data]. *Revista Portuguesa de Pedagogia, 26,* 301–319.

Lourenço, O. (1993a). Toward a Piagetian explanation of children's development of prosocial behavior: The force of negational thinking. *British Journal of Developmental Psychology, 11,* 91–106.

Lourenço, O. (1993b). Da percepção de custos à construção de ganhos: Um estudo longitudinal de 4 anos [From cost-perception to gain-construction: A 4-year longitudinal study]. *Análise Psicológica, 11,* 497–505.

Lourenço, O. (1994a). *Além de Piaget? Sim, mas devagar! [Beyond Piaget? Yes, but slowly].* Coimbra: Almedina.

Lourenço, O. (1994b). What develops in children's development of altruism? *Infancia y Aprendizaje, 67–68,* 185–197.

Lourenço, O. (1997). Promozione del comportamento prosociale del bambini:Um approcio Piagetiano de costruzione-guadagno [Promoting children's prosocial behavior: A Piagetian gain-construction approach]. *Quaderni di Terapia del Comportamento, 41,* 69–83.

Lourenço, O. (2003). Children's appraisals of antisocial acts: A Piagetian perspective. *British Journal of Developmental Psychology, 21,* 19–31.

Müller, U., Sokol, B., & Overton, W. (1999). Developmental sequences in class reasoning and propositional reasoning. *Journal of Experimental Child Psychology, 74,* 69–104.

Perry, D., Perry, L., & Rasmussen, E. (1986). Cognitive social learning mediators of aggression. *Child Development, 57,* 700–711.

Piaget, J. (1926). *La représentation du monde chez l' enfant* [The child's conceptior. of the world]. Paris: Alcan.

Piaget, J. (1957). *Logique et équilibre [Logic and equilibrium].* Paris: Presses Universitaires de France.

Piaget, J. (1974). *Recherches sur la contradiction: Vol. 2. Les relations entre affirmations et negations [Experiments in contradiction: Vol. 2. The relationship between affirmations and negations].* Paris: Presses Universitaires de France.

Piaget, J. (1985). *The equilibration of cognitive structures.* Chicago: University of Chicago Press. (Original work published 1975)

Piaget, J. (1995). *Sociological studies.* London: Routledge. (Original work published 1965)

Severy, L., & Davis, K. (1971). Helping behavior among normal and retarded children. *Child Development, 42,* 1017–1031.

Shantz, C. (1983). Social cognition. In P. Mussen (Series Ed.), *Handbook of child development* (Vol. 3, pp. 495–555). New York: Wiley.

Solomon, D., Ali, F., Kfir, D., Houlihan, K., & Yaeger, J. (1972). The development of demo-
     cratic values and behavior among Mexican-American children. *Child Development, 43,*
     625–638.
Underwood, B., & Moore, B. (1982). The generality of altruism in children. In N. Eisenberg
     (Ed.), *The development of prosocial behavior* (pp. 25–52). New York: Academic.
Weissbrod, C. (1980). The impact of warmth and instruction on donation. *Child Development,*
     51, 279–281.

Wittgenstein's Internalistic Logic and Children's Theories of Mind

Timothy P. Racine
Simon Fraser University

Gauging the impact of the writings of philosopher Ludwig Wittgenstein on developmental psychology is no simple matter. One could make the case that Wittgenstein has held considerable sway given that: (a) elements of his philosophy have been explicitly brought to bear on developmental issues (see Chapman & Dixon, 1987; Hobson, 1994, 2000; Hyman, 1991; Montgomery, 1997; Nelson & Kessler Shaw, 2002); and (b) his conception of a language-game shows up in various forms in developmental theory (e.g., in the social pragmatic approach to language development; e.g., Bruner, 1983). However, it is also the case that his philosophy is rarely applied in a thoroughgoing and cohesive manner. As such, whereas many developmentalists are likely to be familiar with Wittgenstein's strictures regarding language-games, and some may be familiar with his *private language argument*, it is not at all clear that many appreciate that Wittgenstein crafted these tools in opposition to a causal theory of meaning and mind. This seems acutely to be the case in the area of children's social understanding (children's so-called 'theories of mind') where the regnant and default assumptions seem to be that: (a) the mind or brain plays a causal role in learning about the minds of others; and (b) mental states are inner entities with validly statelike properties.

In this chapter, I introduce and attempt to integrate Wittgenstein's ideas within an *internalistic* logical framework. I argue that the underlying logic of Wittgenstein's thought and his opposition to a causal theory of meaning and mind is the wellspring from which the following jointly issue forth: (a) the idea of the impossibility of a truly private language; (b) the need for language-games; (c) the inadequacy of externally related accounts of human conduct; and (d) Wittgenstein's philosophy of psychology. In so doing, I justify a Wittgensteinian view of development and apply aspects of Wittgenstein's philosophy of psychology regarding the ontology of mental states and the logic of mental causation to the theory of mind enterprise.

WITTGENSTEIN'S INTERNALISTIC LOGIC AND ITS MANIFESTATIONS

Wittgenstein is typically considered an ordinarily language philosopher; it is equally typical to group his writings with the works of other analytic philosophers like Ryle (1949) and Austin (1975). Ordinary language philosophers look at the role that words play in our day-to-day activities to delimit what such terms might mean. Astington (1999) brought Austin's ordinary language approach to bear on intention and related terms to see what one can do (in Austin's sense) with such forms. Although there is much to be gleaned from the resultant clarity of Astington's analysis, in her characterization of the rationale for the ordinary language approach she focused on its descriptive methods without mentioning the fact that this approach was a reaction to the insurmountable problems of classical correspondence theories of meaning and reference.

For example, Wittgenstein (1958) began his seminal *Philosophical Investigations* with a discussion of what he characterized as the Augustinian picture (conception) of language wherein a one-to-one correspondence between a word and some aspect of reality is presupposed. It is a picture of language that casts its function as exclusively referential, wherein ostensive definition is the means to discover what words refer to and mean. However, it is obvious that aspects of reality cannot be accounted for ostensively. I cannot point to *hope* in the way that I can point to *red*. Further, it is also obvious that ostensive definition underdetermines meaning and reference in that in my pointing to even a red color sample I might be making a request, issuing a command, and so forth. For Wittgenstein, the solution to this problem of indeterminacy is that meanings are built onto and, thus, presuppose, ways of acting.

Wittgenstein's ordinary language approach was also a reaction to attempts to mend the classical picture. For example, he was critical of Russell's (1921) and Ogden and Richards' (1923) elaboration of what are known as *psychological* or *causal* theories of meaning (Baker & Hacker, 1984, 1985; Button, Coulter, Lee, & Sharrock, 1995; Hacker, 1990, 1996; Savage-Rumbaugh, Shanker, & Taylor, 1998; Schulte, 1993; Shanker, 1991,

1998; ter Hark, 1990). Psychological/causal theories are based on the assumption that the meaning of a term lies in its psychological effect on the mind. Accordingly, a mental verb has been correctly used if it brings to mind the images and associations in the interlocutor that the speaker had intended to communicate. Further, understanding a proposition is assumed to require a mind or brain state to causally mediate between, for example, a thought and some state of affairs. Therefore, understanding is taken to be a mental state bridging thought and action. Wittgenstein objected to this line of reasoning as early as 1932 in his *Cambridge Lectures*:

> Knowing how to use a word is like knowing how to move a chess piece. Now how do the rules enter into playing the game? What is the difference between playing the game and aimlessly moving the pieces? I do not deny there is a difference, but I want to say that knowing how a piece is to be used is not a particular state of mind which goes on while the game goes on. The meaning of a word is to be defined by the rules for its use, not by the feeling that attaches to the words. (Wittgenstein, 1979, para. 2)

Language Games, Forms of Life, and Criteria

As is well known, Wittgenstein argued that terms take on their meanings from the role(s) they play in their respective language-games, which are sets of rule-governed conventions delimiting the relations between linguistic terms and the activities they describe. These activities are rule governed in the sense that a child who learns to use the term *sad* appropriately through correction from her parents is learning the use of the term from parents who have mastered the rules of the sad language game in particular activities. This is to claim that rules could be articulated to describe how terms are employed after a language-game has been learned; this is not to claim that children learn a concatenation of rules that are then applied to make sense of their activities. Rather, through the child's immersion in shared activities with some knowledgeable other, the child develops a mastery of a given set of implicit rules. Wittgenstein argued that one can master such practices because they are embedded in simple day-to-day activities (which he called *forms of life*). Forms of life are the characteristic regularities in human existence that enable intelligible communication with others.

Idiosyncratically, Wittgenstein referred to the use(s) of words—their meaning—as their grammar. In the earlier example, one knows what a chess piece is (its grammar) if one understands how it is employed in the game of chess. Similarly, one knows what an intention is if one understands how it is employed in its respective language-game(s). This necessitates (i.e., presupposes) knowledge of the conventions of how these language-games are played. Were one to observe someone playing chess or using an intention utterance correctly, one would presume (all things being equal) that the individual so playing has mastered the technique or skill required to employ these sets of conventions. From this point of view, although an active agent is required to participate in activities with others to come to understand how linguistic terms are employed in various aspects of the human form of life, the developing agent's mind does not cause these signs to have meaning. My behavior and words (as showing mastery of some practice in a language-game) are intelligible to others because they are grounded in participation in some shared form of life. Shared activities, or social interaction more generally, focus attention on the criteria that one must come to understand to follow what is meant by the use of a term. Chapman (1987) noted that, "criteria are those publicly observable circumstances which might be used in teaching the correct use of [an] expression to a child or someone else learning our language" (p. 105). If public observable criteria for the correct use of words did not exist, then agents could never agree they were using terms correctly. Barring massive nativism, one could interpret the fact that humans successfully interact with another as an existence proof of sorts for a roughly Wittgensteinian position.

Developmentalists who have used Wittgenstein's roughly criteriological approach to semantics (e.g., Chapman, 1987; Montgomery, 1997) have followed a tradition initiated by Baker (1974) wherein meaning and criteria are in one-to-one correspondence. Canfield (1981) argued, however, that five aspects of use can be located in Wittgenstein's philosophy. Although I do not develop this point further in the present chapter, I describe criteria in relation to two of these to guard against a simple criteriological conception of semantics. I stress this because to do otherwise would leave Wittgenstein vulnerable to the criticism that his approach makes implicit commitments to a correspondence theory of meaning (cf. Bickhard, 1987). I have noted that language-games are grounded in the backdrop of everyday human life, activities, and practices. This can be reframed as a basic meaning level because a term in a language game means what it means in part by virtue of the characteristic form of life in which it is rooted (Canfield called these *background conditions*). If these aspects of human existence change, rules of the corresponding language-games may have no application.

Background conditions are to be distinguished from circumstances. Canfield used the latter to implicate the varieties of situations that may serve as criteria (as opposed to the function that a language game might play in the human form of life). For example, sorrow goes along with certain characteristic situations (e.g., grieving, separation, etc.). If a person were not in such a circumstance, one would be much less likely to judge her to be experiencing sorrow. However, if she were to exhibit sorrowful behavior, this might lead one to conclude she is in such a situation. In this sense, meaning and circumstances are inextricably linked. Criteria constitute the third level of meaning for Canfield. Here, we encounter the criteriological conception of meaning. Note, however, that not only need a criterion for a judgment of sorrow be met, but it must also be employed in a sorrowful circumstance *and* with respect to the basic function that sorrow plays in our lives. Therefore, situations and background conditions are not contained in the criterion. Rather, the criterion is employed in these circumstances and in the human form of life. Thus, meaning and criterion are not in one-to-one correspondence.

Internal and External Relations

ter Hark (1990) discussed Wittgenstein's emphasis on internal relations (rather than causal external ones) between criterion and term defined, thought and state of affairs, and so forth (see also Canfield, 1981; Hacker, 1990, 1996; Shanker, 1991, 1998). Quoting from ter Hark (1990):

> Internal relations are characterized by three features: the relation is between two [concepts]; the relation is not mediated by a third term; and the relation exists in a practice and not in the mind or in some abstract medium . . . A characteristic of internal relations is that the two members cannot be identified independently of each other. (pp. 182–183)

Because a criterion and term defined are internally related (e.g., in the way that the angles in a triangle are internally related), a criterion gives an exact definition of the term defined. That is, a criterion and term defined are internally related *because* the criterion gives an exact definition of the term defined. In contrast to a criterion that is internally defined, what Wittgenstein called a *symptom* (an empirical correlate of a defined term) is externally related.

Of course, Wittgenstein did not deny that there are empirical correlates for the meaning of a term in the sense that Russell and company champion (e.g., feelings of correctness when terms are applied, etc.). The problem is that one symptom can be replaced by another symptom. Further, a symptom may be present for some instances of applications of a rule or learning a criterion, but absent in others. For these reasons, Wittgenstein did not endorse Russell's and Ogden and Richards' psychological/causal theories of meaning. Such accounts cannot obtain because they destroy internal relations. That is, an infant or child may or may not feel or think X or Y when discerning a meaningful relationship between two objects or when employing the rule for the use of a term. As such these affective or cognitive states may or may not be empirically correlated with meaning and understanding. However, the internal relation that exists between two objects is exact. It requires and can tolerate no causal input from another source. There is no third term possible in all instances of such a relation.

Despite Wittgenstein's internalistic logic, it seems difficult to shake the view of the mind and brain as causal intermediaries in understanding other agents, generating intelligible behavior, and so forth. For example, although drawing on Wittgenstein (1958) in their work regarding young children's early word use and developing social understanding, Nelson and Kessler Shaw (2002) claimed that, "the bond between word and object is problematic and arbitrary—it is only completed through the mental conception corresponding to the object" (p. 33). They then proceed to build on Ogden and Richards' (1923) theory of meaning, which posits a psychological concept that is claimed to be necessary to anchor word and object. Hobson (2000), who also drew on Wittgenstein (1958) in theorizing about children's social understanding, simultaneously endorsed Wittgenstein as well as Ogden and Richards. However, from my point of view, one should not build on Ogden and Richards, but rather avoid them altogether because they locate the concept in the head as the fulcrum about which word and object are related. It is inconsistent to embrace the language-game metaphor and then render it impotent by relocating meaning back in the mind.

Nelson and Kessler Shaw and Hobson are correct, of course, that an agent must attribute meaning to symbols: What they may not appreciate is that a symbol is not grounded in the agent's mind, but rather in her participation in a shared practice. This is because the meanings of terms and *a fortiori*—the meanings of conceptual terms—exist in the agent's participation in practices. Therefore, this places the meaning of concepts in participation in language-games, not in the agent's psychological activities. Developmental processes still have a clear role to play in the present account, however. The agent must be able to interact with some knowledgeable other who knows how the game in question is played (Chapman, 1991; Piaget, 1932, 1995; Vygotsky, 1978) and negotiate—and even renegotiate with that other—as the child learns the implicit rules of a practice (Turnbull & Carpendale, 1999). One could claim joint attention is required to participate in language games. Whereas this is certainly true in a descriptive sense, I have not employed the term because there is quite a bit of theoretical baggage tied up with its use. Participation in many language-games would also presuppose that the child has constructed the permanence of objects, space, causality, and so forth (Piaget, 1954).

To claim that meaning is grounded in an agent's participation in a practice rather than in the agent's mind, however, is not to take a behaviorist stance, but rather to reject a causal theory of meaning and mind. Although

Wittgenstein has been misinterpreted in this manner, his philosophy would be anathema to a behaviorist enterprise because an associationistic S–R framework could not assimilate an account of word–object mapping based on meaning being grounded and negotiated in participation in a shared practice rather than a simple correspondence between word and object (Racine, 2002). The more sophisticated charge—that Wittgenstein is a logical behaviorist because he claimed that understanding entails discerning the logical relationship between criteria and behavior (e.g., Chihara & Fodor, 1966)—also does not work given that meaning and criteria are not isomorphic and the relation between behavior and criteria is not one of entailment (Canfield, 1981).

The Private Language Argument

Wittgenstein's private language argument (PLA) demonstrates the logical difficulty in being able to refer to an inner mental event outside of a community of language users. In line with the internalistic logic I have framed in this chapter, I note that Russell's and Ogden and Richards' psychological theories of meaning held that inner impressions of, for example, colors could be privately named (Baker & Hacker, 1985; Hacker, 1990; Schulte, 1993; ter Hark, 1990). As with the language-game construct, Wittgenstein's opposition to a causal theory of meaning and mind again provides the impetus for him to, in this case, dismiss private language. Wittgenstein understood that it is easy to inappropriately impose a term employed in a language-game that describes outer objects and, hence, demands referential idioms (e.g., perception) onto another that seems to describe inner objects, but cannot accommodate referential idioms (e.g., introspection). The problem here is that such inner events cannot possibly be observed—despite the *mind's eye* metaphor. Simulation accounts of social cognitive development, however, hold that the developing agent can experience her own internal mental states, understand these, and then apply them to the mental life of others by analogy (e.g., Gordon, 1992; Harris, 1992; Tomasello, 1999). Montgomery (1997) showed the relevance of the PLA to simulation theories because the PLA renders introspection, the lynchpin of simulation accounts, a logically impossible means to learn how terms are employed (Chapman, 1987; Hacker, 1980; Savage-Rumbaugh et al., 1998; ter Hark, 1990; Wittgenstein, 1958).

To demonstrate his points about private language, Wittgenstein used the example of naming sensations to show that private definition could not allow for the verification of whether a symbol (i.e., a psychological stand-in for the private mental event in question) represents what it is taken to represent. In such a case, there would be no way for an agent to know whether she is following the rules implied by a correct use of a term;

if one does not possess a rule of application, one cannot communicate it to others. Some means other than another subjective impression is therefore needed to verify whether the rule has been correctly applied and "in the present case I have no criterion of correctness. One would like to say: whatever is going to seem right to me is right. And that only means here we can't talk about 'right' " (Wittgenstein, 1958, para. 258). Therefore, naming must take place in a shared practice where a child can be corrected when she misapplies the implicit rules governing a term's use (i.e., within language-games).

Thus, an infant or young child cannot introspect on her mental world to conclude she is experiencing mental event A because she possesses no standard with which to know she is experiencing A. To do so presupposes, on pain of circularity, that she is already familiar with the meaning of A. Montgomery (1997) claimed, however, that ". . . the emphasis for Wittgenstein is that the reliability of the introspective process is far from perfect" (p. 298). It is not unreasonable that Montgomery focused on the failings of the human memory system in his interpretation of the PLA in that prominent treatments mention this in passing as did Wittgenstein. Kripke (1982), who was cited by Montgomery (1997), made particular use of this interpretation of Wittgenstein's PLA (cf. Baker & Hacker, 1984, 1985; Russell, 1987; ter Hark, 1990). Wittgenstein's comments on memory, however, are not intended to question the reliability of memory as an end in itself. Rather, they are used to demonstrate the impossibility of an inner criterion for use when one is attempting to name an inner event—an instantiation of his internalistic logic and a bridge to language-games. Therefore, although Montgomery went to some length to review literature demonstrating the fallibility of memory in preschoolers, Wittgenstein's point is a strictly logical one (Baker & Hacker, 1984, 1985; Chapman, 1987; Hacker, 1990; ter Hark, 1990). That is, the fallibility of memory is a symptom to Wittgenstein.

THE ENCULTURATION OF WITTGENSTEIN

Some developmentalists take Wittgenstein's metaphor of a language game as a metaphor for enculturation (e.g., Astington & Gopnik, 1991; de Villiers, 1999; Gopnik, 1993). From this point of view, a Wittgensteinian approach is seen as tantamount to suggesting that a child must learn the culturally relative ways of, in this case, 'talking about the mind'. Chandler (1997), however, pointed out that relativism and developmental psychology make for strange bedfellows for the simple reason that, from a relativistic frame of reference, there can be no development but only change. If this interpretation is correct, a Wittgensteinian approach to development is a nonstarter. However, as previously discussed, language-games are made up of more than language: They include linguistic, paralinguistic, and nonlinguistic elements. In learning a language-game, a child learns a concomitant practice in which she becomes skilled. ter Hark (1990) referred to the *learning to talk about X* interpretation of Wittgenstein as the *actuality fallacy* because the actions that are reciprocally related to the language and that help make the language intelligible are missing or neglected. Absent in such accounts are the activities that ground the language-game. In the case of crucial constructs in theory of mind research, this characterization of language-games seems particularly ill advised given that some 'mental states' (e.g., intention) are often more easily made manifest in nonverbal expressions than in words.

A more sophisticated paraphrase of the prior interpretation might be that children reared in different cultures with different cultural practices and activities would, therefore, learn different language-games. Although this seems to follow from a commonsense understanding of Wittgenstein, it would violate Wittgenstein's internalistic logic because it introduces a cultural third variable into the internal relation between criterion and term defined (Hacker, 1996; ter Hark, 1990). ter Hark (1990) referred to *this* characterization of Wittgenstein as the *sociologistic fallacy*. To repeat, a third variable (sociological, psychological, or biological) cannot be causally related to meaning.

Although there are undoubtedly cultural differences in practices, and therefore the attendant language games, as I understand Wittgenstein, he was working on a different (more basic) level of analysis. For example, before a child learns not to overtly express pain because she comes to realize that it is part of a cultural practice not to do so, the child will still experience and express pain. It is this pain expression that begins the language-game of pain. Any higher level constraints placed on this by cultural conventions would be related to this initial primitive expression. To underscore the rootedness of many language-games, Wittgenstein (1958) described how a member of a language community would learn to use the term *pain*:

> What I do is not, of course, to identify my sensation by criteria: but to repeat an expression. But this is not the *end* of the language-game: it is the beginning ... How do words *refer* to sensations?—There doesn't seem to be any problem here; don't we talk about sensations every day, and give them names? But how is the [connection] between the name and the thing set up? This question is the same as: how does a human being learn the meaning of the names of sensations?—of the word "pain" for example. Here is one possibility: words are used in connection with the primitive, the natural, expressions of the sensation and used in their place. A child has hurt himself and he cries; and then adults talk to him and teach him exclamations and, later, sentences. They teach the child new pain-behavior. (paras. 290, 244; italics original)

The point here is that the language game of pain, like many others, is grafted on to natural expressive behavior (Canfield, 1993, 1999; Malcolm, 1991; Wittgenstein, 1958, 1969). In this sense, primitive language-games are universal because they reflect fundamental human experiences. Concepts like pain presuppose natural expressive behaviors that would by definition not vary across cultures. In such cases, the language in the game is just expressive behavior. Intention is another such psychological concept that is so much a part of the human form of life that it would not vary across cultures. Intention may take on different meanings in more complicated language-games (ter Hark, 1990), but it seems clear that intentional behavior is fundamental to even more than the human form of life: "What is the natural expression of an intention?—Look at a cat when it stalks a bird; or a beast when it wants to escape" (Wittgenstein, 1958, para. 647).

Wittgenstein's (1958, 1976) claim that grammar is arbitrary (or, as he also put it, grammar is not answerable to reality), however, seems to support the enculturation view: "The rules of grammar are arbitrary in the same sense as the choice of a unit of measurement . . . the rules of grammar cannot be justified by [showing] that their application makes a representation agree with reality" (Wittgenstein, 1976, p. 29). This prompted some to conclude that Wittgenstein is an antirealist committed to a form of linguistic idealism—that is, Wittgenstein denied there is a world independent of language or thought. As is often the case when interpreting Wittgenstein, this characterization may be accurate in one sense, but misleading in another. In his criticism of the Augustinian picture of language, Wittgenstein implicitly argued against a realist metaphysics that would presuppose that a proposition could be compared to reality and found to agree with it. However, Wittgenstein was not in the business of theory construction, but was interested rather in whether a proposition makes sense. It is unclear that this makes him an antirealist. Some of his interpreters (e.g., Hacker, 1996; ter Hark, 1990) suggested instead that Wittgenstein cut a swath between the poles of realism and antirealism just as he did with cognitivism and behaviorism. In any event, one should bear in mind that grammar is arbitrary to Wittgenstein in a restricted sense. His point is that one cannot justify a grammatical rule in the same way that one can justify a knowledge claim—for example, by pointing to some further grounds for the claim.

Language-games are grounded in practices, but these practices do not explain why they play a particular role in our form of life. Thus, although particular conventions (e.g., inches, centimeters, cubits) are employed in measurement activities, these are arbitrary because there is not a *further* standard for their correctness. In this sense, there is no reality outside of this practice that justifies it. However, although a variety of conventions are used in measurement practices, a sufficiently complex society would have a need for measurement: It would reflect a universal form of life. In this paradoxical sense, although grammar is not answerable to reality, it reflects pragmatic human concerns. Thus, grammar is not arbitrary in the sense that it is random or dispensable, but simply because no further justification for it can be provided (Hacker, 1996). To claim that one cannot get outside of language games once a member of a linguistic community, however, is not to claim that one cannot get outside of language. Language games are based on regularities in human activity; there is good reason to suspect that humans cannot get outside of the human form of life (Lakoff & Johnson, 1999; Merleau-Ponty, 1962; Wittgenstein, 1958, para. 281).

A LOGICOGRAMMATICAL ANALYSIS OF INTENTIONAL MENTAL STATES

I suggested earlier that Hobson (2000) and Nelson and Kessler Shaw (2002) did not attempt to square their employment of Wittgenstein with more foundational aspects of Wittgenstein's remarks about mental life. It is also not clear whether Montgomery would accept the position I take in this chapter given that he does not distance himself from the view of mental states as inner entities by characterizing criteria as indicating the "presence of mental states" (Montgomery, 1997, p. 295). As I see it, these applications of Wittgenstein's philosophy are conducted in such a manner that readers could easily fail to discern how different a view of the mind Wittgenstein offers. I suggest it is problematic to use the tools in the Wittgensteinian arsenal and ignore the underlying internalistic logic of Wittgenstein's thought and his opposition to a causal theory of meaning and mind because his philosophy issues forth from this wellspring.

The Causal Picture of Mental States

As mentioned before, Astington (1999) drew on Austin's (1975) strain of ordinary language philosophy to discuss the meaning of intention and related terms. Astington subsequently employed Searle's (1983) model of intention to discuss the role of the mind in generating intentional behavior. Although Searle's model may offer Astington a useful way with which to classify children's developing understanding of judgments of responsibility, I argue that the use of Searle's model legitimizes a pernicious and misleading picture of mental states. A survey of literature would also suggest that this is the canonical way to conceive of the role of intentional mental states (beliefs, desires, intentions) in theory of mind research. In brief, according to Searle (1983), an intentional act is intentional because it is coextensive with an intentional mental state (a so-called *intention in action*). Further, an intention in action may or may not be caused by a prior mental state of intention. For Searle, this accounts for the fact that some prior intentions are fulfilled and others are not. Although I offer more specific grounds later on which to reject this picture, I note here that it is incompatible from the outset with a Wittgensteinian view in that intentions and actions interface and are satisfied in language-games, not in the future (Shanker, 1991) or in the head.

To demonstrate that it is impossible to find some mental residue that causes voluntary actions, Wittgenstein (1958) posed the following ironic question: "What remains if I subtract the fact my arm went up from the fact that I raised my arm?" (para. 621). Searle (1979) answered that the difference between my arm going up and my raising it is the causal involvement of an intention in the latter case. Meltzoff, Gopnik, and Repacholi (1999, p. 24) followed suit in their interpretation of Wittgenstein's ironic question. Before looking at intention as a mental state in particular, I give an answer to Wittgenstein's question that is consistent with his philosophy. Schulte (1993) employed a useful analogy to underscore the role that terms play in their respective language-games to make the point that understanding another's intentions is not tantamount to understanding their state of mind. If a person wants to know why another has moved a pawn on a chessboard and he or she does not know how the game of chess is played, then reporting the mental gymnastics that seemed to lead up to the action of moving my pawn will be of no avail: "In order to make him understand my intention I shall have to explain the game of chess to him. And if he grasps what I intended, he will have understood it without my having made any reference to mental processes" (Schulte, 1993, p. 153). If others do not need to understand my mental processes to understand my performance in a game of chess, it is odd to conclude that the ironic subtraction in Wittgenstein's example should lead to the mathematical solution of intention given Wittgenstein's strictures regarding language-games.[1]

The Ontology of Mental States

As I stressed earlier, mental states terms are generally assumed to be referential; that is, they are taken to refer to some internal object on analogy to perceptible objects in the world. Wittgenstein (1958, 1980, 1981) argued that mental state terms like belief and intention do not refer to phenomena

---

[1]As I understand it, Wittgenstein (1958) discussed *willing* as an exemplar of an intentional mental act, and *willing* and *intention* are not coextensive. Willing refers to mental effort applied to achieving a goal; intention refers to the purpose of that goal. To use Wittgenstein's fragment in the context of a discussion of intention, therefore, seems ill advised from the outset.

at all. However, belief and intention can be observed (i.e., in others, not in oneself) if one has developed an understanding of what is criterial for the application of these terms. It is problematic to take mental states and processes on analogy to physical states and processes. Physicists legitimately speak of states and processes; psychologists may perhaps only do so at their own peril. Chapman (1987) pointed out that Wittgenstein conceived of 'mental events' like intentions, beliefs, and desires more like dispositions than states of consciousness because they lack genuine duration, are not interrupted by attentional shifts, and so forth (Wittgenstein, 1980, 1981).[2] Only sensations and emotions obtain as mental states from this point of view. For example, intending to quit smoking or believing you can quit drinking coffee are different than being in a sour mood for half an hour because you did not have a cigarette with your morning coffee. I can monitor the duration of my mood state with a watch; my foul mood might dissipate for a few minutes if I receive a phone call from a friend. None of these would apply to my intentions, beliefs, or desires. Using the example of belief, Hacker (1996) made the grammar of such terms abundantly clear: "There are indefinitely many things that I believe at a given time, but I am not in indefinitely many different mental states at a given time . . . we ask a listener 'Do you believe me?' . . . not 'Are you believing me?' " (pp. 419, 421).

That notwithstanding, as mentioned earlier, psychological concepts are not indiscernible. If they were, we could not communicate about them. However, if mental states like intention, belief, and desire do not obtain, it is not clear how such states could precede actions or be temporally coextant with them (cf. Searle, 1979, 1983). To get around this issue as it applies to intention, one could perhaps invoke Dennett's (1987) intentional stance position that advocates a functionalistic view of mental states in which their ontology is moot. However, the fact that most mental events do not obtain as states is a logicogrammatical truism. Remaining agnostic about the grammar of mental verbs engenders conceptual confusion about the mind. Theories beginning from a logically problematic model of mind cannot help but contribute to the confusion. Theories that posit such mental states at ontological face value run headlong into the monolithic problem of how it is that infants or children could understand such chimera (to understand others) if these states cannot exist. At the very least, this indicates that infants and children must learn about the mind in some other way. I already suggested, in fact, that they do. Fur-

---

[2]ter Hark (1990) would question Chapman's analysis, however, because the former shows that Wittgenstein did not conceive of terms like *intention* and the like as dispositions; Wittgenstein also did not use *disposition* in the same way as, for example, Ryle (1949). Further, Button and his colleagues (1995) pointed out that Ryle's use of the term *disposition* was problematic.

ther, this seems to indicate that theories featuring mental states and/or structures as causal entities are in need of revision.

In contrast, Meltzoff and colleagues (1999) suggested that, although "a few radical philosophers and psychologists may deny the existence of mental states, most regular 'folk' feel sure that they themselves and others have them" (p. 17). The latter is accurate in one sense, but misleading in another. Yes, folk psychological idioms are indispensably intertwined with basic activities and practices in the human form of life. These idioms, practices, and the activities in which they are bound up constitute the nexus of the mind. Wittgenstein (1969) called these the *main thing*. However, when my 4-year-old son declares that a playmate did such and such *on purpose*, I dispute that my son is making a claim about a mental state or that he made his statement because of some computation about the mental state of his playmate. If this is denying the existence of the mental states, then, yes, I deny them—but only when understood on these terms. However, I am not attempting to exclude what people mean when they talk about 'mental states'. Rather, I wish to rehabilitate this view.

Continuing with the case of intentions, Wittgenstein (1958) made the following comment: "An intention is embedded in its situation. If the technique of chess did not exist, I could not intend to play a game of chess" (para. 337). What does it mean to claim that an intention is *embedded in its situation*, and what does this have in common with implicitly rule-governed activities? Consider the following example. My moving forward to stand at a bus stop as a bus pulls closer is an expression of an intention for which the criterion lies in mastery of the particular practice of waiting for a bus. Whether some neurons fired or some psychological events occurred during the execution of my intention is beside the point: If this particular practice did not exist and had I not mastered this skill, my activities would not have constituted my intention. That is, my activities would not mean that I had acted on some intention.

CHILDREN'S ACQUISITION OF A THEORY OF MIND

The dominant theoretical accounts of children's social cognitive development are at odds with the account elaborated earlier. This is not surprising in one sense given that, although Wittgenstein often made reference in his writings to how a child would be taught a term or how a child might understand such and such, Wittgenstein's ideas are not elucidated in the service of understanding development. I have tried to show that children's acquisition of a theory of mind cannot be the result of insight into the mental states of others given that such states do not obtain. I argue presently that the dominant positions in the theory of mind are inconsistent with the account I have advanced because they subscribe to a causal theory of meaning and mind. Wittgenstein's view of concept development is such that concepts are rooted in participation in normative practices. As a corollary, mental activity is not what makes behavior intelligible or what generates intelligible behavior. Of course an active agent is presupposed who is able to jointly engage with some knowledgeable other in basic day-to-day activities. The problem is that an active agent so engaged is just the beginning—not the end—of the story of meaning and mind. However, the dominant assumption in the field seems to be that identification with a conspecific suffices for some rudimentary leg hold on another's mind. However, intentions, beliefs, and desires are not in our head; they exist and are understood in language-games.

As mentioned previously, the simulation explanation of mental life—wherein it is argued that the developing agent comes to understand the mental life of others through first experiencing her own mental contents and then applying these newly discovered states to others (e.g., Gordon, 1992; Harris, 1992; Tomasello, 1999)—relies on a causal view of meaning and mind. Montgomery (1997) used the private language argument to point out the difficulty with relying on introspection to understand inner experiences to be applied to others. I prefer to locate the PLA in the overall context of Wittgenstein's internalistic logic. When framed this way, it is just one manifestation of this basic logic. As such, even if simulation theorists no longer relied on introspective processes, these accounts would still be in difficulty because they place learning about the mind outside mind-related practices. The theory-theory position suggests that children develop a theorylike mental structure that is then used to understand (i.e., decode, mediate between) the mental life of others (e.g., Gopnik & Wellman, 1994; Perner, 1991). Theory-theorists might protest that they sidestep the issue of the ontology of mental states by claiming intentions and the like are hypothetical postulates. However, they do commit to a view of a mental go-between between thought and action and between meaning and definition. As such these accounts also rely on a causal view of meaning and mind in that such a mental structure would be externally related to criterion and term defined, language-game and practice, thought and state of affairs, and so on. Nativist blends of the theory-theory position, which argue for a 'starting-state nativism' also commit to this mediating mental structure view, although the emergence of this mental go-between is anchored in the infant's apparent proclivity for imitation (e.g., Meltzoff, 1999). This account also relies on a causal view of meaning and mind. Ironically, despite the theoretical distinctions between simulation and theory–theory accounts of social cognitive development, there is unanimity regarding the causal role of the mind and ontology of mental events. Further, modular theories (e.g., Baron-Cohen, 1995) quarrel with these two camps not over the causal status of the mind or brain in understanding others, but rather with regard to the modular underpinnings of such an understanding.

There also seems to be some consensus on the causal theory of meaning and mind in opposing camps in infancy research. Tomasello (1999) offered a rich interpretation of infant social cognition wherein infants are said to experience their intentional mental states and then apply these to others. Montgomery's (1997) criticisms of simulation theory as applied to preschoolers' burgeoning grasp of mind would apply here too (see also Müller & Carpendale, chap. 11, this volume). Ironically, Tomasello's (1992) work on language continues in the social pragmatic tradition initiated by Bruner (e.g., 1983), which embodies a roughly Wittgensteinian approach. As I understand it, Tomasello's stand on children's acquisition of a lexicon is at odds with his account of their emerging understanding of mind because he locates the genesis of the latter in the infant mind. Leaner accounts of infant social understanding also seem to rely on a causal theory of mind and meaning. Moore (1998), for example, argued that infants do not understand their mental life outside particular interactive contexts (that are said to provide the infant with an opportunity to match their psychological states with another) until they are able to construct multiple models of self, other, and some state of affairs (e.g., Corkum & Moore, 1995; Moore, 1996, Moore & Corkum, 1994; cf. Perner, 1991). At this point in development, an infant's mind can seemingly begin to understand other minds. From my perspective, Moore was correct that an infant could not have an understanding of her so-called mental states outside interactive contexts—in fact participation in a shared practice could be a reasonable paraphrase of a matched interactive context—but Moore's assumption seems to be that somehow an understanding of mental states will dawn on the infant given the correct form of matched interactive context and information-processing capabilities. As Moore's account stands, the infant mind is a causal one; the problem of other minds is left unresolved.

Canfield (1999) made more explicit the Wittgensteinian point that language, meaning, and understanding have their basis in activity and practice by arguing that, "Wittgensteinian anthropology of word use will recognize a progression in the child from proto language-game through . . . a gestural stage, to the simple language-game, and then on to various elaborations and developments of the latter" (p. 158; cf. Bruner, 1983). Canfield (1993) noted that, "primitive language-games typically grow out of such naturally occurring patterns of behavior as this: baby cries, mother brings it to the breast, baby suckles" (p. 173). Broadly Piagetian activity-based developmental accounts seem well equipped to account for these types of progressions provided that Wittgenstein's internalistic logic is preserved.[3] The reader may, however, note an irony in my chapter in that social interaction is externally related to meaning. Social interaction is, however, noncausally related to meaning and understanding in a different way than, for example, one's mind might be (despite fact that one requires a mind and brain to socially interact). A developing agent cannot directly encode psychological experiences or even objects in their world and then simply unpack their meaning because meaning is inherently social (Goldberg, 1991). It depends on some shared and then mastered practice.

I have tried to show in this chapter that theorists of divergent theoretical stripes assume that mental states can logically obtain qua states. I have suggested that there are difficulties with this assumption. If it is problematic to take mental states at ontological face value, then theories based on such a notion of mental states are in difficulty from the outset. I have also tried to show that causal notions of meaning and mind abound in the theories of mind enterprise. Leaner activity-based accounts like Moore's, which emphasize the role of social interaction in the construction of meaning and mind, however, could be assimilated to a roughly Wittgensteinian perspective. For example, one could reframe the interactive context required in Moore's position and point out that information processing is externally related to meaning without rendering his account unrecognizable. The same could not be said for the dominant positions within the theory of mind enterprise for the simple reason that theory–theory, simulation, and modular accounts are parasitic on a causal theory of meaning and mind. If the criticisms presented in the present chapter of this causal picture are sound, however, then the most popular ways to explain children's social understanding face an insurmountable obstacle.

ACKNOWLEDGMENTS

Preparation of this chapter was supported by a Social Sciences and Humanities Research Council of Canada Doctoral Fellowship. Separate portions of this chapter were presented at the Why Language Matters for Theory of Mind Conference, Toronto, April 2002, and the 32nd Annual Symposium of the Jean Piaget Society, June 2002, Philadelphia. I thank the editors and Bill Turnbull for helpful comments on earlier drafts of this chapter.

---

[3]I use the term *broadly Piagetian* in recognition that Piaget seems to have underemphasized the role of social interaction in the development of knowledge (Chapman, 1991; Müller & Carpendale, 2000). Chapman's (1991) reformulation of Piagetian theory corrects this (see also Piaget, 1995).

REFERENCES

Astington, J. W. (1999). The language of intention: Three ways of doing it. In P. D. Zelazo, J. W. Astington, & D. R. Olson (Eds.), *Developing theories of intention: Social understanding and self-control* (pp. 295–315). Mahwah, NJ: Lawrence Erlbaum Associates.

Astington, J. W., & Gopnik, A. (1991). Developing understanding of desire and intention. In A. Whiten (Ed.), *Natural theories of mind: Evolution, development and simulation of everyday mindreading* (pp. 39–50). Cambridge, MA: Blackwell.

Austin, J. (1975). *How to do things with words* (2nd ed.). New York: Oxford University Press.

Baker, G. (1974). Criteria: A new foundation for semantics. *Ratio, 16*, 156–189.

Baker, G. P., & Hacker, P. M. S. (1984). *Skepticism, rules and language.* Cambridge: Blackwell.

Baker, G. P., & Hacker, P. M. S. (1985). *Wittgenstein, rules, grammar and necessity* (an analytic commentary on the *Philosophical Investigations*; Vol. 2). Cambridge: Blackwell.

Baron-Cohen, S. (1995). *Mindblindness: An essay on autism and theory of mind.* Cambridge, MA: MIT Press.

Bickhard, M. H. (1987). The social nature of the functional nature of language. In M. Hickmann (Ed.), *Social and functional approaches to language and thought* (pp. 39–65). New York: Academic Press.

Bruner, J. (1983). *Child's talk: Learning to use language.* New York: Norton.

Button, G., Coulter, J., Lee, J. R. E., & Sharrock, W. (1995). *Computers, minds and conduct.* Cambridge: Polity.

Canfield, J. V. (1981). *Wittgenstein, language and world.* Amherst: University of Massachusetts Press.

Canfield, J. V. (1993). The living language: Wittgenstein and the empirical study of communication. *Language Sciences, 15*, 165–193.

Canfield, J. V. (1999). Folk psychology versus philosophical anthropology. *Idealistic Studies, 29*, 153–172.

Chandler, M. (1997). Stumping for progress in a post-modern world. In E. Amsel & K. A. Renninger (Eds.), *Change and development: Issues of theory, method, and application* (pp. 1–26). Mahwah, NJ: Lawrence Erlbaum Associates.

Chapman, M. (1987). Inner processes and outward criteria: Wittgenstein's importance for psychology. In M. Chapman & R. A. Dixon (Eds.), *Meaning and the growth of understanding: Wittgenstein's significance for developmental psychology* (pp. 103–127). Berlin: Springer-Verlag.

Chapman, M. (1991). The epistemic triangle: Operative and communicative components of cognitive competence. In M. Chandler & M. Chapman (Eds.), *Criteria for competence: Controversies in the conceptualization and assessment of children's abilities* (pp. 209–228). Hillsdale, NJ: Lawrence Erlbaum Associates.

Chapman, M., & Dixon, R. A. (Eds.). (1987). *Meaning and the growth of understanding: Wittgenstein's significance for developmental psychology.* Berlin: Springer-Verlag.

Chihara, C. S., & Fodor, J. A. (1966). Operationalism and ordinary language. In G. Pitcher (Ed.), *Wittgenstein: The philosophical investigations* (pp. 384–419). Garden City, NY: Anchor.

Corkum, V., & Moore, C. (1995). Development of joint visual attention in infants. In C. Moore & P. Dunham (Eds.), *Joint attention: Its origins and role in development* (pp. 61–83). Hillsdale, NJ: Lawrence Erlbaum Associates.

Dennett, D. C. (1987). *The intentional stance.* Cambridge, MA: MIT Press.

de Villiers, J. G. (1999). Language and theory of mind: What are the developmental relations. In S. Baron-Cohen, H. Tager-Flusberg, & D. Cohen (Eds.), *Understanding our minds: Perspectives from developmental cognitive neuroscience* (pp. 83–123). Oxford: Oxford University Press.

Goldberg, B. (1991). Mechanism and meaning. In J. Hyman (Ed.), *Investigating psychology: Sciences of the mind after Wittgenstein* (pp. 48–66). London: Routledge.

Gopnik, A. (1993). How we know our minds: The illusion of first-person knowledge of intentionality. *Behavior & Brain Sciences, 16*, 1–14.

Gopnik, A., & Wellman, H. M. (1994). The theory theory. In L. Hirschfeld & S. Gelman (Eds.), *Mapping the mind: Domain specificity in cognition and culture* (pp. 257–293). New York: Cambridge University Press.

Gordon, R. M. (1992). The simulation theory: Objections and misconceptions. *Mind & Language, 7*, 11–34.

Hacker, P. M. S. (1990). *Wittgenstein, meaning and mind* (an analytic commentary on the *Philosophical Investigations*; Vol. 3). Cambridge: Blackwell.

Hacker, P. M. S. (1996). *Wittgenstein, mind and will* (an analytic commentary on the *Philosophical Investigations*; Vol. 4). Cambridge: Blackwell.

Harris, P. L. (1992). From simulation to folk psychology. *Mind and Language, 7*, 120–144.

Hobson, R. P. (1994). Perceiving attitudes, conceiving minds. In C. Lewis & P. Mitchell (Eds.), *Children's early understanding of mind: Origins and development* (pp. 71–93). Hove, England: Lawrence Erlbaum Associates.

Hobson, R. P. (2000). The grounding of symbols: A social-developmental account. In P. Mitchell & K. J. Riggs (Eds.), *Children's reasoning and the mind* (pp. 11–36). Hove, England: Psychology Press.

Hyman, J. (Ed.). (1991). *Investigating psychology: Sciences of the mind after Wittgenstein*. London: Routledge.

Kripke, S. (1982). *Wittgenstein on rules and private language*. Oxford: Blackwell.

Lakoff, G., & Johnson, M. (1999). *Philosophy in the flesh: The embodied mind and its challenge to Western thought*. New York: Basic.

Malcolm, N. (1991). Wittgenstein: The relation of language to instinctive behavior. In J. Hyman (Ed.), *Investigating psychology: Sciences of the mind after Wittgenstein* (pp. 27–47). London: Routledge.

Meltzoff, A. N. (1999). Origins of theory of mind, cognition and communication. *Journal of Communication Disorders, 32*, 251–269.

Meltzoff, A. N., Gopnik, A., & Repacholi, B. M. (1999). Toddler's understanding of intentions, desires, and emotions: Explorations of the dark ages. In P. D. Zelazo, J. W. Astington, & D. R. Olson (Eds.), *Developing theories of intention: Social understanding and self-control* (pp. 17–41). Mahwah, NJ: Lawrence Erlbaum Associates.

Merleau-Ponty, M. (1962). *The phenomenology of perception* (C. Smith, Trans.). London: Routledge & Kegan Paul. (Original work published 1945)

Montgomery, D. E. (1997). Wittgenstein's private language argument and children's understanding of mind. *Developmental Review, 17*, 291–320.

Moore, C. (1996). Theories of mind in infancy. *British Journal of Developmental Psychology, 14*, 19–40.

Moore, C. (1998). Social cognition in infancy. In M. Carpenter, K. Nagell, & K. Tomasello (Eds.), *Social cognition, joint attention, and communicative competence from 9 to 15 months of age. Monographs of the Society for Research in Child Development, 63* (Serial No. 255), 167–174.

Moore, C., & Corkum, V. (1994). Social understanding at the end of the first year of life. *Developmental Review, 14*, 349–372.

Müller, U., & Carpendale, J. I. M. (2000). The role of social interaction in Piaget's theory: Language for social cooperation and social cooperation for language. *New Ideas in Psychology, 18*, 139–156.

Nelson, K., & Kessler Shaw, L. (2002). Developing a socially shared symbol system. In E. Amsel & J. P. Byrnes (Eds.), *Language, literacy, and cognitive development: The development and consequences of symbolic communication* (pp. 27–57). Mahwah, NJ: Lawrence Erlbaum Associates.

Ogden, C. K., & Richards, I. A. (1923). *The meaning of meaning: A study of the influence of language upon thought and of the science of symbolism.* London: Routledge & Kegan Paul.

Perner, J. (1991). *Understanding the representational mind.* Cambridge, MA: MIT Press.

Piaget, J. (1932). *The moral judgment of the child.* London: Routledge & Kegan Paul.

Piaget, J. (1954). *The construction of reality in the child.* New York: Ballantine.

Piaget, J. (1995). *Sociological studies* (L. Smith, Ed.). London: Routledge.

Racine, T. P. (2002). Computation, meaning and artificial intelligence: Some old problems, some new models. *Canadian Artificial Intelligence, 50,* 8–19.

Russell, B. (1921). *The analysis of mind.* London: Allen & Unwin.

Russell, J. (1987). Rule following, mental models and the developmental view. In M. Chapman & R. A. Dixon (Eds.), *Meaning and the growth of understanding: Wittgenstein's significance for developmental psychology* (pp. 23–48). Berlin: Springer-Verlag.

Ryle, G. (1949). *The concept of mind.* London: Hutchinson.

Savage-Rumbaugh, E. S., Shanker, S. G., & Taylor, T. J. (1998). *Apes, language and the human mind.* New York: Oxford University Press.

Schulte, J. (1993). *Experience and expression: Wittgenstein's philosophy of psychology.* Oxford: Clarendon.

Searle, J. R. (1979). The intentionality of intention and action. *Inquiry, 22,* 253–280.

Searle, J. R. (1983). *Intentionality: An essay on the philosophy of mind.* Cambridge: Cambridge University Press.

Shanker, S. (1991). The enduring relevance of Wittgenstein's remarks concerning intentions. In J. Hyman (Ed.), *Investigating psychology: Sciences of the mind after Wittgenstein* (pp. 67–94). London: Routledge.

Shanker, S. (1998). *Wittgenstein's remarks on the foundations of AI.* New York: Routledge.

ter Hark, M. (1990). *Beyond the outer and the inner: Wittgenstein's philosophy of psychology.* Dordrecht, The Netherlands: Kluwer.

Tomasello, M. (1992). The social bases of language acquisition. *Social Development, 1,* 67–87.

Tomasello, M. (1999). Having intentions, understanding intentions, and understanding communicative intentions. In P. D. Zelazo, J. W. Astington, & D. R. Olson (Eds.), *Developing theories of intention: Social understanding and self-control* (pp. 63–75). Mahwah, NJ: Lawrence Erlbaum Associates.

Turnbull, W., & Carpendale, J. I. M. (1999). A social-pragmatic model of talk: Implications for research on the development of children's social understanding. *Human Development, 42,* 328–355.

Vygotsky, L. (1978). *Mind in society: The development of higher psychological processes.* Cambridge, MA: Harvard University Press.

Wittgenstein, L. (1958). *Philosophical investigations* (3rd ed., G. E. M. Anscombe, Ed. & Trans.). Englewood Cliffs, NJ: Prentice-Hall.

Wittgenstein, L. (1969). *On certainty* (G. E. M. Anscombe & G. H. von Wright, Eds., D. Paul & G. E. M. Anscombe, Trans.). New York: Harper & Row.

Wittgenstein, L. (1976). *Wittgenstein's lectures on the foundations of mathematics: Cambridge 1939* (C. Diamond, Ed.). Brighton: Harvester.

Wittgenstein, L. (1979). *Wittgenstein's lectures: Cambridge 1932–1935* (A. Ambrose, Ed.). Oxford: Blackwell.

Wittgenstein, L. (1980). *Remarks on the philosophy of psychology* (Vols. 1 & 2; G. E. M. Anscombe & G. H. von Wright, Eds., G. E. M. Anscombe, Trans.). Oxford: Blackwell.

Wittgenstein, L. (1981). *Zettel* (2nd ed.; G. E. M. Anscombe & G. H. von Wright, Eds., G. E. M. Anscombe, Trans.). Oxford: Blackwell.

Author Index

A

Adamson, L. B., 227, 234
Aitken, K. J., 222, 237
Ali, F., 240, 256
Alvarez, A., 101, 109
Anderson, J., 165, 170
Angelopoulos, M., 229, 230, 236
Arievitch, I., 10, 16
Aristotle, 121, 129, 179, 181, 191
Asch, S. E., 52, 53, 65
Asquith, P., 207, 208, 209, 213
Astington, J. W., 258, 264, 267, 274
Austin, J., 258, 267, 274

B

Baillergeon, R., 158, 171
Baird, J. A., 155, 170
Bakeman, R., 227, 234
Baker, G. P., 258, 260, 263, 264, 274
Baldwin, J. M., 32, 41, 219, 221, 222, 235
Barnes, B., 46, 65
Barnett, M., 241, 254
Baron-Cohen, S., 272, 274
Barry, H., 209, 212

Bar-Tal, D., 241, 249, 254
Batson, C., 252, 254
Baumrind, D., 203, 211
Bebeau, M. J., 160, 173
Beilin, H., 25, 41
Bell, S., 227, 235
Bennett, P., 229, 230, 236
Bentley, A. F., 167, 171
Berger, P. L., 4, 5, 16, 114, 118, 120, 128, 129
Berkowitz, L., 240, 254
Bickhard, M. H., 70, 84, 112, 114, 115, 116, 117, 121, 122, 123, 125, 126, 127, 128, 129, 130, 131, 175, 176, 191, 260, 274
Bidell, T. R., 93, 107
Bischof-Köhler, D., 222, 223, 233, 235
Black, P., 186, 187, 191
Blau, P. M., 60, 65
Bloor, D., 46, 65
Boesch, E. E., 5, 11, 16, 33, 36, 41, 166, 170
Bond, T., 187, 191
Boom, J., 68, 69, 70, 73, 75, 83, 84
Bowerman, M., 102, 107
Bowlby, J., 127, 130
Braeges, J. L., 207, 208, 213
Brandtstadter, J., 38, 41
Bransford, J. D., 183, 191
Brehm, J. W., 205, 211

Brehm, S. S., 205, *211*
Bretherton, I., 215, *235*
Bridgeman, D., 202, *213*
Brockbank, M., 226, *236*
Brooks, R., 217, 222, 232, *235, 236*
Brown, T., 165, *170,* 176, 183, 188, *191*
Bruner, J., 1, *16,* 178, *191,* 257, 272, *274*
Bryan, J., 240, *254*
Bryant, P., 184, *191*
Budwig, N., 102, *107*
Bunge, M., 3, 4, 5, 7, 11, *16,* 21, *41*
Butcher, P. R., 226, *235*
Butler, S. C., 232, *235*
Butterworth, G., 223, 227, 228, 229, 230, 231, 232, *235*
Button, G., 258, 269, *274*

C

Cairns, R. B., 93, *107*
Camino, C., 209, 210, *212*
Campbell, D. T., 112, 122, 126, *130*
Campbell, R. J., 125, 126, *130*
Campbell, R. L., 70, *84,* 112, 116, 121, 122, 123, 126, *130*
Campos, J. J., 227, *236*
Canfield, J. V., 260, 261, 263, 266, 272, *274*
Carlo, G., 250, *254*
Caron, A. J., 232, *235*
Carpendale, J. I. M., 164, 166, *171,* 233, *236,* 253, *254,* 262, 273, *275, 276*
Carpenter, M., 215, *235*
Case, R., 101, *107,* 184, *191,* 222, 229, 234, *235*
Chandler, M. J., 5, 13, *16,* 155, 156, 157, 160, 161, 162, 163, 165, 167, *171, 173,* 183, *191,* 264, *274*
Chapman, M., 2, 3, 12, 14, *16,* 68, 72, 75, 79, *84,* 92, 94, *107,* 141, 152, 163, 164, 165, 166, 167, *171,* 175, *191,* 223, *238,* 253, *254,* 257, 260, 262, 263, 264, 269, 273, *274*
Chihara, C. S., 263, *274*
Christopher, J. C., 121, 123, *130, 131*
Churcher, J., 228, *235*
Clark, A., 117, *131*
Cochran, E., 230, *235*
Cocking, R. R., 183, *191*
Colby, A., 156, 164, *171*
Cole, M., 21, 22, *41,* 184, *191*

Coles, M., 189, *191*
Comber, C., 187, *192*
Corkum, V., 215, 216, 222, 224, 227, 228, 229, 230, 231, 232, 233, 234, *235, 236,* 272, 274, 275
Corsaro, W., 202, *211*
Corter, C., 222, *236*
Cosmides, L., 7, *17*
Costello, E. J., 93, *107*
Coulter, J., 258, 269, *274*
Crick, N., 251, *254*
Csordas, T. J., 36, *41*
Cummins, R., 117, *131*

D

D'Entremont, B., 225, 226, 227, 228, *235*
Dahlbäck, O., 4, *17*
Damasio, A., 32, 35, 36, *41*
Damon, W., 164, 168, 169, 170, *174,* 178, *191,* 197, 201, *211*
Darley, J., 240, *254*
Davidson, P., 159, 160, 168, *171, 173*
Davis, K., 241, *255*
de Graaf, J. W., 70, *85*
de Villiers, J. G., 264, *274*
Deák, G., 225, 231, 232, *235*
Décarie, T. G., 215, 225, 228, 229, 231, *236*
del Rio, P., 101, *109*
Demetriou, A., 187, *193*
Dennett, D. C., 37, *41,* 163, *171,* 269, *274*
DES, 187, *191*
Descartes, R., 49, *65,* 217, *235*
Dewey, J., 167, *171*
Dilthey, W., 216, *235*
Dixon, R. A., 257, *274*
Dovidio, J., 241, 251, *254*
Dretske, F. I., 117, *131*
Driver, J., 226, *236*
Dunbar, R. I. M., 113, *131*
Dunn, J., 199, *211*
Durkheim, E., 3, 4, *17,* 55, *65*
Duveen, G., 5, *17*

E

Eckensberger, L. H., 33, *42*
Edelman, G. M., 35, *42*

Eisenberg, N., 239, 240, 241, 250, 251, 252, 254, 255
Elder, G. E., 93, 107
Elias, N., 4, 5, 7, 8, 17
Encarnacion-Gawrych, G., 199, 202, 212
Eysenck, M., 181, 191

F

Fabes, R., 239, 240, 250, 254
Farrell, S., 185, 193
Farroni, T., 226, 236
Fauconnier, G., 104, 105, 106, 107, 108
Feldman, D., 181, 191
Ferrari, M., 180, 182, 191
Fischer, K. W., 93, 107, 227, 236
Flanagan, O., 157, 165, 171
Flavell, J. H., 165, 171, 175, 192
Flom, R. A., 225, 231, 232, 235
Fodor, J. A., 69, 70, 85, 117, 131, 263, 274
Fowler, R. C., 169, 171
Frege, G., 179, 181, 192
Frye, D., 217, 236
Furth, H. G., 168, 171
Furth, H. P., 133, 152

G

Gadamer, H.-G., 126, 131
Gaines, C., 210, 213
Gallese, V., 40, 42
Galton, M., 187, 192
Garcia, R., 26, 43, 47, 66
Garrison, J., 167, 171
Gauvain, M., 11, 17
Gelman, R., 158, 171
Gelman, S. A., 101, 107, 108, 156, 158, 172, 173
Gentner, D., 105, 107
Gergen, K. J., 21, 28, 42
Geuze, R. H., 226, 235
Gibbs, R. W., 104, 107
Giddens, A., 3, 11, 17
Gilbert, M., 55, 65, 114, 131
Ginsburg, H., 186, 188, 192
Girnius Brown, O., 205, 212
Glassman, M., 160, 171
Goldberg, A., 106, 107
Goldberg, B., 273, 275

Goldman, A. I., 47, 62, 65
Goldstein, H., 186, 192
Goody, E. N., 112, 131
Gopnik, A., 158, 171, 217, 218, 236, 264, 268, 270, 274, 275
Gordon, R. M., 263, 271, 275
Gottlieb, G., 40, 42
Gralinski, H., 200, 201, 211
Grene, M., 8, 17
Greve, W., 221, 236
Grize, J.-B., 179, 192
Grover, L., 228, 235
Guerra, N., 202, 209, 212
Gumperz, J. J., 102, 107

H

Habermas, J., 14, 17, 133, 147, 152, 162, 172
Hacker, P. M. S., 217, 218, 221, 236, 258, 261, 263, 264, 265, 266, 267, 269, 274, 275
Hains, S. M. J., 226, 235
Haken, H., 80, 85
Hallett, D., 156, 171
Hampson, R., 252, 255
Handy, R., 167, 172
Hanks, W. F., 102, 107
Hanson, N. R., 163, 172
Harding, S., 28, 42
Hargreaves, L., 187, 192
Harré, R., 36, 42
Harris, P. L., 263, 271, 275
Hasebe, Y., 210, 211
Haugeland, J., 117, 131
Hayes, R., 5, 17
Helwig, C. C., 159, 173
Hespos, S. J., 222, 237
Hiebert, J., 185, 194
Hildebrandt, C., 159, 160, 173
Hirschfeld, L. A., 101, 107, 156, 172
Hobson, R. P., 223, 236, 257, 262, 267, 275
Hoffman, M. L., 223, 236
Hogan, D., 187, 192
Hoijtink, H., 83, 84
Homans, G. C., 3, 17, 60, 65
Hood, B. M., 226, 236
Houlihan, K., 240, 256
Humphrey, N. K., 112, 131
Hutchins, E., 106, 107
Hyman, J., 257, 275

I, J

Ingold, T., 36, *42*
Inhelder, B., 195, *212*
Jackson, E., 227, *236*
Jackson, M., 250, *255*
Jansen, B. R. J., 83, *85*
Jarrett, N., 223, 227, 228, 229, 231, 232, *235*
Jenkins, E., 83, *85*
Johnson, M., 35, *42*, 102, 103, 104, *107*, 267, 275
Johnson, M. H., 226, *236*
Johnson-Laird, P., 178, 182, *192*
Jopling, D., 216, 218, 219, 221, *236*

K

Kalverboer, A. F., 226, *235*
Kant, I., 177, 179, 181, *192*
Karmiloff-Smith, A., 101, *107*, 181, *192*
Keane, M., 181, *191*
Keil, F. C., 156, *173*
Kessler Shaw, L., 257, 262, 267, *275*
Kfir, D., 240, *256*
Kienapple, K., 222, *236*
Killen, M., 159, *173*, 201, 202, 206, 207, *212, 213*
Kitchener, R. F., 1, 6, *17*, 47, 56, 59, 60, *65, 66*, 156, 165, 166, 168, *172*
Knight, G., 250, *254*
Kochanska, G., 205, *212*
Kohlberg, L., 155, 156, 164, *171*, 172, 253, *255*
Kopp, C., 200, 201, *211*
Korthals, M., 78, *85*
Krebs, D., 239, 249, *255*
Kripke, S., *275*
Kuczinski, L., 205, *212*
Kunnen, E. S., 83, *84*

L

Ladd, G., 251, *254*
Lakoff, G., 102, 103, *107, 108*, 267, *275*
Lalonde, C. E., 157, 161, *171*
Lapsley, D. K., 164, *172*
Latané, B., 240, *254*
Latour, B., 28, 30, 33, *42*
Lave, J., 4, *17*, 101, 102, *108*

Lawrence, J. A., 4, 10, *17*, 96, *108*
LeDoux, J., 35, *42*
Lee, J. R. E., 258, 269, *274*
Lee, J. Y., 202, 209, *212*
Legerstee, M., 215, 217, 222, *236*
Leiser, T., 241, *254*
Lempers, J. D., 229, *236*
Lenk, H., 3, 4, *17*
Lerner, R. M., 38, *41*
Levine, A., 117, *131*
Levinson, S. C., 102, *107*
Lewis, D. K., 114, 115, *131*
Lewis, M., 233, *236*
Lewontin, R. C., 40, *42*
Lins-Dyer, T., 210, *212*
Lipps, T., 219, *236*
Longino, H., 62, 63, *66*
Lourenço, O., 2, *17*, 19, *42*, 160, 165, 166, 172, 175, *192*, 240, 243, 244, 245, 246, 248, 250, 251, *255*
Luckmann, T., 4, *16*, 114, 118, 120, 128, *129*
Luhmann, N., 23, *42*
Luria, A. R., 96, *109*
Lyotard, J. F., 160, 161, *172*
Lyra, M. C. D. P., 93, *108*

M

Machado, A., 2, *17*, 19, *42*, 175, *192*
Magnusson, D., 30, 37, *42*
Malcolm, N., 266, *275*
Mantovani, G., 40, *42*, 211, *212*
Marr, D., 157, 163, *172*
Matusov, E., 5, 10, *17*
Mays, W., 183, *192*
McClelland, J. L., 83, *85*
Meacham, J. A., 167, 168, *172, 173*
Mehan, H., 115, *131*
Mele, A., 178, 185, *192*
Meltzoff, A. N., 158, *172*, 217, 218, 222, *236*, 268, 270, 271, *275*
Merleau-Ponty, M., 35, *42*, 218, 222, 223, *236*, 267, *275*
Miller, J. G., 33, *42*
Miller, M., 75, 76, *85*, 133, 147, 149, 150, 151, *152*
Miller, P., 175, *192*, 241, 252, *255*
Miller, P. H., 101, *108*
Miller, S., 175, *192*
Millikan, R. G., 117, *131*

Moessinger, P., 3, 7, *17*
Molenaar, P. C. M., 70, 80, 83, *85*
Montgomery, D. E., 257, 260, 263, 264, 267, 271, 272, *275*
Moore, B., 239, 240, *256*
Moore, C., 216, 222, 224, 229, 230, 232, 233, 234, *236, 272, 274, 275*
Moore, V., 215, 216, 227, 228, 229, 230, 231, 232, 234, *235*
Morissette, P., 215, 225, 228, 229, 231, *236*
Moscovici, S., 50, 53, *66*
Moser, P., 181, *192*
Moshman, D., 156, *172*, 189, *192*
Much, N., 197, 199, *212*
Muir, D. W., 226, *235*
Müller, U., 38, 42, 188, *192*, 231, 232, 233, *236, 237, 242, 255*, 273, *275*
Munn, P., 199, *211*

N

Nagell, K., 215, *235*
Narvaez, D., 160, *173*
National Curriculum, 186, *192*
Nelson, K., 101, *108*, 257, 262, 267, *275*
Newell, A., 117, *131*
Nicolis, G., 80, *85*
Nietzsche, F., 161, *172*
Nucci, L., 196, 197, 201, 202, 203, 204, 206, 207, 209, 210, *211, 212*
Nucci, M. S., 197, 199, 201, 202, 210, *211, 212*

O

Ochs, E., 102, *108*
Ogan, T., 215, *237*
Ogden, C. K., 258, 262, *276*
Orwell, G., 179, 189, *192*
Overton, W. F., 21, 23, 24, 25, 28, 34, 36, 38, 41, *42, 43*, 163, 165, 166, 168, *172*, 188, *192*, 219, 231, 232, *237, 242, 255*

P

Pareto, V., 60, *66*
Pascual-Leone, J., 69, *85*
Pell, A., 187, *192*

Perner, J., 271, 272, *276*
Perry, D., 251, *255*
Perry, L., 251, *255*
Pervez, M., 187, *193*
Phillips, A. T., 217, *237*
Piaget, J., 1, 2, 3, 4, 5, 6, 7, 8, 11, 12, 13, 14, 15, *17, 18*, 21, 23, 25, 26, 27, 28, 29, 31, 32, 33, 37, 38, 40, *43*, 47, 56, 57, 60, 61, 62, 63, 64, *66*, 68, 70, 72, 73, 74, 77, 78, 79, *85*, 88, 89, 91, 92, 94, 95, 96, 97, 98, *108*, 111, 121, 122, *131, 132*, 133, 134, 135, 136, 137, 138, 139, 140, 141, 142, 143, 144, 145, 146, 148, 151, *152, 153*, 155, 156, 159, 161, 165, 166, 167, 168, 169, *172*, 175, 176, 177, 178, 179, 181, 182, 183, 184, 185, 186, 187, 188, 189, 190, *192, 193*, 195, 196, 200, 201, 206, *212*, 220, 221, 222, 223, 224, 226, 227, 228, 229, 230, 231, 232, *237*, 239, 241, 242, 247, 248, 252, *255*, 262, 273, *276*
Piattelli-Palmarini, M., 70, *85*
Pick, A. D., 225, 231, 232, *235*
Pierce, C., 163, *172*
Pinard, A., 180, 182, *191*
Pinker, S., 36, *43*
Plato, 121, *132*, 181, 184, *193*
Plessner, H., 8, *18*, 233, *237*
Poincaré, H., 179, *193*
Popper, K., 122, *132*
Portmann, A., 8, 9, *18*
Prawat, R. S., 70, *85*
Prigogine, I., 80, *85*
Pryor, J., 187, *194*

R

Racine, T. P., 263, *276*
Radke-Yarrow, M., 205, *212*, 223, *238*
Raijmakers, M. E. J., 70, 80, 82, 83, *85*
Rasmussen, E., 251, *255*
Raviv, A., 241, *254*
Reese, H. W., 21, 23, 24, *43*
Reichenbach, H., 176, *193*
Repacholi, B. M., 217, 218, *236*, 268, 270, *275*
Resnick, L., 189, *193*
Rest, J., 160, *173*
Restropo, A., 207, *213*
Reynolds, D., 185, *193*

Ricard, M., 215, 225, 228, 229, 231, *236*
Richards, I. A., 258, 262, *276*
Richie, D. M., 117, 121, *130*
Riegel, K. F., 168, *173*
Rochat, P., 222, *237*
Rogoff, B., 5, *18*, 101, *108*
Rosa, A., 87, *108*
Ross, H., 199, *212*
Rousseau, J.-J., 189, *193*
Rozin, P., 156, *173*
Rumelhart, D. E., 117, *132*
Runions, K., 180, 182, *191*
Russell, B., 216, *237*, 258, *276*
Russell, J., 37, 43, 264, *276*
Ryle, G., 258, 269, *276*

S

Sainsbury, M., 176, 181, *193*
Sameroff, A. J., 167, *173*
Sampson, E. E., 36, *43*
Sapiro, C., 209, 210, *212*
Savage-Rumbaugh, E. S., 258, 263, *276*
Scaife, M., 228, *235*
Scheier, C., 40, *43*
Scheler, M., 218, 219, 220, *237*
Schelling, T. C., 114, *132*
Schlegel, A., 209, *212*
Schmitt, F., 47, *66*
Scholnick, E. K., 101, *108*
Schoner, G., 40, *43*
Schroff, J., 241, *254*
Schulte, J., 258, 263, 268, *276*
Searle, J. R., 25, *43*, 178, 180, *193*, 267, 268, 269, *276*
Sedlak, A., 197, *213*
Severy, L., 241, *255*
Shanker, S. G., 258, 261, 268, *276*
Shanon, B., 37, *43*
Shantz, C., 241, 253, *255*
Sharrock, W., 258, 269, *274*
Shayer, M., 187, *193*
Shephard, L., 187, *193*
Sherif, C. W., 51, *66*
Sherif, M., 51, *66*
Shotter, J., 4, *18*
Shweder, R. A., 197, 199, *212*
Siegler, R., 93, *108*
Simion, F., 226, *236*
Simon, H. A., 117, *131, 132*

Slomkowski, C., 199, *211*
Smetana, J. G., 199, 200, 201, 202, 206, 207, 208, 209, 210, *212, 213*
Smith, L., 2, 5, 13, *18*, 40, *43*, 61, *66*, 70, *85*, 162, 165, 166, *173*, 176, 177, 178, 179, 180, 182, 183, 184, 186, 187, 188, *192, 193*
Smolensky, P., 117, *132*
Soffer, G., 218, 222, 223, 224, *237*
Sokol, B. W., 155, 156, 157, 161, *170, 171*, 188, *192*, 231, 232, *237*, 242, *255*
Solomon, D., 240, *256*
Spelke, E. S., 156, *173*
Springer, K., 156, *173*
Sroufe, L. A., 127, *132*
Stattin, H., 30, *42*
Stern, W., 32, *43*
Stewart, J., 93, *107*
Stigler, J., 185, *194*
Stranger, C., 233, *236*
Straus, E., 222, *237*
Striano, T., 222, *237*
Sugarman, S., 229, 232, *237*
Sullivan, H. S., 32, *43*
Sullivan, M. W., 233, *236*
Suomi, S. J., 40, *43*
Sweetser, E., 106, *107*

T

Tappan, M. B., 1, 13, *18*
Tarde, G., 56, *66*
Taylor, C., 35, *43*
Taylor, T. J., 258, *276*
ter Hark, M., 217, 218, *237*, 259, 261, 263, 264, 265, 266, 269, *276*
Terveen, L., 117, 121, *130*
Thelen, E., 40, *43*
Thom, R., 80, *85*
Thoma, S. J., 160, *173*
Thompson, S., 241, *254*
Tisak, M., 208, *213*, 250, *255*
Tomasello, M., 106, *108*, 215, 217, 235, *237*, 263, 271, 272, *276*
Tononi, G., 35, *42*
Tooby, J., 7, *17*
Torrrance, H., 187, *194*
Trevarthen, C., 222, *237*
Trosper, T., 210, *213*
Tudge, J., 187, *192*

Turiel, E., 159, 160, 161, 170, *173*, 196, 197, 199, 201, 202, 207, 211, *212*, *213*
Turnbull, W., 262, *276*
Turner, M., 102, 103, 104, 105, 106, *107*, *108*
Twain, M., *173*

U, V

Underwood, B., 239, 240, *256*
Valsiner, J., 4, 5, 10, *17*, *18*, 33, *43*, 87, 88, 89, 90, 93, 96, 99, *108*
Van der Maas, H. L. J., 83, *85*
van der Veer, R., 10, *16*, 87, 88, 90, 93, 96, 99, *108*
van Geert, P., 82, 84, *85*
van Haaften, A. W., 78, *85*
Vera, A. H., 117, *132*
Vidal, F., 90, 92, *109*
von Bertalanffy, L., 23, *43*
von Wright, G. H., 38, *44*, 185, *194*, 221, *238*
Vygotsky, L. S., 2, *18*, 88, 90, 91, 93, 96, *109*, 177, 184, 187, *194*, 262, *276*

W

Wagner, E., 223, *238*
Wainryb, C., 155, 159, 160, *171*, *173*
Walden, T., 215, *237*
Wall, D., 187, *192*
Walton, M. D., 197, *213*
Weber, E. K., 199, 201, 203, 204, 207, *212*

Weber, M., 3, *18*, 56, *66*
Weiss, M., 233, *236*
Weissbrod, C., 241, *256*
Wellman, H. M., 158, *171*, *173*, 217, *237*, 271, *275*
Werner, H., 32, *44*
Wertsch, J. V., 11, *18*, 21, 22, *41*, *44*, 70, *85*, 101, *109*, 184, *191*
Wiliam, D., 187, *191*
Wilkerson, W. S., 217, 223, *237*, *238*
Willen, J. D., 226, *236*
Wittgenstein, L., 10, *18*, 218, 219, 220, 221, *238*, 258, 259, 262, 263, 264, 265, 266, 267, 268, 269, 270, *276*
Wood, H., 115, *131*
Wren, T., 78, *85*
Wright, D., 169, *173*
Wynn, K., 156, *173*

X, Y

Xu, F., 210, *213*
Yaeger, J., 240, *256*
Yan, Z., 93, *107*
Yau, J., 207, 208, 210, *213*
Youniss, J., 164, 166, 168, 169, 170, *171*, *173*, *174*

Z

Zahn-Waxler, C., 223, *238*
Zan, B., 160, *171*
Zeedyk, M. S., 217, *238*
Zelazo, P. D., 40, *44*, 223, *238*

Subject Index

A

Abstraction, 101–103, 125, 218
  abductive, 163
  empirical, 73, 95
  pseudoempirical, 73
Accommodation, 26, 38, 74, 96, 98, 135, 211, 226, 254
Action, 182, 223–229, 231, 234, 239, 242, 259, 269, 271
Action knowledge, 148
Action theory, 38, 111–112, 166–169
  interaction, 167–169
  transaction, 167–169
Adaptability, 112
Adaptation, 25–27, 70–72, 89, 91–92, 112
Adolescent–parent conflict, 196, 207–210
  frequent squabblers, 209–210
  placid, 209–210
  tumultuous, 209–210
Affirmation, 13, 72, 239–242, 246–248, 250, 252–253
Altruism, 239–241, 243, 245–246, 249, 251
Analytic attitude, see Reductionism
Argumentation, 75–77, 147–149
Assessment, 182, 186, 190
  criterion-referenced, 187
  diagnostic, 186
  dynamic, 186
  formative, 186
  summative, 186
Assimilation, 26, 38, 74, 89, 96, 98–99, 135, 224, 254
Asymmetry principle of explanation, 46
Atomism, 20, 21, 23, 35, 41
Attachment theory, 111, 127
Authority, 196–197, 199, 205–209
Autism, 90, 91
Autistic, 222
Autokinetic effect, 51, 52
Autonomous morality, 12
Autonomy, 53, 181, 185–186, 189, 196, 204, 206–207, 211, 225, 227, 230–233

B

Background conditions, 260
Behavior-freeze hypothesis, 240–241
Behaviorism, 223, 262–263, 266
Blending theory, 104–106

C

Catastrophe theory, 80, 83
Causal psychology, 176–178, 180–181
Causality, 175–178, 180–185, 188–190
Chaotic, 81
Circular reactions, 229
   primary, 225–226
   secondary, 227–229
   tertiary, 231
Coercion, 152
Cognitive labor, see Epistemic labor
Collaboration, see Cooperation
Collective justification, 55, 56
Collective knowledge, 47, 48, 55–57, 64
Collective learning processes, 134, 147,
   151–152
Collectivism, 55, 67, 75–77, 87, 183–184,
   188–189, 195, 220, see also Holism
Communicative speech, 88, 91–92
Compensation, 72
Competence theory, 144–146
Complexity, 20, 23, 112–113, 115, 118–119
   temporal, 112–113
Compliance, 189, 199–200
Concept learning, 69
Conceptual integration theory, 104–106
Conceptual metaphor, 102, 104
Conformity, 52–55, 61, 62, 185, 199,
   207–208
Consistency, 76–77
Constitution theory, 141
Constraint, 60, 61, 134, 141, 169
Construction, 67, 73, 84
Constructivism, 67–68, 70, 72, 74–75, 122,
   187
Contagion, 223
Convention, 196–205, 207–211
Cooperation, 13–15, 38–39, 52, 54, 56,
   60–62, 75, 77–78, 84, 97, 134–136,
   142–144, 150–152, 169, 220
Coordination, 71, 74, 78, 96–98, 100,
   114–115, 117–118, 120, 134, 140,
   145–146, 232–234, 242, 246–248, 250,
   252
Cost model, 241
Cost perception, 240, 242–247, 249–253
Criteria, 259–265, 267, 269–270, 272
Cultural, 28–32, 36, 202, 208–211, 242,
   245–246, 253, 264–265

D

Decentration, 196, 224, 233, 241
Decomposition, see Reductionism
Dialectical materialism, 21, 99
Dialogicism, 133, 144, 147, 152
Domain
   generality, 157–162, 164–165, 169
   specificity, 156–163, 169–170, 101
Downward causation, 126–127
Dualism, 217
Dynamic systems, 11–12, 30, 67–68, 79–80,
   84, see also Self-organizing systems
   deterministic, 80
   linear, 80, 83
   nonlinear, 68, 80–84
   stochastic, 80

E

Education, 175, 182–184, 186–191
Egocentric speech, 88–94, 96–97
Egocentrism, 94–95, 98, 135, 139, 148, 151,
   188, 195, 221, see also Decentration
   cognitive, 91–92
Embodiment, 34–40
   biological, 35–36
   sociocultural, 36
Emergence, 67, 111, 125–129
Empirical tenability, 149–150
Empiricism, 21, 25, 28, 48, 49, 69–70, 89,
   135–136, 142, 147, 149, 175–178, 180,
   187–188, 190, 215, 218, 222, 225, 234,
   239, 243–244, 247, 261–262
Encodings, 117, 121–122
Enculturation, 264, 266
Epigenesis, 67, 81
Epistemic agent, 117
Epistemic gain, 58
Epistemic labor, 47
Epistemic subject, 27, 32, 37, 47, 63
Epistemic triangle, 14
Epistemic trust, 49, 54
Epistemology, 71, 113–114, 122–123, 156,
   165, 175, 178, 181, 185, 189, 216, 219,
   233
   analytic, 46, 47
   analytic social, 48, 55, 57, 64
   Cartesian, 49

developmental, 175–178, 180–182,
    190–191
individualistic, 49
naturalistic, 61, 64
normative, 176–177, 180
normative social, 46–48
social, 45, 47–50, 52, 56, 64
Equilibration, 26, 58–61, 68, 70–72, 78–79,
    82, 97–98, 100, 136–142, 144–146,
    156, 165, 177, 188–189, 206, 220,
    241–242
Event structure, 103
Evolution, 117, see also Nativism
Exchange theory, 146, 150
Explanatory relevance, 149–150

F

Fallacy
    actuality, 265
    sociologistic, 265
Figurative knowledge, 27, 87, 94–102, 104,
    106–107
Form of life, 259–261, 266–267, 270
Formal, 156–157, 161–165, 167, 169–170
Foundationalism, 20, 21, 23, 28, 35, 40, 41
Frame of reference, 51, 52
Function, 25–26
Functional, 156–157, 161–167, 169–170,
    241–242, 250, 269

G

Gain construction, 240, 242–253
Game theory, 241
Gaze following, 224–233
Generalizability, 76
Generation theory, see Constitution theory
Genetic epistemology, 47, 54–56, 61, 64, 65
Genetic fallacy, 176
Goal directedness, 122
Group pressure, see Conformity
Group think, see Coercion
Groupings, 58, 60, 78–79

H

Heteronomy, 12, 196, 200, 206

Historicity, 94, 118
Holism, 22–24, 33, 55, 56, 60, 61, 64
    sociological, 3–4

I

Identity of opposites, 24–27
Individualism, 50, 52, 53, 55, 56, 60, 61, 64,
    87, 92, 98, 133, 141, 146, 183, 189,
    216–221, 233, 239, 253
    methological, 3–4
Induction, 121
Information-processing frameworks, 111,
    128–129
Inner speech, 91
Intellectual socialization, 97
Intention, 234, 258–260, 265–272
Intentionality, 216–217, 221, 223
Interaction, 67–68, 70, 78, 82–84, 184, 195,
    199, 203, see Relationalism
    adult–child, 200–203, 206
    child–child, 196–197, 199, 201–202
    epistemic, 186
    learner–teacher, 183
    parent–child, 196, 203, 206
    peer, see child–child
    subject–internal, 68, 70, 73, 84
    subject–object, 67, 70–72, 78, 84, 180, 183
    subject–subject, 68, 70, 75, 77–78, 84,
        183
Interiorization, 77, see also Internalization
Internal relations, 261–262, 265
    vs. external, 261
Internal speech, 88
Internalization, 10–11, 75, 96–97, 121–122,
    see also Interiorization, 77
Intuitive reciprocity, 58
Invariance hypothesis, 103

J

Joint activity, 215
Joint attention, 9–10, 215–216, 224–225,
    234, 262
Judgment, 180–181

K

Knowing levels, 122–123
Knowledge, 46, 47, 64, 157, 176–178,
    180–181, 184–186, 188–190, 216–217,
    222
  individualized, 188
  nonmediated, 177
  novel, 181
  operative, 195
  personal, 160
  self-reflective, 195
  social, 195–197, 211
  social conventional, 160, 170

L

Language-game, 257–260, 262–268, 271–272
Learning, 175, 182, 185–188, 190
  group, 187–188, 190
  individualized, 187–188
  peer, 187
  school, 188–189
Learning paradox, 12, *see also* Novelty
Levels analysis, 157
  algorithmic, 106
  computational, 106
  implementational, 106
Logic, 79, 84, 89, 91, 97–98, 134, 136,
    138–146, 152, 156, 158, 161, 163,
    165–166, 168, 176–177, 182, 195, 247
  genetic, 89
  logical inference, 104

M

Meaning, 38, 40, *see also* Theory of meaning
Mental space, 104
Mental states, 217–218, 221, 223, 267–270
Metatheory, 20, 28, 33, 34
  split, 20, 21, 23, 25
  relational, *see* Relational metatheory
Mixed event, 203
Model, 34
Modernism, 160
Modular theories, 272–273
Moral reasoning, 155–156, 164–165, 168–169
Morality, 157, 160, 170, 195–198, 202–203,
    210

N

Nativism, 7–8, 21, 25, 67, 70, 160, 260, 271
  neo-, 156, 170
Naturalism, 46, 50
Negation, 13, 70, 72–73, 77, 239–242,
    246–248, 250, 252–253
Nonequilibrium thermodynamics, 80
Normativity, 14–15, 112, 119–120, 175–178,
    180–185, 187–190
  social, 119–120
Norms, 121, 137–139, 142–143, 145–146,
    151, 177–178, 181–182, 187–188, 190,
    195–202, 207–208, 210–211, 240,
    250–251, 271
  epistemic, 57, 61, 62, 65
  instrumental, 121
  logical, 59
  noninstrumental, 121, 123–124
  of obligation, *see* Rules
  social, 51, 52, 55
Novelty, 67, 70, 74–75, 77–79, 84, 96, 104,
    112

O

Object relations theory, 127–129
Objectivity, 76–77, 62, 63
Observables, 71
Ontological hermeneutics, 126
Ontology, 93, 111–113, 118–119, 121,
    125–129, 162, 177, 217, 258, 268–269,
    271–273
Operations, 5, 13, 60–61, 68, 73–74, 78–79,
    94, 97–99, 136–150, 156, 220, 239,
    242, 250
Operative knowledge, 27, 87, 94–98,
    100–102, 104, 106–107
Operatory reversibility, 59
Organization, 25–27

P

Paradigm, *see* Model
Parenting, 209
  authoritarian, 210
  authoritative, 203
Peer interaction, *see* Interaction,
    child–child

Personal, 197, 202–211
Perspective taking, 241
Perspectivism, *see* Decentration
Postmodernism, 160–161, 170
Poststructuralism, 160
Pragmatics, 147–148, 150
Private language argument, 257–258, 263–264, 271
Probabilistic melange, 56
Projection, 74
Prosocial behavior, 239–242, 245, 248–253
Prosocial reasoning, 250–251
Prudential, *see* Personal
Psychological subject, 27, 32, 37

R

Rationality, 46, 48–54, 60–64, 134–136, 139, 143, 146, 148, 150
  procedural, 150, 152
Realism, 266
Reasoning, 155, 178, 180–182, 186, 189–190, 218–219
  abstract internalized, 250
  approval-oriented, 250
  intellectual, 156
  needs-oriented, 250
  physical, 164
  secular, 155, 164–165
Reciprocity, 59–61, 134–135, 137, 139, 141, 144, 156, 195–197, 206
Reductionism, 21, 35, 41, 134–135, 141, 143, 146
Reflecting abstraction, 68, 73–75, 77, 79, 84, *see* Reflective abstraction
Reflective abstraction, 26, 38, 95, 195
Reflexion, *see* Reorganization
Regulations, 58, 60, 78–79
Relational metatheory, 20, 22, 23–27, 28, 30, 33, 34, 40
Relational structuralism, 3, 6–7
Relationalism, 55, 56, 64, 168–169, 215–216, 219–221, 223–224, 233–234, 251
  reciprocal relations, 168
  unilateral relations, 168
Relationships, 124
Relativism, 5, 13, 28, 264
Reorganization, 74, 82–84
Representational redescription, 181
Responses, 180–181

Rhythms, 58, 60, 78–79
Rules, 57

S

School, 184, 186, 201–202, 206, *see also* Learning, school
Self-organizing systems, 23, 25, 30, 37, 39, 41, 79, 81–83
Set theory, 136
Signs, 57
Simulation theories, 263, 271–273
Situation convention, 113–119
  institutionalized, 115–116, 118
  noninstitutionalized, 115–116
Skepticism, 48, 64
Social contract theory, 55
Social psychology of trust, 51
Socialized directed thought, 90
Socialized speech, 89, 91–93
Sociocultural, 21, 28, 36
Sociogenesis, 96
Solitary child, 183, *see also* Solitary knower
Solitary knower, 48–50
Speech act theory, 145
Spontaneity, 185–187
Structural metaphor, 103
Structuralism, 6, 89
Structure, 8, 12, 23, 25–26, 37, 136, 138–146, 150–151, 155–158, 160–170, 189, 234, 250, 271
Structure mapping theory, 105
Subpersonal level, 37
Symptom, 261, 264
Synergism, 80

T

Teaching, 175, 182, 184–187, 189–190
Theory of meaning, 262, *see also* Meaning
  causal, 258–259, 261–263, 267, 271–273
  correspondence, 260
  psychological, *see* causal
Theory of mind, 234, 257–258, 262–263, 265, 267, 270–273
Theory-theory, 158–161, 170, 271, 273
Thought
  communicable, 89
  noncommunicable, 89–90